The Oxford Guide to Card Games

The Oxford Guide to
Card Games

DAVID PARLETT

With cards I while my leisure hours away,
And cheat old Time, yet neither bet nor play.
Engraving by W. J. Linton, c.1848

Oxford   New York

OXFORD UNIVERSITY PRESS

1990

Oxford University Press, Walton Street, Oxford OX2 6DP

Oxford New York Toronto
Delhi Bombay Calcutta Madras Karachi
Petaling Jaya Singapore Hong Kong Tokyo
Nairobi Dar es Salaam Cape Town
Melbourne Auckland

and associated companies in
Berlin Ibadan

Oxford is a trade mark of Oxford University Press

British Library Cataloguing in Publication Data
Parlett, David
The Oxford guide to card games: a historical survey.
1. *Card games, history*
I. *Title*
795.409
ISBN 0–19–214165–1

Library of Congress Cataloging in Publication Data
Parlett, David.
The Oxford guide to card games: a historical survey   David Parlett.
p. cm.   Includes bibliographical references.
1. *Cards—History.* 2. *Cards–Social aspects.* I. *Title.*
795.4'09—dc20   GV1233.P37 1990   89–77641
ISBN 0–19–214165–1

Text processing by the Oxford Text System
Printed in Great Britain by
Butler & Tanner Ltd.
London and Frome

To
Andrew Pennycook

Acknowledgements

A book of this sort will inevitably consist, in about equal parts, of plunderings from other sources, helpful contributions from correspondents, and a residue of bridge passages linking one to the other. As to the first, my gratitude to the authors and sources plundered for relevant information cannot be individually specified but may be measured from the notes and quotations appearing throughout. As to contributions, I must make blanket acknowledgement of the many interesting and informative letters I have received since I have been writing on the subject, originally in my 'On the Cards' articles for *Games & Puzzles* magazine in the 1970s, and subsequently in a variety of card game compendia. A much missed contributor was the late Robin Goodfellow, who left me a legacy both of books and of an invaluable ten-year correspondence on facts and speculations on card-game history.

For the present book, I wish to record my thanks to notable members of the International Playing-Card Society who were not only patient enough to read through the manuscript and save me from many errors of fact and interpretation, but also generously furnished additional data which they might quite properly have retained for eventual publication under their own names. Michael Dummett especially (probably better known as the Wykeham Professor of Logic in the University of Oxford) has contributed more help and encouragement than will be apparent from the extensive references I make to his researches, as have card-game historian Thierry Depaulis (Paris) and historian and field-researcher John McLeod (London). Particular thanks are also due to Giampaolo Dossena (Milan), Dan Glimne (Vittsjö), Kishor Gordhandas (Bombay), Frank Jensen (Copenhagen), Alois Nasadil (Hlucin), Jaime Poniachik (Buenos Aires), and Wolfgang Suma (Leipzig).

In dedicating the end-product to Andrew Pennycook, I accord him no more than his due and considerably less than his worth. To say merely that, on hearing of my intention to embark on such a book, he promptly lent me all the notes he had compiled over the years with a similar end in view, and subsequently applied his editorial expertise to turning my shapeless first draft into something with an apparent sense of direction, will be a severe understatement of the extent of his contribution.

Contents

List of Colour Plates

List of Black and White Plates

Abbreviations

References in the notes to *JIPCS* denote the *Journal of the International Playing-Card Society* (latterly known as the *Playing-Card*). The Society's address is 188 Sheen Lane, East Sheen, London SW14 8LF.

References to Dummett, unless otherwise stated, denote *The Game of Tarot* (London, 1980).

Introduction

In order to form a just estimation of the character of any particular people, it is absolutely necessary to investigate the sports and pastimes most generally prevalent among them. War, policy, and other contingent circumstances, may effectually place men, at different times, in different points of view; but, when we follow them into their retirements, where no disguise is necessary, we are most likely to see them in their true state, and may best judge of their natural dispositions.

Joseph Strutt, *The Sports and Pastimes of the People of England* (1801)

A game may be as integral to a culture, as true an object of aesthetic appreciation, as admirable a product of human creativity as a folk art or a style of music; and, as such, it is quite as worthy of study.

Michael Dummett, *The Game of Tarot* (1980)

This is not a book of card games but a book about them. Other books on card games tell you how to play them or teach you how to play them well, but few offer more than sketchy and misinformed notes on where they come from, how they have developed, where, when, and by whom they are or were played, what (if anything) they mean, and how (if at all) they fit together. My aim is to put this right by exploring the realm of card games and reporting back on how they work and how they have come to be what they now are.

This may appear a risky if not reckless undertaking. Such field reports as may be drawn on are widely scattered, sometimes contradictory, and not always reliable, and I cannot guarantee to have tracked them all down, resolved the contradictions, or verified my every supposition. But there are several sound motives for making the attempt. The main one is that, although the field is rich enough to be worth exploring for its own sake, it has not yet formed the subject of a single book—apart from Dummett's voluminous *The Game of Tarot*, which bears a different emphasis. Another is to show those who don't play cards what valid pleasures they may be passing up for possibly all the wrong reasons, and those who do that there are more games in heaven and earth—especially earth—than they probably have ever dreamed of.

I especially want to counter traditional misconceptions about cards and games still perpetuated by entertainers, occultists, and hacks who don't consider the subject important enough to write about accurately. Many popular myths cannot be exploded often enough. That card games are by definition a form of gambling; that cards are rooted in fortune-telling; that they were introduced into Europe by Marco Polo, or gypsies, or crusaders returning from the east; that the earliest cards were Tarots; that Bridge is the only intelligent card game; that Poker is a game of chance; that all card games are blessed with official rules divinely revealed through the prophet Hoyle . . . are notions fanciful and often picturesque, but all entirely false.

The following guide is subject to two intentional limitations. First, it covers only card games of the western world. A different type of book would be needed even to touch upon the venerable traditions of the Middle East, India, China, and Japan, and I am not qualified to attempt it. Second, it is not a book of rules. Where I describe games in sufficient detail to enable you to try them out, I plan to save space by omitting the fine print of procedure and scoring, and may deliberately over-simplify for the sake of clarity. Regular card-players can be left to fill the gaps on the basis of general experience, and the pernickety entrusted to track down further details from the sources quoted.

An underlying contention of this book is that most card games are folk games, that informality forms much of their appeal, and that local variability is the hallmark of a truly living game.

1

Players please

I am sorry I have not learned to play at cards. It is very useful in life: it generates kindness and consolidates society.

Dr Johnson, in *Tour to the Hebrides* (11 Nov. 1773)

Cards are not 'a game' but equipment used for playing different types of game, and are therefore widely popular because they appeal to different types of player.

A poll commissioned by Waddingtons Playing Card Company in 1981[1] showed that half the adult population of Britain regularly played cards and another quarter at least had cards in the house, that players were evenly spread between men and women and married and single, and that the games they mostly played were Rummy (32 per cent having recently done so), Whist (28 per cent), Pontoon (26), Brag (23), Cribbage (17), Newmarket (15), Solo Whist (9), Poker (9), Bridge (8), Canasta (4), 'Other' (26). The last category must have included Nap, Euchre, some form of Patience, All Fours, and Hearts, perhaps even some children's games. Unfortunately, only ten games were specifically asked about, and under-sixteens were excluded from the survey.

No comparable survey of American card games has, I think, been published later than 1946, when the US Playing Card Company discovered the most popular games to be, first, Bridge, then Pinochle, Rummy, Five Hundred, Poker, Whist, Solitaire (Patience), and Hearts.[2] Women preferred Bridge and Rummy, men Poker and Pinochle. This was shortly before the Canasta craze and shortly after the Contract Bridge boom detonated by Ely Culbertson in the 1930s. In 1953 an American book specifically on 'the most popular card games' covered, in this order, Bridge, Poker, Gin Rummy, Canasta, Pinochle, Blackjack (Pontoon), Hearts, Crib, and Pitch.[3] Even less seems to have been published for other western countries. Examining the order and relative treatment of games covered in indigenously published gamebooks is of doubtful value, as most would-be Hoyles only write about

well-known international games and perhaps the most formal specimen of their own national repertoire. Their frequent unawareness
of truly popular games is illustrated by the British Poker expert who,
invited to appraise the synopsis of a book on Poker and Brag, adjudged
the inclusion of Brag pointless as it was 'an old game that nobody
played any more'![4]

Contrary to the impression conveyed by Hoyles of various na-
tionalities, there can be little doubt that most Europeans play the
particular game of the country, region, or even village they live in,
and only a small percentage such international games as Bridge and
Poker. Just what those national and local games are may be left to
arise of their own accord in the course of our survey.[5]

Haunts and habitats

Every game has a character of its own appropriate to the company
it keeps and the place where it is played. Often, the same basic game
is played in different versions according to circumstance. For instance,
Rummy is a multi-player social and family game particularly enjoyed
by women, whereas its sharper and snappier two-handed relative,
Gin, is much favoured by (almost invariably male) professional
gamblers. Partnership Whist, which once occupied the social and
intellectual position since usurped by Bridge, is a genteel four-player
partnership game popular with the older generation. It is largely
encountered in the 'Whist Drive', a competitive event held either as
a local weekly club or as a one-off fund-raising exercise in the village
hall. Knockout Whist, on the other hand, which the Waddington
survey unfortunately failed to distinguish, is a juvenile quasi-gambling
game mainly encountered in pubs and school playgrounds.

Pub games are a peculiarly British genre equivalent to continental
café games and student drinking games. The archetypal pub game is
Cribbage, or 'Crib' for short, an ancient two-hander of apparently
English origin. Courtly and aristocratic in its youth, it has since
retired to pipe and slippers and may now be venerated as a national
folk game. But it is vigorous enough to spend all its evenings in the
local pub, where it boasts itself the only form of cards playable in
licensed premises without special permission from the local magistrates.[6] Others often permitted in pubs include Whist, Solo, Nap,
Rummy, Pontoon, Brag, and a fascinating variety of other local and
ethnic games.[7]

If pub games are mostly played for money, it doesn't follow that
they are technically gambling games. A 'technical' gambling game

is one which, because the pay-off varies according to the amount staked, can only be conveniently played for a 'hard score', that is cash, or cash substitutes such as chips or counters. Non-gambling games, however—technically speaking—have a fixed scoring schedule enabling pay-offs to be recorded as a 'soft score' of notional points, which may be kept in writing and may or may not subsequently be translated into monetary settlement.

Gambling games do not constitute a single social genre but fall into various categories. Pontoon and Brag are sociable games popular in schools, colleges, working-men's clubs, and the armed forces, though Pontoon has wider appeal, being played as a family game for pennies or matchsticks and as a tightly controlled casino game under the name Twenty-One or Blackjack. Other domestic gambling games include Newmarket and Michigan, respectively the English and American descendants of such defunct but classic games as Hoc, Comet, Pope Joan, and Yellow Dwarf.

Domestic gambling games shade off imperceptibly into what are now described as children's games. Strange as it may seem, such harmless amusements as Battle, Snap, and Beggar my Neighbour undoubtedly derive from primitive gambling games—as indeed do solitaires or Patience games, which may be regarded as a genre in themselves.

At the opposite extreme we must recognize casino games—Blackjack, Baccara, Faro, Rouge et Noir, and suchlike—as a distinctive gambling genre. Games of this sort, designed for rapid turnover with a minimum of social interaction, are characteristically faster, sharper, more solitary, and altogether less friendly than the likes of Newmarket and Pontoon. Incidentally, casinos do not officially exist in Britain: the equivalent establishments are generally known as 'clubs', entry being restricted to 'members'.

Solo differs from Whist proper in being a non-partnership game. It can be played as seriously as Bridge, but lacks a scoring system and is therefore usually played for cash or counters, which gives it the appearance of a gambling game. Equally popular in private and public houses, Solo is also the chief representative of the distinctive genre of 'commuter games'. These are characteristically found in trains, as the American game of Railroad Euchre suggests by its title. The chief requirements of a commuter game are that it should have sufficient intellectual bite to appeal to 'city gents' and that different players should be able to cut in and out of the game, without disturbing its flow, as they get on and off the train. Thus a given Solo school at the end of a journey may consist of four entirely different people from those who started it, with none of them conscious of the fact that any great change has taken place.

Other genres include workplace games and drinking games. The former are associated with particular occupations or places of work, as suggested by the American game of Firehouse Pinochle for a variety easily picked up and dropped again between calls on duty. Gin Rummy, 'the game of the stars', was popular with Hollywood film actors of the 1940s as a good way of passing time between takes, and in the 1970s I was assured that London taxi-drivers mostly played Kalookie in their moments off. (Whether this was a temporary craze or still obtains I cannot say, as I can never find a taxi when I want one.) Drinking games—the term evokes a romantic vision of German student princes carousing in half-timbered bierkellers—are characteristically fast and funny and produce no winner. Their purpose is to yield a loser, whose privilege it is to pay for the next round.

Contract Bridge is a formal, not to say institutionalized, partnership game comparable to Chess in depth, complexity, and social status. Played by men and women and young and old alike, it is the only British card game able to boast professional tutors, nationwide clubs devoted to its practice, regular columns in the press, and at least a modicum of television coverage. In any given year more books are published on aspects of Bridge than on all other card games put together. If, as has been said, the Church of England is the Conservative Party at prayer, Contract Bridge may perhaps be described as the Conservative Party at play.

Poker may be categorized as a gentleman's gambling game, or at least as one played by executives, crooks, and yuppies with pretence in that direction. It is not a gamble in the mindless way of Bingo and casino pastimes, but a game of considerable depth and variety, and, contrary to popular belief, essentially one of skill. Professional Poker-players exist, but the only people who make a living from casino games are casino owners.

Canasta is a highly elaborate and complicated form of partnership Rummy, said—truly—to have been 'invented by the ladies of Montevideo as a counter-attraction to Poker, which, in their opinion, took up too much of their menfolk's time'.[8] A fast and flighty fad game of the 1940s and 1950s, it has since added a few inches to the hips and settled down into domestic respectability, from which position it still succeeds in tickling the fancy of many a jaded Bridge-player in his lighter moments.

From folk to famous

Though differing markedly from one another in make-up and character, Bridge, Poker, and Canasta taken collectively confront us with a paradox. They are all famous games which even the most dedicated non-card-players must at least have heard of, yet from the figures quoted in the survey above it would appear that relatively few people actually play them. Bridge-players will undoubtedly claim a foul in the method of survey (which certainly suffers from other defects), but it seems too great a coincidence that comparably low figures should emerge for games of such comparably high social prominence.

Perhaps 'social prominence' affords a clue to the answer. These three are prominent because in depth and complexity they appeal to the most prominent levels of society, that is, the educated and literate upper socio-economic classes and those who pretend or aspire to them. Many of the games mentioned so far have been informal or folk games of regional or at most national extent, being known little or not at all outside Britain and her former colonies. Bridge, Poker, and Canasta, by contrast, are essentially formal and upper-class games, and international in extent—extending even into those people's republics where upper classes are supposed not to exist. They are not only games played for enjoyment but also desirable social accomplishments of high prestige value. Generally speaking, in any given country the players of national games may well be expected to outnumber those of international games. It is only when the whole card-playing world is taken into account that international games have the weight of numbers on their side.

This offers another perspective on the natural history of card games additional to that of genre, namely, that of formal development. Traditional card games, at root, are essentially products of folk art comparable to ballads, legends, and (more similarly) dances. The earliest form of any such game is necessarily irrecoverable, but all the evidence suggests that it typically starts off as a gaming motif, or combination of motifs, which spreads through the population engendering local embodiments of an unformulated game which is 'everywhere different, yet everywhere the same'.[9] To a certain degree, this level is still occupied by such folk games as All Fours, Brag, and Cribbage, which, despite the artificial appearance of formal rules in formal gamebooks, in fact are played in a wide range of variations, often under different names, in different localities.

Many card games remain fixed at this level. Sometimes, however, a remarkable thing happens. A game played in a prestigious cultural centre undergoes a significant change which seizes the imagination of its players. Inevitably, their enthusiasm communicates itself to a gradually widening public. A wider public wishes to share the experience of those at the centre of the cultural storm, and in no time at all the game has reached what Michael Dummett happily likens to the 'nova' state of an exploding star. Perhaps the greatest centre of all time was the Bourbon Court of Versailles in the seventeenth and eighteenth centuries, from which emanated a whole series of such brilliant card novae as Hoc, Ombre, Comet, Basset, and Quadrille. The fashionable resort of Bath, in the west of England, proved a cultural centre for Whist in the eighteenth and nineteenth centuries, and Paris and New York for Bridge in the twentieth. We might go further than Dummett and draw a distinction between 'novae' and 'supernovae'. A mere nova is one which achieves the status of national card game, such as French Belote, the Germans' Skat, Switzerland's Jass, Sweden's Vira, Hungary's Ulti, Italy's Scopone, Spain's Tute, and Argentina's Truco. A supernova is one which sweeps at least a continent, as did Piquet in the sixteenth century, Ombre in the seventeenth, Tarot games in the eighteenth, Whist in the nineteenth, and Bridge, Poker, Gin, and Canasta in the twentieth.

Nova status entails well-attested consequences. More and more people wish to play it against more and more other people. Clubs are established to provide a greater variety of gaming opportunities, tournaments are organized at regional or national levels. It is obviously desirable that players from different localities and walks of life should all be playing the same game by the same set of rules. To this end a body of interested parties will come together for the purpose of drawing up a definitive code of practice. What they produce—if sufficiently competent to be accepted as authoritative—may then be accepted as the formal embodiment of the game in question. At this point it ceases to be a folk game and becomes a formal game. It no longer evolves fluidly, but at most undergoes a few lurches before eventually settling down to the sort of definitive fixity currently exhibited by Contract Bridge. Eventually, the game passes out of fashion, in which case it either reverts to folk status, like Whist ('clogs to clogs in three generations'), or becomes a fossil, like Piquet.

But this digression still leaves unexplained why such national games as Skat in Germany and Jass in Switzerland achieve the depth of club organization and media coverage which in Britain is reserved for Bridge at the expense of such native games as Whist and Crib.

The answer, I suggest, lies in the peculiar cultural symbiosis of Britain and the United States. For while Bridge, Poker, and Canasta are international luminaries as far as Britain is concerned, all three are 'national' games when viewed from the opposite side of the Atlantic. Canasta certainly, and its ancestral Rummy probably, originated in Latin America and migrated northwards. Poker was invented in the United States and Contract perfected there, and both are clearly most at home in their country of origin, being played over broader reaches of society than probably anywhere else in the world. American Poker may be classless in its native country, but elsewhere is an upper-class game, being complemented by such 'folk' equivalents as Brag in Britain, Primiera in Italy, and Mus in Spain.

Disconcertments

With so many card games to choose from, it is surprising how may people still don't play cards from one year's end to the next—four in ten of the British population, according to the survey. Some, presumably, do not discriminate against cards specifically but merely lack interest in games generally—either because they are 'game-dumb' in the way that others are colour-blind or tone-deaf, or because they are lucky enough to lead lives which afford them sufficient opportunity to exercise the skills and faculties that would otherwise atrophy if particular games had not been devised to engage them. Others may be so enthusiastically wedded to a single game like Chess or Draughts, or to an area such as fantasy games, that all their recreational needs are fully met and they have no time for anything else.

Yet others, on being introduced to cards for the first time, may have found the particular game at issue not to their taste or ability, and jumped to the conclusion that card games as a species are not for them. This could be due to an inherent feature of card games disconcerting to those who have not played cards from childhood but come to them from other types of game—namely, a general lack of openness or *clarity*.[10] In most board games, whether abstract or thematic, you can usually see from the outset what sort of things are likely to happen, and can plan your play by visualizing the probable or possible results of prospective moves. In card games, you normally know only the cards dealt to you. You can see that other players also have cards, but don't know what they are. This prevents you from judging the relative merits of prospective moves until you are sufficiently experienced at play to learn what sort of situations are likely to arise from them, and how to select moves in such a way as to engineer good positions, avoid bad ones, or cope with those you cannot directly control. Beginners at cards are therefore playing blindly by comparison with those whose experience has accustomed them to the relatively dim light of incomplete information, and who have begun to develop that intuitive faculty known as 'card sense'. Hence it is not surprising if beginners at cards—especially adults (who have lost the knack of learning new experiences)—lack the self-confidence or blind faith necessary to carry one through the phase of trial and error from which derives that basic grasp of 'what it's all about'.

Another possible source of disconcertment is starting with an uncongenial game. Many would-be card-players may have been put off cards in general because the specific game to which they were first introduced was not suited to their particular tastes and talents. Perhaps it was a gambling game like Poker, which they didn't take to because they are not by nature gamblers, or a social accomplishment like Bridge or Canasta, which they couldn't cope with because it is too complex for beginners. In fact, to attempt Canasta without previous experience of Rummy, or Bridge without a basic grounding in Whist, is like learning to run before you can walk, and Bridge-players who seek to instil their enthusiasm for the game into someone void in basic card experience have a lot to answer for. Bridge, in short, should not be crossed until you come to it.

You may even be forgiven for not coming to it at all. There are games to suit every taste; and if, in exploring them, you discover a preference for card-building over trick-taking, or two-player to multi-player games, or solo to partnership play, then you will have a perfectly good reason for setting off in some other direction. Not all card games have complicated rules, take years of experience to play well, and call for a phenomenal memory, uncanny powers of deduction, and the ability to feign hour-long facial paralysis without breaking into hysterics. No one can cope with more than two of these requirements at once, and few card games require them to do so. The important thing is not to reject all card games, like all members of the opposite sex, on the basis of an unhappy experience with one or two of them. There are plenty more where Bridge and Poker come from, and one can spend a lifetime falling in and out of love with different card games. Unlike other bits of life, there is no virtue in remaining monogamously wedded to any of them.

The devil's picture-book

Perhaps the greatest resistance to card-play still emanates, especially in Protestant countries, from those who have been brought up to shun gambling, and to identify cards—'the devil's picture-book'—as nothing else. This error arises from the unquestioned assumption that all card games are gambling games because some are, and partly from a muddled notion as to what constitutes 'gambling' in the first place.

Whether or not a game counts as gambling depends more on the motivation of the players than on the substance of the game. Gambling means 'playing for money'; but since anything can be played for money, from Chess to Hopscotch, players are only gambling if they are using a game primarily for this purpose, and not if they are playing it primarily for some other purpose—such as to pass the time, to enjoy being sociable, or to exercise the reasoning faculties. While it is true that all card games *can* be played for money, and some, like Poker, can *only* reasonably be played for money, 'gambling' nevertheless defines the motivation and interest of the players, and cannot be held binding on the definition of card games as a whole.

Objections that may be validly raised against gambling mostly derive from secondary associations of the word—for example, that of excess. Even the childish 'Snap' could rightly lay itself open to a charge of corruption if played by adults for excessive stakes—that is, real wealth which, financially or morally, they are not entitled to lose.[11] Gambling here implies an excessive degree of interest in the outcome of the game. Compulsive gamblers are held by some psychologists to suffer from a pathological condition akin to masochism, in that they unconsciously need to lose in order to punish themselves.[12] All this is alien to the nature and function of games, which, rightly used, are played for pleasure, not pain; are designed for the exercise of social intercourse, not for the working out of solitary obsessions; and are, by definition, intended to be won.

Another association is that of chance, or lack of control over the outcome. Some card games are undeniably more like lotteries than skilled exercises, and only scrape into the category of games by an act of semantic generosity. They can hardly be condemned for their triviality, except in so far as mindlessness may lead to recklessness. But most card games involve some degree of skill, and some a very high degree. The higher the degree involved, the greater the intrinsic interest of the game; and the greater its intrinsic interest, the less need players feel to derive an income from its outcome. This is not to say that skill and monetary interest are mutually exclusive. Poker, one of the most skill-demanding of all card games, is inevitably played *for* money because it is necessarily played *with* money: cards themselves are not the instruments of play but represent measures of value on which the skills of money management are exercised. On the other hand, skilled trick-taking games such as Bridge and Skat are played *with* cards, and may or may not be played *for* money. The fact that some do play them for money, or at least convert the final score into some sort of settlement—such as who pays for the refreshments—does not make them gambling games by definition. Rather, the fact that many people do not play for money specifically releases them from this charge.

If the practice of converting notional points into a trifling monetary settlement is not to be tarred with the same brush as vicious gambling, then why, it may be asked, do it at all? Some reply that keeping a written account ('soft score') is burdensome to the appointed scribe and open to error, whereas settling each deal in cash ('hard score') is quicker, more accurate, and involves no complex calculations at end of play. To this it may be retorted that a scoresheet can be kept in duplicate, remains a checkable record for future reference, and generally takes up less space on the table; furthermore, if hard score is still preferred, intrinsically valueless counters will do the job equally well. Others argue that if a player has no 'real' stake in the game he may spoil the others' pleasure by playing recklessly and taking pointless risks; but the remedy for this, surely, is to choose your company carefully and ostracize silly players. The great nineteenth-century card expert, 'Cavendish' (Henry Jones), justified playing a rubber of Whist for small stakes on the ground that it served 'to define the interest of the players'. This is more subtle. It certainly serves to realize (literally) the interest of the players, which takes us back to playing sensibly and carefully; but, so far as definition is concerned, the same effect may be achieved on paper by always ensuring that the final scores are converted to or expressed in zero-sum format—that is, the amounts that would be paid if money were actually involved.

Most games originally were played for money, which is why 'gaming' does not just mean 'playing games' but is actually syn-onymous with 'gambling'. The practice of not doing so—an historically recent development—may be explained by a variety of social factors. To the influence of Protestant morality, traditionally strong in Britain, and to a consequent tightening of legal restrictions on gambling, may be added such humane considerations as a reluctance to damage social relationships by inflicting loss on other members of the group, and, if players are of unequal skill or experience, a feeling that stakes would be unfair.[13] If, in fact, monetary stakes discourage some from spoiling the game by playing recklessly, it may just as easily cause others to spoil the game by playing nervously and hence badly.

This process has paralleled, and been reinforced by, the development of games of skill in which the interest attaching to the outcome has been diverted into the mental challenges induced by greater sophistication in the mechanics of play and scoring. It is widely held that games originated in the process of lot-casting and divination, which partly explains the depth of fundamentalist objection to it. As games of chance arose from casting lots by the replacement of religious interests by mercenary ones, so games of strategy arose from games of chance by the gradual replacement of chance determinants by those of skill. If it is surprising to learn that Chess was once a gambling game and sometimes played with dice, it is because modern Chess has completely ousted its dice-determined variants. Strategic card games, however, have not ousted chance-determined gambling games, and may therefore still be influenced by their persistent example. Perhaps, then, the most blameless justification for nominal stakes lies in tradition. The harmless vestige of an ancient practice, it no more forces a classification of card games as gambling than the military origin of Chess forces its classification as a war-game. Except in technical gambling games like Poker, playing for money is not an essential but only an optional extra, and whether or not it is exercised is a matter of taste and habit.

Vindications

As a source of mental and social recreation to millions of players world-wide, cards offer the unrivalled merits of being small, neat, inexpensive, and full of ideas. ('Ideas', to misquote an image from Gerald Abrahams, 'inhabit the pack, to be seen or missed, as animals inhabit the forest.')[14] They are pleasant to hold and manipulate, and exhibit an attractive balance of basic concepts like number, colour, abstract symbolism, and human archetypes. They offer games suitable for any number of players of any age from five upwards, of any required degree of depth or triviality, and engaging any combination of talents from the intuitive to the intellectual. They are also fast. Unlike board games, card games do not keep you in suspense or boredom waiting for your turn to come around. They are good practice for those who like, or need, to exercise their capacity for making rapid decisions on a basis of part information and part judgement.

Where games are valued as a means of bringing people together for the enjoyment of a common social activity, cards may be treasured for the breadth of their appeal and the depth of their sociability. Contradictory images—the nervous, eye-glazed fluttering of the casino Blackjack addict, the film-studio Poker set-up apparently staged by the local Mafia—represent the more newsworthy pathology of card-play rather than its general practice. I take particular issue with the underlying sentiment of John Scarne's assertion that 'Nobody plays [cards] only with close friends.'[15] While the definition of 'close' may give him an out, it seems a matter of common experience and observation that card games are mostly played by people who know and get along with one another, whether family, friends, neighbours, fellow-travellers, club members, or workplace colleagues.

The pleasures of card-play may stem from the unconscious, and therefore largely unremarked, satisfaction of participating in a ritual governed by conventions—'rules', perhaps, though agreed from within rather than imposed from without.[16] Convention implies co-operation, and this imbues them with a marked educational value. The competitive nature of games is easily exaggerated and often confused with aggression, especially by those who would do away with all but so-called co-operative games. 'Playing to win', in a civilized society, should be a self-contained concept restricted to the field or framework of the game itself. Only the disturbed and maladjusted embark on games to demonstrate their superiority (or adequacy?) in the 'real world' outside.

This is not to deny that winning is the legitimate object of a game. On the contrary, playing without seeking to win threatens the stability of the group by failing to perform one's own role in the ritual and thereby degrading everyone else's. Do not be misled by a rule often encountered in gamebooks which states 'The object of the game is to win the pool'. It isn't. The object of the game is to compile a hand of matched cards, win a majority of tricks, or whatever, and winning the pool is the pay-off for achieving that object.[17] Some may make it the object of playing the game, but it is not the object of the game itself. A better one is to enjoy the shared exercise of talents and values held in common. Card games, therefore, rightly exercised, may well come to fulfil Dr Johnson's expectation of 'generating kindness and consolidating society'.

2

What's in a game?

M. I know a game I always win.

X. If you can't lose, it isn't a game.

M. I can lose. But I always win.

    S. Distoeff and G. Albertazzi, in *Last Year at Marienbad* (1962)

The way I do it, it isn't gambling.

    Robert Mitchum, in *His Kind of Woman* (RKO, 1951)

What you play with governs what you play, as you will soon discover if you try playing football with a shuttlecock or ping-pong with a puck. We therefore start our exploration of card games with the nature of the gaming material itself.

Cards are flat and flexible objects made from layers of pasteboard pressed together and printed on both sides. One side is marked in such a way as to give each card an individual identity; the other is either blank or carries a design common to every card, so that none can be identified from the back. This two-faced nature of the cards themselves generates two basic characteristics of all natural card games, namely, *randomness* from the front, in that the cards are shuffled before play, and *secrecy* from the back, in that their identities are revealed only to those who hold them. (As Cardano put it in 1564,[1] 'There is a difference from play with dice, because the latter is open, whereas play with cards takes place from ambush, because they are concealed.') A game in which backs and fronts are irrelevant, like pitching cards into a hat or building card houses, does not count as a natural card game. Hardly more natural are games of 'perfect information', in which all cards remain face up throughout the play.

Randomness and secrecy are not unique to cards but are shared by dominoes and Mah-jong tiles. All have known and unknown sides and evidently derive from a common ancestor, probably in dice. Neither Mah-jong tiles nor Chinese dominoes are used for the positional games associated with western dominoes. Mah-jong is basically Rummy, and Chinese dominoes are mostly used for games related to Cassino.

Chance and skill

A major attraction of card games is that they are in general neither wholly mindless, like most dice games, nor excessively cerebral, like Chess, but offer a reasonable balance of chance and skill. The actual balance varies from game to game, enabling well-informed players to select from the vast repertoire of card games the one or two best suited to their tastes and talents.

Because card games normally start from a random and secret opening position, with cards dealt face down from a shuffled pack, they are often collectively dismissed as games of chance as if there were nothing more to them than that. Some compound the error by confusing chance with luck. Chance is equivalent to the mathematical concept of probability, which is a precisely measurable factor enabling the accurate prediction of average outcomes over long runs of random events—the longer the run, the more accurate the predictions. Luck is at best a platitude and at worst a superstition. To describe anyone who wins a lottery or game of pure chance as lucky, after the event, is merely platitudinous; but to believe that some people win with predictable consistency because they are lucky by nature, or exert some mystic influence over the gaming materials, is unsupportable, in our present state of knowledge. It is true that card-players often have runs of good or bad hands, but this is as mathematically natural as the fact that a surprisingly long sequence of heads or tails may turn up in a sufficiently prolonged bout of coin-tossing.

A game of skill is indicated when certain players win more consistently than others. The shorter the run of games over which they do so, the greater the skill or strategy likely to be involved. Strategic card games vary not only in the degree of skill they bring into operation, but also in the type of skill or skills engaged. Memory is most quoted in this connection, though it is much exaggerated. While it is true that some degree of memory is useful to some games, it is equally true that others make no particular demand on this ability—apart from the need to remember the rules of play and how to tell one card from another. Other skills, such as observation and deduction, may involve memory but should not be mistaken for it. Certain games call for highly specific skills. Pelmanism is by definition a memory game, while Snap tests reaction speed, I-Doubt-It is pure bluff, and Gops pure psychology. Even cheating is a variety of skill.

What most concerns us in card games, however, is strategic skill. The extent to which it obtains in various games depends on several factors, of which the following may be usefully singled out.

Chance

Because cards are shuffled before play, the opening position of a card game is always unpredictable (because governed by chance), unknown (because players can only see the backs of one another's cards), and unequal (because some may be dealt a better hand than others). This contrasts in every respect with most board games—Chess, Backgammon, Monopoly, Snakes and Ladders, etc.—whose opening position is defined by the rules, known to everyone, and theoretically equal.[2] But starting from a random or 'chance-determined' position does not necessarily mean that chance prevails throughout—Chess, for instance, remains a game of skill even if players agree to start from move 10 in a game selected at random from *Modern Chess Openings*. Card games promote equality by other means. Typically, a 'game' consists of many deals, so that in the long run each side or player will have been favoured and unfavoured to about the same extent. In Duplicate Bridge, pairs play as teams, and the partners at one table are presented with the same hands of cards as those received by the opponents of their team members at the other. One can hardly expect to go any higher in cancelling out the effect of chance on the outcome of a game. Duplicate Bridge, of course, is an extreme end of the spectrum. At the other are simple card games for children or gamblers in which the whole course of play is governed by chance, with chocolate buttons and other fortunes literally won or lost on the turn of a card. Other card games lie at various points between the two extremes, with Twenty-One/Pontoon/Blackjack nearer the chancy end, Bezique and Rummy somewhere round the middle, and Solo, Whist, and Skat closer to the top.

Choice

The essence of strategic skill lies always in choosing the right move. The reason why Snakes and Ladders is a game of pure chance, despite starting from a known and equal position, is that the player in turn has no choice but to roll the dice and move as directed. But choice alone is not enough: it must be *significant* choice. Ludo is a game of chance, despite its choice of moves, for the very reason that there is no point in having a choice if players have no way of telling whether one move is likely to be better than another. Briefly, then, the fact that card games involve some element of chance does not by definition exclude them from the realm of skill. The defining feature of a game of skill is not the absence of chance but the presence of significant choice.

Coherence

By this I mean both the extent to which one's play affects or restricts that of other players ('player interaction') and that to which what happens early in the game affects what happens later ('consequentiality'). Coherence is essential to strategy, which implies the ability to formulate a plan designed to produce a situation envisaged in advance—not necessarily an exact and predetermined sequence of moves, but at least an overall plan of campaign which can be used to guide and inform the choice of subsequent moves. The skills it calls for are those of vision and foresight, and, in the deepest examples, notably Chess, of creative imagination.[3] The deepest card games are those like Bridge, Skat, and Piquet, in which play begins with a fair degree of information as to the lie of cards, and is pursued without the interruption of random events beyond that of the deal.

Strategic card games might be thought less 'coherent' than strategic board games because the formulation of an opening strategy is—surely?—hampered by lack of information as to the lie of cards. Many modern trick-taking games, however, overcome this objection by starting with an 'auction', whose purpose is not just to determine the conditions and object of the game but also to convey more information as to the opening position and players' intentions before any card is played. Some might further object that even if a game does not involve events as random as the roll of dice, it may be just as indeterminate in that, if you do not know which of several probable cards an adversary has until he plays one of them, its appearance might just as well be a random event as far as you are concerned. This is countered by emphasizing that such uncertainty is essential to the enjoyment of cards, and that the strategic content of a card game differs not in degree but in kind from that of a completely open board game. The key to that difference lies in the question of information.

Information

If choice is essential to a game of skill, then information can hardly be less important, since an uninformed choice is no choice at all. This is where card games differ most distinctively from most board games. Typically, board games are games of 'perfect information', in that the situation resulting from every move is entirely open (and 'above board') to all players. As games of 'imperfect information', cards are sometimes assumed to be naturally less skill-demanding than those of perfect information—even though the latter include Snakes and Ladders as well as Chess! This error arises from a failure to see that different games test different types of skill, and goes with an unwarranted assumption that the skill of Chess—which takes perfect information for granted and is therefore essentially positional—is the only one worth exercising. But information is not absent from strategic card games: rather, it is released gradually as cards are played or announcements made, and much of the information that has not yet been revealed is to be deduced or inferred—or even 'intuited'—from that which has. The acquisition of information is as much the goal of strategy in strategic card games as the positional moves made as a result of the knowledge acquired. Indeed, in the higher trick-taking games positional moves may be made specifically for the purpose of acquiring information, even at the expense of loss of material—a device equivalent to the gambit at Chess. To recognize this as a defining feature of card games is to expose the fallacy of Mortimer Collins, who, in *Attic Salt* (1887),[4] observes: 'There are two classes of men, those who are content to yield to circumstances, and who play Whist; and those who aim to control circumstances, and play Chess.'

Card games play many variations on the theme of information, for example in the amount of it they make available, the speed at which they give it out, and the ways in which it may be ascertained. It is always gradually revealed by the play of cards. It is sometimes openly revealed at start of play, as in the dummy feature of Bridge, the spread misère of Solo, and the face-up tableaux of many Patience games. It may be 'declared' in exchange for a score, as at Piquet and Bezique. It may be conveyed between partners in accordance with accepted conventions, whether of play (at Whist), of bidding (at Bridge), or even of facial gestures, as in many Spanish games (Truco, Mus, etc.). And always it may be gained by applied psychology: by watching, studying, and knowing the habits of partners and adversaries—above all, of oneself, so as not to give the game away. Hence the Poker face. Poker is largely a game of psychology, and Gops of nothing but.

If we look at the introduction of bidding, of conventional leads, of exposed hands, of Stud at Poker, of the dummy feature of Bridge, and so on, we find that the evolution of card games has tended to increase the amount of information available at start of play. The logical conclusion would appear to be a game of perfect information, in which everyone plays with hands exposed. Yet although such games have been invented, none has ever become widely popular.[5] Then why increase the initial information at all? Evidently, because so many different combinations of cards may be dealt from a shuffled pack that there is not enough strategic space in which to make and act upon deductions before the hand is over. The more information provided at start of play, the more rapidly and accurately can further information be acquired once play begins; but to reveal all at the outset would then leave nothing to be achieved.

We may therefore conclude that card games are, by nature, not so much games of imperfect information as games about imperfect information, and about its acquisition or perfectibility, and that this character derives directly from the basic two-faced nature of the cards themselves—mysterious on one side and self-evident on the other, and therefore 'played from ambush, because they are concealed'.

Counting the cost

We had a very pleasant game of cards, though I lost four shillings and Carrie lost one, and Gowing said he had lost about sixpence: how *he* could have lost, considering that Carrie and I were the only other players, remains a mystery.

'Mr Pooter', in G. and W. Grossmith, *The Diary of a Nobody* (1892).

Another attraction of card games is that they produce more interesting results than the simple win/lose outcome of games like Chess and Ludo. In fact, the scoring systems of sophisticated games like Bridge, Skat, and Piquet are so interesting that they require some effort to master.

At base, card games are technically 'zero-sum' games, in that one player's gain is another one's loss, and all wins and losses sum to zero—as Mr Pooter (above) was intuitively aware. This is inevitable in gambling games and clearly reflects the original purpose of card-play. But while it remains obvious in hard-score games, which are mostly gambling games by definition, it is often less apparent in soft-score games played for purely notional points. Thus, if at the end of a two-hand game one player has scored seven points and the other ten, one's immediate impression might be that the rest of the universe has made a net loss of seventeen. However, since the rest of the universe is not playing, the final account will, in practice, be expressed as the difference between the 10 and 7, i.e. 3. The loser actually or notionally pays the winner an amount equivalent to this difference, thereby transposing into zero-sum format (one scores minus 3, the other plus 3) and restoring the universal status quo.

Card-game books often give the impression that hard-score games can only be recorded on paper by zero-summing at each deal—that is, writing down the complete transaction between all players. This is true in a technically gambling game like Poker or Pontoon, where play consists in varying the stakes. But it does not apply in a pseudo-gambling strategy game like Solo, where previously agreed amounts are attached to particular bids and feats. Therefore, contrary to popular belief, it is not necessary to record every detail of a series of transactions at Solo as shown in the 'hard-score' section of Table 1.

TABLE 1

	Hard score (zero-sum)				Soft score (points on credit)			
	A	B	C	D	A	B	C	D
C wins solo worth 16	−16	−16	+48	−16			16	
A loses solo worth 12	−36	+12	+12	+12	−12			
BD win prop/cop worth 10	−10	+10	−10	+10		5		5
D wins misère worth 20	−20	−20	−20	+60				20
Actual totals	−82	−14	+30	+66	−12	5	16	25
Zero-base totals	0	68	112	148	0	17	28	37

It is because this is so complicated that Solo players tend to stick to coins or counters even if they are not seriously playing for money, thereby destroying its appeal to those who dislike even the appearance of gambling and prefer to play for a written score. Yet exactly the same result is easily achieved by scoring on paper as at Whist or Bridge. As illustrated by the 'soft-score' section, you need only record the nominal value of the game won or lost by the individual bidder (half that amount in the case of a prop-and-cop, because it is shared by two). Although at end of play the four scores no longer sum to zero—in this example they total 34—they still record precisely the same proportional relationships as those obtained in hard score. This is easily demonstrated by reducing both sets of scores to 'zero-base', that is, setting the lowest score to zero and adjusting the others accordingly. Here it means adding 82 to the first set and 12 to the second, from which it will be seen that zero-based soft scores equal zero-based hard scores divided by the number of players. This will always be so, regardless of how many play, and whether the individual soft scores are positive or negative.

If players wish to keep written scores for convenience but ultimately convert them into a hard score for cash, the soft scores may be zero-summed as follows:

(1) total the scores (34, in this example);
(2) multiply each player's score by the number of players (−48, 20, 64, 100);
(3) anyone with less than the total (34) pays the difference into a pool; anyone with more takes the difference out of the pool.

Here, A pays 34−(−48)=82, B pays 34−20=14, C draws 64−34=30, and D draws 100−34=66. These amounts sum to zero and exactly match the final totals in the first method. Alternatively, each player pays anyone with a higher score than himself a sum equivalent to the difference between their two scores. Thus A pays B 17, C 28, and D 37 (see right-hand zero-base line on the scoresheet), making a total of 82 . . . and so on.

Even if players do not wish to translate points into cash, it is still worth reducing all actual scores to zero-base format, as this will clarify their relative positions as accurately as if they had been settling up in hard score as they went along. They may, of course, not be interested in relative positions. Greater interest may attach to making record scores, and some games, like Strip Poker, are by nature designed to produce only a single winner or a single loser. In such cases, players must agree in advance on what their objectives are, otherwise they may employ different strategies, and so, in effect, be playing different games.

Many card games retain relics of their staking origins even though played for notional points. Where games were originally played for a single fixed stake, certain outcomes might result in the stake's being lost double or treble. In Short Whist, played up to five points, the losing side would pay a double stake if it failed to reach three, a treble if it scored none. At Cribbage, if the loser fails to reach half the target score, he is 'in the lurch' and pays double. At Piquet, the loser is 'rubiconed' for failing to 'cross the Rubicon' of 100 points. In games of the Skat family, a player or side is made *schneider* ('clipped', 'tailored', 'cut down to size') for failing to gain a specified level of card-points, and *schwarz* ('blackened') for losing every trick.

The scoring-objects used in hard-score games—apart from cash itself—are varied and intriguing. Counters were formerly called 'fish' and actually so shaped, and one might suppose some natural connection with the 'pool', i.e. the receptacle in which they reposed until won. However, 'fish' is equivalent to the French word *fiche*, literally a pin or similar object of small value, and 'pool' to the French word for the same thing, *poule*, literally a 'hen'. The hen may date from more agricultural days as symbolic of plunder or booty, though another explanation relates it to the traditional French egg-container shaped like a hen, from which the monetary stakes were drawn like eggs (nest-eggs, perhaps?). If 'pin' brings 'point' to mind, we may note that the 'points' for which menials played in the fifteenth century were ribbons, being of purely nominal value, like modern matchsticks. The actual points of point-scoring games hark back to the points or *puncti* literally 'punctured' on the sides of dice.

The written points of soft-score games are not necessarily recorded on paper. Chalk-marks on table-tops and scratches on slates do equally well. Charles Cotton, in 1674, refers to setting up so many 'chalks' for a game, and the German game of Schafkopf ('Sheepshead') is so called because the nine points needed to win are recorded as lines gradually building up to the representation of a sheep's head. Soft scores may not be written down at all. In Cribbage they are recorded by moving pegs round a scoreboard; the Basques use pebbles for the game of Mus; Euchre is traditionally recorded by revealing or covering pips on low numerals cards not used in play; and elaborate mechanical markers have been devised in their times for Whist, Bezique, and Piquet.

The play's the thing

If at cards 'a game' is defined as everything that happens between one deal and the next, and if brevity be the soul of wit, then card games are notably wittier than board games. Simple gambling games run as fast as dice, because simple gamblers require only a rapid succession of outcomes to bet on, while strategic card games last a little longer, because it naturally takes time to make decisions. Even so, it rarely takes normal people more than five minutes to bid and play a hand of Bridge or Solo. This may suit Solo in its capacity as a pseudo-gambling game, but will not do for what we have already described as a social accomplishment appealing to the thinking levels of society. They will certainly be looking for something with more substance and structure—partly to satisfy those for whom 'the play's the thing', rather than the pay-off, and partly to ensure that the consequently much-delayed eventual outcome more fairly reflects the cumulative skill involved. A single deal may be won on the strength of a lucky hand; but, the more deals there are to a game, the more certainly will good and bad hands even out among the players, leaving skill the convincing explanation for consistent wins.

There are various ways of structuring deals into games, or games into sessions. (English lacks convenient terms for whole and part-games. A part-game may be referred to as a deal, hand, or round, though each of these has a more specific meaning. For whole game, 'rubber' is too specific to Whist and Bridge, and the French *partie* does not transplant well into English.) The simplest method is to keep playing until at least one player has had enough and wishes to close the account. Such an *ad hoc* structure typically obtains at Skat, whose length is only constrained by the agreement that everyone should have dealt the same number of times. The Hungarians have a curious method of bringing to a close their national card game Ulti. As John McLeod reports:[6] 'When a player wants to end a session soon he says "The Ace of hearts deals and does not deal"(!) The meaning of this is as follows: At the end of the following hand it is noted who originally held the Ace of hearts . . . Play continues until it is the next "Ace of hearts" player's turn to deal. Three more hands are played (beginning with his deal) and then the session ends'.

The simplest predetermined structure is that whereby the game consists of a specified number of deals (e.g. six at Rubicon Piquet) or is played up to a specified total (e.g. 121 or 181 at Crib). Several games are named from their usual target score. Piquet was formerly known as Saunt or Cent from its target of 100, while 'Five Hundred' and Cinq Cents denote respectively a development of Euchre and a variety of Bezique.

More sophisticated structures obtain at Whist and Bridge. A 'game' at Whist is won by the first side to reach five (GB) or seven (US) points, which can be done in one deal but usually takes several. At Bridge, it is won by the first side to reach 100 points scored 'below the line'—that is, for tricks won by contract, as opposed to incidental bonuses. In both, a 'rubber' is the best of three games. If one side wins the first two, it scores an extra bonus and the third is not played. Card-game scoring systems are often strategically significant, in that any change to the scoring exerts its influence on the strategy of play. This is indicated by the phrase and concept 'playing to the score', and by the time it has taken to develop such sophisticated systems as those of Skat, Contract Bridge, or even Gin Rummy. It may well be that the failure of Solo Whist to attract the attention it deserves reflects its failure to develop a scoring system of comparable refinement.

Two's company, three's ideal

Yet another attraction of card games is that they are playable by any reasonable number. For centuries they have proved a uniquely sociable activity against the alternatives of two-player games requiring exclusive concentration, such as Chess, Draughts, and Backgammon, or dice, which appeal almost exclusively to male gamblers and cannot, with the best will in the world, be described as 'sociable'. Playing-cards, perhaps partly for their aesthetic qualities, have always appealed as much to women as to men, and their sociable nature is enhanced by the fact that whole games consist of relatively brief part-games with opportunities for talk and relaxation in between.

The popularity of games for two needs no explanation. As far back as the fifteenth century most depictions of card-play show two at a table, many of them apparently married couples or lovers.[7] Classic two-handers include Cribbage, Piquet, Bezique, Sixty-Six, Klaberjass, Belote, and Gin.

Three is recognized as an ideal number almost everywhere except in Britain, where the tyranny of Whist and Bridge has always militated against the trinity of Ombre, Skat, and suchlike. A particular merit of three is that all the cards can be dealt without anyone having perfect information as to their distribution, while the fact that only two hands are unknown enables deductions to be carried out early in the game, thereby increasing the element of skill. Another is the opportunity afforded for alternating solo with partnership skills, an ideal format being that in which at every deal one player—anciently the dealer, latterly the highest bidder—plays alone against a temporary alliance of the other two.

The popularity of four-handers is no more in need of explanation than the four-sidedness of most tables, but it is worth pointing out that they occur in several formats:

1. In *cut-throat* games, each plays for oneself and there is little or no opportunity for co-operative effort. Few cut-throats are designed specifically for four: most, like Black Maria, Nap, and simple forms of Rummy, can be played by any number from three up.

2. In *alliance* games, one person either plays alone against the other three, who therefore play as temporary allies, or engages another to act as a temporary ally for a two-against-two contest. Many different games of this type are known as 'Solo'. Other classics include Quadrille and Boston.

3. The *fixed-partnership* format of two against two has tended to oust three as the most natural number of players under the influence of Whist and Bridge. (This has also affected such three-handers as Skat, which are often played by four at a table with each in turn sitting one hand out.) Partners normally sit opposite each other, with

North–South playing co-operatively against East–West. In German-speaking countries such games are described as 'cross' games because players sit 'a-cross' the table from each other. Thus Gaigel, the partnership version of Mariage, is also known as Kreuzmariage. It is natural in partnership games for partners to stick together for tournament and social play. Bridge, in particular, was promoted in the 1930s as a game played between married couples—with Ely Culbertson, its chief exponent, dedicating his famous *Blue Book* to 'My wife and favourite partner'.

One by-product of rivalry between three and four-hand play has been its interesting effect on the size of the pack. In Britain, the 52-card Whist/Bridge pack has long been standard equipment, thirteen being an ideal number of cards per player. This has tended to favour the introduction, development, and persistence of any game played with 52 cards in preference to games played with any other number, and this in turn has reinforced a preference for four-hand play. In Europe, by contrast, packs have gradually decreased in length from 52 to 48, 40, 36, 32, and even 24 cards, all of which are increasingly convenient for three-hand play.

Beyond four, every increase in the number of players correspondingly decreases the amount of initial information available and so tends to reduce the efficacy of strategic skill over chance. Many are gambling games by definition, five or six being an ideal number for Draw Poker and seven for Stud. Others, especially Rummies, are playable without modification by any number from three up. Such games are generally described as 'round' games, a term that arose in the late eighteenth century with the technical perfection of circular tables designed to accommodate an indefinite number of players.

Attempts to adapt strategy games for more than four players have met with varying degrees of success. A natural approach for five is to follow the alliance principle, with one player becoming the soloist and seeking the assistance of a temporary partner to play against the other three. An early instance is provided by the five-handed version of Hombre practised in late seventeenth-century Spain under the name Cinquillo, later revived by the French in an extension of Quadrille called Quintille. Many such five-handers have been devised for Tarot games, which are more suitable for the greater number of cards involved. Six-hand partnership games are a natural extension of those for four, being playable between either three pairs or two trios—as, respectively, in the French games of Sixte and Sizette.

3

A joke of cards

'Who cares for *you*?' said Alice . . . 'You're nothing but a pack of cards!'
Lewis Carroll, *Alice's Adventures in Wonderland*

Playing-cards as we now know them could not have originated before
the economic production of paper, which in Europe dates from the
thirteenth century. The very word is from medieval Latin *charta*, 'a
sheet of paper', and survives as the standard term for the object
throughout Europe—variously written *cart*, *carte*, *karte*, *karta*, *kartya*,
etc.—except in Spain, where *naipe* is preferred to *carta*, though both
are used.[1] That cards are not a game but equipment for playing
different types of game is underlined by the varied and sometimes
picturesque words adopted as the collective noun for them. Fifteenth-
century English players spoke of a 'pair' of cards, Shakespeare later
uses 'deck', and his contemporary Harington, 'pack'. 'Pack' has been
the standard British word since the seventeenth century, when 'deck'
became dialectal and American. Russians speak of a *korona* or 'crown'
of cards, Poles of a *talia* or 'waist', Czechs of a *balicek* and Hungarians
of a *csomag*, both meaning 'packet', and Italians of a *mazzo* or 'bunch'
of cards. Curiously, a special word for 'pack' is by no means universal.
Those who first needed to refer to it in writing normally wrote in
Latin, which left them no alternative to *ludus chartarum* for 'pack' as
well as 'game'. This deficiency is reflected in many modern languages.
The French speak of *un jeu de cartes*; in German it is *Kartenspiel*, in
Dutch *kaartspel*, and in Danish *spil kort*. On reaching the Romanian
joc de carts we realize that had English here not shed its Norman
French overlay we might now be playing with, and at, 'a joke of
cards', thereby making jokers of us all.

Standard and non-standard cards

If we discard advertising packs, commemorative packs, pornographic
packs, educational, political, satirical, and other novelty packs, what

we are left with are the standard cards that regular card-players prefer for playing games with. A quick glance through a standard pack, with its heraldic suitmarks and medieval courtly figures, rightly suggests that it goes back a long way and can hardly have changed much over the centuries. Trevor Denning does not overstate the case when he writes: 'Playing-cards are unique . . . in their resilience to change. Nowhere else can be found examples of an imagery which the passage of centuries has left . . . so little altered in form. No detailed study of popular taste could fail to single out playing-cards as artefacts of unrivalled stability.'[2] Does this mean that card-players are die-hard traditionalists opposed to change on principle? Such is the burden of this anecdote from E. S. Taylor's *The History of Playing Cards* (1865):

One of the large card-makers in London told the writer that many years ago . . . the head of the firm introduced a scarcely perceptible modification in the colour of the knave's garter . . . Very soon the steward of one of the considerable clubs came rushing down in a great hurry to the shop. 'The Committee can't think what you have been doing to the cards! All the members are complaining that they keep losing! What have you done?' At first the card-maker said 'Done? Why, nothing!', not thinking the trifling change of any importance; but on further enquiry it was found that the indescribable something the clubbists had detected confused them, and he was obliged to take back all his cards, and supply those of the former old fashioned sort. Such is the influence of a trifle!

Exaggeration apart, traditionalism alone will not account for the persistence of playing-card design. The practical explanation is that players tend to concentrate on the game rather than the cards, whose appearance they so take for granted that any visual deviation is likely to be distracting. In fact, players do not 'read' the individual elements of a card any more than they read the individual letters of a word, but unconsciously take in the whole shape at a glance. If the design is, so to speak, misspelt, they may well be disconcerted without necessarily being able to put their finger on the disconcerting element. This may be less true today since the introduction of indices—those numbers, letters, and miniature suitmarks in the top left corners of the cards enabling their rapid identification in a tightly squeezed hand—but the fact remains that regular card-players still prefer to play with the regular design or 'standard pack' to which they are accustomed.

Different localities have different standard packs. This discovery often surprises British players, whose own national pack of cards happens to have achieved currency as the international standard associated with globally popular games like Poker, Bridge, and Rummy, and who are therefore unaware that there is anything local about it. To understand card games properly it is helpful to know that traditional games are often inextricably linked to the packs used for them. Thus the 52-card international standard is also variously referred to as the Whist or Bridge pack, the 32-card French-suited pack as the 'Piquet' pack, and the 36-card Swiss-suited pack as 'Jass'-cards from the games traditionally associated with them. It is for similar reasons that the everyday Greek word for 'pack', *trapoula*, was originally the name of a particular card game. When a game achieves such popularity that it spreads to neighbouring countries using different packs, it either brings its own pack with it, as in the case of Piquet, Whist, and Bridge, or else undergoes modifications to accord with the pack and playing habits of the newly conquered country. This explains why so many clusters of similar games are played in slightly different ways with packs of different length. Bezique, for instance, which in England and France is played with a double 32-card pack, is equivalent to American Pinochle played with a double 24-card pack, to Germany's Sixty-Six played with 24 cards, Austria's Schnapsen played with 20, Spain's Tute played with 40, and so on. Perhaps it is not surprising that so many languages equate a game with a pack of cards.

Five main types of standard pack are current in Europe, each distinguished by its suit system, its court characters, and its selection of numeral or 'spot'-cards.

1. *French-suited cards.* The suits are spades, clubs, hearts, diamonds; the courts are King, Queen, and a male menial called Knave or Jack; and numerals One to Ten. The One is usually called Ace and often ranks higher than the King. Although the full pack therefore comprises 52 cards, many traditional continental games use packs stripped of lower numerals from Two upwards. The commonest short pack comprises 32 cards, with Seven low (omitting Two to Six). The French-suited pack, besides that now regarded as the international standard, is also the standard national pack of France, Britain, the Low Countries, Scandinavia, much of northern Germany, and parts of Switzerland. Each country has its own distinctive design or pattern of French-suited cards. Many derive from the Paris pattern of French cards. The most widespread or international design is that of Britain, which in turn derives from France's now extinct 'Rouen' pattern.

2. *German cards.* Unlike French cards, which have an air of refinement and courtliness about them, traditional German cards are

of a more rustic and military character. The suits are leaves, acorns, hearts, and bells (spherical hawk-bells), and the all-male courts are King, Ober, and Unter. The last two are often taken to mean 'Over-Officer' and 'Under-Officer', though the terms originally referred to the position of the suit-signs. The numerals are Seven to Ten inclusive and a Deuce—usually referred to as 'Ace', since it behaves like one. The traditional German pack therefore now comprises 32 cards, though deriving, like the French Piquet pack, from an earlier 36-card model by suppression of the Sixes. Other lengths are produced for particular games, such as 36 for Tarock, 24 for Sixty-Six, double-24 for Gaigel. German cards appear in a variety of regional patterns. They are used mainly in the German south, but are also current in Poland, Czechoslovakia, Hungary, Austria, and other eastern European countries.

3. *Swiss cards.* These are closely related to German cards, as might be expected. The suits are shields (actually escutcheons), acorns, flowers (called roses), and bells; the courts are King, Over, and Under, and the numerals theoretically Six to Ten plus Deuce. The Ten in fact is known as 'Banner', and actually depicts that object, with the appropriate suitmark on it. The Swiss pack therefore comprises 36 cards, though a 48-card pack (lacking only Aces) is still produced for the ancient Kaiser-game, formerly known as *Karnöffel*. Swiss-suited cards are also known as *Jasskarten* from the principal game played with them, to distinguish them from the indigenous Swiss design of French-suited cards or *Piquett-Karten*.

4. *Spanish cards.* By comparison with French and German cards, both Spanish and Italian cards might perhaps be characterized as noble and ceremonial. The suits are swords, clubs (real ones, with knobs and leaves), cups, and coins; the courts are King, Knight or Cavalier, and a male Servant or Valet. The numerals are normally One to Seven, making a 40-card pack in all, though 48-card packs are also produced with numerals One to Nine. Spanish cards, in a variety of designs and patterns, are used throughout the Spanish-speaking world, including South and Central America, as well as in Catalan France (Roussillon), the Balearics, Morocco, and central and southern Italy.

5. *Italian cards.* These are basically the same as Spanish cards, with suits of swords, batons, cups, and coins; courts of King, Knight (Cavalier), Footsoldier; and numerals One to Seven, making a 40-card pack, though 52-card packs are also manufactured. The main difference lies in the representation of swords and batons. Italian swords are curved (like scimitars), depicted at full length, and

interlaced with one another at top and bottom to produce an integral design, whereas Spanish ones are straight, depicted separately, and on higher numerals are shortened into what look like daggers in order to avoid overcrowding the space. Italian batons and Spanish clubs are both basically sticks, but whereas Spanish sticks look as if they have just been hewn from trees, those of Italy are narrow and neatly turned ceremonial objects best described as batons. They are long, thin, straight, and interlaced into a pattern reminiscent of trellis-work. Italian-suited cards are restricted to the north of the country, where they appear in a variety of local or regional patterns.

This outline will do for a general appreciation of the cards employed in European games, though a more thoroughgoing classification of the various national and regional standards has been devised by the International Playing-Card Society for the specialist requirements of collectors.[3] From this viewpoint it should be added that Spanish and Italian cards are collectively classed as Latin-suited cards, which also include a now extinct Portuguese variety and the highly specialized Aluette cards of western France. Tarot cards, as we shall see, are basically French or Italian-suited standard cards with the addition of a fifth suit.

Other traditional packs survive which do not fit into any of the categories above because they lack suits in the normal sense of the term. An Italian pack employed for Cuccú (literally 'Cuckoo'; the equivalent English game is called Ranter-go-Round) dates back to the seventeenth century. From it derive the Scandinavian Gnav pack, known as Killekort in Sweden, for which various other games have since been devised. Mercante in Fiera, or 'Fairground Trader', is another traditional game with cards of its own. Jewish Kvitlakh cards have numbers without suits and are used for a gambling game equivalent to Pontoon or Twenty-One.

On the cards

The identification marks sited at diagonally opposite corners of each card, called indices, did not appear before the mid-nineteenth century. Some such cards were marketed as 'squeezers' from the way in which they could be easily read though squeezed tightly into a protective fan. Previously, as old illustrations show, cards were often larger than today's and would have been either spread between two hands or passed rapidly from one to another to enable a proper survey to be made of the player's holding. On French-suited cards the individual

symbols—technically called pips, or peeps—were widely separated
and placed close to the edge, so that not too much of the card had
to be exposed for recognizability. The same applied to Spanish
suitmarks, which were long produced by French card-makers and so
affected by the same design considerations. German, Swiss, and Italian
suitmarks were separated in some cases and in others conjoined into
a single design unit. An integrated design is no problem: once you
know the overall shape of a given numeral card, you don't have to
count the pips.

A noteworthy consequence of the invention of corner indices
concerns the word now used in English for the lowest court.
Previously, the English equivalent of French *valet* was normally
known as Knave, in the sense of 'serving-lad'. In the seventeenth
century it came to be called Jack, from the name properly applied to
the Knave of trumps at All Fours. All Fours being a low-class game,
the use of 'Jack' for 'Knave' was long considered vulgar. ('He calls
the Knaves *Jacks*!', remarks Estella contemptuously in Dickens's *Great
Expectations*.) When indices came in, it was obviously preferable to
use 'J' rather than 'Kn' to avoid confusion with 'K' for King. Jack
has since become the normal title of the lowest court, though 'Knave'
can still be heard.

The index 'A' for 'Ace' needs little explanation. Originally, the King
was the highest card in the pack; but from an early date—perhaps
late fifteenth century—special significance began to attach to the
nominally lowest numeral, so that it often rose to a position above
the King, leaving the Deuce or Two as the lowest-ranking card.
(Except, as we have seen, in Swiss and German packs, where the
missing Ace has been replaced by Deuce.) These by origin are dicing
terms from Anglo-Norman French, the first going back to Latin *as*,
the smallest unit of coinage. Of those that follow—*trey, quater, cinq,
sice*—only 'Trey' is likely to be encountered over the card-table.

Not all traditional packs have succumbed to corner indices. Some
lack them entirely, others incorporate them only partially. Spanish
cards present a novel variation on the theme. Only ranks are indicated
in the corner, for which purpose the three courts are numbered 10,
11, 12. (Tens, remember, are omitted from the Spanish pack.) Suit
is quietly indicated by the number of breaks or gaps in the shorter
edges of the thin-lined rectangle enclosing the main design: three
breaks denote clubs, two swords, one cups, and an unbroken line,
coins.

Court cards have always depicted human figures bearing, or at
least looking at, the appropriate suit symbol. The figures are variously

depicted standing, enthroned, or mounted on a horse, and on the earliest cards were always shown full length. For this reason they were formerly called 'coats' from their most obvious feature, 'courts' being an obvious corruption. They are known technically as *têtes* or 'heads', and colloquially as 'face' or 'picture' cards. (In Damon Runyon stories they are 'paints'; consequently, anyone of great age or wealth is described as being 'up in the paints'.) There must have been a natural tendency for players to arrange their cards, automatically or absent-mindedly, in such a way as to present the courtly characters right way up. As there was no such need for numerals to be reversed, observant players could gain much useful information by noting the number of cards their opponents reversed while sorting their hands. It was evidently to overcome this problem that designers hit upon the notion of making 'double-ended' courts by halving the figure at waist level and repeating the halves, so that a head always came at the top. By the end of the nineteenth century this practice had spread to many regional patterns, though even today some continue to resist it. Some patterns are produced in both single and double-ended versions.

Given the need for cards to be indistinguishable from the back, it is not surprising to find their backs now printed with complex, abstract patterns comparable to those found on banknotes, though often more decorative and highly coloured. The value of such a pattern is that it effectively masks the tiny blemishes which quickly accrue with intensive play, and which would otherwise serve as identifying features to players with sharp eyesight and a good visual memory—like the fifteenth-century Parisian card-sharps we shall meet in Chapter 7. Back-patterns are often highly decorative and printed in more colours than Joseph's coat. On the whole, though, serious players favour cards with fairly abstract, sober, and discreet backs. Those with pretty or pictorial designs, unless special issues for collectors, are mostly bought as presents by people who are not themselves regular card-players and so have no other basis of selection than the pattern on the back. What is surprising is that such back-patterns did not become widespread until the nineteenth century. Before that, backs were largely plain, or bore at most the repetition of a simple pattern such as spots or fleurs-de-lis. Most Tarot cards still bear a tartan-like pattern of eighteenth-century origin described in French as *taroté*.

Ironically, the simpler patterns afford greater protection against cheating than highly complex ones. An elaborate floral pattern, for example, makes it easier to differentiate between individual cards by means of tiny design variations following a code known only to the user. Marked cards or 'readers' are, as is well known, used only by professional magicians and bona fide conjurors, and for this purpose are obtainable in plain brown-paper packages from discreetly sited mail-order houses.

Which brings us, finally, to the Joker, Juggler, Fool, and downright Mountebank. The international 52-card pack usually contains one or more extra cards known as Jokers and depicting what appears to be the traditional idea of a court jester. As the similar figure of a medieval Fool is also an important card in most forms of Tarot, the Joker is often said to derive from it. This is quite fallacious; nor is it even likely that whoever invented the Joker was influenced by acquaintance with the Tarot Fool. The first true Joker was added to the American pack in the mid-nineteenth century to act as the 'Best Bower' or top trump in the game of Euchre, a position it still holds in the derivative game of Five Hundred. Poker-players then used it to spice up their game by treating it as wild, its holder counting it as any natural card he wished for the purpose of improving the value of his hand. In this capacity it has since been adopted into other games, especially those of the Rummy family. In the simpler games it is optional, but Canasta and its relatives positively require a minimum of two Jokers to every 52 naturals.

The Tarot Fool, if not the Joker, has its real-life medieval archetype in the popular public performer of one or more of a variety of entertainments, as suggested by the synonym 'mountebank', one who mounts a platform or stage, and such names as English *juggler*, French *jongleur*, Spanish *juglar*, these meaning 'minstrel' and deriving from Latin *ioculator* meaning joker or player. Ultimately, as Peter Burke observes, 'A "player" . . . might play instruments, play a part, play the fool, or all of these.'[4]

Strange are the ways of words! We started this chapter by discovering that a pack of cards (ludus chartarum) might easily have been called a joke of cards, and end by learning that a school of players (ludus ioculatorum) is nothing more than an academy of jokers.

4

A good deal of history

Hinc est quod quidam ludus, qui ludus cartarum appellatur, hoc anno ad nos pervenit, scilicet anno domini mccclxxvii.

Thus it is that a certain game, called the game of cards, has reached us in the present year, namely AD 1377.

John of Rheinfelden, 1377

An amazing fact of card-game history is how rapidly the craze hit Europe. Cards are first mentioned in Spain in 1371, described in detail in Switzerland in 1377, and by 1380 reliably reported from places as far apart as Florence, Basle, Regensburg, Brabant, Paris, and Barcelona.[1] References are also claimed for earlier dates, but these are relatively sparse and do not withstand scrutiny. A problem with ancient manuscripts is that many are not original but survive only in later copies. Copyists, being human and overworked, were prone to error, and often consciously or unconsciously 'improved' on their models. A fifteenth-century Civil Servant reissuing a fourteenth-century gaming prohibition in which cards are the only game unlisted (being then unknown) would be quite likely to add it for completeness. There is nothing dishonest about this—it merely acts as a warning not to take old documents as gospel just because they are old.

Three of the earliest references describe cards as 'new', a description which is strengthened by a good deal of negative evidence. They are notably absent from appropriate passages in Petrarch (1304–74), Boccaccio (1313–75), and Chaucer (1343–1400), despite the authors' evident interest in games. Nor do they occur in *Confort d'Amy*, a poem by Guillaume de Machau addressed to Charles V on his accession to the throne in 1364, which denounces gaming in general and dice in particular, but says nothing of cards. Two equivalent ordinances from Paris dating from 1369 and 1377 respectively omit and include reference to card games, as do two others from St Gallen dated 1364 and 1379.

Most early mentions of cards occur in prohibitions or restrictions on gambling. One of the first comes from a statute of the city of Florence dated 23 March 1376 (1377 by today's calendar), wherein the city elders prohibit by 98 votes to 25 the playing of 'A certain game called *naibbe*, [which] has recently been introduced into these parts'. *Naibbe*, variously spelt, is the earliest word for cards: it first appears as *naip* in a Catalan document of 1371[2] and still survives as modern Spanish *naipes*. A German ordinance, enacted in Regensburg on 23 July 1378, declares various games, including 'spilen mit der quarten', punishable by fine if played for stakes higher than those expressly permitted.[3]

Two other documents relating to cards are more specific and more interesting, if at the same time rather more problematical. One is a Chronicle of the City of Viterbo, now lost in its original form but credited by later copyists to Cola di Covelluzzo. The relevant entry probably ran: 'Anno 1379: fu recato in Viterbo il gioco delle carte, che in saracino parlare si chiama nayb' (In the year 1379 there reached Viterbo the game of cards, which in Saracen speech is called *nayb*). Stories crediting cards to a 'Saracen named Hayl' derive from the garblings of a later copyist, who misread this as 'il gioco delle carte da un saracino chiamato Hayl'.[4] The other, even more remarkable for its age, detail, and sympathetic interest in the subject, is the Tractatus de moribus et disciplina humanæ conversationis, an allegorical treatment of the game of cards composed at Basle by a monk now known as John of Rheinfelden (though he actually declares himself born at Fribourg).[5] An oft-quoted passage referring to the introduction of cards appears at the head of this chapter. Amongst other things, we also learn that:

In the game called cards, the cards are painted in different designs and are played with in various ways. In the commonest manner—the one in which they first reached us—four cards depict four kings, each of whom is seated on a royal throne. Each of them holds a certain sign in his hand, some of these signs being considered good but others signifying evil. Under these kings come two marshals, of whom the first holds the sign upwards, as the king does, but the other holds the same sign downwards in his hand. After this are ten other cards, of the same overall size and shape. The king's sign appears once on the first of these, twice on the second, and so on with the others up to and including the tenth. Thus the king is the thirteenth card, and there are fifty-two cards altogether.

(Reference to the ways in which the two marshals hold their suit symbols probably indicates the original meaning of 'Over' and 'Under' for the two male figures themselves.)

Unfortunately, John reneges on his promise to explain how cards are played, and hereupon embarks upon his allegory without even describing the suit-signs to which he has tantalizingly referred. Further details are provided, but may not be authentic. John's text, though dated 1377, is not known at first hand but comes from a manuscript copy made in 1429, of which further copies were made later in the same century. The surviving texts go on to describe alternative packs, some with Queens instead of Kings, or additional to Kings in a 56-card pack, and some of 60 cards in all—though still with no indication of the suits involved. These are suspected of being additions made by the first copyist. While such variety of packs undoubtedly existed in 1429, they can hardly have been extant when John was writing, since the text one moment states 'cards have just come to us in this year 1377', and the next distinguishes between the form in which they first arrived and a variety of forms into which they have since evolved.

Early cards were individually hand-made and painted, which made them expensive to produce and may at first have restricted the market to the well-to-do. Such is suggested by an entry dated 14 May 1379 in the Register of Duke Wenceslas of Brabant and his wife Jeanne, recording the disbursement of four peters and two florins 'to buy playing-cards with' (quartespel met te copen). It is reinforced by an oft-quoted entry in the now lost account-book of Charles VI ('the Mad') of France: 'Donné à Iacquemin Gringonneur, peintre, pour trois ieux de cartes à or et à diverses couleurs, de plusieurs devises, pour porter devers le dit seigneur roi, pour son ébatement, cinquante-six sols parisis' (Paid to Jacquemin Gringonneur, painter, for three packs of cards in gold and colours of various designs, to present to his said Majesty for his entertainment: 56 Parisian sous).[6]

The fact that this remained the earliest known reference to cards throughout the nineteenth century and much of the twentieth is responsible for several of the myths still perpetuated about their origins. The suggestion that Gringonneur actually invented cards— 'for the amusement of a mad king'—is quite gratuitous, as is the claim that the cards in question were Tarots, which are now known to be a later invention. Nor does it follow that only the rich were card-players; for those who could easily afford new cards could probably afford to lose old ones in the direction of servants, menials, and hangers-on. Town ordinances of Paris (1377) and St Gallen (1379) prohibit card-play in contexts clearly directed at the working classes, and a wide public may be inferred from the anecdote about early fifteenth-century Parisian card-sharps (see Chapter 7). This anecdote also supports the view that early card-play was restricted to the relatively sophisticated town-dwellers. Countryfolk may have resisted the degree of concentration required for even simple card games, cleaving rather to their homelier, faster, and less demanding dice games for decades to come.[7]

The belief that cards were only for the rich is also inspired by the fact that the surprisingly large number of cards surviving from the fifteenth century are mostly luxury items produced by the expensive process of hand-painting or (later) metal-engraving. Probably, though, they survive mainly because they were acquired and preserved as works of art or collectors' items rather than as playthings. Cheaper products for everyday use are well attested, but they must have disintegrated rapidly and been thrown away in thousands daily, just as they are today. The records make it clear that cards were popular at all levels of at least urban society throughout the fifteenth century. Bernardine of Sienna preached against gaming at Bologna in 1423 so persuasively that the populace consigned their cards in thousands to a public bonfire. In 1452, at Nuremberg, his disciple John Capistran sparked off an even bigger bonfire reportedly fuelled by 76 sledges, 3,640 backgammon boards, 40,000 dice, and a comparable quantity of cards.[8]

Eastern origins

The pack described by John of Rheinfelden as structured into four suits comprising ten numerals and three dignitaries each sounds too well developed to have resulted from an act of spontaneous generation. One would expect an earlier form with just ten numerals and perhaps a King, or a suit of twelve cards rather than the numerologically suspect thirteen. Doubts are reinforced by the historical background. Europe had only recently been ravaged by successive attacks of the Black Death: its population was almost halved, civil order was strained, people were poor, and labour scarce. This seems hardly the place or time for the unheralded creation of a novel but refined game played with such delicate objects as painted pieces of paper. Now if cards were not invented in Europe they must have come from the east. But as the east is rather large, the question is—which part?

The old idea that cards reached Europe from China in or following the thirteenth-century voyages of Marco Polo is no longer credible. It is true that playing-cards were then known to the Chinese, and probably invented by them; but trade with China had petered out long before John of Rheinfelden described them as new, and, more significantly, Chinese cards themselves seem too different in kind to have been directly ancestral to the European model. Those which can be dated New Year's Eve, 969, when the Emperor Mu-tsung is reported to have played them with his wives,[9] were evidently domino cards. Domino cards, or tiles, bear at each end a pattern of spots corresponding to the fall of two dice, for example 1–2, 6–5, etc. A difference from western dominoes is that whereas our 1–6 domino (for example) is 1 at one end and 6 at the other, a Chinese 1–6 is 1–6 all over, just as a western Ace of hearts is ♥ A all over. Hence they are used not for positional games but for what we should recognize as card games.[10]

Western playing-cards more closely resemble Chinese 'money cards'. In their oldest embodiment these have four suits: cash, strings (of cash), myriads (of strings), and tens (of myriads), with numerals 2–9 in the first three suits and 1–9 in the fourth. The pack was sometimes extended by the addition of special ranks in one or more suits. Modern three-suited versions lack the tens suit but are doubled or quadrupled to 60 or 120. Mah-jong, a nineteenth-century invention, is clearly a version of the three-suited money-card pack. It is tempting to view money cards as the ancestor of western playing-cards, since cash is comparable to coins, and strings to sticks or staffs or batons—vaguely. Some associated games are even of the trick-taking variety, with 'upside down' ranking in the cash suit, a feature recalling the upside-down ranking of coins and cups in such ancient western card games as Hombre.[11] Even so, the jump from Chinese money cards to western suited cards is both abrupt and pushed for time, and, although there must be some connection between the two, it has yet to be explained.

A theory placing cards in the baggage of 'crusaders returning from the east' amounts to unsupported guesswork. Crusading was effectively over by 1300, but there is no substantiated evidence for the existence of cards in Europe before 1371, which leaves far too long a gap. Yet another suggestion, that they were introduced by the gypsies, fails for the opposite reason that gypsies did not appear in Europe until some forty years after cards themselves. An even more untenable theory derives card games from a Persian (Iranian) Poker-like game called As-Nas. Despite fantastic antiquity often claimed on its behalf, As-Nas only became popular in the eighteenth century and is not recorded earlier than the seventeenth. Sixteenth-century Persians describe themselves as playing Ganjifeh, the ancestor of Ganjifa, which in various forms remains the national card game of India. This is a trick-taking game played with circular cards (usually), comprising from eight to twelve suits with ten numerals and two dignitaries in each. The suits, which in one version (Dasavatara) represent the various incarnations of the Hindu deity Vishnu, bear no plausible relation to those of either Chinese or European cards. Ganjifa cannot be traced back any earlier in India, and, although it may form a link in the chain somewhere along the line, its distinctive cards cannot be seen as directly ancestral to those of Europe. A more imaginative idea, proposed by Hellmut Rosenfeld, roots the origin of playing-cards in Indian four-sided Chess. This has not won great support, despite several plausible parallels, and does not mesh well with generally accepted historical outlines.[12]

After all these negatives and flights of fancy, it is a relief to record a positive answer to the question 'Where did European cards come from?'—namely, 'From the Mamelukes of Egypt'.

The undisputed evidence is an almost complete pack of Mameluke playing-cards which L. A. Mayer discovered in the Topkapi Sarayi Museum, Istanbul, in 1939. Mayer's discovery remained little known until his original paper was posthumously republished in book form in 1971, together with photographs of most of the cards.[13] By this time it was possible to include details on the fragment of a similar card subsequently identified in a private collection. The pack itself does not predate 1400, but the 'private' fragment is tentatively dated to the twelfth or thirteenth centuries. The reconstructed pack[14] consists of 52 cards, with suits of swords, polo-sticks, cups, and coins, numerals from one to ten, and courts labelled *malik*, *nā'ib malik*, and *thānī nā'ib*—respectively King, Viceroy or Deputy King, and Second or Under-Deputy. This is virtually identical with the Italian variety of Latin-suited pack, and the date of the other fragment (identifiable as one quarter of the four of cups) clinches the argument that the Mameluke pack came first. Furthermore, the Arabic *nā'ib*, 'deputy', suggests the origin of Italian *naibbe* and Spanish *naipes* for the name of the game—'the Game of Deputies'.

As to whether cards reached Spain first and migrated to Italy, or vice versa, or both more or less at once, the evidence is conflicting. Priority has long been accorded to Italy, partly because cards always spread along major trade routes, and Venice was the tradesman's entrance to medieval Europe. Furthermore, the design of traditional Italian cards more closely reflects that of the known Mameluke pack, while that of Spain suggests a later simplification. The translation of Mameluke polo-sticks into Italian batons is explained by noting that polo was then unknown in Europe, and that on some Mameluke cards the sticks are sometimes straightened rather than curved in order to fit the pattern better. Batons are therefore a logical transformation, whereas the equivalent Spanish suit of clubs—cudgels, in fact—represent a radical design departure made for the sake of clarity. On the other hand, an old theory crediting cards to the Moors of Spain has recently been reinforced by the discovery, in Barcelona, of an uncut sheet of cards dating from the fifteenth century and bearing designs remarkably similar to those of Mameluke cards.[15] This makes it equally possible that Mameluke-style cards reached Europe via Spain, and thereafter migrated to Italy before giving way to the now distinctive Spanish packs. On the whole, though, the balance of evidence and argument still favours Italy.

To draw these threads together, Professor Dummett outlines a possible 'working model'[16] of relationships between European, Mameluke, Persian, and Indian cards. There may, he suggests, have existed in Persia or central Asia a prototypal 48-card game involving four suits with ten numerals and two courts in each. Known as 'Ganjifeh' to the Persians, it was transmitted by them to both eastern and western neighbouring cultures. In India the name was taken over as 'Ganjifa' and the pack later elaborated by doubling the number of suits (to $8 \times 12 = 96$). In Arabia it became 'Kanjifah'— a word appearing in an inscription on one of the Mameluke cards— and was expanded by the addition of a third court card ($4 \times 13 = 52$). Similarities between the two systems suggest a prototypal suit of money or coins and a non-trump trick-taking game in which the numerals ranked upside down in half the suits; but certain differences in the mode of trick-play[17] suggest that Indian and Arab cards derive from a common ancestor rather than either from the other.

The origin of species

Card-making rapidly became a growth industry in the early fifteenth century, and by the beginning of the sixteenth, through vigorous export drives from the principal card-making centres of France and Germany, cards had conquered most of Europe short of Greece, Russia, and northern Scandinavia. Because they were still too great a novelty to have developed any substantial tradition, both their individual designs and the constitution of the pack at first varied enormously over this vast area. Local manufacturers invented suits and courtly figures at whim, or to satisfy a perceived demand for novelty and variety, and it is not until the latter part of the fifteenth century that we see relatively standardized versions of the major national packs beginning to emerge from a state of designers' anarchy.

By 1420 German and Swiss card-makers were producing packs in thousands, first by stencil, soon by woodblock, and subsequently by metal-engraving, for a relatively restricted up-market product. From the outset they felt no need to perpetuate any particular form of suits or figures, and rapidly embarked on an orgy of imaginative variation on that simple basic theme. In designing suitmarks they forsook the ceremonial abstractions of Mameluke and Italian models in favour of concrete objects drawn from everyday life, whether animals (hounds, deer, hares, bears), birds (ducks, falcons, herons, parrots), flowers (pinks, roses, lilies, columbine), or hardware (shields, helmets, banners, bells, keys, purses, thimbles, etc.). A pack would often contain one each of several categories linked by a chosen theme, typically hunting—though it is hard to spot the connection between those of my particular favourite, namely, cupids, goats, harps, and millstones. Many packs were lengthened by the incorporation of a fifth suit, but there is no record of a five-suited game and they may have been collectors' items rather than functional pieces. Alternatively, one suit might have been kept back to replace another when one of its cards got lost or torn.

Experimentation extended also to the courtly figures. The original over and under-marshals variously appear as Knights and Knaves, the Knaves sometimes as Maids. Queens are mentioned in the 1429 copy of John of Rheinfelden's treatise, and in the earliest surviving German cards (1440s) do not come second to Kings in the same suit but head two of the suits in place of Kings. Fifty-six-card packs headed King, Queen, Knight, Valet were common throughout the fifteenth century. This arrangement, recommended as ideal in the 1429 copy of John of Rheinfelden, was evidently current when Tarots were invented, since the Tarot pack retains its four courts to the present day. When three courts again became the norm, all but the French restored the original male hierarchy by dropping the Queen in favour of the Knight.

Despite the persistence of imaginative and one-off packs, standardization had shown itself inevitable well before the end of the fifteenth century, partly because standard packs are cheaper and quicker to manufacture, and perhaps also because regular players who had grown up with cards were now growing less amenable to novelty. (One wonders to what extent the natural conservatism of old age is linked to feelings of insecurity induced by failing eyesight.) Nearly all the suitmarks of traditional Swiss and German packs appear individually before 1450 and in complete systems perhaps by 1475. On visual grounds, it is vaguely possible to derive the German suit of acorns from the Latin suit of swords, leaves from clubs, hearts from cups, and bells from coins; but the preceding chaos renders such equations less than meaningful.[18]

The standardization of what is now regarded as the Spanish variety of the Latin suit-system is less clear-cut. (Amongst other things, Spanish sword and club suitmarks are depicted as plain, simple, discrete objects rather than as component parts of an elaborately integrated design. If a Spanish Nine of swords unmistakably depicts nine swords, its Italian counterpart looks more like a nest of vipers.) The distinctively Spanish system as a whole did not win out over a host of variations in the Spanish style much before the end of the sixteenth century, even if individual elements of it appear a hundred years earlier. Dummett now considers over-simplified his suggestion that Spanish suitmarks originated north of the Pyrenees as a French variety of the Latin suit-system.[19] Latin suitmarks were, however, certainly current in France throughout the fifteenth century, and quite possibly underwent evolutions of design now specifically associated with the Spanish pack. This idea is strengthened by the curious French game of Aluette, played with special cards of a distinctly Spanish type. As there is nothing to connect it with Spain, it may perpetuate a tradition of the fifteenth century when the French themselves used Latin suitmarks.

France's greatest contribution to the world of cards was her invention of spades, hearts, clubs, and diamonds, which first appear as such about 1480. These simple, abstract shapes, while products of artistic genius, were probably motivated by practical and even mercenary considerations, in that they enabled the forty numerals constituting the bulk of the pack to be produced by the sweep of a colour-loaded brush across a single stencil, leaving complex three- or four-colour stencilling to the twelve courts. Despite a fanciful story deriving the four suits from emblems of the four estates of medieval life (military, peasantry, clergy, bourgeoisie), they surely represent a simplification of the German series.

Pique, literally 'pike(-head)', clearly echoes the German 'leaf' suitmark. Its English name 'spade' is thought to derive from Italian *spada* or Spanish *espada*, 'sword', and to reflect an earlier use of Latin-suited cards. But the shape is in fact that of an obsolete all-wood spade tipped with iron, and this literal use of the word is supported by the still current German use of *Schippen* or *Schaufel* (cf. 'shovel') for the suit of leaves.

Trèfle literally means 'clover'—compare Dutch *klaver* for the leaf and the suitmark. It may have been suggested by the shape of the German acorn or Spanish club suit symbol. The latter idea is supported by the English word 'club', which, again, perhaps perpetuates the word formerly associated with the Latin-suited pack.

Cœur comes directly from the German heart symbol for the suit called *Rot(h)*, 'red'.

Carreau commonly means 'paving-tile', but the underlying sense is any four-sided lozenge shape. (It is basically the same word as 'quarrel', the similarly shaped head of a crossbow bolt.) 'Diamond' may reflect the use of that shape to represent the said stone in heraldry. The shape was surely invented first and the word then chosen to illustrate it, not the other way around. It does not naturally derive from the German suit of bells, though these may have had some visual bearing on the fourth suit of the oldest surviving French-suited pack, which actually appears as crescents.

By dividing the four suits into two red and two black, our unknown designers not only facilitated rapid card recognition but also retained the twofold nature of the Latin pack, which had been lost from the German. The distinction in Latin-suited cards between 'long' or 'male' suits (swords and clubs/batons) and 'round' or 'female' ones (cups and coins) is significant in such games as Hombre, where numeral cards rank normally in long suits but upside down in round. Upside-down ranking in half the suits is characteristic of early trick-play: it applies to Chinese money cards and Indian Ganjifa games, is implied by inscriptions on some of the Mameluke cards, remained current in Italy and Spain up to the early sixteenth century, and survives in many Tarot games to the present day.[20]

French court cards are equally inspired in their selection and rationalization of established elements. King, Queen, and Valet are not only more distinguishable than a King and two officers as individuals, but also form a natural and more human grouping as a whole, unconsciously suggestive of the family unit.[21] Modern French packs retain the delightful and archaic feature of court cards bearing individual names, typically:

spades	David, Pallas, Hogier
clubs	Alexandre, Argine, Lancelot
hearts	Charles, Judith, La Hire
diamonds	César, Rachel, Hector

Although the French named-card tradition goes back to the sixteenth century in principle, in practice the actual names have varied enormously and the most constant of them have not applied consistently to the same cards. David, Judith, and possibly Rachel appear to be biblical; Alexander, Caesar, Hector, and Pallas are classical, as also is Argine, whether regarded as an anagram of regina or a corruption of Argea; Lancelot must have been drawn from the Matter of Britain. Charles may be Charlemagne, and Hogier his distinguished cousin. Alternatively, he may head a trio comprising (1) Charles VII of France, (2) Rachel, the pseudonym of his mistress, Agnès Sorel, and (3) la Hire, an illustrious knight of his court. Or is Rachel a corruption of the Celtic Ragnel, relating rather to Lancelot?[22] There certainly seems to be scope for further research on this topic.

English postscript

No one knows when cards reached England. Pre-fifteenth-century references sometimes claimed for them are either misunderstandings or later additions, and we have already noted their apparent absence from Chaucer's experience. Their passage across the English Channel can hardly have been delayed by the so-called Hundred Years War with France, which was barely simmering at the end of the fourteenth century. Isabella, daughter of the King Charles who paid 56 sous for a pack of hand-painted cards, was married to Richard II in 1396, and in 1401 the usurper Henry IV married Joan of Navarre. Either queen may be suspected of including cards in her courtly train, even if there is no evidence for a conviction. Failing them, we recall that the Battle of Agincourt in 1415 was followed by a succession of English administrators in occupied France, some of whom would surely have discovered the delights of card-play. It is hard to believe that cards would have been either unknown or uninteresting to so colourful a character as Humphrey of Gloucester, and impossible to believe that they were not well established by the time Paris reverted to France in 1436. Thereafter, the English were too engrossed in such domestic affairs as the Wars of the Roses to have much truck with foreigners, which may explain why Tarot games never reached these islands, or made no headway if they did.

Even early fifteenth-century references can be misleading, as 'a pack of cards' was then called 'a paire of cardes', which also happens to mean a pair of instruments for carding wool. (The 1418 reference quoted in the *Oxford English Dictionary*, though attributed to gaming implements, from its context almost certainly refers to carding.) The first certain and unambiguous reference to playing cards occurs in one of the many fifteenth-century letters and documents relating to the Paston family. One letter in particular, addressed by Margaret

Paston to her husband John, reports on her enquiry into what Christmas amusements would be permitted at the home of her recently widowed neighbour Lady Morley. There were to be, she learnt,

Non Dysgysings, ner harping, ner lutyng, ner syngyn, ner no lowde dysports; but pleyng at the tabyllys, and schesse, and cards; sweche dysports sche gave her folkys leve to play and no odyr.

For many years this popular reference has been dated (in the *OED* and elsewhere) to 1483–4; but Keith Turner has convincingly argued that the deceased referred to in that letter is Sir John Fastolf, who died on 5 November 1459. As the latter is dated 'Crystemes Evyn', (sc. 1459), it must antedate by two years the previously earliest known record of cards in England, also discovered by Turner, in the records of Edward IV's first parliament (November 1461–May 1462).[23] Paragraph 5 reads:

And also that noo Lorde, nor other persone of lowere astate, condicion or degree, whatsoever he be, suffre any Dicyng or pleiyng at the Cardes within his hous, or elles where he may let it, of any of his servauntes or other, oute of the XII dayes of Christmasse; and yf any presume to doo the contrarie at any tyme, that he avoid hym oute of his hous and service.

The progress of card-play in fifteenth-century England is largely charted by further enactments. The next is from a 1463 statute of Edward IV forbidding the import of cards. Its protectionist tone leads some to believe that they were already being produced in significant quantities by native craftsmen. Later, in 1495–6, an edict of Henry VII 'expressly forbids the practice of card-playing to servants and apprentices, excepting during the Christmas holidays, and then only in their masters' houses, under the penalty to the householder of six shillings and eightpence for every offence . . . It would appear that these games, cards included, were not forbidden from any evil tendency in themselves, but because they engrossed too much of the leisure and attention of the people, and diverted their minds from pursuits of a martial nature.'[24]

Although card games were well established in England by 1500, we do not know what sort of cards were used or what games were played with them. No unquestionably English game is mentioned before the 1520s, and the oldest surviving English cards date from 1590. These are all French-suited; but as French suits were not invented until after 1470, and none of the English suit names is recorded earlier than 1522, we must assume that early English cards bore Latin suitmarks of swords, clubs, cups, and coins.

5

Hoyle on troubled waters

We have strict statutes and most biting laws.
    Shakespeare, *Measure for Measure*

Whatever the rules are, I'll play them.
    Robert Mitchum, in *My Forbidden Past* (RKO, 1951)

Do not read the rules as they are too confusing.
    Wergin, 'How to Become a Popular Card Player', in *Wergin on Skat and Sheepshead* (1975)

To the making of rule-books there is no end, and books on card games are no exception to the rule. Many claim to be the last word in 'Official Rules', and to this end disguise themselves under the name of HOYLE as an earnest of proof and authority. It may therefore be rather surprising to learn that Hoyle died over 200 years ago, and positively disconcerting to find that most card games do not actually have official rules. What's more, the original Hoyle, an eighteenth-century Whist tutor, only described some half-dozen card games, and in not a single instance did he write any rules explaining how the game is played.

What does it all mean? Perhaps we had better start by asking what is meant by 'rules', as the word seems to be used in several different ways.

First, there are the specific or 'definitive' rules of a game, that is those which serve to define it. They will tell us, for instance, the equipment used (e.g. 'cards'), number of players, mechanics of play ('trick-taking'), objective ('to win most tricks'), score ('one per trick taken in excess of six'), and so on. They 'define' the game in so far as, if you change any of the rules, you change the game by definition, and ought in theory to give it a different name. 'All play has its rules', notes Huizinga in *Homo Ludens*;[1] but he might equally have said 'Every game is its rules'.

Next, there are the rules of good and proper play. These are better referred to as the 'laws' of a game, its definitive rules being taken as read. (Many laws, far from being specific, are common to a variety of games.) Laws are of various sorts. Corrective laws specify remedies for repairing the course of play, or penalties for upsetting it, when such things go wrong as failing to follow suit when required to do so. Preventive laws often come under the heading 'etiquette' because they seem to deal 'only' with matters of polite behaviour. But they may be based on very practical considerations. For example, it is not merely bad manners to start picking your cards up before the deal is over, for in doing so you may put your hand in the way of the next card dealt, thereby causing it to fall face up and necessitating another deal. Good behaviour, in any case, is a thing to be encouraged, as it makes the game more enjoyable and keeps it running smoothly. I would also classify as laws, rather than rules, certain conventions that exist merely to save argument. Whether the turn to play passes to the left, as in Britain, or to the right, as in Spain, does not affect the way the game is played; but it has to be known in advance, if only to save the trouble of taking a democratic vote on the issue before play begins.

Thirdly, for any given game, there are so-called rules whereby you may 'attain to the playing it well', as Hoyle expressed it in 1742— or which tell you, in the words of a book title of 1953, *How to be a Consistent Winner in the Most Popular Card Games*. These might be more suitably termed 'guide-lines': they are not rules in the normal sense of the word, which implies some degree of moral imperative. In passing, though, we ought to mention as a dubious case the concept of bidding conventions at Bridge. Theoretically, any system of bids or plays devised not for their face values but as a way of conveying coded information might be classed as rules of winning play, and, as such, set outside the scope of moral legislation. In fact, the laws of Bridge specifically restrict their use to published and recognized systems, and if a team or partnership introduces significant variations, these must be declared beforehand. In other words, bidding systems—Acol, Two-Club, Goren, or whatever—have now become virtually integral to the definitive rules of the game, and thereby turned it into as many different games as there are systems.

In sum, the rules of a game normally consist in its definitive rules (how the game is supposed to go) plus its associated laws (how to ensure that it does). In the world of play, such rules are of the essence—'The rules of a game are absolutely binding and allow no doubt', as Huizinga puts it. That this reflects an everyday perception is demonstrated by the apparent appeal of any book labelled 'Official Rules', and by the steady stream of letters to authors and card manufacturers seeking clarification or arbitration on tricky points that have given rise to problems over the card-table. Players might reasonably be expected to discuss and agree their own remedies in such matters, and probably many do—though how many is an open question, since we only ever hear of those who seek guidance from a supposed external authority.

Such everyday perception is further supported by the fact that universally accepted definitive rules do exist for a handful of formal games like Chess and Contract Bridge. Bridge, however, is exceptional. Card games, for the most part, are not played formally, and few are governed by universally accepted official rules. The most popular card games are best described as folk games, being played with greater or lesser degrees of variation from place to place—so, if you move from place to place, you must be ready to acquaint yourself with local rules before becoming too involved. This applies even to such well-established traditional games as Crib and Solo, for which there may appear to exist a standard set of rules coincident with that perpetuated in all the gamebooks. Close examination of the books concerned will usually throw up differences of detail as between themselves (except where one has cribbed entirely from another) and, even more, as between their bookish theory and actual practice. The latter differences arise because living games evolve, whereas gamebook writers generally do not, many remaining unaware that evolution is a fact of card-game life. Books on card games therefore date rapidly, in part if not in whole. A notorious instance is the game of Brag, which most currently obtainable gamebooks describe in an eighteenth-century version recorded by the original Hoyle, though it must have been extinct by the end of the nineteenth century, and bears practically no relation to what is played under that name today.

This is not to deny that 'The rules of a game are absolutely binding'. A school of players round a given table will certainly be conscious of playing in accordance with absolutely binding rules. (Even if they are cheating! For, as Huizinga pertinently continues, 'The player who trespasses against the rules or ignores them is a "spoil-sport". The spoil-sport is not the same as the false player, the cheat; for the latter pretends to be playing the game and, on the face of it, still acknowledges the magic circle. It is curious to note how much more lenient society is to the cheat than to the spoil-sport. This is because the spoil-sport shatters the play-world itself [by] withdrawing from the game.') With this consciousness may go the unconscious belief that everyone in the world plays that game to exactly the same set of absolutely binding rules. The belief may be pandered to and reinforced by books of rules, but, except for a tiny handful of formal games, it is mistaken. Whether players in Pontefract play the way they do in Pittsburgh or Perpignan, or in *Foster's Complete Hoyle* of nineteen-umpty-ump, is really unimportant. All that counts to their enjoyment of the game at hand can be summed up in Parlett's Universal Rules of Card Games, which are two in number and read:

1. Everyone at the same table should be following the same rules at the same time.
2. Everyone at the table should know which rules they are supposed to be following.

How they achieve this is up to them. Theoretically, they constitute their own authority, and should agree beforehand on all the details of the rules of play. In practice, problems tend to arise in the middle of a hand, giving rise to disputes upon which it is practically impossible to be both creative and impartial at the same time—though in this connection attention may be drawn to the assertion of Aquarius, in *Spanish Card Games* (London, 1890):

[The Spaniards'] way of referring to the dealer to settle every doubtful point or dispute is very marked. A book is never mentioned. The decision of the dealer, right or wrong, settles everything or anything, without a murmur, during outplay. Thus little hitches are readily disposed of, and any game can continue. A dealer can ask advice or consult with others, but his decision is his own, and must be immediate. Players come in and leave a game with a substitute very suddenly, and agree to anything done for them. The coolness, courtesy and skill of the Spaniard at card playing renders him in such things superior to card players of other nations.

In our less idealistic and relatively literate age it is probably more expedient to follow the rules of a printed gamebook, for which purpose the best and most practical Hoyle will be the nearest one to hand, provided it is comprehensive enough to cover points of question likely to arise. Even then, the book itself should not be thought of as bearing intrinsic authority, beyond that of the author's own competence and experience: it can only be invested with an authority which, by their very submission to it, actually derives from that of the players themselves.

Higher levels of authority are those of the club or federation of clubs within which the players practise—like the Portland Club, the

American Bridge League, the German Skat Federation, and so on. These levels bring us from the realm of folk to that of formal games. Such rules as they promote are evidently as authoritative as one can get. Even so, I think it worth asserting that the rules drawn up by any official body should be regarded not as the official rules of the game in question, but as the official rules of the body concerned, be it the International Bridge Federation or the Whist-Drive Committee of the Friends of the Village Hall. And they are still only authoritative to the extent that players agree to abide by them.

Proto-Hoyles

A book that tells you how to play any game covered seems such an elementary and desirable necessity of everyday life that it is hard to believe there was ever a card-playing time when no such thing existed. It therefore comes as something of a surprise to find that books of this sort did not appear until the mid-seventeenth century, some 300 years after the appearance of cards themselves. Surprise diminishes when we note that this period saw an information explosion comparable with that of the late twentieth century, with an accompanying increase in literacy. It was, for example, also the time of the earliest newspapers. Previously, true folk games were played by truly illiterate folk, while those of the literate classes were simply picked up like any other social accomplishment.

This makes it difficult to recover information about the earliest card games. It is not entirely impossible, for there remains plenty of early writing on cards and card games: the problem is that most writers, being ecclesiastics, were more interested in moral than technical instruction—not so much 'how card games should be played' as 'why card games should not be played'. A notable near miss was John of Rheinfelden, whose treatise of 1377 was intended to describe card games for moral (i.e. allegorical) purposes. Unfortunately, he did not fulfil that promise, beyond remarking that 'they are played in various ways', and even this could be a later interpolation.

In the 1430s a certain Meister Ingold of Alsace wrote a treatise called *Das güldin spiel* ('The Golden Game'). From this we learn that the 52 cards of the pack represent the 52 weeks of the year in which we fall into sin, the sins in question being symbolized by the four suits (roses, crowns, pennies, rings) and thirteen ranks depicted on the cards.[2] We also learn that the ranks represent various medieval characters who 'win' one another in a given order of precedence, suggesting the mechanics of a trick-taking game—possibly Karnöffel.

Similar moral allegory occurs in a sermon datable to about 1470, in which the game of 'Triumphs' (tarots) is distinguished from games played with the ordinary pack, though all are equally inventions of a devil called Azarus ('Hazard').[3] Several games are named, some with comments of varying degrees of informativeness. Perdi o vinci, 'Win or Lose', sounds much like a still popular modern Italian game, though the title could apply to almost any procedure. Crica is specifically described as a three-card game, Milaneso as one in which the object is to be the first to reach a total of 50 on the cards. 'Sequentia' evidently means a sequence or straight, 'Fluxo' a flush. The latter, we learn, signifies the instability of money, which it 'flushes out of gamblers like an issue of blood'.

A celebrated list of sixteenth-century card games occurs in Chapter 22 of Book I of Rabelais's *Gargantua*, the 'fearsome' but garrulous history of a rather jolly giant, first published in 1534. 'Having sluggishly mumbled over some scraps of grace', runs J. M. Cohen's translation,[4] 'Gargantua rinsed his hands in fresh wine, picked his teeth with a pig's trotter, and chatted gaily with his people. After which a green cloth was laid, and a stock of cards, of dice and of games-boards were laid out.' Then he played some 195 games, of which the first thirty-five appear to be at cards: le flux; la prime; la vole; la pille; la triomphe; la picardie; le cent; l'espinay; la malheureuse; le fourby; le passe-dix; le trente et un; pair et sequence; trois cens; le malheureux; le condemnade; la charte virade; le maucontent; le lansquenet; le cocu; qui a, si parle; pille, nade, jocque, fore; le mariaige; le gay; l'opinion; qui faict l'un faict l'autre; la sequence; les luettes; le tarau; coquinbert, qui gaigne perd; le beliné; le torment; la ronfle; le glic; les honneurs. (Passe-dix is a dice game, but may also have been a card game, as many early gambling games were adapted from one to the other.) An equivalent German list appears in Fischart's *Geschichtklitterung* ('History-Twistery'), a creative German-language adaptation of Rabelais's story by a later sixteenth-century Alsatian writer. Through three editions, 1575, 1582, and 1590, the author expands the gaming list from a variety of sources to truly Gargantuan proportions, eventually totalling over 600 items.[5]

The earliest technical details of card games occur in the *Liber de ludo aleae* (Book on Games of Chance), written in 1564 by Girolamo Cardano, a 63-year-old Italian scholar and former playboy. This is basically a manual on gambling, which he approaches like the true doctor of medicine that, amongst other things, he was. 'Even if gambling were an evil,' he argues,[6] 'still, on account of the very large number of people who play, it would seem to be a necessary evil. For that very reason it ought to be discussed by a medical doctor like one of the incurable diseases . . .' His aim is to help reduce one's loss of fortune—and time—by showing that outcomes are determined not by a personification of 'luck' ('I have never seen an astrologer who was lucky at gambling, nor were those lucky who took their advice') but by the rigorous if unpredictable logic of mathematics—not to mention the inexorable logic of cheating, which he also examines in detail. To this end he quotes the probabilities of achieving certain outcomes on the throw of various numbers of dice or turns of cards, and explains how these figures are reached. This entirely novel exercise was performed a century in advance of Pascal, who is normally regarded as the father of probability theory.

More relevantly to our enquiry, Cardano mentions many games current in his lifetime—Basset, Primero, Trappola, Triumphus, Geleus, Cricones, Cent, Romfa, Scaltara, etc.—pointing out how they differ from one country to another. He expatiates perceptively on their nature in relation to other games: 'It is more fitting for the wise man to play at cards than at dice, and at *triumphus* rather than other games . . . [for] this is a sort of midway game played with open cards, very similar to the game of Chess.' His descriptions of Primero and Trappola are remarkably detailed for their time, and it is a great pity that nothing survives of the gamebook Cardano claims to have been drafting in the 1520s. Whether it would have served as an instruction manual seems doubtful. Pre-seventeenth-century card-game references, as we have seen, consist of prohibitions, allegories, lists, and, in Cardano's unique work, practical advice on play. None give 'the rules' of any given game from which either the basic mechanics or the proprieties of play may be learnt, all assuming such knowledge to be acquired by word of mouth and practical experience.

One of the earliest books of instruction was published at Rouen in 1647. *Le Royal Ieu du Piquet plaisant et recreatif*, an elementary treatise on the truly royal game of Piquet, marks the starting-point of two distinct but often interrelated pre-Hoyle traditions, one French, the other English. In France, the text was incorporated (probably without permission) in Denis la Marinière's *La Maison académique*, a 'general collection of games', with instruction in Piquet and Hoc, besides such non-card games as Tric-Trac, Billiards, and the Royal Game of Goose, published at Paris in 1654. Subsequent editions—at least five by 1700, and retitled *La Maison des jeux académiques*—considerably expand the text by the addition of Tarots, Triomphe, Ambigu,

Romestecq, Impériale, Homme d'Auvergne, Homme, Reversis ('Currently in use in the highest reaches of society'), and one or two 'family games' to complement those played in the 'highest reaches'.

As instruction manuals they leave much to be desired. The effective communication of basic game mechanics requires not just the ability to think logically and write simply—which is obvious, and can be perfected by practice—but, more importantly, that of anticipating on the part of the learner elementary queries and misunderstandings about things that experts take for granted. This is an unteachable talent, and the requisite skills were yet to be understood and developed. One respect in which these proto-Hoyles may be considered superior to many of their twentieth-century descendants lies in their intuitive grasp of the distinction between formal or court games and informal or folk games. The 1718 *Académie universelle des jeux* includes a lowly game called Ma commère accommodez-moi with the comment 'It is true that this game is very old [implying "and therefore not fashionable"], and that it is little played outside the "populace". But we are not writing here solely for the upper crust . . .'

Wits and gamesters

The English gamebook tradition starts in 1651 with *The royal and delightfull game of Piquet*, an anonymous translation of the French book mentioned above. Piquet had long been played in England under the name Sant or Saunt (from *Cent*, 'Hundred'); but of others current in the previous century—Trump (ancestor of Whist), Noddy (of Cribbage), Primero (of Poker), Gleek, Maw, Thirty-One—little is known beyond miscellaneous and not always explicit references from various literary sources. Henry VIII, who acceded in 1513, is known to have played cards from records of his expenses at the card-table. Shakespeare represents him as playing Primero (*Henry VIII*, v. i), which is quite possible: it was certainly played at the court of Elizabeth I.[7] Shakespeare's acquaintance with card games is variously demonstrated. He most frequently alludes to Primero, either directly or through the phrase 'to set one's rest', meaning to stake everything (*Romeo and Juliet*, IV. v. 6). Noddy is implied in *Troilus and Cressida*, I. ii. 212, by 'Will he give you the nod?', and Thirty-One in *The Taming of the Shrew*, I. ii. 32, by 'Two-and-thirty, a pip out'. A sustained metaphor based on terms employed in Trump, occurs in *Antony and Cleopatra*, IV. xii, from 'My good knave Eros' to 'She . . . has | Pack'd cards with Caesar, and false-play'd my glory | Unto an enemy's triumph'.

Cards were equally favoured at the Scottish court. A note in Leyland's *Collectanea* represents Henry VII's daughter Margaret as playing cards in Edinburgh shortly after her marriage to James IV in 1502. When James VI of Scotland became James I of England a century later Elizabeth's Primero found itself usurped by the Scottish game of Maw. According to Chatto, he played it 'just as he played with affairs of state—in an indolent manner, requiring in both cases some one to hold his cards, if not to prompt him what to play'.[8]

The longest list of early seventeenth-century card games occurs in John Taylor's *Taylor's motto: et habeo, at careo, et curo* (1621). It surveys the gambling activities of what appears to be the original sucker:

> The prodigalls estate like to a flux,
> The Mercer, Draper and the Silkman sucks.
> . . . At Irish, Tick-Tacke, Doublets, Draughts, or Chesse,
> He flings his money free with carelessnesse.
> At Novum, Mumchance, Mischance (chuse ye which),
> At one-and thirty, or at Poor-and-rich,
> Ruffe, Slam, Trump, Noddy, Whisk, Hole, Sant, New-cut.
> Unto the keeping of four Knaves he'll put
> His whole estate; at Loadum or at Gleeke,
> At Tickle-me-quickly, he's a merry Greeke;
> At Primifisto, Post-and-payre, Primero,
> Maw, Whip-her-ginny, he's a lib'ral hero;
> At My-sow-pigg'd: but (reader, never doubt ye)
> He's skill'd in all games, except Look about ye . . .
> And thus the Prodigall, himself alone,
> Gives sucke to thousands, and himself sucks none.

Primero, Maw, Sant, and Tromp are listed in Dekker's *The Belman of London* (1608), while his contemporary Sir John Harington mentions Primero, Maw, Lodam, Noddy, La Volta, Post and Pair, and Bankerout. From Dodsley's collection of *Old Plays* may be extracted references to Gleek, Crimp, Mountsaint, Post and Pair, Ruff, and 'Knave out of Doors'. John Hall, in *Horae Vacivae* (1646), remarks 'A man's fancy would be summed up at Cribbidge; Gleeke requires a vigilant memory; Maw, a pregnant agility; Picket, a various invention; Primero, a dexterous kinde of rashness.' In 1656, one F. Jackson, MA, published a pack of 'Schollers Practicall Cards' for what we should now call 'educational' purposes, although, as Chatto wryly comments, they 'must have formed an almost unsurmountable obstacle to the unlettered, unless they were previously well grounded in Gleek, Ruff,

Post and Pair, Saunt, Lodam and Noddy,—the games to which he chiefly refers in his instructions'.

The text of *The royal and delightfull game of Piquet*, quoted above as the first English-language booklet devoted to a specific card game, soon found itself cribbed for use in the earliest English games compendium, which constitutes one chapter of the second edition (1662) of John Cotgrave's *Wits Interpreter: the English Parnassus*. This extraordinary book can only be described as a sort of Idler's Vademecum, or possibly the Ancestral Playboy Annual. The first edition (1655) contains eight sections: The Art of Reasoning, Theatre of Courtship, Labyrinth of Fancies, Love Songs, Description of Beauty, Poetical Fictions, Letters ala mode, and Richelieu's Key to his Cyphers. The Theatre of Courtship presents various he–she dialogues which, if now mildly erotic, may well have been hot stuff in their day, while the Labyrinth of Fancies gives instruction in such social accomplishments as 'How to make an egg flye about'. For the second edition, the Art of Reasoning has been pensioned off (not surprisingly) to make way for a new chapter on 'Games and Sports now used at this day among the gentry of England'—to wit, l'Ombre (that 'noble Spanish game'), Picket ('ingenious'), Gleek ('noble and delightful'), Cribbidge ('gentile' [*sic*]), and 'the Princely Game of Chesse'. Chess, being followed by an article entitled 'How to cure corns', presumably brings the gaming section to a close.

The first English book entirely devoted to indoor games, *The Compleat Gamester*, was published anonymously in 1674. A later editor (Seymour) plausibly ascribes its authorship to Charles Cotton: the title is evidently modelled on Izaak Walton's *The Compleat Angler*, of which Cotton himself produced a greatly expanded edition in 1668. It is a strange mixture of plagiarism and originality. The opening chapter—'Gaming is an enchanting witchery, gotten betwixt Idleness and Avarice: An itching Disease, that makes some scratch the head, whilst others, as if they were bitten by a Tarantula, are laughing themselves to death . . .'—had already appeared as a pamphlet entitled *The Nicker Nicked: Or the Cheate of Gaming discovered* (1669); and such card games as had already appeared in *Wits Interpreter* were merely copied out for retransmission, not always accurately. (The chapter on Piquet, therefore, goes back to the French booklet of 1647.) To these, however, Cotton added a number of other card games, some unknown from any other context, which he evidently wrote himself. A change of style is discernible after the four chapters lifted from Cotgrave. The latter plunge straight into practical matters ('Deuces and treys must be cast out as useless in this game'), are written impersonally, and try to cover all the learner needs to know. Left to his own devices, Cotton becomes anecdotal, personal, and apologetically incomplete. His first original chapter begins 'All-Fours is a Game very much play'd in Kent . . . and . . . may be lookt upon as trivial and inconsiderable, yet I have known Kentish Gentlemen and others of very considerable note, who have play'd great sums of money at it . . .'. As to the play of the game, 'Now you must play down your Cards, but to what advantage I cannot here prescribe, it must be according to the Cards you have in your hand managed by your judgment to best advantage.' In other words, 'You're on your own.'

All Fours is followed, in similar style, by English Ruff and Honours, and Whist; French-Ruff (= Triomphe); Five-Cards ('an Irish game'); Costly-Colours (a sort of Cribbage); Bone-Ace (a trivial gambling game); Put; Wit and Reason (a childish adding-up game with a forced win for the first player); The Art of Memory (a drinking game); Plain-dealing ('I cannot commend this Pastime for its ingenuity'); Queen Nazareen (an ancestor of Newmarket with extra-curricular attractions: 'The Queen of diamonds is Queen Nazareen . . . the Knave of Clubs is called Knave Knocher . . . If women play among men, it is customary for Knave Knocker to kiss Queen Nazareen'); Lanterloo; Penneech; Post and Pair (= Brag); Bankafalet (a betting game); Beast (a relative of Triomphe). Further chapters are devoted to various sports and pastimes, from Chess to cock-fighting.

Few games are described in sufficient detail to be playable without further research or creative thinking. Like most authors hitherto, Cotton takes some grounding for granted. His stated purpose, which we may or may not take at face value, appears in an introductory Epistle to the Reader as follows: 'It is not my intention to make Gamesters by this Collection, but to inform all in part how to avoid being cheated by them: If I am imperfect in my discoveries, impute it to my being no profest Gamester, and the hatred I bear that Hellish society, by whom I know I shall be laught at . . .'.

Further editions of Cotton's work were produced after his death in 1687, and in 1734 Richard Seymour merged it with his own *The Court Gamester*. First published in 1719, this was ostensibly compiled for the instruction of 'the young Princesses' (daughters of the then Prince of Wales), though he later admits to thoughts of a wider audience, since 'gaming had become so much the fashion among the beau-monde, that he who in company should appear ignorant of the games in vogue would be reckoned low-bred and hardly fit for conversation'. Seymour covers only Ombre, Piquet, and 'the royal game of Chess', the first two in considerably more detail than had yet been seen in English. Several editions followed, until in 1734 Seymour produced a *Compleat Gamester* in three parts: (1) games chiefly used at court and in the assemblées, viz. Ombre, Quadrille, Quintille, Picquet, Basset, Faro, Chess; (2) the most usual games at cards—Whist, All Fours, Cribbage, Put, Lue, Brag, etc.; (3) games played within and without the tables. In the 1739 edition, Parts 2 and 3 were combined as 'The City Gamester'.

By now, individual treatises were appearing on other games, and Hoyle was waiting upon ladies of quality in their own homes prior to remodelling the gamebook tradition along lines which would eventually reduce him to a household name. Countless Hoyles and *Académies universelles* appeared at the hands of more or less competent and increasingly less original writers throughout the nineteenth century. German-language collections also appear throughout the eighteenth century, the *Académie* being paralleled by *Das neue Königliche l'Hombre* ('The New Royal [Game of] Ombre'), which covers much more than its title implies.

Edmond Hoyle, Gent.

Of the most illustrious name in the history of card games little for certain is known beyond newspaper reports of his death in London on 29 August 1769, at what is now called Welbeck Street. No age is quoted, but later researchers variously place him in his ninetieth or ninety-seventh year. He is said to have been buried in the parish church of St Marylebone and to have left his estate to his sister Eleanor, with bequests to his niece Fanny and a variety of women of no specified relationship. A barrister by some accounts, he is not reliably reported to have practised at the bar, and styles himself 'Gentleman' in his first book, which he published at an age most of us are now as thankful to reach as to retire at. The lengthy title of that little work, of which only one first edition survives, begins *A short Treatise on the Game of Whist, containing the laws of the game; and also some Rules whereby a Beginner may, with due attention to them, attain to the Playing it well* . . . .

Hoyle may have figured among Lord Folkestone's clique of gentlemen who frequented the Crown Coffee-House, Bedford Row, and there effected upon the humble game of 'Whisk' a similar transformation to that which Shaw's Professor Higgins was later to perform upon the person and manners of Eliza Doolittle. The newly refined game rapidly attracted so large a following that Hoyle conceived the novel plan of offering his services as a professional Whist tutor, attending persons of quality in their own homes, as did masters of music, dancing, drawing, and other social graces. In parallel with personal instruction he also reduced his methods to writing, offering his first manuscript treatise of the game for sale to his clients at one guinea apiece, with the promise of personal explanation of any case therein illustrated on payment of a further guinea each.

The manuscript treatise was as valuable as it was novel. Everybody wanted it, but few could afford it. Inevitable pirates soon appeared, finding it profitable to make their own manuscript copies or summaries of the original work and to sell them at more popular prices. To protect his interests, Hoyle had his manuscript printed and officially entered at Stationers' Hall (that is, copyrighted) in November 1742. The book proved as successful as the manuscript: it went through five editions in its first year, and his copyright was attacked by pirates yet again. A later edition carries the warning 'Whoever pirates either of these works will be sued. The proprietor has already obtained an injunction against nine persons for pirating or selling pirated editions of them.' By way of certification, and to ensure that he should not find himself called upon to 'personally explain any case' not constructed by himself, every copy of the book was individually signed by Edmond Hoyle and his publisher Thomas Osborne.

Hoyle now found himself a celebrity. As early as 1743 he is caricatured as 'Professor Whiston' in an anonymous pamphlet entitled *The Humours of Whist, a dramatic Satire* . . . . Other characters include Lord Finesse, Sir George Tenace, and the enthusiastic but plod-brained Sir Calculation Puzzle, who cannot see the wood of the game for its trees. ('We were nine all', he drools. 'The adversary had 3 and we 4 tricks. All the trumps were out. I had Queen and two small clubs, with the lead. Let me see; it was about 222 and 3 halves to—'gad, I forget how many—that my partner had the Ace and King; aye, that he had not both of them, 17 to 2; or that he had not one, or both, or neither, some 25 to 32 . . .') A sidelight on Hoyle's tutoring activities is thrown by a letter from a lady to the *Rambler* magazine of 8 May 1750 which reads in part: 'Papa made me drudge at Whist till I was tired of it; and far from wanting a head, Mr Hoyle, when he had not given me above forty lessons, said I was one of his best scholars'. Another, from the February 1755 issue of the *Gentleman's Magazine*, more darkly adds: 'Hoyle tutored me in several games at cards, and under the name of guarding me from being cheated, insensibly gave me a taste for sharping'.

Not slow to cash in on his own success, Hoyle lost little time in producing similar treatises on other games—Backgammon in 1743; Piquet, with some observations on Chess, 1744; Quadrille, 1745; Brag, 1751; Chess, 1761; and various of these were combined in compendium editions from about 1750. These, too, were autographed; but in the fifteenth edition his autograph is woodblocked and in the seventeenth his death admitted.

With the passing of Hoyle, piracy found itself elevated into plagiarism, and plagiarism into tradition. Editions of *Hoyle's Games* have been produced by an endless variety of authors and publishers ever since, the only connection between them being that of promiscuous cribbing. All include games that Hoyle had never heard of, and most adopt approaches alien to his. The curious thing is that what, if anything, we now understand by 'the rules according to Hoyle' is a detailed statement of the definitive rules of a game, from which we may most reliably learn how to play it, whereas this is precisely what Hoyle himself never set out to do. His *Short treatise on the Game of Whist* says nothing as to how the game is played. Such knowledge is taken for granted. As stated in the further reaches of its meandering title, the author's interest and genius lay in devising and presenting the laws of the game, together with some 'rules' *whereby a Beginner may attain to the Playing it well*. Not until the later nineteenth century do Hoyle's successors go so far as to explain intelligibly how any given game is actually played.

In Britain, the habit of attaching Hoyle's name to a book of games is practically extinct. It fares better in the United States, where so many editions have appeared since the mid-nineteenth century that it has degenerated into little more than a household term for a book of indoor games. To what extent any of them may be regarded as authoritative depends entirely upon the authority of the compiler, as it is plainly absurd to pretend that that of Hoyle did not pass with him to the grave.

6

Happy families

To explore the vast realm of card games coherently we first need some sort of classification to serve as a guide or map. This sounds easy. First, collect all the games you can find; next, arrange them in families whose members have so many features in common that they must have evolved from a single ancestor; finally, name the families.

The trouble with such a 'genealogical' exercise is that the more games you discover, the less clear-cut the boundaries are between them, and you end up with either one big family, or as many families as there are members. This is because card games are not solid objects like rocks and stones and trees, but patterns of human behaviour, ranging somewhere in complexity between, say, languages at one extreme and limericks at the other. The similarities we are looking for therefore resolve themselves into the gaming elements of which each game is comprised. Just as atoms are not indivisible units but bundles of elementary particles bound together by sub-atomic forces, so card games may be regarded as bundles of elementary gaming features acting in harmony towards a common end—'the complete consort dancing together'.

It helps to sort these gaming elements (or 'ludemes', to quote an eminently dispensable term proposed by Pierre Berloquin)[1] into three types: (1) mechanical, i.e. those governing the physical process of play, such as trick-taking or discarding to a sequence; (2) purposive, i.e. those defining the aim or objective of play, such as card-capture or penalty-avoidance; and (3) decorative, i.e. cultural motifs which are not essential to the gaming content but add a measure of human or real-life interest to it, rather like the 'programmatic' elements of non-abstract music.

Decorative motifs are unreliable guides to classification, as they migrate so easily from one type of game to another. A particularly nomadic and persistent example is the attachment of peculiar significance to the Knave, which pops up like a jack-in-the-box in a variety of unrelated games brandishing special powers and often a distinctive name—Karnöffel in the game of that name, 'his knob'[2] in Cribbage, 'Jack' in All Fours, 'Mistigris' in Bouillotte, 'Pamphilus' or 'Pam' in Loo. This traditional figure has to some extent become reincarnated as the modern Joker. Equally nomadic is the scoring combination of King–Queen of a suit, known as 'marriage', which occurs in such disparate games as Poch, Guimbarde, and Pope Joan, though it also serves as a defining feature of a family of trick-taking games headed by Mariage. Perhaps also classifiable as a cultural motif is the practice of conveying information to a partner by means of winks, nods, and related grimaces following a statutory code of conventions. This element characterizes many unrelated games of Spanish practice, though it is also found in odd games outside Spain.

We will probably do best to ignore decorative elements and take 'mechanics of play' as a first line of classification, with 'objectives' as a secondary subdivision. This has the merit of making primary groups of games that go together because they 'feel' the same in play—whether, for instance, they all involve the playing of tricks, as at Whist, or the draw-and-discard principle of Rummy, or whatever. The secondary nature of 'objectives' is confirmed by games like Solo and Skat, where the basic mechanism of play—trick-taking—remains constant, while the objective varies from deal to deal according to the bid of the soloist. It could be argued against this approach that varieties of poker, for example Draw and Stud, clearly represent different mechanisms applied to a constant objective. Poker, however, is untypical of card games, in that cards themselves are not the instruments of play.

Classification is complicated by the existence of compound games consisting of basic games welded together, rather like molecular compounds formed from atoms of different elements. By 'basic game' I mean one whose procedure and objective remain the same from deal to deal. In Whist, for example, it is to win a majority of tricks with a given suit as trump. Misère, in which the object is to avoid taking tricks, also counts as a basic game, though it is never played alone but only as on occasional contract in a compound game.

Basic games are compounded in various ways. In Cribbage, all deals are the same, but each deal consists of two basic games: first, arranging cards into scoring combinations; second, playing them out to a sequence. Similarly, Piquet consists of (1) an exchange and declaration of card combinations followed by (2) outplay to tricks. Both may be described as simple compounds, in that their component parts are played within the same deal, and the whole game consists of a repeated sequence of identical deals: $(G = d_1 + d_1 + d_1 + \ldots)$. Others, such as Bismarck or Sergeant Major, may be described as cyclic compounds, in that a sequence of different basic games is played in a statutory order, and the sequence is then repeated indefinitely. $(G = (d_1 + d_2 + d_3) + (d_1 + d_2 + d_3) + \ldots)$. More interesting, more advanced, and more 'modern' are variable compound games, in which the object or conditions of play follows no fixed order but at each deal is determined by one of the players—for instance, by the highest bidder in auction games, or by the dealer in Poker. $(G = d_{1/n} + d_{1/n} + d_{1/n} \ldots$, where 'n' is the number of bids available and '1' can be any of them.) Other structures are possible—compare le Barbu in Chapter 22.

Clearly, no compound game can be classified as a whole: it must first be decomposed into its basic games, and then, perhaps, considered under the heading of its most significant element.

Games may be sorted by mechanisms of play as follows:

1. *Null*. This covers gambling games in which cards themselves are not the instruments of play (e.g. Faro).
2. *Exchange*. Each in turn puts out one or more cards and takes in a corresponding number. Exchange may be made as between players' hands (Old Maid), or between one's own hand and either a spare hand (Commerce) or the whole pack (Rummy).
3. *Matching outplay*. Each in turn plays to a sequence or pool a card that matches one or more of those in place, whether to continue the sequence (Newmarket, Jubilee) or to make a capture (Cassino, Scopone).
4. *Competitive outplay* (*trick-taking*). Each in turn contributes one card to a specialized sequence called a 'trick', which is captured by the player of the highest card.

They may also be sorted by objectives as follows:

1. *Null*. For gambling games where the 'aim' is to have bet on the

right card (Faro), or to have the best hand (Pontoon), or to persuade others that one has the best hand (Poker).

2. *Penalty avoidance.* To avoid holding a penalty card or cards at end of play (Hearts, Old Maid, Cuckoo).

3. *Card elimination.* To be the first to play out all one's cards (Newmarket, Earl of Coventry, Durak).

4. *Card combination.* To form sets of matching cards, whether as the sole objective (Rummy) or as a contributory factor (Piquet, Cribbage).

5. *Card capture.* The usual object of trick-play (Whist) and 'fishing' games (Cassino, Scopone).

Though possible, it would not be very helpful to construct a diagrammatic table of games with mechanisms as one set of headings and objectives as the other, as some intersections are practically empty while others are over-full and require further subdivision. In any case, means and ends are not always mutually exclusive. For instance, it is clearly desirable to keep most forms of Poker together, though Draw Poker, by definition, slips out of the 'null-play' class by involving an element of 'card-exchange'. In Rummy games the object is both to form combinations and to go out, with different emphases in different varieties, and much the same might be said of typical Patience games. Compound games like Piquet and Bezique involve both capture and combination.

Nevertheless, this approach offers a logical and practical way of structuring our guide to card games, and may be taken as a field-guide to the realms of exploration embarked on in this book. Its broad outlines are as follows.

'Null-play' (gambling) games: betting, banking, vying

The most primitive games—which does not necessarily mean the most ancient, historically speaking—involve little or no competitive play in any meaningful sense of the term. Instead, to all intents and purposes, cards are merely turned up to see who wins the stake. Thus drinking games, in which the player ending up with the worst card pays for the drinks, amount to simple lotteries. A children's game like Beggar my Neighbour, though affecting some semblance of card-play (quasi-trick-taking), at root is nothing but a simple turn-up gambling game. Banking games like Basset and Faro bear some veneer of sophistication, if only in so far as they are more tightly controlled. Since the bank may be held in turn by individual players or permanently by the organizers of the game, these tend to be synonymous with casino games.

A modicum of skill, mainly mathematical, enters point-count banking games of the Pontoon/Blackjack family, where success is determined by the total face value of the players' cards. Such games are played all over the world with a variety of packs (Jewish Kvitlakh, Indian Naqsh, Japanese Kabu, Melanesian Laki, etc.). A derivation from dice games is suggested by the fact that few attach any significance to suits. Typically, only numbers count.

The most sophisticated null-play gambling games are those embodying the vying principal of Poker, whereby players can force a win without necessarily holding the best cards. The essence is that players vie with one another as to who holds the best hand of cards before they are revealed in a 'showdown'. Stakes are not fixed but variable within certain agreed limits, and players are not obliged to stay until the showdown but may drop out of the contest to avoid further loss. This provides the range of choice which is essential to any game of genuine skill. Those who have a favourable hand (or at least pretend they have) can gradually raise the stakes until those who haven't (or at least fear they haven't) relinquish their stakes and gracefully retire. If it comes to a showdown, the best hand wins; but if all retire but one, that one sweeps all the current stakes without revealing his hand, even if was the worst. This is why Poker is described as a game of bluff. It is not a strategic card game in the sense applied to trick-taking games, or others in which cards are the instruments of play. In Whist or Bridge you actually play with cards, whereas in Poker and relatives you only play at them.

Card-exchange games: scapegoats and collectors

The simplest card-play mechanism is that of exchanging cards with each other one at a time. Typically, each in turn passes a card to the left and receives a replacement from the right, or vice versa.

One branch of these comprises negative or 'scapegoat' games centring on the avoidance of a bogy-card or similar penalty, as suggested by the title la Condemnade for an old French game presumably of this type. The English exemplar is Old Maid, in which players exchange cards with a view to discarding them in matching pairs as and when obtained. Since one Queen has previously been 'slyly finger'd from the deck' the end result is one player left over with an unmatched Queen in hand. In other traditions the missing card is a Jack, the game being known in French as le Vieux Garçon and in German as Schwarzer Peter. These are technically negative games in that there is no winner: the aim is to avoid being the loser, or scapegoat. In practice, if losers pay a forfeit, it is a children's game; if they remove an article of clothing, it is an adult game; if they buy the next round, it is a drinking game; if they pay everyone else, it is a gambling game; and if they be cast into the pit, it is a method of divination by lot.

Marginally more sophisticated than Old Maid is Ranter-go-Round, or Chase-the-Ace. Players are dealt one card each, and each in turn may stand pat or demand to swap cards to the left. The neighbour may not refuse a demand unless holding a King, which must be revealed. The dealer plays last and may exchange with one drawn at random from the stock. Cards are then revealed, and the player with that of lowest rank is cast into the pit—or, at least, loses one of three lives. This game is widely played throughout Europe under the name Cuckoo. Its age and popularity are suggested by, respectively, the fact that Ace counts low, and the number of non-standard packs that have been designed uniquely to play it. These include the Cuccú pack of seventeenth-century Italy, the Gnav packs of Denmark and Norway, Sweden's Killekort (the Scandinavian packs still extant and used for a variety of other games), and Germany's now extinct Hexenkarte.

The positive equivalent of negative (scapegoat) exchange-games is represented by simple collecting games, where the object of exchanging is to collect combinations of matching cards, typically three or more of the same rank, or in suit and sequence. Such combinations are sometimes called melds, from German *melden*, 'to declare'. These include a number of children's and simple gambling games such as Donkey and Go Fish, in which cards are exchanged between neighbouring players, and Commerce and Whiskey Poker, in which exchange is made through a spare hand ('widow') belonging to no one in particular. Since the beginning of the twentieth century, however, they have been chiefly represented by the vast family of Rummy games, from the relatively simple Gin to the unashamedly elaborate Canasta, in which exchange is made by means of drawing from a stock and discarding to a waste-pile.

Simple outplay: matching games

These are games in which each player starts with a hand of cards and plays them out one by one until the hand is empty. (Some may involve a degree of exchange as well, but, generally, outplay is of the essence.) They may be referred to as matching games, since, typically, each card played must match the previous one by rank or suit. Matching may be considered a definitive feature of Rummy games and other collectors, but there is a clear distinction between the two. Since collectors are exchange games, the aim is to form matched sets within the hand. They are therefore 'matching-in' games, as opposed to those of the following category, which may be described as 'matching-out'.

The usual object of matching games is to be the first to run out of cards, as in children's games like Snip-Snap-Snorem, or Earl of Coventry. Classics of this type include Comet, Yellow Dwarf, Pope Joan, Newmarket, Crazy Eights, Pink Nines, and suchlike, sometimes called the 'Stops' family. Typically, each in turn plays a card of the same suit and higher in sequence than the previous one. The sequence does not continue indefinitely because it is 'stopped' by certain cards left out of play. When a stop is reached the last player starts a new sequence. Fixed stakes may be won for playing certain cards, and the game ends when someone wins by running out of cards.

Dimly related to Stops, but of a distinctly higher intellectual order, are eastern European games typified by the Russian Durak and Svoyi Koziri, which latter attracted a following at Cambridge in the 1950s as 'Besicovitch's Game', from the Professor who introduced it, and as 'Challenge' from the pen of Hubert Phillips. Their simple object is to go out first, but in accordance with rules of sufficient complexity and flexibility to require considerable forethought.

Going out is not the only possible objective in games of the matching variety. There is a distinctive group of 'adding-up' games in which the total face value of the sequence is increased by that of each card played and the object is to make or avoid specific totals. In such eastern European games as Fifty-One and One Hundred a player wins by bringing the sequence to the said total, or loses if forced to exceed it. The same principle is seen in Cribbage, where the limiting total is 31 and a score is made for making 15, in addition to scores for forming certain combinations on the way.

Games in which players capture cards by matching one or more from the hand to one or more on the table have been graphically described as 'Fishing'—a term used by the Chinese, who play them as avidly as westerners play trick-taking games. They are not greatly played in the west, except by the Italians, whose national card games of Scopa and Scopone are of this type. The only example regularly recorded in English-language Hoyles is Cassino.

The matching-out classification also applies to the most usual forms of Patience, in which the object is to eliminate all cards from hand by playing them out to matching sequences.

Trick-taking games (Tricksters)

Most western card games involve trick-taking. It is the underlying principle of such major games as Bridge, Whist, Solo, Nap, Bezique, Pinochle, Skat, and every form of Tarot, and has given rise to probably more significantly different games than those of the gambling and other non-trick categories put together. I call such games 'tricksters', to avoid hyphenated circumlocutions.

The basic mechanism is very simple. One player *leads* a card by playing it face up to the table, and the others *follow* by adding a card each to it. The cards so played constitute a *trick*, which is won by whoever played the highest card of the same suit as the one led. The winner turns the trick face down and continues play by leading to the next trick. Cards taken in tricks are no longer playable, and the game ends when all cards have been played and won in tricks.

This simple procedure is usually enlivened by the appointment of certain cards—normally all those of a particular suit—to the status of *trumps* ('triumphs'). Trumps provide an alternative way of winning a trick, in that if a *plain* suit is led, the play of a trump will beat it. This device obviates the potentially boring inevitability of one player's winning all the tricks in a given suit because he happens to hold the best ones in it and systematically leads them out from the top down. In trick-and-trump games the rule of capture may therefore be expressed: The trick is taken by the highest card of the suit led, or by the highest trump if any are played.

Tricksters are distinguished by the high degree of creative strategy to which the best of them give play. The play of cards to early tricks, when choice is at a maximum, may be so shaped as to influence the lie and play of cards to later tricks when choice has been whittled down to a minimum. The final outcome of a hand may balance on the last card played, and whether it is a winning or a losing card may have been determined as far back as the opening trick. Thus the course of a hand in a well-balanced trickster follows a connected pathway through a network of strategies, which to some degree (depending on the structure of the game) experienced players may foresee, control, or work towards. Successful trick-play, while demanding varying balances of foresight, judgement, and calculation, also depends on the employment of specific techniques—on which, in turn, depends the continued employment of professional Bridge tutors.

A further, and consequent, characteristic of tricksters is the degree of player interaction they afford. In this respect tricksters are beaten only by vying games like Poker, which, since they involve no card-play at all, are games of nothing but. In most non-trick games, especially those for three or more and notably in forms of Rummy, players more often seem to be competing against the pack or circumstances of play rather than against each other—or else multi-player interaction, where it does exist, devolves into a series of two-player contests. (Since Rummy is widely observed to be more popular with women than with men, it might not be too fanciful to relate the Rummy family to a collecting-gathering lifestyle and tricksters to a hunting-capturing background.)

Certain ground rules of western trick-play are remarkably constant. Typically: the leader is free to play any card,[3] each player in turn must then contribute exactly one card,[4] the trick is taken by the highest card of the suit led, and the winner of one trick leads to the next. This seems to imply a common origin for European trick-games, for the rules themselves, despite their constancy, are conventional rather than logically inevitable. In the Ganjifa games of India, by contrast, the leader is obliged to play a top sequence of cards if possible, and there are several in which each player contributes more than one card to a trick.[5] Other possibilities have appeared by way of experiment. In Hoffman's game of 'Quinto', all 52 cards rank in a single hierarchical series from ♥ A (high) to ♠ 2 (low). From my collection of *Original Card Games* (1977) come 'Anarchy', where everyone plays simultaneously and the highest card of each suit captures any others of the same suit that may be played; 'Welsh Whist', where everyone plays in turn regardless of who won the last trick; 'Sex', where the lead may be passed to the next player; and several games in which one needn't play to a trick at all, so that tricks contain varying number of cards.

Despite this degree of constancy, western tricksters vary enormously in the rules governing what cards may be played when following to a trick (which may support the theory that trumps did not come in with the oldest pack but were a later European invention). Given that the only possibilities are

f = follow suit to the card led,
t = play a trump, or
r = renounce, i.e. play from some other suit,

we find the following variations:

1. The laxest rule is that a follower may play any card at all, i.e. follow suit, trump, or renounce ad lib, which we may express as *ftr* for short. This rule is typical of two-hand trick-and-draw games such as California Jack, Honeymoon Bridge, and Bezique.
2. Under the somewhat tighter rule of All Fours, Pitch, and related games, players may freely follow suit or trump, but may only renounce if unable to follow. This may be expressed *ft,tr*, with a comma marking off the first degree of obligation.
3. Most western games exhibit 'Whist' rules: follow suit if possible, otherwise play any desired card. This may be expressed *f,tr*.
4. A much tighter rule, typical of Tarot games, may be expressed *f,t,r*—follow suit if possible, otherwise trump if possible, otherwise play any card.
5. In some games, notably Ecarté, it is obligatory not only to follow suit but also to 'head' the trick if possible, that is, to play a higher card from that suit. This may be indicated by capitalizing the appropriate initial, thus *F,t,r*. In others, a player unable to follow suit and wishing or having to trump, must play a higher trump than any so far played to the trick—*f,T,r* or *F,T,r* as the case may be.

Further variations will be encountered in the course of our survey.

One might expect the laxest rule of trick-play, *ftr*, to make the greatest demands on skill because it offers maximum choice of play, and the tightest rule, *F,T,r*, to limit severely the players' scope for creative strategy. In fact, the laxest rule is *too* lax: its lack of discipline prevents both the formulation of foreseeable lines of play and the drawing of logical deductions from what already has been played, and it is therefore mainly associated with gambling games. The Whist rule, *f,tr*, seems to offer the best balance between freedom of choice and logical restraint, as suggested by the fact that it has been adopted into so many different tricksters.

Rules of trick-play do not provide a useful basis for classifying tricksters, as they vary somewhat loosely and unpredictably between different games of obviously the same basic type. More helpful is the variation they display in the extent to which cards are concealed, or known, or made knowable in course of play, which is another determinant of skill. At the more chancy extreme come part-pack or short-hand games, such as Pitch, Nap, and Loo, in which only a few cards are dealt to each and the rest remain permanently out of play. As the scope for deduction is thereby much reduced, such games are mostly played as gambling games. At the opposite extreme lie whole-pack games, such as Whist, Bridge, and Solo, in which the whole pack is distributed. Here, the skill involved in deducing the lie of unplayed cards from the earlier course of the game is not nullified by uncertainty as to which cards are out of play, and whole-pack games are therefore largely games of skill. Between the two extremes lie games in which not all the cards are dealt initially, but some or all of those omitted from the deal come into play eventually. For example, in 'trick-and-draw' games, such as California Jack, Bezique, and Sixty-Six, each time a card is played from hand another is drawn from stock to replace it. In 'stock-exchange games' such as Piquet, Ecarté, and Ombre, every player may discard and draw replacement cards before beginning play. In 'widow' games, such as Skat, Pinochle, Five Hundred, and many forms of Tarot, most of the cards are dealt initially, but two or three of them go face down to a 'widow' (or 'skat' or 'blind'), which the highest bidder may take into hand before the play begins.

The most useful way of classifying tricksters is by reference to the basic objectives of play. While the obvious object of a trick-taking game is to win as many cards as possible (or, what comes to the same thing, as many tricks as possible), there are in fact several possible objectives, each of which defines a distinct class of game:

1. In *plain-trick* games, all cards are of equal value, and what counts towards winning the game is the number of tricks taken.
2. In *point-trick* games, different cards have different values, and what counts towards winning the game is the total value of the point-scoring cards captured in tricks.

    (Plain-trick and point-trick games are sometimes designated, respectively, 'simple' and 'complex' trick-taking games; but the technical use of non-technical words can be confusing. For instance, Boston Whist is a highly complex 'simple' trick-taking game, whereas Sueca is a very simple 'complex' one.)

Games in each class can also be played either positively or negatively, which theoretically makes four classes altogether. In practice, though, negative games are relatively rare and so similar in play as to justify the establishment of a third category:

3. In *negative trick-taking* or *trick-avoidance* games the object is to avoid winning tricks, whether penalties apply to the tricks themselves (plain-trick avoidance) or to particular cards contained within them (card-point avoidance). In either case the ideal outcome is to win no tricks at all.

Tricksters will necessarily claim most of our attention in the course of our survey, and will be approached as follows:

1. Primitive tricksters, including Karnöffel and Piquet, characterized by an absence, or imperfect development, of trumps (Chapter 14).
2. Plain-trick games characterized by short hands—typically 'five-card' gambling games such as Ecarté, Nap, and Loo (Chapter 15).
3. Plain-trick games of the whole-pack variety, notably Ombre, Solo, Whist, and Bridge (Chapters 16–17).
4. Primitive point-trick games, starting with Tarot (Chapters 18–19).
5. Point-trick games of the 'Ace-11, Ten-10' family, such as Skat, Pinochle, and Jass (Chapters 20–1).
6. Trick-avoidance games—Reversis, Hearts, and suchlike (Chapter 22).

7

Betting and banking

He [Bragadin] gave Casanova two sound pieces of advice—only to play for cash; and never to punt, only bank.

John Masters, *Casanova* (1969)

LABORATORY VISITOR. Is this some kind of mathematical experiment?
ROBERT MITCHUM. No. It's a gambling game. I made my way through college with it.

My Forbidden Past (RKO, 1951)

The most primitive games are of the blind bet variety, in which there is no real play of cards and the outcome depends entirely on chance. Some, like Find the Lady, are so intimately associated with side-show swindles as not to count as games at all. What might be called the father and mother of all such swindles has been unearthed by Thierry Depaulis[1] from the records of court appeals of 1408. It describes a real-life incident in which two Parisian layabouts inveigle a travelling merchant into an inn on the offer of a favourable currency deal. One of them subsequently draws from his pocket 'unes quantitées de papier pour jouer' and demonstrates a harmless little diversion based on guessing the identity of a card seen only from its back. The merchant, having been allowed to spot that one of the cards has an almost imperceptible but distinctive stain on the reverse, is eventually invited to play for money. When the marked card turns up, the dupe puts his shirt on it, only to find that the front of the card is not quite what it was before. Needless to say, the pack contains two cards bearing the same carefully engineered distinctive mark.

This is obviously more of a swindle than a game. Depaulis relates it, at a slightly higher level, to the game of Condemnade mentioned several times in literature of the period, notably in Rabelais's list of Gargantuan games. It probably consisted in merely dealing cards around until someone is 'condemned'—perhaps to pay for the drinks—

by receiving a predetermined 'bogy' card. Even this can hardly be accounted a game. It isn't even a gamble, more a method of drawing lots. The history of cards is puddled with drinking games, some of which have at least the merit of being jokes. In Four of a Kind, the dealer deals cards around one at a time. As soon as any rank is repeated, the player receiving the duplicate orders a drink. Whoever gets the third card of that rank pays for the drink, and whoever gets the fourth drinks it. As Geoffrey Mott-Smith puts it: 'The cards are then shuffled and cut for a new deal by the next player in rotation. Every player antes before each deal, and the entire pot goes to the last player on his feet.'

Many primitive gambling games, long abandoned by serious gamblers, survive, cleaned up, as children's games. Such exercises as Great Expectations, Lottery, Bango, I Fancy My Cards, Blind Hookey, Speculation, and the like, go back a long way and are too elementary to have changed much in essentials throughout their history. Many conveniently keep the children occupied by involving them in some sort of active card-play, without, however, offering sufficient choice of moves to enable anyone to show off by being clever. Because the outcome is random, everyone does their fair share of winning. But, because they also involve a modicum of apparent card-play, they no longer appeal to serious gamblers, who prefer a more rapid succession of outcomes and pay-offs, and regard any actual playing with cards as a profitless waste of time.

A simple specimen is Battle. The cards are all dealt out and players hold their piles face down in hand. At each round the topmost cards are exposed, and whoever has the highest wins those of the others and places them all at the bottom of his pile. In case of equality the cards are put to one side, and there is a battle royal of further rounds until a best card does appear. This wins all cards held in abeyance, and play continues until somebody has won the lot. Although French legend supposes Bataille to have been played by Charles VI (d. 1422) and Odette de Champdivers, the game is not actually attested earlier than 1828.[2]

Marginally more sophisticated is Beggar my Neighbour, or Beat your Neighbour out of Doors. Two players start with half the pack face down and take turns to play their top card face up to the table. When an honour appears, the opponent has to 'pay' for it at the rate of one card if the honour is a Jack, two for a Queen, three for a King, or four for an Ace. Unless the pay-off cards themselves contain an honour—thus turning the tables—the payment cards are added to the other's hand, and play continues until either of them has won all the cards. We may perhaps equate this with the 'Knave Out of Doors' referred to in Heywood's *A Woman Killed with Kindness* (1607).

Snap and its relatives (Slapjack, Farmyard, etc.) are forms of Battle upgraded by the addition of skill—not strategic skill, but in speed of reaction to card recognition. Gops, to my knowledge unrecorded before the second half of the twentieth century, may be regarded as a form of Battle upgraded by the element of choice and so entirely released from fatalistic outcome. Each of two players (or, with complications, three) takes all thirteen cards of a suit. An unused suit, say diamonds, is shuffled and placed face down between them. The object is to capture the greatest value of diamonds, counting Ace to Ten at face value and courts 11, 12, 13. At each move the top diamond is turned face up and players bid for it by selecting one of their hand-cards and laying it face down on the table. When both are ready, their cards are revealed and the higher ranking of them captures the diamond. The bid cards are then thrown away and the next diamond turned. In case of equality the contested diamond is held in abeyance and goes to the winner of the next. Though childishly simple and well suited to gambling, Gops is clearly a game of skill, though of what type it is hard to specify. Its title happens to be an acronym of 'Game Of Pure Strategy', which is either a coincidence or a misnomer, as the skill involved is more like that of extra-sensory perception.

Banking games: Lansquenet, Basset, Faro, etc.

Banking games are not necessarily more complicated than those described above, but they are more tightly controlled and organized. They are also, by definition, distinctly unequal in format. On one hand stands the banker, who deals the cards, operates the knobs and levers of play, and acts as a centre for the redistribution of wealth. On the other are the punters, who exercise no player interaction amongst themselves but oppose the banker on an individual basis. In effect, the banker plays a series of two-player games simultaneously.

Inequality consists in the fact that ties and special cases are invariably designed to favour the banker, who is thereby assured of a small but cumulative profit or rake-off. This makes banking games ideal activities for casinos, in which the bank is held by the management and the game is dealt and controlled by its agents. In the past, it made them equally ideal for easing the perpetual problems of royal insolvency—Cardinal Mazarin, for instance, is said to have turned the seventeenth-century French court at Versailles into one vast casino, virtually operating it as an instrument of state. Played informally, such games may be equalized by causing the bank to pass from player to player—whether by rote, outcome, or auction—so that each theoretically has the same opportunity to recoup in the banker's role what he lost in that of the punter.

That banking games are little more than dice games adapted to the medium of cards is suggested by the fact that they are fast, defensive rather than offensive, and essentially numerical, suits being often irrelevant. They are divisible into two broad classes: (1) turn-up games, in which stakes are literally won or lost on the turn of a card, and (2) face-count games, in which the players' object is to draw cards whose combined face value most nearly reaches but does not exceed a given total or 'point'. We start with turn-ups.

An archetypal banking game is the celebrated Lansquenet, from German Landsknecht, which first appears in the fifth edition of Rabelais's *Gargantua* in 1542. *Landsknechte*, literally 'country knights', were German mercenaries who roamed fifteenth and sixteenth-century Europe in quest of short-staffed wars, maidens not yet in distress, and opportunities to play an inane but highly romanticized gambling game with cards. The game itself may have taken its name from the special cards produced for mercenaries, which were small enough to be carried conveniently in a backpack and bore the figure of a *Landsknecht* for each Jack. So romantic were the associations that Lansquenet often found itself spoken of as Germany's national card game, leading Cavendish to expostulate 'It is hardly a game at all, but a complicated way of playing Pitch and Toss with cards . . . to elevate it to the dignity of a national card-game is to treat it with a respect it does not deserve.'[3] Attempts were made to revive the game in nineteenth-century France, probably under the influence of the Romantic movement. An introductory passage from *L'Académie des jeux* of 1876 sets a characteristic tone:

It is a game of good repute whose very name evokes the cavalier ways of 17th-century gentlemen and soldiers of fortune . . . Chronicles of the time tell us that d'Artagnan and his musketeers were dedicated Lansquenet players . . .

To business. The banker, having made a stake and engaged one or more punters to match it in whole or part, begins by dealing a card face up to the left and to the right. If they are of the same suit, he wins the stakes, calls for more, and deals the next two. If not, he continues dealing individual cards to the middle until one appears that matches the left or right starter. A left-card match wins for the banker, a right-card for the punters. If the banker loses, the bank statutorily passes to the next in turn; if not, he may sell it to the highest bidder if he wishes.

More notorious than illustrious was the Italian game of Basset, frequently recorded from the mid-fifteenth century onwards. It escapes the notice of Rabelais and his French contemporaries, but was introduced to the French and English courts towards the end of the seventeenth century, where its pursuit, especially by the mistresses of Charles II, became a craze of scandalous proportions. In his *Court Gamester* of 1725, Seymour describes

BASSET, a French Game, [as] amongst all those on the cards, . . . accounted to be the most courtly, being properly, by the understanders of it, thought only fit for Kings and Queens, great Princes, Noblemen, &c. to play at, by reason of such great losses, or advantages, as may possibly be on one side or another, during the time of play.

It may read like a complicated game, but the complications are superficial, relating mainly to its elaborate staging and the multiplicity of technical gambling terms required for its 'proper understanding'.

Basically, each punter has a layout of thirteen cards in front of him and lays stakes on one or more ranks. The banker starts by turning up the bottom card of his pack and winning all the stakes placed on cards of the same rank in the layouts. He then deals cards face up from the top of the pack alternately to two piles. After each two he receives all stakes wagered on the rank of the first of them, and pays out matching stakes to all those wagered on the second. His last card, like the first, wins all stakes on the corresponding rank. A punter who is due for payment (having staked on a rank matching the banker's right-hand turn-up) may decline it and bet on the same rank again, indicating this option by turning up one corner of the appropriate card and leaving his stake intact. This bid, called *sept-et-le-va* from the fact that it pays seven times the stake made, can in theory be repeated three more times, another corner being turned for each and the relevant payments being 15, 30, and 60 times the amount staked. The prospect of such enormous pay-offs, however remote, presumably accounts for Basset's fatal attraction to the simple-minded, and certainly reflects some sort of evil genius on the part of its inventor. As Seymour rightly concludes, 'The dimmest eye may easily see, without a pair of spectacles, how much and considerable the design of this court game is in the favour of the Banker.'

By the mid-eighteenth century Basset had given way to its simpler relative le Pharaon, supposedly so called because one of the cards of the pack in use at the time bore the picture of a pharaoh. This exercise had the advantage of requiring one communal layout instead of one per punter. The procedure was similar to that of Basset, with the additional refinement that when both cards of a turn formed a pair the banker won half the stakes applying to their rank. Under new spelling, Faro developed such further refinements as the ability of punters to bet simultaneously on two or more ranks, and to bet for or against the appearance of a given rank. Casanova, when not more profitably engaged, played Faro wherever he went, and by the nineteenth century it had become the world's most widespread casino game. Its particular popularity in the United States led to the development of a simpler and more informal variant called Stuss. In the twentieth century it has been ousted by Blackjack and Baccara.

Still played in French casinos is the less frenetic game of Trente et Quarante, also called Rouge et Noir or 'R. &. N.' Its age is uncertain, partly because there seems no way of proving its identity with such fifteenth/sixteenth century game-names as 'a la terza, a la quarta', and partly because later reports often confuse it with Trente-et-Un. It was certainly known in 1650 and may have been introduced by Mazarin.[4] In Trente et Quarante the banker first deals cards face up in a row marked 'rouge', then again to a row marked 'noir', stopping each row when it reaches or exceeds a point of thirty-one. The players will have previously bet on which row will come closer to 31, or that the first card dealt will or will not match the colour of the winning row, or both. The game has not spread elsewhere, and is probably diminishing in France. It suffers from a low house percentage, the bank's only certain win being a 31-point tie.[5]

A full survey of informal banking games belongs less to the history of card games than to that of gambling, if not of crime. Bingo, Bango, Blind Hookey, Butcher Boy, Monte Bank, Lottery, Put and Take, Racing Aces (or Minoru, after a race-horse of Edward VII), Red Dog, Shoot, Skinball, Slippery Sam, Speculation, Stitch, and Ziginette are but a few of the most frequently recorded in English-language Hoyles.

Face-count games: Twenty-One

Vingt-et-Un, Pontoon, and Blackjack are respectively the French, British, and American variants of a globally popular banking game best referred to as Twenty-One. The name 'Pontoon' dates back to the First World War and probably derives from Vingt-un, as the French name usually appears in English. Presumably this first became 'vontoon' by the same sort of soldierly mispronunciation that transformed billet-doux into 'Billy-do', and was then assimilated to 'pontoon' as being the nearest meaningful equivalent. (Another reported anglicization of the French name is 'Van John'.) 'Blackjack' is said to reflect an early twentieth-century American practice of increasing the reward for a hand consisting of an Ace and a black Jack. I can find no contemporary support for this, though it could have been inspired by the role of a black Jack as *mistigris* or wild card in Poker.

In the oldest and simplest form of Twenty-One the dealer distributes two cards face down to everyone including himself. Each in turn, having examined his cards, may pass or call for another card to be dealt face up. He may keep calling for cards so long as the combined value of all his cards does not exceed twenty-one. This continues until he either 'sticks' with cards totalling 21 or less, or 'busts' with 22 or more, which costs him his stake. Cards count face value, with courts 10 each, and Ace 1 or 11 ad lib. A twenty-one made on two cards—an Ace plus a Ten or court—is variously known as a 'natural' or a 'pontoon' and pays double. The dealer then exposes his own cards and may stick immediately or else draw more until he either sticks or busts. If he busts, he pays the stakes of those who didn't; if he sticks, he pays those whose cards count more than his and wins from those with an equal or lesser point.

The dealer/banker clearly has all the advantages. Playing last, he has already won against those who have bust; he can be guided in his own play by the number of punters left in and the part-total visible on their faced cards; and he always wins a tied hand. Arrangements are therefore usually made to distribute the bank equitably, a common method being to cede it to a punter who wins on a natural.

Pontoon is largely played as an informal family game. It is popular with schoolchildren, students, manual workers, and, especially, the armed forces. Informally, it has given rise to a number of playing features designed to add greater interest to what is otherwise a rather boringly repetitive exercise. Any given form of the game may now include one or more of the following features: (*a*) Punters must increase their stake before their second card. (*b*) The dealer, on examining his first card, may demand all stakes to be doubled before the seconds are dealt around. There may also be provision for punters to double the pay-off. (*c*) If the first two cards are of equal rank, they may be split and used as the basis of two entirely independent hands, a second card being immediately dealt to each. (*d*) Punters may acquire their third and subsequent cards either by purchase, in which case they increase their stake and receive the card face down, or by 'twisting', in which case the card is dealt free but face up. (*e*) A five-card trick is a hand containing five cards without a bust, and wins double. (*f*) Three Sevens is a 'royal pontoon' and wins treble.

The casino version of Twenty-One, a necessarily more formal activity, has spread—not without variation—from its home in Nevada to most western countries under its American name Blackjack. A notable reason for its popularity is that it is one of the few casino games at which the punter can (theoretically) hold his own by the application of skill, or at least considerably reduce the house advantage of never ceding the right to deal. Unfortunately, the skill involved— 'card-casing'—is more like hard labour than a real day's work, as it involves prodigious feats of memory to keep track of the cards dealt and of analysis to take effective advantage of that knowledge.[6] A more practical problem is that casino managements are inclined to exert self-protection against unusually consistent winners.

Vingt-et-Un appeared in about the middle of the eighteenth century and was to number amongst its early enthusiasts such unlikely bedfellows as Madame Du Barry and the Emperor Napoleon. Vingt-et-Un, Whist, and Faro were the chief court games when Madame Du Barry succeeded Pompadour as the mistress of Louis XV in 1764. Taylor, translating from d'Ambly, reports an occasion on which the king called for a Vingt-et-Un party for the amusement of his new favourite, whose favourite game it was, and later observes 'It is on record that Napoleon preferred Vingt-et-Un to any other game of cards'.[7]

Thirty-One

Twenty-One was preceded by one or more games called Thirty-One, first mentioned by name in a 1464 French translation of a sermon preached by Bernadine in 1440, and reported throughout the sixteenth century in all major gaming sources including Rabelais and Cardano. If it is the same as the 'trenta un per forza' mentioned by Citolini in 1561, it may also relate to the 'al trente per forza' listed in the late fifteenth-century Steele manuscript—though *per forza*, 'by force', might imply a mode of play more akin to that of Cribbage. In any case, we do not know how the original Thirty-One was played. Later French books describe two games under this title, one played like Pontoon, the other like Commerce. The basic numerical feature of Thirty-One has also been adopted into other card games, which to some extent complicates the issue. Drawing to 31 constitutes part three of many old three-stake gambling games such as Post-and-Pair and Belle, Flux et Trente-et-Un, and the play to 31 in Cribbage and its sixteenth-century forerunner Noddy may also be inspired by the same principle.

The early popularity of Thirty-One in both Spain and Ireland is underlined by Chatto, who quotes from Cervantes's *Comical History of Rinconete and Cortadillo* as follows:

with these [cards] I have gained my living at all the publick houses and inns between Madrid and this place, playing at One-and-Thirty,[8] and though they are dirty and torn, they are of wonderful service to those who understand them, for they shall never cut without leaving an ace at the bottom, which is one good point towards eleven, with which advantage, thirty-one being the game, he sweeps all the money into his pocket.

Chatto also quotes from a commentary on *A Kerry Pastoral* of 1724, in which 'The favourite game of the Kerry men is said to have been One-and-Thirty', and goes on to observe that 'as the intercourse between the two countries was frequent, and the favourite game in both was One-and-Thirty, it is not unlikely that the Irish obtained their knowledge of cards from the Spaniards'.[9]

Seventeenth-century English references to the game are somewhat ambiguous. The identity of Thirty-One is not clarified in *Taylor's Motto* (1621), where it is merely listed as one of the games on which the prodigal squandered his money. Florio, in *The World of Wordes* (1611), glosses *Trentuno* as 'One-and-Thirty . . . also called Bone-Ace'. Cotton does not mention Thirty-One in *The Compleat Gamester* of 1674, but does describe Bone-Ace as a three-part game in which the stakes are won respectively by the best card, the best triplet, and drawing the nearest to thirty-one (as in Belle, Flush, and Thirty-One). He also describes the hitherto unrecorded Wit and Reason, wherein one player has all the red cards and one all the black, each in turn plays to the count as at Cribbage, and the player who makes it 31 wins.

Twenty-One may have resulted from a deliberate speeding-up of Thirty-one, effected by first permitting players to count Ace as 1 or 11, and then reducing the target by 10 so that it could be reached on just two cards.

Baccara and others

Unsupported protestations of mythic antiquity notwithstanding, Baccara ('Baccarat' in British and Nevadan casinos) does not grace the realms of recorded history before the nineteenth century, when it became firmly entrenched in French casinos. It embodies an interesting variation on the face-count theme by replacing a best total (21) with a best remainder after division, thereby eliminating the possibility of 'busting'.

Two cards are dealt and a third may be drawn. Numerals count face value and courts zero, and the aim is to get closer to a point of 9 than the banker, for which purpose 10 or more counts only as its last digit. There are three main varieties of play. In Baccara à un tableau, or Chemin de Fer ('Chemmy'), any player may act as banker-dealer; in Baccara à deux tableaux or Baccara-Banque, the casino holds the bank and provides the dealer-player; and in Punto Banco, the Spanish-American version played in Nevada, the casino holds the bank but players may act the part of the banker by dealing cards and playing on its behalf. This makes them feel important and is quite safe from the casino's point of view, as the banker is obliged to follow choice-defeating rules of play.

'To say that the actual play of Baccara is simple is an under-statement,' observes Barrie Hughes in *The Educated Gambler.* 'Most children's games are infinitely more complicated, and it is doubtful if Baccara played without stakes could hold the attention of any but the most backward child.' Adding this to the Tranby Croft Baccara scandal,[10] which heaped such lovable disrepute upon the Prince of Wales in 1891, may lead one to conclude that the difference between Baccara and Pontoon/Blackjack is more social than anything else— the one plush but mindless, the other semi-skilled but vulgar.

Other members of the family may be mentioned in passing. Macao is a one-card version of Baccara, possibly ancestral to it, and named from that Portuguese corner of the Chinese world sometimes described as 'the Monte Carlo of the east' (as over the opening credits of *Macao,* RKO, 1952). Quinze, dating from the late eighteenth century, is a two-hand equivalent of Twenty-One played to a point of fifteen. In Onze-et-demie ($11\frac{1}{2}$) and Sette e mezzo ($7\frac{1}{2}$) courts count half a point each. Seven-and-a-Half is played with the Italian 40-card pack lacking Eights, Nines, and Tens, as also is Trenta Cinque, 'Thirty-Five'. This might be described as a banking game without a banker. Numerals count face value and courts 10 each. A pool is formed, each receives nine cards, and a four-card 'widow' is dealt face down to the table. The widow is auctioned and the highest bidder discards four cards and takes the widow in their place. If he can now show cards of the same suit totalling 35 or more he wins the amount of his bid from the pool, otherwise he pays it in. Anyone initially dealt 35 or more in a suit wins without further ado, and bonuses are awarded for various other combinations.

The American game of Farmer and the German Pächter may be traced back to la Ferme, first described in Oudin's *Recherches italiennes et francoises* of 1640.[11] It is not a rustic game, as sometimes claimed: 'farm' is metaphorical for 'bank', and the proprietors of Parisian gaming-houses were known as 'farmers', a jocular term first applied to professional tax-collectors. Farm was played with a 45-card pack made by removing the Eights and all the Sixes except that of hearts, known as 'le brillant'. This choice of absentees will be understood from the point of the game, which was to make sixteen. The best result was a sixteen consisting of le brillant and a court or Ten. Next best was any other two-card sixteen, followed by one of three cards. A sixteen won the pool and relieved the current farmer (dealer) of his farm (bank). If no sixteen appeared, the highest point below it won the pool but not the farm.

Face-count gambling games make only limited use of the definitive features of western playing cards: suits are irrelevant, and the translation of court cards into numerical values—however interesting to the mathematician—can only be regarded as an evolutionary step backwards. That they might as well be played with a set of purely numerical cards is indicated by the Jewish game of Kvitlakh (in various versions and spellings). The modern 'Quitli' pack produced by Piatnik of Vienna contains twenty-four cards in two series of numbers from 1 to 12. The object is to reach but not exceed a point of 21, for which purpose a Twelve may count anything from 9 to 12 at its holder's discretion. Deuces and Elevens are special cards and appropriately decorated, as a pair of either rank wins outright. Kvitlakh packs in several different constitutions are known, some exhibiting numerals of a design current in eighteenth-century Germany. The name probably derives from Quittel, 'a Yiddish word for a slip of paper, pawn ticket, receipt, bill of exchange, or a petition handed to a miracle working rabbi'.[12]

Similar face-count games are played with various local packs throughout the world. The Indian Naqsh, played mainly by women,[13] employs Ganjifa cards and hinges on a point of 17; the Japanese Kabu uses a distinctive pack deriving ultimately from the Portuguese, though now heavily modified, and resembles Baccara in setting as its target a point ending in 9.[14] Don Laycock describes[15] a possible Baccara relative played at Sepik, New Guinea, with European cards under the name Laki ('Lucky'), which is simplified by the omission of a banker and by the lack of opportunity of improving one's hand.

A version of Lucky played at Rabaul and Buin features a point of 10 instead of 9 and recognizes certain winning combinations known as *kung*—namely A-A-A, 3-3-3, K-K-K, Q-Q-Q, 10-10-10, three courts, two courts and a Ten, and one court and two Tens. 'Another game known to one Arawe informant, but certainly not current,' adds Laycock, 'approximates the European game of Baccarat more closely— with some possible contamination from Pontoon.' Intriguingly, the first cards are dealt respectively face up and face down, which is in fact the reverse of Pontoon but equivalent to the practice of Japanese Kabu. Apparently unaware of Kabu, Laycock adds 'This is . . . known as *Kawu*; it was said by the informant to be "Japanese Lucky" (*laki bilong Siapan*), but it is almost certainly European in origin.'

8

Vying and bragging

The first or eldest says, *I'le vye the ruff*, the next says *I'le see it*, and the third *I'le see it and revie it* . . . then they show their Cards, and he that hath most of a suit wins six pence or farthings according to the Game of him that holds out the longest.

Cotgrave, *The Wit's Interpreter* (1662)

The nature of it is, that you are to endeavour to impose upon the judgment of the rest that play, and particularly upon the person that chiefly offers to oppose you, by boasting of cards in your hand, whether *Pair Royals*, *Pairs*, or others, that you are better than his or hers that play against you . . .

Seymour, on Brag, in *The Compleat Gamester* (1725)

Having surveyed relatively simple-minded gambling games, in which cards are turned up but not 'played' in any meaningful sense of the term, and moneys staked in advance of the deal are won or lost on the turn of a card rather than by the application of any skill, we turn now to gambling games involving some degree of strategy. Here, stakes are not bet blindly but may be varied under the control of the players, and are won not entirely on how cards turn out in the deal but on how skilfully the players have handled their investments according to the strength of their hands and the relative skill of their opponents. Poker is the most illustrious example of what I here term 'vying' games, from an old use of the word illustrated in the first quotation above.[1]

Basically, players are dealt a hand of cards and then 'vie' with one another, by progressively raising the stakes, as to which of them is holding the best card-combination according to an agreed scale of values. At each turn a player may match the previous stake (*see* or *call*, in the language of Poker) or increase it (*raise*), or else drop out (*fold*), thereby relinquishing whatever he has so far paid to stay in. There is no card-play as such, though there may be some exchange of cards with a view to improving the hand at some stage in the proceedings. There are two possible outcomes. Either a *showdown* is reached, in which case those left in reveal their cards and the player with the best hand wins the *pot* (all the stakes); or players may keep folding until only one is left in play, whereupon he wins without having to reveal his hand. In this case he will have done so by a process of vying, or psychological warfare, or *bluff*, since he might not hold the best hand and would therefore have lost if the game had reached a showdown instead.

The vying principle must be older than cards themselves and was probably transferred to them from dice, as the earliest cards were clearly designed for playing with rather than merely betting on. Poker and suchlike are therefore not so much card games as gambling games which happen to be played with cards. The principle can be applied to any sets of things capable of being arranged in order of agreed value, from dice, dominoes, and Scrabble tiles to precious stones or the entire contents of the National Gallery. Playing-cards just happen to be the quickest and most versatile source of things of unarguable relative value: unarguable, because value is a function of rarity, and the relative rarity of any given card-combination is a mathematically demonstrable fact rather than a matter of opinion or convention. Hence every country, in every age, has developed a vying game proper to its design of cards and national temperament: English Brag, French Bouillotte, German Poch, Italian Primiera, Spanish Mus, and so on. Poker itself is basically the national vying game of the United States, and its international prominence is as much due to the prominence and influence of American culture as to its own individual merits. What these are, and how the game developed over the years, will require a separate chapter. Here we survey its ancestors and surviving cousins.

From Poch to Poque

The word 'Poker' can be traced back via French Poque to one or more fifteenth-century German games variously recorded as Boeckels, Bocken, Bogel, Bockspiel, etc., which, when not denoting one of similar title played with balls or stones[2] (or conkers?) was the original of the still-played game of Poch, or Pochen. (The -en form is a verb. In German you do not 'play Poch', or whatever the game may be, but 'do Poching'.) Its basic meaning is 'bash' or 'pulverize', and, by extension, 'knock, provoke, brag, vie', and suchlike.

A family game perhaps equivalent to Newmarket or Michigan,

Poch is played with a distinctively designed and decorated circular board containing labelled scoops in which stakes are set against the contingencies of the game. (Two early sixteenth-century Poch boards may be seen in the Bavarian State Museum, Munich, and one of 1535 in the Victoria and Albert Museum, London.) The rules of play have been variously recorded at different times and places, but Poch in essence has always been a compound game in three parts, of which only the second involves 'vying' in the true sense of the word.

Poch (*German, traditional*). Any reasonable number can play, using 32 cards (or 52 if necessary).

In Part 1, players 'dress the board' by placing chips in the first seven of eight compartments labelled Ace, King, Queen, Jack, Ten, Marriage, Sequence, and *Poch*. Five cards each are dealt and the next is turned for trump. Anyone dealt the Ace of trumps wins the contents of the 'Ace' compartment, and so for the other compartments. The contents of the 'marriage' pool are won by anyone dealt both King and Queen of trumps, in addition to those of the separate 'King' and 'Queen' pool, and that of 'sequence' similarly for holding the 7–8–9 of trumps. If any of these winning cards or combinations is not won, the appropriate pool is carried forward to the next deal.

In Part 2, players vie as to who holds the best combination. A quartet beats a triplet, a triplet a pair, and a pair an unpaired hand, with ties determined by the highest card. The first to bet does so by placing a stake in the *poch* compartment, saying 'Ich poche eins' ('I bet one', or however many). Each in turn may match it or pass, and the opener may raise it when his turn comes round again.

In Part 3 the cards are played out in sequences after the manner of Stops games (Newmarket, Michigan, etc.), but without following suit. A player ending a sequence is paid by the others and starts a new one, and the first out of cards wins one for each card left unplayed in all the others' hands.

First recorded at Strasburg in 1441, Poch is one of the oldest identifiable card games and has evidently influenced the pattern of many others. One of the most frequently attested French games of the fifteenth and sixteenth centuries—first mentioned in the accounts of Charles VII in 1454 and again by Villon in 1461—is Glic, whose virtual identity with Poch is demonstrated by the equivalent technical terms marked on a late fifteenth-century Glic board preserved in the Museum at Cluny. Glic had vanished from the French scene by about

1600, but another version of Poch appears under the name 'Poque' in the 1718 edition of the *Académie des jeux*, dying out about a hundred years later, and yet another from 1855 under the name Bog, which remained popular up to the early 1900s. Possibly related to Poch are the original three-stake form of English Brag, its ancestor Post and Pair, and the substantially similar French game of Belle, Flux et Trente-et-Un, also known as Les Trois Jeux (and in German as Dreisatz, literally 'Three-Stake'). The structural similarity of all these games will be appreciated from the (simplified) listing of their essential features in Table 2.

TABLE 2

Game	Cards	Stake 1	Stake 2	Stake 3
Poch (Ger. 15–20 C.)	12/52, 5/32	sweepstake	vying (pairs)	stops (31?)
Poque, (Fr. 18–19 C.)	5+/36	turn-up	vying (pairs)	stops
Bog (Fr. 18–19 C.)	5+/32	turn-up	vying (pairs)	stops
B.F. & 31 (Fr. Ger., 17–18 C.)	3/52	best upcard	best flush	draw to 31
Post & Pair (Eng. 16–17 C.)	3/52	best upcard	vying (pairs)	draw to 31
Brag (Eng., 18–19 C.)	3/52	best upcard	vying (pairs)	draw to 31

In original Poch, a 'trump' is turned, and players holding trump cards or combinations corresponding to those marked on the board sweep the appropriate stakes. In Poque and Bog the dealer turns up a card, and, if it corresponds to one of the specific winning cards marked on the board, scoops the appropriate pool. The other stakes relating to individual cards are taken if and when the appropriate cards are played out in the third part of the game. In 'vying for pairs', a pair is beaten by two pair, two pair by three alike, and threes by four alike.

In the others, each player receives two cards face down and one face up, and the first stake is won by the player with the best upcard, unless tied, when it is carried. On the face of it, these three bear only a superficial resemblance to Poch. I believe the resemblance was once much greater, however, in that the third stake for Poch would originally have been decided by a draw to 31 rather than by playing out sequences. Drawing to 31 is well known as a fifteenth-century game in its own right, whereas 'Stops' play is not positively recorded before the seventeenth century, when—to judge from the sudden popularity of games based solely on that principle—it must have been something of a novelty. The change probably took place under the influence of Hoc, a multi-stake vying game much favoured by Cardinal

Mazarin at the court of Versailles in the mid-seventeenth century. In Hoc, each received twelve cards from a 52-card pack, three stakes were contested by vying as to point, sequence, and threes or fours of a kind (compare Piquet), and the cards were then played out in the manner of Stops.

From Flush to Prime

Passing from compound games in which vying was just one of several gaming elements to those in which it formed the whole point of play, it will be interesting to note in how many different ways cards may be matched to produce 'viable' combinations whose relative values derive directly from their mathematical rarity. Various ways in which cards can be matched together may be outlined as follows:

1. Suit-based

Flush = two or more cards of a suit; or, in some games, a complete hand of suit-matched cards.

Prime = one card of each suit. In effect, this is only recognized in games based on four-card hands such as Primiera, though the term could be applied to a hand of different suits in a three-card game. Poker freaks have invented the 'Flash', which consists of a Joker plus one card of each suit.

2. Rank-based

Set = two or more cards of the same rank, hence basically = pairs, triplets, and quartets. Compounds appearing in hands of more than four cards include two pair and pair-and-triplet ('full house').

Sequence or *run* = three or more cards in numerical sequence or ranking order ('straight').

Point—Numerical total of point-values assigned to component cards, such as Ace + Ten = 21 in Pontoon and Blackjack.

3. Suit–rank compounds

The commonest is the self-explanatory *straight flush* of Poker or *running flush* of Brag, of which great play is also made in Rummy games. A highly specific combination is the *marriage* of King and Queen in (usually) the same suit, which appears in a wide variety of games. Even more specific is the eponymous ♠ Q- ♦ J pair of Bezique and Pinochle. Multi-pack forms of Bezique, in which it is possible to acquire more than four of a rank, occasionally recognize (under various names) such a thing as a *prime quartet*, i.e. four of a kind, one of each suit. The combination described above as *point* most often appears in combination with a flush: in other words, it usually means 'total value of cards in any one suit' (as at Piquet), and therefore should be referred to technically as a 'flush-point'.

If Poch took its name from the actual process of bragging or vying, others took theirs from the most characteristic winning combination. Sequence, Flush, Prime, and Gé ('Pair') are all names of early European games, and are later encountered as elements of such compound games as the J'ai (gé), flux et séquence (sixteenth century), and J'ai, point, flux et séquence (seventeenth). A primitive feature is that they are multi-stake games, in that separate pots are built and won in sequence for the various types of combination, as opposed to hierarchic games like Poker, in which a single pot is won for the best hand as determined by a mathematically arranged hierarchy of different types of combination.

Gé is evidently the 'Geleus' whose title derives, according to Cardano in 1564, from *geleo*, 'I have (it)!'. It also appears as Gilè in Italian, which in Florio's 1611 dictionary is glossed as 'like our poste and paire'. The Gilet of eighteenth-century France[3] was a three-card game of two deals, the first for a fixed stake won by the best pair or triplet, the second vied for in respect of the best-held flush-point. (We will also encounter it as Giley when we come to Spanish games.)

Nothing is known of the game referred to as 'Sequence' in fifteenth to sixteenth-century France and Italy, except that it might be synonymous with its oft-mentioned German contemporaries Quentzen and (perhaps) Schwentzlen.[4] Even more tantalizing is 'Flush', which has a long history but is not technically described before the nineteenth century. It first appears in fifteenth-century Italy as Flusso, Frussi, etc. and reached France as Flux before 1500, being played by, amongst others, Charles VIII and Anne de Bretagne. Rabelais, in 1534, gives it pride of place in his list of games played by Gargantua. By 1513 it had reached Germany, where Gengenbach describes it as a new game ('ein nüwes spyl'), imported from foreign parts ('der welsch Flüss'). A Swiss engraving of about 1514[5] shows it to be a three-card game, and the caption to a contemporary French copy of it suggests an element of vying. Something of the sort is sporadically reported in France as late as the nineteenth century, and to this day there is played in Muotatal, in the Swiss canton of Schwyz, a highly distinctive variety called Flüsslen.[6]

Possibly related to Flush was the fifteenth-century French game of Ronfle, later recorded in Italy as Ronfa, and described as 'still played in the Vosges' by Boiteau d'Ambly in 1854.[7] Its nature is suggested by the fact that *ronfle* also means the 'point' (strictly, flush-point) at

Piquet, being equivalent to Cotton's use of the word 'ruff' for the same thing.

One of the most elegant combinations, that consisting of just one card in each suit, gives its name to an illustrious and well-known game called Prime in French, Primiera in Italian, and Primero in English:

> LOVELL. Came you from the king, my lord?
> GARDINER. I did, Sir Thomas; and left him at primero
> With the Duke of Suffolk . . .
>
> Shakespeare, *Henry VIII*, v. i 8–10.

Primero was the fashionable game of the Tudor court and certainly played by Elizabeth I,[8] though there is no evidence to support Shakespeare's idea that Henry was so engaged on the night of her birth in 1533, or even that it was his game at all. (Catherine of Aragon, his first and longest-lasting wife, played Gleek.) Nor, despite the Spanish flavour of its English spelling, does there appear to be any solid evidence supporting a Spanish origin for the game, which in Spanish is Primera. On the other hand, it has long been, and still remains, the major native vying game of Italy, and involves a distinctive card-point system common to several Italian games but unknown elsewhere.

Primiera is often described as 'the' ancestor of Poker. This over-simplification is correct at least to the extent that the game embodies the hierarchical principle whereby several different types of combination compete against one another in a single series of relative values. In this, together with the distinctive combination from which it takes its name, may lie the novelty required to explain the remarkable veneration accorded to the game by early Italian writers. Berni's *Capitolo del gioco della primiera* was published at Venice in 1526, and Cardano, in his *Book on games of chance* (1564), describes it as the 'most noble' game of all. Reference to the modern game enables it to be reconstructed along the following general lines.

Primiera (Italian, sixteenth century). Four or more players, 40-card pack lacking Eights, Nines, and Tens. Players ante to a pot, are dealt two cards face down, stake again, and receive two more. The winning combinations are, from lowest to highest:

1. Point (*numerus*): two or three cards of the same suit. A point of higher card-value beats one of lower value, for which purpose courts count 10 each, Two 12, Three 13, Four 14, Five 15, Ace 16, Six 18, and Seven 21.

2. Prime (*primiera*): four cards, one of each suit.
3. Fifty-five (*supremus*): the highest possible three-flush, i.e. Ace-+Six+Seven (= $16+18+21 = 55$) plus an unrelated fourth card.
4. Flush (*fluxus*): four of a suit.
5. Quartet (*chorus*): four of the same rank.

Anyone holding a prime or flush may call 'Vada!' ('Go!'), which brings an immediate showdown won by the best hand. Failing that, there is a draw and another betting round. If no one bets, the stakes are carried forward to the next deal; but if one stays in, at least one other must contest the pot, this obligation ultimately falling upon the player immediately ahead of the last bettor if everyone else has folded.

In a showdown the better of equal combinations is that with the higher point. Thus a quartet of Aces ($4 \times 16 = 64$) beats a quartet of Fives (60) but is beaten by four Sixes (72). Four Kings will not beat four Queens or Jacks, as these hands all count 40. Such ties are broken in favour of the eldest hand competing.

Players 'vie' by stating how high a hand they are claiming to have, and may 'bluff' by overstating it. What they apparently must not do is to underbid their hand; for, as Cardano puts it, 'If anyone wins with the greater point, he is obliged to show another card; otherwise he loses his deposit because he could have a flush . . . Similarly, if he vies on the basis of point, he is obliged to show two different cards and one of a matching suit, so that no one may suspect him of having a flush or prime.'[9]

Modern Primiera appears under various guises and names, including Goffo and Bambara. Most retain the same card values and basically the same combinations, though the simple point has been downgraded and the rare quartet counts only as a prime. The hands have therefore been reduced to the series *primiera*, *cinquantacinque*, and *flusso*. Other simplifications have also taken place. Players now ante a fixed amount and receive four cards immediately, dealt two by two. Various rules apply if in the final showdown no one has a prime or better. The pot may be won by the highest counting two or three-card flush, or the result is a stand-off and a new deal ensues, or players keep drawing till someone knocks or the pack is exhausted. Equal-ranking combinations are still decided by reference to card-points, but any further equality is settled on a 'best suit' basis—typically hearts best, then diamonds, clubs, spades (or cups, coins, clubs, swords).

From Glic to Gleek

Glic is one of the most frequently recorded games of fifteenth to sixteenth-century France. Its apparent identity with Poch has already been noted by reference to a gaming board in the Museum at Cluny, whose staking compartments are labelled as shown in the left-hand column of the list below. Their German Poch-board equivalents, as analysed by Thierry Depaulis,[10] are shown alongside.

roys	könig
roynes	obermann
valletz	untermann
dix	zehner
mariage	braut
sequence	sequens
glic	poch
mornifles	. . .
le mains	sau

The first four are obvious (roi, reine, valet, dix), as also is sequence. If it seems odd that the German equivalent of mariage is Braut, literally 'bride' or 'fiancée'—their two lower courts both being male— this may be explained by noting that Poch dates back to the first half of the fifteenth century when either of the lower courts was as likely to be female as male, and that Queens are known earlier in German packs than in French. The words glic and mornifle denote, respectively, three-alike and four-alike (*Drittgleich, Viergleich*, in Swabian dialect). They are therefore collectively equivalent to Poch, which in the German game was won on either of these combinations. In this connection, Depaulis points out that the Swabian terms suggest a derivation of glic from *gleich*, '(a-)like', rather than from *Glück*, 'luck'. The last term, le mains ('the least'), evidently denotes the Ace, or lowest card, as it still was in the fifteenth century). Similarly, the German Sau ('sow'), denotes the lowest card in the late fifteenth-century German 48-card pack, namely the Deuce, which usually bore the picture of a pig.

Glic may or may not be related to the contemporary Italian Cricca, and if the latter is to be identified with 'Cruca', described in the Steele document as 'a three-card game', then its resemblances lie rather with the branch represented by Les Trois Jeux and proto-Brag. It must, however, underlie the curious English game of Gleek—curious because of the remarkable transformation it seems to have undergone by the time of its first detailed description in *The Wits Interpreter* of 1662.

Gleek first appears in Watson's *Chirch of the Evill*, 1522, and is often mentioned throughout the sixteenth and early seventeenth centuries. It was presumably identical with Glic in the form played, according to the lines from Sir William Forest,[11] by Catherine of Aragon:

> With stoole and with needyl she was not to
> seeke,
> And other practiseinges for ladyes meete,
> To pastyme at tables, tick tacke, or gleeke,
> Cardis and dyce . . .

According to Cotgrave's 1662 description, however—subsequently regurgitated in Cotton's *The Compleat Gamester* and Lucas's *Lives of the Gamesters*—it has become a specifically three-hand game of tricks and combinations with some distinct resemblances to Piquet and Hombre. Of a 44-card pack lacking Deuces and Treys, twelve are dealt to each player in batches of four and the remaining eight laid aside with the topmost turned for trumps. If the turn-up is a counter, the dealer wins its value in pence from each opponent (assuming stakes are set in units of one penny). Counters are certain cards of the trump suit, namely: Ace (Tib) 15, Jack (Tom) 9, Six (Tumbler) 6, Five (Towser) 5, Four (Tiddy) 4, King 3, Queen 3. All other cards, including unlisted trumps, count 1 each at end of play but do not entitle the dealer to payment on turning them.

There follows a round of bidding to buy the seven face-down cards in return for seven discards, which must be made before the draw. The object here is to acquire, as far as possible,

(1) the best holding of cards in any one suit, thereby winning the 'ruff', or flush;
(2) three or four Aces, Kings, Queens, or Jacks, thereby scoring for gleek (three) or mournival (four);
(3) a strong trick-playing hand.

The first to bid offers 12 pence, and each succeeding bid must be one penny higher. When two pass in succession, the third pays half the stated amount to each opponent, any odd penny going to the player at his left (or to a pool if previously agreed). He then discards seven cards and takes the unseen stock. Next, players bet on who holds the longest suit by raising stakes in the manner of Poker. Cotgrave's example runs: 'I'll vie the ruff'—'I'll see it.'—'I'll see it and revie it.'—'I'll see your revie.'—'I'll not meddle with it.'

'They then shew their cards', our author continues, 'and he that hath most of a suit wins six pence . . . of him who holds out longest, and four of the other that said he would see it, but after refused to meddle with it.'[12] If two players fold, the third wins the ruff without showing it. If neither of the first two will start the vie, the third does not win but may double the stakes of the next deal. From Cotgrave's later comment that a player may bluff the others out of the pot when he has 'not above thirty in . . . hand, and the rest may have forty or fifty', it seems likely that ruff is won on the highest value of cards held rather than simply on the length of the suit.

If any player has four Aces, he may count it as the best ruff and bet accordingly, not revealing it until the others have folded. This seems somewhat unfair, but Cotgrave is quite explicit on the point.

Assuming four Aces has not been announced, players now declare their best gleek or mournival. A mournival beats any gleek, and a mournival of higher cards one of lower cards. Whoever wins this is paid at the appropriate rate, to wit for Aces 4 or 8 (for gleek or mournival respectively); for Kings 3 or 6; for Queens 2 or 4; and for Jacks 1 or 2.

Finally, the cards are played out in tricks—possibly as at Whist, though no rules of play are given. Each player adds together the face values of all the cards he has won in tricks and calculates the difference between this total and 22 points. If he has taken less than 22 he pays the difference to each opponent; if more, he receives the difference from each.

Geoffrey Mott-Smith, in *Culbertson's Card Games Complete*, p. 82, makes the players win or lose the difference between the number of cards they have taken and the twelve they started with. In case he has missed the significance of 22, we may note that the seven counters total 45 points, which, added to the 37 others, makes 82 points in all. Thus the mean value of a single card is about 1.86, and of the original hand 12 times this amount, or 22.36. Anyone with 23 or more has therefore gained on the deal.

The French connection: Brelan, Bouillotte, Ambigu

The descent of Poker may partly be traced through the supposedly ancient French game of Brelan and its certainly more advanced offspring Bouillotte.

Brelan is not actually recorded as a card game earlier than 1634.[13] The word originally meant a gaming-table (from German *bretling*), and, subsequently, a place where gaming is done—thus Nicot's French Dictionary of 1606, 'locus in quo alea luditur', and Cotgrave's 1611 French–English Dictionary, 'A common tipling house; a house of gaming or of any other disorder'. And when François Villon, the vagabond poet, speaks of 'berlanc' in his *Grand Testament* of 1461, he does so in its further extension to cover a gambling game in general, including one played with dice. From the second half of the seventeenth century to the end of the eighteenth it is a frequently mentioned and clearly most popular card game, whose apparently down-market status is reflected in its omission from the *Académie des jeux* series (except for passing references), and in a remarkable paucity of working descriptions before that in Diderot and d'Alembert's *Dictionnaire raisonée* of 1751.

In essence, three or more players receive three cards each from a pack of any length from 24 to 36, and another is turned from the stock. The best hand is a *tricon*, three of a kind, which is even better if matched by the rank of the upcard, which makes it a *tricon carré*, or 'triplet squared'—i.e., a quartet. By the end of the eighteenth century Brelan had evolved into Bouillotte, apparently by governmental decree, as suggested by the oft-repeated but eminently repeatable anecdote involving the lovely Madame Tallien. The French revolutionary government of 1795–9 (the 'Directory'), itself with another threatened revolution on its hands when it restored the prohibition on Brelan, is said to have met in conclave at the Palais de Luxembourg to devise a new but legally acceptable game to replace it, Bouillotte being the not very dissimilar end-product. Tallien, promenading herself in the gardens of the palais, reportedly observed: 'Up there are five kings, sweating blood and tears to make a triplet [*brelan*] of knaves'.

Bouillotte—the word means 'hot-water bottle', though some say it commemorates Geoffrey de Bouillon—remained popular throughout nineteenth-century Europe, eventually being displaced by Poker in some circles and Baccara in others. It evidently contributed a number of features to Poker, and, in a detailed appreciation written shortly before its demise, Foster observes 'By many persons Bouillotte is considered superior to Poker, because it offers the player many opportunities to speculate on winning by the aid of cards that are not in his own hand'.

Bouillotte (French, nineteenth century). Four players, 20-card pack consisting of A, K, Q, 9, 8 in each suit. The first two players ante, three cards are dealt to everyone, and the thirteenth is turned face up as a *retourne*. Players may pass until someone bets, after which they must either fold or bet. If all pass there is a new deal, and if an opener or raiser is not called he wins without a showdown. The rules of calling and showing are complex but not without strategic point. At a showdown the hands are decided by the best brelan, or, if none appears, by the best point. Best of all is a *brelan carré*, or four of a kind made up of three in hand plus the retourne. If, against a *brelan carré*, anyone has a higher-ranking brelan in hand, he may turn up the second card of stock, and, if this matches, he wins by *brelan carré à l'anglaise*. Either coup wins a payment of four chips in addition to the pot. Next best is a simple brelan, which is either three of a kind in hand or a pair in hand matching the turned card—a *brelan de retourne*. A simple brelan wins an extra chip from each player other than anyone else holding a brelan, a *brelan de retourne* earns a further chip, and the highest-ranking brelan wins the pot. Failing brelans, the best point wins. This is determined in a peculiar way. First, the 'winning suit' is defined as that showing the highest combined value of cards in the hands of all players remaining in the pot (Ace 11, courts 10 each, others face value). The pot is then won by the player holding the highest card of the winning suit. Ties are broken by position, the 'eldest' relevant player having priority.

An interesting feature of Bouillotte is that players need not equalize to stay in, but may bet a proportion of their *cave* (the amount they have left). Pots are therefore split accordingly. The fact that one card is dealt face up and may form part of another's hand brings to mind the communal-card feature of modern Poker, though in Bouillotte it is not in fact communal. The game also often featured a wild card, the club Jack (or Queen), known as *mistigris*. This was held to form a brelan if held in conjunction with two cards of the same rank and colour (not necessarily suit).

No account of the French connection would be complete without reference to the eccentric Ambigu. Its first appearance, in the 1674 edition of *La Maison académique*, is prefaced by a letter describing it as a recently discovered game and dedicating its discovery to 'Madame la Comtesse de V.' by its discoverer 'P.P.B.' It appears that this man with no name got it from another man with no name, but that this other man was 'un Seigneur Esclavon', and the name of the game, in its native Slavonian, was 'Prispistrihoc'. Understandably, 'P.P.B.' finds this a bit of a mouthful, and has taken the liberty of renaming it Ambigu, or le Meslé ('banquet'), because it is a mixture of several existing games. Amongst its many points of superiority is the fact that it can last for any agreed length of time, a common way of marking a time limit being to stick a pin in a candle and play for as long as it takes the flame to reach it.

Two or more players are dealt four cards each from a 40-card pack consisting only of numerals A–10, and vie as to who holds the best combinations. The lowest of these is point, followed by a prime, a three-card suit-sequence (bobtail), *tricon* (triplet), flush, *tricon*-prime (triplet plus card of fourth suit), flush-sequence (four-card straight flush), and *fredon* (quartet). As a final flourish, four Tens or Sixes beats everything, including a pig with wings.

Ambigu's eccentricity, plus the fact that it appears only in the *Académie* gamebook series and is not even mentioned in passing in contemporary literature, suggests a one-off invention, if not a deliberate spoof. Thierry Depaulis derives the preposterous 'Prispistrihoc' from a mixture, or 'banquet', of Prime, Piquet, Tricon, and Hoc. Not so much a banquet, perhaps, as a dog's dinner.

Spanish relations: Giley, Golfo, Mus

Spanish gamebooks record several vying games clearly related to those of the European mainstream, and one, Mus, of considerable originality.

Giley, described by Barnes[14] as much played at horse fairs—and hence, by association, a gypsy game—deals four or more players four cards each from a 28-card pack and a showdown is won by the best flush-point. With Ace 11, courts, treys, and deuces 10 each, and Seven worth 7, a four-flush will be worth 37–41 points, a three-flush 27–30, and so on. Not dissimilar is Golfo, declared by Barnes to be the king of gambling games—'el rey de los juegos de envite'—and played also as Goffo in Italy and Gofo in Uruguay. Only three of the four players are active at a time, and the 28-card pack consists solely of numerals 3–9, which count face value. Although five cards are dealt, the best hand is the highest-valued four-flush, ties being broken by 'age' (the player nearest the dealer has priority).

A rival to Golfo in the Spanish-speaking worlds of both Spain and South America is Mus, an extraordinary game of Basque origin and terminology which in many ways is quite unique. As I know of no previous English-language account I will describe it in some detail, though space precludes a complete description of so complicated a game.

The uniqueness of Mus begins with its basic structure, for, even though it is a gambling game and includes vying, it is normally and best played as a partnership game for four. Not only that, but partners are permitted to indicate the nature of their hands by means of conventional signals! (Try introducing that into the 'official rules' of Poker.)

Its next peculiarity is that despite the vying element, a game is played up to a fixed target of 40 points over as many deals as it takes. Points are represented by *piedras*, 'stones', which we can call chips. As chips are won, they are taken from a central pool by one member of each partnership. For every five chips his side wins, he returns four to the pool and passes one to his partner. This one is called an *amarraco* (Basque for 'five'). Players therefore judge the state of play by noting the number of *amarracos* on the table in front of the relevant member of each side, plus any odd chips in front of his partner. Each player in charge of *amarracos* must announce when he has seven of them, for obvious reasons.

The cards of the 40-card Spanish pack count at face value from Ace (1) to 10 each for courts (King, Caballo, Sota). In the most widespread version of the game all Threes count as Kings and all Deuces as Aces, as to both rank and value. The game is therefore said to be played with eight Kings and eight Aces.

Four cards are dealt to each player and the game begins with a possible draw. Each in turn announces 'mus' if he wishes to draw or 'No hay mus' if satisfied with his hand. At each round, either everyone draws or no one does. If everyone calls 'mus', all may exchange from one to four cards, and further rounds ensue until someone eventually says 'no'. If the stock runs out before all draws are completed, a new one is formed from the shuffled discards.

This is followed by four rounds of possible betting and vying, each for a particular class of combination. These four classes are followed in an invariable order and there is no showdown until all four have been gone through—except in the case of an *órdago*, which is a bet amounting to all the chips either side requires to make up 40 and so win, if accepted, on a single coup.

The four classes of combination are treated in the following order:

1. *Grande.* The highest holding of cards regardless of point-value wins the stakes, or one chip if no bet has been made or accepted. (Example: K-3–7-6 beats K-C-S-S, as Threes are equivalent to Kings.)
2. *Chica.* As above, but won by the lowest holding of cards regardless of value. (Thus K-6–2-A beats C-4–4-A because, Aces being equal, its second-lowest card beats the other's Four.)
3. *Pares.* Two or more cards of the same rank. There are three types. The lowest is *par*, a pair, with a basic 1-chip value; then

medias, triplet, basically worth 2; then *duples*, defined as any two pair or four of a kind, and basically worth 3 chips. (Since quartets count only as two pair, K-3–2-A would beat C-C-C-C because it is equivalent to K-K-A-A and Kings beat Caballos.) In this and the following rounds the best hand wins the basic value plus the value of the last best accepted—or, if none, 1 chip extra.

4. *Juegos.* Subdivided into *juego* or *juego sí* ('play') and *punto* or *juego no* ('no play'). Juego is won by a hand counting exactly 31, which carries a 3-chip base-value. Failing that, 32 wins for a 2-chip base-value. Failing either, there is a 1-chip bonus for 40, 37, 36, 35, 34, or 33, which is the lowest hand of its class. (It is impossible to make 39 or 38.) Punto, 'no play', only applies if no one opens the betting on *juego*, and carries a 1-chip base-value. It is won by the highest-counting hand under 31, i.e. 30 best, then 29, and so on down to 4, the worst possible.

On each round players may pass or open for a minimum of two chips. An opening bet may be declined, matched, or raised by either opponent. If declined, the bidder takes the appropriate bonus from the pool, 'porqué no'. If raised, it may be raised by any amount. If *órdago* is announced, the other side may either accept, in which case the best hand wins the whole game outright, or decline, in which case the other side wins only the bets made on the hand under consideration, plus any appropriate bonus. When all bets are declined or equalized, the next round begins. On a showdown, no ties are recognized. As between identical combinations the higher-ranking beats the lower, and, if still equal, the elder hand beats the younger.

Partners may signal to each other the holding of certain combinations, provided they stick to accepted convention. At *grande*, for instance, you can show two Kings by biting your lower lip. To show four Kings, do the same thing twice!

Mus is equipped with a tremendous array of protocols, conventional jokes (if an adversary misbehaves, you can claim a 'Bonus of one chip for playing properly'), technical terms, and basic Basque vocabulary: *bi* 'two', *hiru* 'three', *lau* 'four', *amarraco* 'five', *bay* 'yes', *ez* 'no'. There is a version in which the Caballo of clubs and Sota of coins are wild cards, known respectively as 'Perico', and 'Perica', and a non-partnership version for four to eight players called Mus Ilustrada.

Although Mus as a whole seems unique, its individual elements are recognizably drawn from common stock. Visual signals are a distinctive feature of other Spanish games such as Tute and other European gambling games such as Watten and Flüsslen. Staking all on a single hand is a feature shared with Truco, and has parallels in Tute. Its unusual structure, whereby bets are made in different classes on a single showdown, may conceivably have evolved from a three-stake game in which the first stake was won by the best card dealt (giving rise to *grande*), the second increased by vying on pairs and triplets (retained in *pares*), and the third determined by drawing cards up to 31 (the basis of *juego*).

From Post to Brag

Brag is the longest-standing British representative of the Poker family. The Waddington survey of 1981 (see Chapter 1) rated it fourth in numerical popularity after Rummy, Whist, and Pontoon. Of its type, it is the everyday game of workers, students, and the armed forces, and, despite theoretical restrictions applying to all card games other than Cribbage, it is most at home in the pub. Arthur Taylor reports that some licensees take steps to ban it, or to circumvent its most dangerous effects, by 'allowing seven or nine-card Brag, but insisting that it is scored round a crib board, with a maximum of 10p per game [this was in 1976] and no kitty'.[15]

From an historical point of view the most remarkable feature of Brag is how much it has changed over the centuries. As now played it is virtually three-card non-draw Poker with no 'calling' until only two players remain in the pot—in other words, the stakes can theoretically be raised indefinitely up to that point. The winning combinations are pair, flush, run (sequence), flush-run or running flush, and three of a kind, or *prial*. (From 'pair-royal'. The spelling 'pryle' enjoys no literate support.) For two of these hands special significance attaches to the Threes. Three Aces is beaten by a prial of Threes, which is therefore absolutely unbeatable, and a run of A-K-Q by one of 3–2-A. One or more cards may be designated wild: sometimes Jacks, nowadays often Deuces. The traditional 'braggers' of classical Brag were the Jack of clubs and Ace, Nine of diamonds. In America, where the game achieved some vogue in the nineteenth century, all eight Jacks and Nines were made wild. Interesting features of Brag include the practice of betting blind—i.e. without looking at one's cards for several rounds—and of not shuffling between deals until a hand has been won on a prial.

Countless variants of the game are currently played. In Seven-Card Brag each player selects six cards out of seven dealt and forms them into two Brag hands. Each player's higher hand is exposed first, then his lower, and the stake is either won by the player with both hands best or carried forward for as many deals as necessary for this to occur. A prial of Sevens beats everything, except that anyone dealt four of a kind sweeps the pool. Nine-Card Brag extends this principle to a deal of nine cards, which are formed into three Brag hands. In the Lancashire game of Crash[16] four players each receive thirteen cards, discard one, form the others into Brag hands, then play them out like tricks. One point per trick is pegged in a square Crash board—like a Cribbage board, but with twenty-five holes drilled in the shape of a cross of St Andrew. Six points brings one from the corner to the centre and so wins the game, though winning all four tricks in one hand brings sudden victory. Another variant, known as 'Stop the Bus' in some quarters and 'Bastard' in others, is the Brag equivalent of Whisky Poker or Commerce. Players receive three cards each and play at draw and discard through a three-card dummy dealt face up at start of play.

Originally, however, Brag was a three-stake game comparable to Poch, the first stake going to the player dealt the highest upcard, the second to the winner of a round of vying on pairs and triplets, the third to the player drawing cards totalling closest to 31. Such appears to be the format of its earliest direct ancestor Post, later called Post and Pair. Post first appears in conjunction with 'Glyeke' in 1528.[17] An epigram by Harington (d. 1612) bespeaks its social status:

> The first game was the best, when, free from crime,
> The courtly gamesters all were in their *Prime*:
> The second game was *Post*, until with posting
> They paid so fast, 'twas time to leave their boasting;
> Then thirdly followed *heaving of the Maw* . . .

Since Prime (Primero) was played at Elizabeth's court, and Maw at James Stuart's, Post presumably reached its courtly prime round about the first decade of the seventeenth century. For its unknown origin a possible Spanish connection has been suggested[18] by the derivation of 'post' from *apostar*, meaning to bet, or, in its original strict sense, 'to place in the hands of a third party a sum of money (or equivalent) for the winner'.

Post and Pair is mentioned in *Taylor's Motto* of 1621, and Cotton offers a somewhat garbled description in 1674. He adds that it is 'very much played in the West of England'—as might be guessed by pronouncing 'prial' in west country accent and comparing it with 'pair-royal'. The essentials of Cotton's game read:

You must first stake at Post then at Pair; after this deal two Cards apiece, then stake at Seat, and then deal the third Card about. The eldest hand may pass and come in again, if any of the Gamesters vye it; if not, the Dealer may play it out, or double it.

The Ace of Trumps, as at Ruff and Honours, is the best Card of all, and so the rest in order. At Post the best Cards are one and twenty, viz. two Tens and an Ace, but a Pair-royal wins all, both Post, Pair, and Seat. Here note, that he who hath the best Pair or the best Post is the winner . . .

The third card is dealt face up and the stake for *seat* won by that of highest rank. The reference to 'trumps' is unclear, unless it means the Ace of diamonds, as in Seymour's 'Bragg'. The second stake, for *pair*, is evidently contested by vying, and that for *post* won by the player whose cards total nearest to 21 without busting. Cotton may be in error here: 31 is the usual target for games of this type, and remains so in the virtually identical game of 'Bragg' first described in Seymour's 1721 edition of *The Compleat Gamester*.

The quotation from Seymour heading this chapter is surrounded by further enlightening observations on the name and nature of the game:

The next principal matter, and the main thing by which the second stake is to be won, is called the *Bragg*, which by the ingenuity of its management, gives the game its name. The nature of it is . . . [*etc.*]. Here you are to observe, that the witty ordering of this Bragg, is the most pleasant part of this game; for those that by fashioning their looks and gestures, can give a proper air to their actions as will so deceive an unskilful antagonist, that sometimes a pair of Fives, Treys, or Deuces, in such a hand, with the advantage of his composed countenance, and subtle manner of overawing the other, shall outbragg a much greater Pair Royal and win the stakes with great applause and laughter on his side, from the whole company.

The translation of Post and Pair into Brag was clearly synonymous with the introduction of wild cards or 'braggers'. Seymour declares the Jack of clubs to be a 'principal favourite', as in the game of Loo, and adds 'some very nice players at this game, make the Nine of diamonds a second favourite'.

Such is the classical game of Brag as described by Hoyle himself in 1751, and so it remained, at least in the books, for some time after.[19] By the time of the 1847 edition by 'G. H————, Esq.' the hands include 'pairs, flushes, sequences of flushes, and so on, similar to Cribbage, excepting fifteens'. Such hands may have been added to the original schedule under the influence of Cribbage, perhaps from a train of thought engendered by the draw to thirty-one. It is described as being 'not near so much in vogue as formerly', though 'at present much patronised at the Oriental Club, in Hanover Square'. By 1863 it had been dropped from *Hoyle's Games Modernized*, and thereafter rarely occurs in British gamebooks, except in a regurgitation of the three-stake form.

Single-stake Brag is described in various nineteenth-century American Hoyles, the earliest I have seen being that published by Excelsior, New York, 1887. Dick and Fitzgerald's 1868 Hoyle described only three-stake Brag, though it agrees with Excelsior in designating all Jacks and Nines wild. American writers of this period tend to derive Poker from Brag, but the two are clearly cousins rather than parent and child. No one plays the three-stake game today, and it seems likely that Brag shed its irrelevances and became a single-stake game under the influence of Poker. Amongst its borrowings from Poker is that of forcing a showdown by equalizing the bets. It is by tradition a 'freeze-out' game, in which at least one player is obliged by law to keep raising until all but two have either folded voluntarily or been completely ruined.

9

Bluffing and poking

It is a game in which there is a right technical play in every situation, and the winning player should know this correct technical play. But the winning player must go further. He must deliberately make the wrong technical play on a sufficient number of occasions so that the other players in the game will never be certain as to what he is doing.

Oswald Jacoby on Poker

Is that the game where one receives five cards? And if there's two alike that's pretty good, but if there's three alike that's much better?

W. C. Fields

Poker is the most highly evolved and widely played member of the 'vying' family introduced in the previous chapter. It is also the most widely misunderstood and blighted by myth.

Poker is not so much a card game as a game that happens to be played with cards, which themselves have little part to play beyond sitting around looking pretty. The true instruments of play are coin of the realm, or representations of it called 'chips', and a move consists in transferring one or more of them from one's personal stack into a communal pool or 'pot', which is eventually won by the player who either has the best hand or has persuaded everyone else that he has. 'Technical play' basically involves weighing the probability that one has the best hand against the odds currently offered by the pot, and betting boldly if these odds are greater, otherwise cautiously or not at all. Because the situation changes with each move, such evaluation requires considerable flexibility and mathematical expertise. This doesn't mean it has to be carried out analytically or with computer assistance: experienced players do so intuitively and may well be unable to express their reasoning in numbers. Technical play, however, is not itself the essence of the game. The point of Poker lies in the exercise of competitive psychology, which is the essence of game-play whether in 'real life' or over the card-table. Real-life Poker is a theme explored in many books, from Yardley's *The Education of a Poker Player*,[1] to Berne's *Games People Play*[2] (which is about 'The Psychology of Human Relationships'—nothing to do with formal games), to Spanier's *Total Poker*,[3] in which the Poker factor of everyday life is illustrated by reference to a variety of historical, political, and fictitious events.

Myth-representations of Poker are particularly prevalent in films. As Spanier perceptively observes, those centring on Poker games, like *The Cincinnati Kid* or *Big Deal at Dodge City*, often fail to convey the essence of Poker as well as others in which it is not the principal subject—notably *The Hustler*, which is nominally about Pool. It is a pity that Spanier wrote before *The Driver* was released in 1978. The game itself makes only a fleeting appearance at the beginning of this unlauded masterpiece,[4] where it is portrayed as dull and mechanical by comparison with the real-life Poker subsequently played out by all its characters, from leads to bit-parts. What it proves is the inadequacy of bluff alone as the distinguishing feature of Poker, whether at cards or at life. The fact is that the consistent bluffer loses consistently, because the losing factor lies not in his bluffing but in his consistency. And that, although Jacoby expresses it more elegantly, is what it's all about.

Varieties of Poker

Poker is not a homogeneous game like Bridge but, like Rummy, a close-knit family of games based on several basic principles. The most characteristic of these is the particular range of card combinations, or 'hands', on which stakes are made. By definition, a Poker hand contains exactly five cards, even if a greater or lesser number happens to be dealt, and even though not all five may actively contribute to a valid combination. Another defining feature is that these values are arranged in a single hierarchy reflecting their mathematical rarity. There is no question, as in some ancestral games, of vying on different types of combination in a series of separate pots. Yet another is the principle of 'calling' for a showdown by equalizing the stakes—a feature from which Poker derives most of its strategic potential, and whereby it distinguishes itself from more primitive games in which players can either bet only once (which is boring) or go on raising the stakes indefinitely (which is silly).

Standard Poker hands are listed below from lowest to highest. The figures following each one show the odds against receiving such a combination in five cards dealt cold from a properly shuffled 52-card pack:

Nothing (1–1): five unmatched cards;
One pair (1½-1): two cards of the same rank, three unmatched;
Two pair (20–1): the fifth card unmatched;
Triplets (46–1): three cards of the same rank, two unmatched;
Straight (250–1): five cards in numerical sequence but not all the same suit; for this purpose only, Ace may count low, so the lowest possible straight is A-2-3-4-5;
Flush (500–1): five cards of the same suit but not all in sequence;
Full house (700–1): triplets plus a pair (competing fulls are decided by the rank of triplets);
Four of a kind (4150–1): four cards of the same rank, the fifth any;
Straight flush (65,000–1): five cards of the same suit and in numerical sequence. Ace may count low again, as in an ordinary straight. An Ace-high straight flush—A-K-Q-J-T in suit—is known as a royal flush. It is unbeatable, but is equalled by a royal flush in another suit, as no suit is better than another.

One hand beats another if it represents a higher-ranking type of combination. If both contain combinations of equal type, the better is that containing higher-ranking matched cards, or, if equal—and where possible—higher-ranking unmatched cards. For this purpose cards rank downwards from Ace high to Deuce low.

The betting procedure of Poker is essentially as follows.

1. Players *ante* (i.e. make an initial stake in advance of the deal): this ensures that there is always a pot to play for and discourages underplaying.
2. Each player in turn may bet or *fold* (drop out). If he folds, he loses what he has already staked and can win no share of the pot, but is not otherwise penalized further.
3. A player who does not fold must increase his stake to at least the level of that of the last player to raise it. To equalize the stake is to *call*.
4. While matching the stake, he may simultaneously *raise* it by adding more. This sets a new level for subsequent players to match.
5. If after a raise all subsequent players either call or fold but do not raise it further, no more raises may then be made. If two or more remain in play, there is a showdown and the pot is

won by the best hand, or shared by equal best. If no one calls, the last raiser wins the pot without showing his hand.

Additional rules will often be imposed. Legal restrictions may be placed on the amount players may bet initially or by which they may raise. The opener may be allowed to fold immediately, or to pass (*knock* or *check*) and come in later; or he may be required to make an initial bet regardless of his hand, or to bet (or not) if his hand is above (or below) a minimum level—typically, in American Draw Poker, a pair of Jacks. Always, though, the player has five basic options: to fold, pass, bet, raise, or call. Note that a showdown can be forced by equalizing the bets—in other words, you can always call an opponent's bluff. In Primero, at least one player was obliged to stay in if anyone before him made a bet; in Brelan, equalizing the bets did not prevent the last from raising them again, and this remains the custom in Brag.

Given these basic essentials, Poker can be played in a variety of formats:

Flat Poker. The earliest, simplest, and most reckless form, in which five cards each are dealt and there is a single betting interval followed by a showdown. (Or an uncalled raise, as will henceforth go without saying.)

Draw Poker. Five each are dealt and there is a betting interval. If two or more stay in, there is a draw, each player making one or more discards and being dealt a like number of replacements. A second betting interval follows, terminated by a showdown. This is the classic form of Poker, and on a global basis still the most widely played. It suffers from the average mediocrity of winning hands, every other pot being swept by one or two pairs, and anything higher than a flush calling for something of a celebration. Draw has been largely superseded in its country of origin by more varied forms of play described below, but remains the basic standard in Europe, where the custom of playing with short packs increases the incidence of interesting hands by sheer force of mathematics.

Stud Poker. In classical Five-Card or 'Short' Stud, the simplest and, by general consent, dullest variety, each player receives a card face down (his *hole* card) and another face up. There is a betting interval. The next three are dealt face up with a betting interval after each, the last one ending in a showdown. The fact that everyone can see four out of everyone else's five cards considerably increases the psychological over the mathematical element of the strategy. The winning hands still tend to be low, but this situation can be brightened up by playing Seven-card or 'Long' Stud. Its basic format is: deal two down and one up, bet; a fourth, fifth, and sixth upcard, each followed by a betting interval; and a seventh card face down, followed by a final betting interval and showdown. (In which, of course, only five cards count.)

Spit Poker. Modern developments of Poker mostly involve communal cards or 'spits'. (I take this term from a variety of Draw called Spit in the Ocean, wherein four cards are dealt to each player, and an odd card—the spit—is dealt face up, counting as the fifth card in everybody's hand.) As with Stud, this basic idea has given rise to a whole range of games which pass in and out of fashion with varying degrees of rapidity. In Hold-'em—the professionals' game—each player receives two down-cards and there is a betting interval. Three communal cards, collectively called 'the flop', are dealt face up to the table and another betting interval ensues. Then two more spits are dealt face up one at a time, with a betting interval after each. In a showdown, each player counts the best five cards out of the seven consisting of his two hole cards plus five spits. The average winning hand here lies within the straight to flush range, but the real excitement of such games derives not so much from the frequent appearance of high hands as from the suspense that builds right up to the last card, which can make or break many a promising hand.

Other Poker variants are based on the recognition of low hands, the use of wild cards, the invention of new combinations, and the reduction of pack sizes, as follows:

Low-hand games. In Hi-Lo Poker the pot is equally divided between the highest and the lowest hand; in Lowball it is won exclusively by the lowest. In deciding which is lowest, Poker hands are always evaluated from the top down, not from the bottom up. Thus the lowest possible hand under normal Poker rules is 7–5–4–3-2 of mixed suits. It isn't 6–5–4–3-2, because that would be a straight, nor 6–4–3–2-A, because an Ace is always high by definition, except in a low straight.

In Lowball, where high hands don't count, straights and flushes are ignored and Ace always ranks low. In this case the lowest possible hand is 5–4-3–2-A flush or mixed, known as a *wheel*. Inexperienced players should not allow themselves to be misled into thinking that low hands are easier to get than high ones. The odds against being dealt a wheel are about 2,500–1, which puts it somewhere between a full house and fours at high-card Poker. At a table of five in Hi-Lo Draw a Jack-high hand can easily lose.

Wild-card games. A wild card is one that can be used to stand for any desired rank and suit. Wild cards have been customary in gambling games since long before Poker. The oldest and simplest device is to add a Joker to the pack and count it wild. This upsets the mathematics and produces some curious anomalies—notably that two pair and three of a kind are each a higher combination than the other! The number of possible natural threes is 54,912, of natural two pairs 123,552, of hands containing one pair and the Joker 82,368. If you count the wild hand as threes, the number of possible threes is thereby increased to 137,280, making them commoner than two pairs. The usual solution to this problem is to rank hands normally, ignoring the wildness, though a better one is to count the said wild hand as a combination ranking midway between two pair and threes. ('Mathematically correct, sir, but . . .', as Sidney Greenstreet observes in *The Maltese Falcon*, threatening Humphrey Bogart with a loaded cigar.) Another peculiarity is that the highest hand is five of a kind, making five Aces absolutely unbeatable. As it is considered unethical to be able to bet on absolute certainty, in species of Poker where such high hands actually occur players prefer to rank five of a kind between fours and a straight flush. (Though it would satisfy mathematics as well as principles to rank it between a King-high straight flush and a royal flush.) A commoner and better way of introducing wild cards is to play 'Deuces wild', or any other specified rank, or to nominate particular cards such as 'one-eyed Jacks'—i.e. that or those depicted in profile. In communal-card Poker, one or more of the spits may determine wild ranks. Wild cards may even be variable and personal. In Stud, for instance, it is not uncommon for each player's hole card to count as wild for him alone, together with any more of that rank he may acquire.

Freak-hand games. Poker based on unusual combinations or 'freak hands' tends to be looked down on. Freaks were originally introduced to liven up the low to middling range of winning combinations at five-card Draw, but, in the United States at least, have been made redundant by the replacement of Draw by Stud and Spit games, in which high hands are commoner. At a time in the nineteenth century when even straights were not always admitted into the game another contentious hand was the so-called 'blaze', consisting of five court cards of which not more than two were of the same rank. A surprisingly vast array of freaks can be devised. Those most commonly recognized include the self-explanatory four-flush, the Dutch or skip straight (e.g. 2–4–6–8–10), and big or little bobtails (four or three-card straight flushes).

Short-pack games. Poker players do not normally go out of their way to strip low cards out of the 52-card Bridge or Poker pack, but in countries where short packs are the norm the game is naturally played with them, with the mathematics adjusted accordingly and with other distinctive rules of national repute.

The genesis of Poker

Poker was born in what had been, until the Louisiana Purchase of 1803, French territory centred on New Orleans. Its cradle was the gambling saloon in general and, in particular, those famous or notorious floating saloons, the Mississippi steamers. The future genius of the game lay in its simple composition and capacity for development rather than in any of its individual playing elements, all of which, as we have seen, already existed in a variety of European games.

It is first mentioned in print in 1836, in *Dragoon Campaigns to the Rocky Mountains*; but that the prototype of Poker was played as early as 1829 is independently confirmed by the reminiscences of two witnesses, the reformed gambler Jonathan H. Green (*Exposure of the Arts and Miseries of Gambling*, New York, 1843, republished in 1857 as *Gambling Exposed*) and Joe Cowell, an English comedian (*Thirty Years Passed Among the Players in England and America*, New York, 1844). Both describe as Poker a version of the game played with a 20-card pack (A-K-Q-J-T) evenly dealt amongst four players. There is no draw, and bets are made, raised, and called on a narrow range of combinations: one pair, two pair, triplets, 'full'—so called because it is the only combination in which all five cards are active—and four of a kind. Unlike modern Poker, in which the top hand (royal flush) can be tied in another suit, Old Poker's top hand (four Aces, or four Kings and an Ace) was absolutely unbeatable.

Twenty-card Poker is well attested. Green, again, in *The Reformed Gambler* (1858), refers to its being played at a house in Louisville in 1834, and a vivid account of a Poker game played on a Mississippi river boat in 1835 appears in Sol Smith's *Theatrical Management in the West and South for Thirty Years* (Harper, New York, 1868), with an anecdote hingeing on the two players switching from 'low' cards to 'large cards', i.e. Tens and over.[5]

By the time Poker reached the American Hoyles it was also being played with the full 52-card pack. Its earliest working description occurs as a brief supplement to the 1850 reprint of a Philadelphian Hoyle by Henry F. Anners under the title 'Poker, or Bluff', with '20-deck Poker' mentioned in passing.[6] In a Boston Hoyle of 1857

Thomas Frere describes 'The Game of "Bluff", or "Poker"', with so brief a reference to the 20-card game as to suggest it was becoming obsolete. The gradual adoption of a 52-card pack was made partly to accommodate more players, perhaps partly to give more scope to the recently introduced flush (the straight was unknown), but chiefly to ensure there were enough cards for the draw—anther relative novelty, and one that was to turn Poker from a gamble to a science.

The fact that Old Poker involved 20 cards, five-card hands, and rank-only combinations led some nineteenth-century researchers to derive it from the Persian game of As-Nas, as described by General A. Houtum Schindler in Culin's *Chess and Playing Cards* (1896).[7] This theory, accepted with a caution amounting almost to reluctance by R. F. Foster in *Practical Poker* (1904), has since attracted such uncritical enthusiasm as to be in danger of forfeiting whatever modicum of credibility it may reasonably be held to possess. The story that As-Nas was played by Columbus's sailors is pure invention, and the claim that certain Persian references to it date back thousands of years quite ludicrous.

As to its alleged antiquity, the facts of the case have been painstakingly researched by Michael Dummett[8] and may be outlined as follows. Iran (formerly Persia) is indeed the home of As-Nas playing-cards, so called from the game principally played with them. Actual cards survive from the seventeenth century which are consonant with various subsequently published descriptions of the game. There are twenty or twenty-five to a pack, depending on the number of players, consisting of four or five each of ranks designated Ace (or Lion and Sun), King, Lady, Soldier, and Dancing-girl. Each rank is sometimes associated with a colour, but there are no suits as such. Players receive five cards each and vie on them as at Flat (non-Draw) Poker. The only recognized combinations are, naturally enough, pairs, triplets, fulls, and quartets. As Dummett shows, however, claims of amazing antiquity are not based on any solid foundation. Despite expert research undertaken at his behest, no one has been able to show that As-Nas is mentioned in Persian literature at any date earlier than that of the oldest surviving cards, i.e. the eighteenth century; nor do we have any rules of the game earlier than the late nineteenth. The kinship of As-Nas can be more plausibly explained as a borrowing from European games than vice versa, especially when it is observed that 'As' is not itself a relevant Farsi (Persian) word, but does happen to be the French for 'Ace'.

If Poker derived from an amalgam of vying games current at its time and place of origin, its immediate ancestors would have been

Poque and Bouillotte, and possibly As-Nas. The latter may have been played by Iranian sailors visiting this cosmopolitan port, or, as Louis Coffin avers,[9] by 'French inhabitants who had been in the French service in Persia *circa* 1800–20'. Not that As-Nas is absolutely necessary to account for the characteristic features of Old Poker: four-handed Bouillotte was itself played with a 20-card pack,[10] and Poque was based on five-card hands restricted to one pair, two pair, triplets, and four of a kind. As-Nas can be invoked for the invention of the 'full'—but then, so can logic. Poque is certainly the likeliest candidate for the name of the game. Betting is carried out by announcing 'Je poque de dix' (or whatever the sum involved; compare German 'Ich poche zehn'), with two syllables to the key word. It has been suggested[11] that 'poque' so pronounced was interpreted by English-speaking southerners as 'pok-ah', which is a fair phonetic rendering in the local accent of the word normally written 'poker'.

From the middle of the century Poker experienced rapid changes and innovations as it became more widespread through the upheavals of the Civil War. Stud, or 'stud-horse' Poker, a cowboy invention said to have been introduced around Ohio, Indiana, and Illinois, first appears in *The American Hoyle* of 1864,[12] and Jack-pots date from 1870, reportedly in Toledo, Ohio. All appear in the 1875 edition of *The American Hoyle*,[13] together with Whiskey Poker, which is a form of Commerce based on Poker combinations, and Mistigris, which is Poker with a 53rd card 'wild', namely 'the blank card accompanying every pack'. By this time, too, the full range of Poker combinations was widely recognized, though not universally so. *The American Hoyle* notes that four of a kind is the best hand 'when straights are not played'. Curiously, the introduction of the straight was not as straightforward as might be expected. The 1864 *American Hoyle* gives the hands as: one pair, two pairs, straight sequence or rotation, triplets, flush, full house, fours, and adds 'When a straight and a flush come together in one hand, it outranks a full.'

The problem with straights, here ranked in the wrong order, was partly mathematical but largely one of principle. A nice example of the mathematical deficiency of everyday players occurs in a letter to the editor of *The Rambler and Dramatic Weekly*:[14] 'Now in our pack of playing cards, there are 52 combinations only of "threes", and at least one hundred of "straights". Hence "threes" should beat "straights". There is no getting over this mathematical fact.' But even those capable of grasping that 54,912 five-card hands rank as threes and only 10,200 as non-flush straights were likely to come up with another objection. If you ignore straights, and hence straight flushes too, the highest possible hand is a top four of a kind, which is not just unbeatable but cannot even be tied. Thus led to a tussle between the traditionalists, who clung to the unbeatable four Aces of Old Poker, and the innovationists, who found the game more interesting with straights. In this light, the acceptance of straights ranked in the wrong order may be seen as a temporary compromise. As late as 1892, John Keller defended his view that the straight 'should be allowed. My authority for this is the best usage of today, and my justification is the undeniable merit of the straight as a Poker hand.'[15] He clinches this with the moral argument that has prevailed ever since—namely, that it is unethical and ungentlemanly to bet on such a sure thing as four Aces. If the best hand is a royal flush, there is always the outside chance that it may be tied. However minute that measure of doubt, it has to be morally superior to betting on a certainty.

Equally contentious was the introduction of 'jack-pots'—a rule of the game whereby a player must open the betting if he holds at least a pair of Jacks, and may not open if he doesn't. (At a full table of five-card Draw about half the players, on average, will be dealt Jacks or better.) Two complementary motives for this innovation were, first, to impose discipline on the game by driving out wild players who would bet on anything; second, to encourage cautious players who did have something not to be frightened out of the pot by openers who didn't. Opposition to the idea was pithily expressed by Blackridge, who declared it 'equivalent to a lottery except that all players *must* buy tickets'. He adds that the rule is thought to have originated at Toledo and that it is played in the west, to some extent in the east, and not at all in the more conservative south. It remains a standard feature of American Draw that players may not open without Jacks or better (but are no longer obliged to open if they can)—thereby reducing one element of chance by increasing the information available at start of play. At the end of the nineteenth century, Foster summarized the situation thus: 'The jack-pot, with its accompanying small-limit game, has completely killed bluffing—that pride and joy of the old-timer . . . Modern Poker has gradually become more of a lottery than anything else.' Nevertheless, he adds, 'The two great steps in the history and progress of Poker have undoubtedly been the introduction of the draw to improve the hand, and the invention of the jack-pot as a cure for cautiousness . . . It has come to stay.'[16]

The introduction of Poker into English society is often credited, if only on his own claim, to the American ambassador General Schenck. Blackridge quotes a letter from Schenck to General Young of Cincinnati describing a weekend retreat to the Somerset country home of a certain 'Lady W.' in the summer of 1872, when he was prevailed upon by the other guests to teach them this peculiarly American game. As part of the exercise he drew up a written guide for them. Some of his pupils subsequently had these rules printed in booklet form, much to Schenck's surprise when he received a copy upon his return home. Schenck's rules were circulated in the United States and variously approved or opposed according to temperament. (Some opposition may have been provoked by Schenck's informality. He opens: 'The deal is of no especial value, and anybody may begin. The dealer, beginning with the person on his left, throws around five cards to each player . . .'.)

Poker's position as America's national card game in the twentieth century may not have been foreseeable towards the end of the nineteenth. As late as 1897 Foster wrote:

There is no authoritative code of laws for the game of Poker, simply because the best clubs do not admit the game to their card rooms, and consequently decry the necessity for adopting any . . . In the absence of any official code, the daily press is called upon for hundreds of decisions every week. The author has gathered and compared a great number of these newspaper rulings, and has drawn from them and other sources to form a brief code of Poker laws . . .[17]

American society of the time was notoriously more Victorian than the Victorians. Opposition to the game is wittily put down by Blackridge in the introduction to his *The Complete Poker Player* of 1880:

This opinion operates in the United States to such an extent as to produce an almost total outlawry of games of chance in social circles . . . and especially all games in which stakes are an essential element. This is evidenced by the immense number of childish and frivolous games which are everywhere sold at the shops, in which people contrive to mingle a slight flavor of the intellectual diversion that real playing cards afford, with a great deal of useless lumber in regard to painters and authors; ancient English and Choctaw kings; famous poets and pickpockets, and the thrilling details of the private life of the Dr Busby family . . .

'To my own knowledge,' he elsewhere concludes, 'so many cultivated men *love* this game, that it is impossible for me to do other than respect it.'

10

Matching and cribbing

Isabella Wardle and Mr Trundle 'went partners', and Emily
Wardle and Mr Snodgrass did the same; and even Mr Tupman
and the spinster aunt established a joint-stock company of fish
and flattery . . . Then, when the spinster aunt got 'matrimony',
the young ladies laughed afresh . . .

Dickens, The Pickwick Papers (1836–7)

The games surveyed so far have involved no real play of cards, and
hence are technically 'gambling games' since there is no other respect
in which they can properly be said to engage the player's interest.
The rest of the games in this book are technically 'strategic' games,
in that (*a*) cards are always the instruments of play, and (*b*) players
usually, or at least sometimes, have a choice of plays to make.

We start with a group of rather elementary examples which,
though not demonstrably related to one another, may be broadly
described as 'matching games'. Their common feature is that everyone
in turn adds a card to a sequence gradually built up on the table. In
some games, each new card must match the previous card by rank
or suit; in others, it may or may not be required to match but must
always 'beat' it in some way; in yet others, it is not obliged to match
or beat the previous one, but only earns a score if it does. As to
objectives, we may distinguish between 'eliminators', in which the
simple object is to be the first to go out by playing off all one's cards
(Newmarket, Eights, Durak, etc.), and 'adders', in which a running
total is kept of the face values of all the cards played out, and scores
accrue for making certain totals. To the latter may be attached the
compound game of Cribbage and its more obscure relatives. We shall
also encounter games in which the sequences are so like tricks as to
make one wonder which came first in the evolution of card games.

Many games in this section, being of low strategic interest, are
played as children's, family, or mild gambling games, though one or
two—notably in the 'Durak' branch—are remarkably challenging.

Stops

That Cribbage is the only card game playable in pubs without special permission presents no problem when it comes to games well known to latter-day Hoyles, but, as Arthur Taylor recounts in *Pub Games*, 'The real headaches occur when the authorities are asked to pass judgement on games which haven't reached those hundreds of reference books'—as illustrated by a little vignette which took place in 1971 at Bletchley Magistrates Court:

The Court had received a list for its approval which included Solo, Bridge, Nap, Pontoon, Nine-card Brag and, perhaps surprisingly, Poker-Dice. So far so good, conditional approval granted. They were also asked to allow Pink Nines, but unfortunately no-one knew what it was; the police solicitor said rather plaintively that he had been trying to find out about it for several days, but no-one had been able to enlighten him. In the end, after what seems like a period of total bewilderment, the chairman of the bench said that they could *not* give permission for it, since after all 'it might be something we would deplore later on' . . .

In fact, Pink Nines turns out to be a thinly disguised variant of the eighteenth-century royal game of Comet. Everyone contributes to a pool, four cards are dealt face down as a 'dead hand', and the rest are evenly distributed, any remainder being added to the dead hand. The aim is to get rid of your cards first by playing them out in numerical sequences regardless of suit. Leader begins by laying out as many cards as he can in a run. Suppose he plays 3–4–5, then stops because he has no Six. Next in turn then continues from Six if possible, or else passes. Each 'pink nine' (♠9 and ♦9) is wild and may stand for any card. Ace is high: whoever plays one immediately starts a new run. If no one can continue a run, the player who ended it starts a new one. First out wins the pool.

Games like this are generically known as Stops, from the distinctive feature that players find themselves stopped from getting rid of unwanted cards by lacking the next in sequence. No fresh cards are drawn during play, which ends as soon as one player goes out. The pay-off is then often determined by the number or value of cards left in other players' hands. Most are mild, unskilled gambling games suitable for family play, the best-known modern representatives being Newmarket (GB) and Michigan (US). In recent years they have been displaced in popularity by games of the Eights branch.

Stops games go back to the seventeenth century game of Hoc, sometimes called Hoc de Mazarin after its supposedly most illustrious player and by way of distinction from its contemporary Hoca, which was a cross between Basset and Bingo. Cardinal Mazarin, Louis XIV's Prime Minister, was a passionate card-player who turned the royal court of Versailles into a virtually non-stop casino as a means of filling the royal purse, though there in no hard evidence to suggest that he wasted his own money on the game. Hoc was a three-part gambling game similar to Poch, except that the third stake was contested by matching cards to a sequence with a view to being first out. For this purpose players were assisted by certain 'wild cards' called *hocs*, namely the four Kings, spade Queen, and diamond Jack. For all its popularity in France, Cotgrave's French–English dictionary of 1611 refers to 'Hock' as 'a Dutch card game', and references to it abound in Dutch literature before its first French appearances in 1620–30.[1]

Later, the last part of this game was isolated for play on its own and the *hocs* were replaced by a single wild card, the Nine of diamonds, known as *manille*, which gave the game its new name. It also became known as Comet following the appearance of Halley's comet in 1682, perhaps from its vague resemblance of the gradually lengthening line of cards to the tail of a comet. Its earliest mention under this name seems to be English; for Hartmann, in his Introduction to *Games & Gamesters of the Restoration*, avers 'In 1684 a friend at Court wrote to the Countess of Rutland: "Play is grown the predominate passion even of the ladies . . . Comette now reigns though Bassette still keeps in creditt at her Grace of Portsmouth, the Duke of Norfolk, the Lady Poltney, and Mrs Morine . . ."'.

Manille or Comet is played with a 51-card pack lacking ♦8. Two to five players receive (respectively) 20, 14, 11, or 9 cards each and form a pool to be won by the first to go out. The leader plays a sequence as far as he can regardless of suit, the next in turn continues it when the previous player gets stuck, and so on. The sequence is cyclic, King being followed by Ace, Two, etc. The ♦9 may be played at any time and followed either by the next above the rank it represents or by a Ten (thereby ending the turn, in later forms of the game). If a stop is reached, the current player may start a new sequence with any card. Additional scores include a penalty for holding the Comet (♦9) when someone else goes out or a bonus for going out oneself by playing it.

Comet waned after the death of Louis XIV, but from about 1748 a more elaborate version came into vogue. This was played with two 48-card packs lacking Aces, and re-formed in such a way that one contains all black cards except for a single red Nine, the other all reds except for a single black Nine. Packs are alternated in successive games, each odd-coloured Nine being a Comet.

A game still recorded in Italian gamebooks as Stoppare divides the Italian 40-card pack evenly amongst four players and is played like original Comet but without a wild card. It begins, however, with a round of vying as to who holds the best three-card flush (as at Hoc), for which purpose cards bear the face values associated with Primiera. Depaulis traces this back to Stuppa, first described in 1695.

Eighteenth-century France also produced an elaboration which continues the Poch/Poque feature of a board with special betting compartments, though without the first two phases of play. This was le Nain Jaune or 'Yellow Dwarf', also known as 'Lindor', which *Le Guide Marabout* explains—if that's the word for imparting a piece of information as baffling at it is useless—as the name of a popular clown in the Comédie Espagnole. Depaulis more plausibly offers 'lin d'or' as a corruption of 'nain d'or'.

The Yellow Dwarf tableau has five compartments, the corner four being marked ♥K ('Charles'), ♠Q ('Judith'), ♣J ('Lancelot'), and ♦10. The centre depicts a costumed dwarf ('Lindor'?) holding the ♦7 in one hand. These represent the *belles cartes* or 'boodle' cards. From three to eight may play, each receiving from a 52-card pack an equal number of cards such as to leave a face-down widow of four to seven undealt cards. Players 'dress' the board by placing one counter on the ♦10, two on the Jack, three on the Queen, four on the King, and five on the ♦7 or Dwarf. Play proceeds in Stops fashion, not necessarily following suit and with the player of a King or any other stop beginning a new sequence at any point. Playing a boodle card promptly wins any and all the stakes in its compartment. The first to go out sweeps all remaining counters off the board—after any other player stuck with a boodle card in hand has forfeited its value to the appropriate compartment. My nineteenth-century *Salon des jeux* refers to sweeping the board as doing a 'Grand Opera', and adds that in a few circles the winner also receives one counter for each pip left in other players' hands.

Though occasionally played in England under the name 'Commit', Comet was eventually ousted in popularity by Pope Joan, the equivalent of Nain Jaune. How this came to be named after a legendary female Pope of the ninth century is uncertain—perhaps 'Nain Jaune' was misinterpreted as 'Nun Joan' and then turned into something more meaningful. The *OED* quotes a reference to Pope Joan from as early as 1732, though it does not seem to have come into its own until nearer the nineteenth century, first reaching the pages of Hoyle in 1826.

Pope Joan soon acquired the character of a mild and homely gambling game for all the family, including clergymen's. 'I cannot condemn the Vicar of Broad Hembury for relaxing now and then among a few select friends with a rubber of sixpenny Whist, a pool of penny Quadrille, or a few rounds of twopenny Pope-Joan', wrote Augustus Toplady, Vicar of Broad Hembury, towards the end of the eighteenth century.[2] The game also figures prominently in the 'old-fashioned card party' depicted in chapter 6 of *The Pickwick Papers* and quoted at the head of this chapter.

Pope Joan (English, nineteenth century). Players: three to eight. Equipment: a 52-card pack stripped of diamond Eight, and a layout of eight compartments labelled Ace, King, Queen, Jack, Pope (diamond Nine), Matrimony (trump K + Q), Intrigue (trump Q + J), Game.

Dealer starts by dressing the board with six counters to Pope, two each to Matrimony and Intrigue, and one to each other compartment. He then deals all the cards round one at a time to one more hand than there are players, the dead hand remaining unrevealed throughout play. It doesn't matter if some have more cards than others. The last card dealt is turned for 'trump', and dealer sweeps the stakes of the appropriate compartment for turning the Ace, King, Queen, or Jack of trumps, or the Nine of diamonds (Pope). (*Variant*: for turning Pope, he also wins the stake for 'Game', the cards are gathered up without play, the board is further dressed, and the deal passes on.)

Eldest leads by playing the lowest card he has of any suit he chooses (Ace is low). Whoever holds the next higher card of the same suit plays it, and this continues until a stop is reached. Kings are always stops, and so are cards which no one can follow because the next in sequence is in the dead hand. The player of a stop then continues by playing the lowest card in hand of any preferred suit. (*Variant*: the new suit must differ from that of the stop.) Whoever plays the Ace, King, Queen, or Jack of trumps, or ♦9, wins the counters in the appropriate compartment. Anyone holding and playing both Jack and Queen of trumps wins the contents of Intrigue; for Queen and King they win Matrimony; for Jack, Queen, and King they win both. (*Variant*: if the two cards are played from different hands, the stake is divided between them.)

Play ceases as soon as somebody goes out. The winner takes the contents of 'Game', plus as many counters from each opponent as they have unplayed cards in hand. The holder of Pope unplayed is excused payment. (Or, variant, pays double). Unclaimed stakes are carried forward to the next deal, so that it is possible for large quantities to build up on Matrimony and Intrigue.

A feature apparently novel to Pope Joan is that the sequence is now required to follow suit, and, since only one card will continue it, the turn to play jumps around instead of circulating predictably. Its King-Queen, Queen-Jack combinations derive from those of a simple staking game called Matrimony, which, according to a rough guess of 'Captain Crawley' in *The Card-Player's Manual* of 1867, 'came into vogue with Adam and Eve, and is, therefore, the most ancient and primitive of games'.

By 1890 Pope Joan was losing in popularity to the simpler derivatives known as Spin or Spinado, and Newmarket, both of which dispensed with the need for elaborate staking equipment. Spin had only three pools—Game (for the first out), Matrimony, and Intrigue— and featured the Ace of diamonds as an automatic stop, playable at any time. Newmarket, named from the race-track frequented by royalty, has proved the more enduring game. It has no trumps, no Pope, and no two-card combinations, and stakes are made to a simple layout consisting of four cards from a spare pack, namely an Ace, King, Queen, and Jack of four different suits. A dead hand is dealt to provide the stops, play proceeds as at Pope Joan except that Ace is high, and whoever plays a card matching one in the layout collects the appropriate stake. In America, where the name Newmarket lacks significance, the game was known as Stops or Boodle and the favoured cards as boodle cards. By 1920 it had developed into Michigan—also commemorating a race-track—with some additional features from which minor variations have since been derived. Another race-track is featured in the modern English game of Epsom, which I know only from Andrew Pennycook. It has a four-card layout as at Newmarket and everyone receives an equal number of cards, any spares being stops. Each in rotation must either play the next higher card of the current suit-sequence, or a card of the same rank as any already played to the sequence, or else must pass. Playing the fourth card of a given rank entitles one to start a new sequence.

Eights

The game known as Eights, Crazy Eights, or Swedish Rummy does not appear in English-language gamebooks before about 1940. It has engendered many variants, all of which involve more skill in play than Stops games. The most distinctive feature of this branch is that players may, or must, draw more cards when unable to continue the sequence.

Eights itself is a good two-hander, though any number may play. Each receives seven cards, the rest are stacked face down and the topmost turned for starter. (If more than four play, deal five each or use a double pack.) First in turn must match the starter, and each thereafter must either play a card which matches the previous one by rank or suit, or draw fresh cards from the stock (if any) until able and willing to play. When the stock is empty it is obligatory to play if possible. An Eight may be played at any time, its holder specifying what suit is to follow it if the next card is not also an Eight. The winner is the first out, or the player with cards of lowest value if play ceases because everyone is stopped. The winner scores the value of unplayed cards in other players' hands, counting Eight 50, courts 10, Ace 1, other numerals at face value.

Almost identical is Rockaway, in which Aces are wild and count 15 against. In a later development played as a pub game called Switch (or Crazy Jacks, or even Black Jack), each starts with twelve or ten cards, Aces are wild, and certain other cards have special powers. The play of a Deuce forces the next player to miss a turn and draw two cards from stock—unless he also plays a Deuce, which forces the next in turn to do likewise or draw four cards, and so on for six or even eight cards. Playing a Four has the same effect, but doubles the number to be drawn by the next player. Playing a Jack reverses the current direction of play—if you play one, it forces the person who played immediately before you to come back in again. Of course, if he also plays a Jack, he thereby turns the tables.

A game similar to Eights is played in Austria under the name Neuner, 'Nines', using a 32-card pack plus Joker. It is best for four; each receives five; Joker and Nines are wild; and, so long as any remain in stock, the player in turn may draw as often as possible before playing his next card, even if able to follow immediately. The penalties are Joker 20, Nine 15, Ace 11, King 4, Queen 3, Jack 2, 10–7 face value. A development of Neuner paralleling that of Switch became popular in the 1960s under the name Mau-Mau, in which Sevens and Eights force the next player to miss a turn, a Seven additionally forcing him to take two from stock.

Various games now classed as 'for children' may be ancestral to Stops and Eights. In Snip-Snap-Snorum (or -Snorem), or Earl of Coventry, the pack is dealt as far as it will go and the leader plays any card. The next in turn able to do so pairs it and says 'Snip', the next also matches rank and says 'Snap', and the next plays the fourth of its kind, announces 'Snorum!', discards the quartet, and leads afresh. Anyone unable to match the previous card misses a turn, and in some versions plays a counter to its player. If two or more are able to play consecutively, the first of them is 'snipped' and pays one counter to a pool if he played the first of its rank; if he played the second he is 'snapped' and pays two, if the third, he is 'snored' and pays three. The pool goes to the first out of cards, who also receives one counter from each opponent for each card left in hand. Earl of Coventry is the same, except for the announcements: (1st card) 'There's as good as [Ace] can be', (2nd) 'There's an Ace as good as he', (3rd) 'There's the best of all the three', (4th) 'And there's the Earl of Coventreeeee' . . . The game is apparently referred to in a 1782 quotation from Fanny Burney: 'I suppose he'll shilly-shally till somebody else will cry snap, and take her.'[3]

In the German game of Schnipp-Schnapp-Schnurr-Burr-Basilorum each in turn plays the next higher card of the same suit and the player of the fifth starts a new sequence—which is cyclic, Ace counting high and low. The equivalent English game is Jig, with only four cards per sequence. A two-dimensional matching game is represented by Parliament, also called Card Dominoes or (wrongly) Fan Tan. The first plays a Seven to the table; the second plays either the Six or the Eight of the same suit adjacent to its long side, or another Seven adjacent to its short. The aim is to run out of cards by adding them to the layout, which gradually builds up towards a four-tier tableau of thirteen-card suit sequences. Each new card must, of course, be laid adjacent to an existing one.

Quasi-trick games

In some games the sequences played are so short, consisting of one card from each player before the next begins, as to look almost like tricks. The only real difference is that it is not the object to 'win' completed sequences, which are either swept aside as irrelevant or added to one player's hand as a penalty.

Go Boom, for instance, looks at first sight like a matching game related to Newmarket or Crazy Eights. Players are dealt seven cards apiece. At each round the leader starts a sequence to which each in turn contributes a card matching the previous one by rank or suit. Anyone unable to play must draw from stock (if any left) until able to do so, or, if still unable, misses a turn. The sequence ends when all have played one card; the player of the highest card of the suit led takes the sequence—or throws it away, since it is of no value—and leads to the next. Go Boom is probably best attached to the Eights branch, in that the aim is to run out of cards first and players must draw if unable to play; yet the resemblance of sequences to tricks is quite remarkable.

Rolling Stone is similar, except that each must follow suit if possible. If everyone follows, the winner of the 'trick' throws it away and leads to the next; otherwise, the first unable to follow must take the trick, add it to his hand, and lead to the next. This game is known as Enflé in French and Schwellen in German—equivalent to English 'Inflation'. Rolling Stone, if accurately played, usually goes on for ever.

Its exact reverse, in that the object is not to go out but to stay in, is called Linger Longer, Sift Smoke, or Lift Smoke—possibly from Tupper, *Proverbial Philosophy 1838–42*: 'He who would lift the smoke must needs provide himself with a pair of bellows.' (I prefer the second title and propose a new proverb by way of explanation: 'He who would play with the devil must first sift him out of the smoke.') Tricks are played as at Whist, the winner of each throws it away and draws a card from stock, and the last player with a card in hand wins. An elaborate Spanish game related to Linger Longer is described by Andrew Pennycook under the name Tardar.[4]

A rather more advanced variation on a theme is represented by the apparently modern Baltic game of Cucumber (Polish Ogórek, Scandinavian Gurka, etc.).

> *Cucumber (Swedish, twentieth century)*. Two or more players receive six cards each. The leader plays any card, and each in turn must then play a card of equal or higher rank than the one before. Suit is irrelevant, Ace counts high, and anyone unable to play a higher card must play the lowest he has. The player of the highest card removes the sequence, or trick, from the table and leads to the next one. This continues until all have played five cards. Those unplayed cards are then revealed and the holder of highest rank (or holders if tied) is penalized according to its face value. Jack counts 11 against, Queen 12, King 13, Ace 14.

Cucumber seems to form a transition to various Scandinavian trick-taking games—notably Swedish Femkort ('Five-Card')—which are won, or in some cases lost, by taking the last trick.

In eastern Europe, quasi-trick games are considerably more sophisticated and call for a high degree of strategy. The only one to have made its appearance in English books is Challenge, Hubert Phillips's rendering of the Russian game Svoyi Koziri, 'Personal Trumps', which was introduced into Cambridge circles by Prof Besicovitch in the early 1950s.[5] The classic member is Russia's national card game Durak, 'Fool', also played in Finland as Durakki or Hörri. The Czech equivalent, Dudàk, literally means 'Bagpiper'—either as the nearest word to *durak*, or perhaps because a bagpiper is regarded as a bumpkin.

Durak (Russian, twentieth century). Two players use a 36-card pack ranking Ace high, Six low. Deal six each in threes; stack the rest face down; turn the top card for trumps and slip it half under the pack. The game consists of several bouts, each followed by a draw of fresh cards if necessary. The aim is to be first out of cards when the stock is exhausted. The loser is *durak*—'a fool'.

In each bout, one player attacks and the other defends. Non-dealer attacks first; thereafter, the winner of each bout attacks in the next. Each bout proceeds as follows:

Attacker leads any card. Defender responds with a higher card of the same suit, or any trump if a non-trump was led. Attacker continues with any card of the same rank as either of the first two, and, again, defender plays higher or trumps. This continues till all twelve cards are played, or one player can't or won't make a legal continuation. Note that the two follow different requirements: the attacker's lead must always match the rank of any card so far showing, the defender's reply must always be higher in suit or a trump.

If all cards are played out, the attacker draws six cards from stock, waits for the defender to do likewise, then starts a new bout with any desired lead.

But a bout more commonly ends because one player fails to play the next card. If the attacker fails, he concedes the bout by turning the played cards face down and pushing them to one side, where they remain out of play for the rest of the game. He then becomes the defender in the next bout.

If the defender fails, he does so by gathering up all cards so far played to the bout and adding them to his hand. He will continue to defend in the next bout.

Before the next bout begins, each player (starting with the attacker) must, if necessary and able, restore his hand to six cards by drawing from stock. The last card drawn from stock will be the turned trump, after which play continues without further drawing until one player goes out.

Social climbers

Formally related to the Durak branch, but with single cards replaced by card combinations, is the extraordinary Chinese game of Zheng Shàng Yóu, first described in English by John McLeod.[6] When Depaulis subsequently reported it in the French magazine *Jeux et stratégie*, he was surprised to receive reports of virtually the same game from two different areas of France. This may not make it a French game, but it suggests French Indo-China as a possible link, and justifies our dwelling here upon a game of possibly oriental provenance. (The Japanese Dai Hin Min is similar.)

To judge from its Japanese and French counterparts, Zheng Shàng Yóu, literally 'Climbing Up', is perhaps better rendered as 'Social Climber'. In Japan, the winner of each deal is designated 'king', the runner-up 'nobleman', the third 'poor man', and the loser *dai hin min*, 'very poor man'. As reported to Depaulis, the French equivalents are 'le patron' (the boss), 'le contremaître' (foreman), 'l'ouvrier' (worker), and 'le trouduc' (which may be bowdlerized to 'dogsbody'[7]). The significance of these terms will become apparent.

Zheng Shàng Yóu (Chinese, contemporary). A 54-card pack including a red and a black Joker is dealt out as far as it will go between four players (or five, but four is assumed below). The highest card is the red Joker, followed by the black Joker, then Deuces, Aces, Kings, and so on down to Threes. Within certain limits, Deuces and Jokers are wild.

A game consists of several rounds of play and the object is to get rid of all one's cards. The first to do so is the boss (winner), but the others then play for position until only one has any left in hand, he being the dogsbody (loser).

The leader to a round may lead one of the following: a single card; two, three, or four cards of the same rank; a single sequence of three or more cards; a multiple sequence of six or more cards. Whatever he leads establishes the pattern to be followed by the other players. i.e. a pair can only be followed by a pair, a single sequence with a single sequence of the same length, and so on. Each subsequent player must either play a higher-ranking combination of exactly the same pattern, or pass. A player who passes although able to play is allowed to come in later if the turn reaches him again. However, as soon as a play is followed by a pass from everyone else, the last player disposes of the cards so far played and leads to a new round.

The following rules govern the constitution and relative values of the playable patterns:

Singleton. Any single card is beaten by one of higher rank, suit being irrelevant. A Deuce can only be beaten by a Joker, and the black Joker only by the red.

Pair. Two cards of the same rank can be beaten only by a pair of higher rank, Jokers being highest. A Deuce or Joker may be used 'wild' to form a pair with a natural card, but a natural pair beats a wild pair of the same rank. (Deuce–Joker counts as a wild pair, and is therefore beatable by two natural Deuces.)

Triplet, quartet. The same, with the additional note that a wild set can only be beaten by a higher rank or a natural set of the same rank, not by a wild set containing fewer wild cards. Note: If a three-card lead contains both jokers, the leader must state whether it is to be counted and followed as a triplet or a three-card sequence.

Single sequence. A sequence is three or more cards in numerical order, for which purpose the order runs Three (low) to Ace (high). Deuces may not be used in sequences at all, but either or both Jokers may be used 'wild' to make one up. All sequences must be of the same length. A higher-ranking sequence beats one of lower rank, and a natural sequence beats one of the same height containing one or more Jokers; but both cases are overridden by the fact that any flush sequence beats any mixed-suit sequence regardless of height or naturalness. For this purpose either or both Jokers count as belonging to the desired flush suit.

Multiple sequence. Two or more sequences of the same length and rank—or, to put the same thing another way, three or more pairs, triplets, or quartets of consecutive ranks. The lowest possible multiple sequence is therefore 3-4-5; 3-4-5. All Deuces and Jokers may be used wild, and suits and flushes are irrelevant. A multiple sequence is beaten only by one of higher ranks, except that, as between sequences of the same height, an entirely natural one beats one containing any wild cards.

The first player to run out of cards ('the boss', in the equivalent French game) scores 2, and the second (foreman), 1 point. The others score nothing, but the third (worker) has the slight advantage of leading to the next round, to which the loser (dogsbody) has the onerous task of dealing. After the deal, but before the opening lead, the two losers must each place the highest-ranking card from their hand face up on the table. (If they have a choice of suits they may choose freely.) The boss takes whichever of these he prefers, and the foreman the other, each laying out any single card face up in exchange. Of these two discards, the worker adds whichever he prefers to his hand, and dogsbody takes the other.

There are many variations in procedure and scoring. In Trouduc, which is played with only one Joker and omits sequences, players occupy significant positions around the table and change places throughout the session accordingly. From north to west, assuming clockwise play, the actual seats are respectively designated boss, foreman, worker, dogsbody, and after each game the players take their places according to rank. The respective scores are 4, 3, 2, and 0; dogsbody deals and the boss gets the opening lead. Before leading, however, the boss gives dogsbody his two lowest-ranking cards in return for the latter's two highest, and the foreman exchanges his one lowest for the worker's one highest. (Jokers, however, are always exempt from surrender.) This ingenious representation of class privilege tends to ensure that positions do not change very easily, in accordance with a well-known principle of life best summed up in Matthew 25: 29.

Cribbage, and other Adders

Adders, in which the face value of each card is added to the previous total, are common in central and eastern Europe but rarer in the west, whose nearest equivalent is that phase of Cribbage in which cards are played up to thirty-one.

A typical adder is the game of Hundred, played by three or more with a 32-card pack counting face value from Seven to Ten, then Jack 2, Queen 3, King 4, Ace 11. The pack is evenly dealt, any odd cards going face up to start the total. Each in turn adds a card to the sequence and announces the new total. Whoever takes it over 100 loses, though making it exactly 100 wins instead. Not surprisingly, there are many variations. Cards may have alternative values, including zero and negative numbers, and there may be scores for making part-totals such as multiples of 25, as in the Czech game of Jubilee.[8]

The old English game of Crib abdicated from its courtly role some 250 years ago and now retains a devoted following throughout the country in homes, pubs, and clubs. Apart from the change from five to six-card Cribbage, which began in the nineteenth century, it has remained remarkably stable in format, though individual schools spice it up with side payments for various features that can occur during the course of play. Though adaptable for three or four, it remains essentially a classic two-hander.

Cribbage (English, traditional). A two-part compound game played with the full 52-card pack. Players take turns to deal, dealing six cards each in ones.

In Part 1 each player discards two face down to a 'crib', leaving four cards in each hand and four in the as yet unseen crib. Each player's aim is to retain in hand cards which form scoring combinations. Any combinations contained in the crib will count in favour of the dealer when it is revealed at end of play. For this reason the dealer will try to put in it cards that are likely to make combinations, whereas the non-dealer will throw out two cards which are unrelated to each other and unlikely to match anything else. As there are fifteen ways of discarding two cards from a hand of six, considerable interest attaches to their selection. Cribbage combinations and their scores are:

Fifteen (2 pts.): two or more cards with a combined face value of 15, counting Ace 1 and courts 10;

Pair (2 pts.): two of the same rank;

Pair royal or *'prial'* (6 pts.): three of a kind;

Double pair royal (12 pts.): four of a kind;

Run: three or more cards in numerical sequence, worth 1 per constituent card;

Flush: four cards of the same suit, worth 1 each.

The non-dealer then cuts the pack. The dealer takes the top card of the bottom half and lays it face up on the table as a 'starter'. If it is a Jack, he scores 'two for his heels'.

In Part 2 each in turn, beginning with non-dealer, plays a card face up from hand to table, announcing its face value in the case of the first card and thereafter the combined total of all cards so far played. Points are scored for playing any card which forms a pair, prial, or run when taken in conjunction with its immediate predecessor(s). Bringing the combined total to 15 scores 2 points. If a player can add a card without exceeding 31 he must do so, otherwise he says 'Go' and the other continues to add cards as far as possible without exceeding 31. The player of the last card scores 1 point, or 2 for making 31 exactly. Whoever did not play the last card then leads to a new sequence if he has any cards left in hand. The same procedure is followed until all eight cards have been played out.

Finally, each gathers up his hand and scores for it, counting the starter as a fifth card as if it were held along with the others. Non-dealer scores first and dealer second, the latter then turning over the crib for the first time and scoring for it as a five-card hand taken in conjunction with the starter. (A four-card flush in crib does not count unless the starter makes it five.) An additional '1 for his nob' goes to the holder of the Jack of the same suit as the starter, whether in hand or crib.

Game is usually 121 up, play ceasing as soon as either player reaches or exceeds that total.

Because Cribbage attracts scores in constant dribs and drabs throughout play it is played with a special scoreboard to obviate the inconvenience of fiddling about with coins, counters, or writing. In shape a narrow rectangle, it has a double row of holes along each side in groups of ten. Each player has two pegs (often matchsticks) and records each new bunch of scores by removing the trailing peg and replacing it the appropriate number of holes ahead of the previously leading peg. Thus the leading peg always indicates the current total, while the distance between it and the trailing peg reveals the amount just scored. This enables checks to be made in cases of doubt, and prevents a player from removing a peg and forgetting where it came from before reinserting it. A circuit of the double row accounts for 60 points, the old five-card game being played up to 61. The modern six-card game calls for playing twice round the board (to 121). The last point is marked by getting the trailing peg into an odd hole at the end and so 'pegging out'.

Cribbage is said to have been invented by Sir John Suckling (1609–42), 'the greatest gallant of his time and the greatest gamester, both at bowling and cards', according to a contemporary; for all of which, after being implicated in a plot to rescue the Earl of Stafford from the Tower, he fled to France and there, apparently, pegged himself out. Such invention is at least consonant with the game's courtly status throughout the seventeenth century. 'God send you', wrote Charles II in exile to his friend Ormonde,[9] 'better lucke at pickett than I have with Harry Bennett at cribbadge.' By the eighteenth century it seems to have lost this social cachet, for Seymour at first excludes it from his *Court Gamester* of 1719, and in 1732 classes it as one of the 'usual' games along with Whist, All Fours, and Put. In 1768 Goldsmith looked back to 'men that would go forty guineas on a game of cribbage';[10] and Dickens subsequently portrays it as a game at which Little Nell's grandfather helps himself along the road to perdition in *The Old Curiosity Shop*.

Three-sided tables were specially designed for the play of Hombre (English 'Ombre'). From a painting by J. E. Nilson.

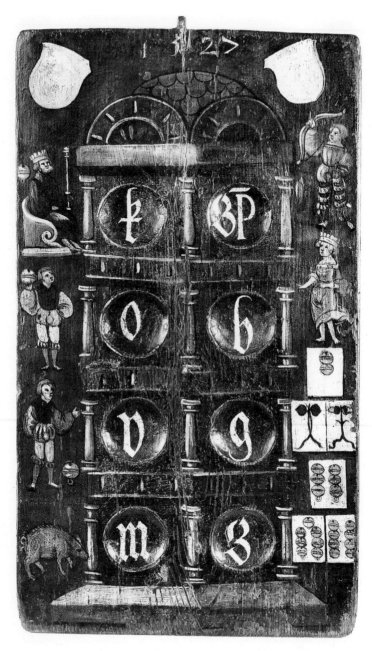

Top view of early sixteenth-century German Poch board, with compartments marked for (reading counter-clockwise from top left) King, Queen, Jack, Ace, Ten, Gleek (three alike), Marriage, *Poch*.

The Skat Fountain, no longer extant, was erected in 1903 at Altenburg, home of Germany's national card game. It portrays the four top trumps (Jacks) in contest.

The highest card should always be played from the greatest height. (*The Skat Players*, late nineteenth-century engraving.)

Card-playing at the French court under Louis XV (1710–74). Cardinal Mazarin (1602–61) had virtually turned Versailles into a non-stop casino in order to keep royalty in funds.

Whatever Sir John did to Cribbage, he can hardly have invented it from scratch. Neither of its twin components is entirely original, and Crib is not the only game of its type. References to Noddy, an earlier form of the game, appear in the sixteenth century, and many later ones make it sound synonymous with Cribbage, even to its scoring device being known as a Noddy-board. (It is an interesting coincidence that Noddy should mean 'fool', as does the Russian Durak.) In various card games it applied particularly to the Jack of the suit turned for trumps, or 'Knave Noddy'. The Jack is of obvious significance in Cribbage, even though trumps do not apply, and the association of Jack with fool—especially, on the continent, the Jack of bells—is another gaming feature lost in the mists of time. Perhaps Sir John's contribution was to tidy up the rules of play, to draw attention to some hitherto overlooked skills inherent in the game, or by his tastes and force of personality to render it popular in fashionable circles. He may also have been responsible for the name of the game, which the *OED* does not record before 1630 when Suckling was twenty-one. 'Cribbage', amongst other things, basically means the gaining of an unfair advantage by 'cribbing', an idea that may be considered applicable to the dealer's advantage of scoring from the crib. Crib also means 'box', and it is interesting that the dealer is customarily said to be 'in the box'.

A relative of Cribbage and Noddy is Costly Colours, briefly described in *The Compleat Gamester* of 1674, occasionally mentioned in the eighteenth century, and played in parts of the country into the nineteenth. Some years ago a correspondent[11] kindly sent me a copy of an article in *Shropshire Folklore* beginning: 'The following digest of the game of Costly, now (1874) obsolescent, was made partly from oral instructions given by "old players", and partly from rules set forth in a scarce hand-book . . . entitled *The Royal Game of Costly Colours* (Shrewsbury, 1805).' The game described amounts to an extraordinary elaboration of Cribbage, involving ideas and terms borrowed from other games. These include the valuation of Ace as either 1 or 11 (possibly from Vingt-Un) and the term 'right Jack' for that of the suit matching the turn-up, which is reminiscent of Euchre.

Our survey of adders would be incomplete without reference to Twenty-Nine, a fairly recent game of unstated origin.[12] Four players receive 13 cards each and play to cumulative sequences, with courts and Aces counting 1 each and numerals at face value. Each sequence, containing anything from three to eight cards, is won (like a trick) by the player making it exactly 29, and a new sequence is begun by the next in turn to play. With the eighth and last sequence completed, the player who has taken most cards wins. The game is playable in partnerships or by other numbers, and lends itself to many ingenious arithmetical variations.

11

Gone fishin'

There are two kinds, sorts, descriptions, species, manners, classes, natures and qualities of Casino. As you love me, child, avoid that which contains but a single 'S'.

Lady Chesterfield's Letters to her Daughter[1]

Cassino is the only example regularly encountered in Anglo-American Hoyles of a game family little heard of in the west but played widely in the east. The Chinese, who play them more avidly than trick-taking games, refer to them collectively as 'Fishing'.[2] The title is apt. A few cards lie face up on the table as a 'pool', and players each in turn try to capture one or more of them by matching them with a card from hand. If unable, they end their turn by throwing one of their own cards into the pool—thereby, so to speak, converting bait into fish.

The origin of European fishing games is unknown. Nowadays they are largely restricted to Italy and the Balkans, but they may first have appeared in seventeenth-century France—the earliest, Culbas, is described in the *Maison académique* of 1659. It was much enjoyed by the dauphin, who is said to have possessed a large triangular table designed for its practice.[3] The first English description is given in Piggott's 'Hoyle' of 1797 under the name Cassino, which is for ever being castigated by purists as a misspelling for Casino. If so, it is a good one.

Scopa forms perhaps the best, certainly the simplest, introduction to the family. Its title means 'broom', one of the main objects of play being to capture all the cards in the pool with a single card from the hand. This is called making a 'sweep'—or, to use the cognate English word, a 'scoop'. It should be played with the 40-card Italian pack, though in the following account—from Dossena's *Giochi di Carte Italiani*—I translate Italian suits into Anglo-French equivalents.

Scopa (*Italian, current*). Two or three players, 40-card pack. In each suit cards count face value from Ace 1 to Seven 7, followed by Jack (*Fante*) 8, Queen (*Cavallo*) 9, King (*Re*) 10.

Deal three cards each and four face up to the table. Each time the players empty their hands deal three more each from stock. Continue until all cards have been used and captured.

Each in turn plays a card from hand with a view to capturing one or more table cards. Table cards may be captured either by *pairing*—e.g. a Seven from the hand captures a Seven from the table, a Jack takes a Jack, and so on; or by *combining*—e.g. a Seven from the hand captures two or more cards totalling 7 (A + 6, 2 + 2 + 3, etc.), a Jack two or more cards totalling 8, and so on. The play of a single card can capture only a single combination: thus, if the table cards include 1, 2, 4, 5, a Six will capture either 1 + 5 or 2 + 4 but not both. If the played card can capture by either method it must do so by pairing: thus, if the table cards include 3, 4, 7, the play of a Seven captures only the Seven.

Both the captured and the capturing cards are stacked face down in front of the successful player, whose turn then ends. If the capture results in a sweep, so that no cards remain to be captured, the capturing card is left face up in the player's pile and will count one point at end of play.

A player unable to make any capture must 'trail' by adding one of his cards to those on the table. The player following a sweep can only trail.

When no cards remain in stock, whoever makes the last capture takes all the other table cards with it. This does not count as a sweep, even if, technically, it happens to be one.

At end of play, each player examines his won cards and scores as follows:

1 for having captured the most cards. If tied, no one scores.
1 for having captured ♦7, *sette bello*.
1 for having captured the most diamonds. If tied, no one scores.
1 for *primiera* (see below).
1 per sweep, as indicated by face-up cards.

Game is 11 points and the winner is the player with the highest score when this is reached. (*Variant*: points are remembered as they accrue and the winner is the first to claim correctly that he has reached 11. A false claim loses the game.)

The point for *primiera* goes to the player who has captured the four best numeral cards of their suits. For this purpose only, cards count as follows: courts 10 each, Two 12, Three 13, Four 14, Five 15, Ace 16, Six 18, Seven 21. Each extracts the highest-scoring card he has in each of the four suits, and the player whose four have the highest combined value wins. A player unable to show one card in every suit cannot compete. If equal, no one scores. (*Variant*: King counts 10, Queen 9, Jack 8. This is followed by the Federazione Italia-Svizzera Gioco Scopa, but rejected by the Associazione Napoletana Scopone.)

Partnership Scopa, or Scopone, follows a similar procedure except that all the cards are dealt and there is no stock. There are two versions of the game: either nine cards are dealt to each player and four to the table, or all four receive ten cards each and the first player is obliged to trail since there is nothing to capture. Each game has its devotees, all of whom call their version 'lo Scopone scientifico' as opposed to the hazardously 'unscientific' game indulged in by their rivals. (*Lo Scopone Scientifico* is even the title of a film made by Comencini in 1972 with Alberto Sordi and Bette Davis. Its English version is less explicitly listed as *The Scientific Card-player*.) It is interesting to look through Italian gamebooks and see which authors favour which variety. Nine-carders maintain that the ten-card game, by forcing the first player to trail, gives him no point of attack on which to exercise skill, so that the game is more chancy than it need be. Ten-carders maintain that the nine-card game gives the first player an unfair advantage, so that the game is more chancy than it need be.

In this dispute, relating as it does to matters of national honour, it is not merely inadvisable for foreigners to take sides: it could also be dangerous. Scopone has long been popular with the Italian military, and is only now growing out of an image of both male and nationalistic chauvinism which enveloped it during the 1930s and 1940s. A specimen of fiery enthusiasm quoted by Dossena from *Giuochi e Sports*, Turin, 1945, may be translated as follows: 'It is a game for men, real men—not for drips or blithering women or people who want to make it big and pay their way into high society . . .'[4]

It is more helpful to point out that both versions of Scopone prove to be subtler games of strategy than might appear to the casual reader entirely unacquainted with fishing games.[5] Several variations devised to add interest and excitement to the game are worth mentioning. One attaches special powers to Aces. An Ace may be used to sweep the board, unless the board contains one already, in which case it may be only paired. Alternatively, the holder of an Ace need neither capture nor trail, but may simply show it and add it to his pile of captures, rather like 'the Fool' at Tarot in its capacity as an 'excuse'. In Scopa di Quindici it is possible to capture with one hand-card one or more table cards whose face value, combined with the capturing card, totals 15. Other optional extras include a score of 3 for capturing the Ace, Two and Three of diamonds—a combination known as *bazzica*, which adds further food for thought to the mystery of what this term signified before it attached itself to the game now called Bezique. These and many other variations occur in Cirulla, much played in Genoa and Liguria. In Rubamazzo, a two-hand game, each player's won cards are stored face up on the table and can be captured as if they were table cards.

The point for *primiera* is a peculiarly Italian feature, lacking from varieties of the game played in other countries, and associated with a Poker-like vying game of the same name. Primiera being one of Italy's most ancient native games, this feature was presumably grafted on to an original form of Scopa from which it was absent. Such a form is embodied in Scarabociòn, a fishing game popular in nineteenth-century Venice until the advent of Madrasso, and now played mainly in the Venetian hinterland. Scarabociòn has the further distinction of being played with 52 cards—in fact, it is about the only game for which the 52-card Trevisane pack is still manufactured and employed. More remarkable is Calini, a fishing game played with Tarot cards.[6]

Another early member of the series, played with 52 cards and lacking a score for prime, is the French game Papillon ('Butterfly'), introduced as a novelty in the 1730 edition of the *Académie des jeux*, but referred to in letters and literature from about 1707. Papillon contains an extensive range of scoring features bearing picturesquely entomological names. A sweep, for example, is called *sauterelle* ('grasshopper'), and the capture of three like cards is a *hanneton* (or 'cockchafer'). In both Papillon and another 52-card game described by Anton under the name Callabra the Jack counts 11, Queen 12, and King 13.

Cassino exhibits a number of distinctive elaborations. The basics are straightforward enough: deal four each and four to the table; courts count 11, 12, 13; and the scoring points are 3 for cards, 2 for Great Cassino (♦10), 1 for Little Cassino (♠2), 1 for spades, 1 per Ace, and 1 per sweep. Complication has set in with the additional feature of 'building'. Suppose there is a Three on the table and you hold a Two and a Five. You may on this turn unite the Two to the Three, announce 'Building Fives', and on your next turn capture both with the Five—unless, that is, your opponent also holds a Five and captures it first, or else increases the build by playing another card to it and announcing a higher total. A 'build' on the table counts as a single entity: the cards comprising it are no longer capturable as individuals. It is also possible to make multiple builds; but at this point my powers of description fail. Cassino is usually presented as a simple game for children, which surprises me greatly, as I have never been able to follow the rules myself. I do not know when or where the building elaborations originated, but believe them to be an American invention of the mid-nineteenth century. Its earliest description known to me occurs in Dick and Fitzgerald's New York 'Hoyle' of 1868, and its first in England in *Cassell's Book of Indoor Amusements . . .*, 1881. Several nineteenth-century English Hoyles omit the game altogether, and it is not until the twentieth century that all accounts include the building feature.

Cassino crops up in unlikely places and guises. Gerver, in *Le Guide Marabout* (Verviers, 1966), writes of 'Le Whip' as a 'local Flemish game . . . whose origins are unknown and whose rules are transmitted orally'. The game described is virtually unadulterated Cassino. Don Laycock, in *Three Native Card Games of New Guinea*, correctly identifies as Cassino a game played under the name of Pilei Swip, or Sweep, and adds: 'One is inclined to speculate on the route by which this game reached New Guinea, as the game of Casino does not seem, today, to be played extensively by any European community, though it may well have had a vogue among Australian or American soldiers in wartime.' It seems possible that wartime (1914–18) was also responsible for its introduction into Flanders and that 'Whip' is a corruption of 'Sweep', though I have no direct evidence that the game has ever been known as 'Sweep' by English-speaking players.

Escoba, the principal Spanish member of the family, resembles Scopa di Quindici in that one or more cards are captured by combining with a card from hand to total 15. No other type of capture—even pairing—is admitted. As 'Escoba de Quince' is also played in the Spanish-speaking New World, it is conceivable that the apparently American idea of building derives from this feature. Baciga is an extension of Escoba in which each time a player is dealt three more cards he may score for any combination they contain. The Seven of coins (cf. *sette bello*) is wild, and the game is influenced in various other ways by Mus and Truco.

Other fishers include Tablanette, described by Phillips and Westall in *The Complete Book of Card Games* and said to be of Russian origin, and two or three Balkan games described from oral sources by Robert

Harbin in *Waddingtons Family Card Games*. Pishti or Pashta is reportedly Turkish, and 'the Dry Game' or 'the Ladies' Game' Greek.

All in all, fishing games form a rich hunting ground for researchers in quest of a challenge.

12

The realm of Rum

I will not attempt to describe Gin Rummy in detail as you can
call up any insane asylum and learn all about it in no time, as
all lunatics are bound to be Gin players, and in fact the chances
are it is Gin Rummy that makes them lunatics.

Damon Runyon, *The Lacework Kid*

Rummy is a twentieth-century phenomenon. Unheard of before 1900,
it has since engendered some of the most popular card games of all
time, typically simple in structure, easy to learn, and fast to play.
Though ranging socially from snappy gamblers' games like Gin and
Pan to elaborately ornamented accomplishments like Canasta, the
vast majority lie somewhere in between, as interesting but not too
strenuous family games especially popular with women and children.

Rummy is hardly 'a game' as such. It really denotes a vast family
of games based on a particular way of playing with cards, namely
by 'draw and discard', which is almost a definition of Rummy in
itself. This consists in drawing cards one by one from a central
stockpile and throwing out unwanted cards in return, with a view
to forming one's hand into matching sets of cards, or *melds*. A meld
is normally either three or four cards of the same rank, or three
or more cards in suit and sequence, such as ♥A-2-3-(etc.) or
♥A-K-Q-J-etc. Rummies are therefore matching games, but in a different sense from those already considered under that heading. Newmarket, Eights, and so on might be described as 'matching out'
games, in that each card you play must in some way match the one
played out before, so that matches or sequences are formed com-
munally on the table. By contrast, Rummies are 'matching in' games,
in that what you are trying to do is build up a matching set or
sequence in the privacy of your own hand.

Given this basic procedure, Rummies fall into several groups
according to their respective aims and rewards. In the original forms,
nowadays best represented by Gin, the aim is to be the first to go out

by matching all one's cards, and the score is determined by the penalty value of opponents' cards left unmatched in other players' hands ('deadwood'). In a later branch, including Michigan and its relatives, melds themselves also attract scores. In the most developed forms, such as Canasta, all the emphasis is placed on scoring for melds, and the main purpose of going out is to quit when you're winning.

If any single game can be described as archetypal Rummy, it runs more or less as follows:

Seven-Card Rummy (notional). Three or more players each receive seven cards from a 52-card pack, the next is dealt face up to start the waste or discard pile, and the rest are stacked face down beside it. Each in turn draws either the down-card heading the stock or the upcard heading the waste-pile, and makes a single discard face up to the waste-pile.

The aim is to get rid of all one's cards by laying them face up on the table in melds. Between drawing and discarding, a player may make a complete meld of three or more cards, or 'lay off' one or more cards to a meld they have already started, provided that such card or cards fill the quartet or continue the sequence.

The winner is the first to run out of cards, whether by melding or laying the last one off, and with or without making a final discard. Other players are penalized according to the face value of unmelded cards remaining in their hands. If the stock runs out before this happens, the waste-pile is turned (without being shuffled) to make a new one.

Innumerable variants have been produced by the addition of extra features in various combinations. For instance: (1) two or more packs may be used, all being shuffled together; (2) the packs may include Jokers or other wild cards; (3) different numbers of cards may be dealt; (4) scores may be made for melds made, as well as, or instead of, penalties for unmatched cards; (5) players may or may not be permitted to lay off cards to other players' melds; (6) they may be allowed to draw more than one card from the waste-pile, or even take them all, so that hands are constantly varying in size; (7) constraints may be placed on the order in which various types or sizes of meld may be declared; (8) melds may be broken up and re-formed . . . and so on. The varieties and variations are virtually endless.

It has to be said that Rummy suffers from a basic character defect. When three or more are playing as individuals, there is a distinct lack of gaming interaction between any two players, except to the extent that a player may hinder the one immediately next in turn by holding back discards the latter requires. You can do nothing effective to the player who plays immediately before you, and if there are more than four around the table then half your opponents might as well be playing on the moon. Multi-player games therefore tend towards triviality, leaving as the most strategic forms those for two players (notably Gin) or two partnerships (notably Canasta).

Uncertain ancestors

Although Rummy itself is relatively recent, the idea of exchanging cards with a view to collecting matched sets within the hand is not.

The simplest format has players exchanging cards one by one with their immediate neighbours. In the children's game of Pig, or Donkey, the winning combination is four of a kind; in My Ship Sails it is nowadays seven of a suit. To strengthen our suggestion that children's games derive from former gambling games, we find a probable ancestor in *Taylor's Motto* (1620), where the list of games at which the Prodigal squanders his wealth includes 'My Sow Pigg'd'.

Another way of acquiring cards is to ask for them. In Happy Families, the aim is to collect and declare 'families' of four of a kind. At each turn you ask a particular person for a particular card: if they have it they must give it to you, and you get another turn; otherwise your turn ends. A nineteenth-century version of Happy Families was played under the name Spade the Gardener, with five members in each family, and another, Authors, with cards representing famous writers and their works.

In Go Fish (or Go and Fish, in British English) a player does not ask for a particular card but for any and all cards of a particular rank. A challengee who has none says 'Go fish' (or 'Go and fish', as the case may be), and the challenger has to draw from stock. That this may also descend from an ancient gambling game is suggested by the appearance, in an Italian list of 1585 (Garzoni), of 'Andare à Piscere'.

A variation on exchanging cards with your neighbour is to exchange them with a spare hand or 'widow'. A version of Thirty-One is of this type. Three cards each are dealt to the players and another three to the table, and each in turn exchanges a card from hand with one from the table until someone knocks. The winner is the player then showing cards of the same suit with face values totalling 31 or the nearest under (Ace 11, courts 10). As an additional refinement, three of a kind counts $30\frac{1}{2}$.

An extension of Thirty-One called Commerce, or Brelan de Famille, was first described in the *Académie des jeux* of 1718 and subsequently became popular throughout Europe. Three-alike was now the best hand, followed by a straight flush, followed by the highest flush-point; later, pairs and sequences were sometimes added. The name Commerce was, confusingly, also applied to an early nineteenth-century variant better known as Trade-or-Barter, which heads for the same combinations by a different route: each in turn may either 'trade' by buying a replacement from the dealer, or (as in Cuckoo) 'barter' by forcing the next player into a blind exchange.

In the later nineteenth century the popularity of Poker and (Old) Commerce led to a combination of the two called Whisky Poker, in which the object of exchanging through the widow was to collect a Poker combination strong enough to justify calling for a showdown ('knocking'). Whisky Poker has been proposed as the parent of Rummy, but this is unlikely. For one thing, it is quite different in kind, constitution, and relative sophistication from Conquian, the earliest known Rummy. For another, Foster traces Conquian back to the early 1860s, whereas the earliest description of Whisky Poker occurs in *The Modern Pocket Hoyle* of 1865.

Conquian

The earliest true Rummy, a kind of proto-Gin, was first described briefly in 1887 under the name 'Coon Can', and at length in 1897 as Conquian.[1] 'The etymology of this word is very doubtful', says Foster, 'and of the origin of the game it stands for, little is known except that it is a great favourite in Mexico, and in all the American states bordering upon it, especially Texas.'

Conquian, or Coon-Can (Spanish–American, late nineteenth century).- Two players receive ten cards each from a 40-card pack ranking A-2–3-4–5-6–7-J-Q-K. The other twenty are stacked face down. Ace being low and Seven–Jack consecutive, 6–7-J is a valid meld but Q-K-A is not. The winner is the first to go out by melding eleven cards, including the last one drawn. Non-dealer starts by facing the top card of stock. He may not take it into hand, but must either meld it immediately (with two hand cards) or else pass. If he melds, he must balance his hand by making a discard face up. If he passes, dealer must either meld it himself, leaving a discard face up in its place, or else also pass by turning it face down. In the latter event it then becomes his turn to draw from stock.

Play continues in the same way. Whoever turns from stock has first choice of the card turned, and must either meld it, extend one of his existing melds with it, or pass. If both pass, the second turns it down and draws next. Whenever a player melds, his faced discard becomes available to the opponent, who may either meld it himself or turn it down and make the next draw. When melding, it is permissible to 'borrow' cards from other melds to help create new ones, provided that those thereby depleted are not reduced to less than valid melds.

The game ends when one player melds both the faced card and all the remaining cards of his hand, whether by adding to existing melds, making new ones, or both.

If a player declines a faced card which can legally be added to one of his existing melds, the opponent may 'force' by demanding that he meld it. In this way, it is sometimes possible to force a player into a situation from which he can never go out, a point of considerable interest to the strategy of play.

If neither is out when the last available card has been declined, the game is drawn and the stake carried forward.

As Conquian is played with the typically Spanish 40-card pack and is the earliest known game of its type, it may reasonably be traced to the Spanish of Mexico or the south-western states and preferred under its Spanish name, however uncertain the etymology. (It sounds like *con quién*, meaning 'with whom', under which spelling Culin records it as played by Apaches in 1896.)[2] This may make it a Mexican invention; but it is evidently not a Spanish one, as the earliest forms of Rummy appearing in Spanish card-game literature (as Ramy) are obvious twentieth-century transatlantic imports.

A likelier origin may be sought in the Orient. The Rummy principle of drawing and discarding with a view to melding out is as common in Chinese games as trick-play is in western games; furthermore, it is not restricted to cards but also occurs in domino and tile games—it is, in fact, the essence of Mah-jong. In 1891 one W. H. Wilkinson, enthusing over a Chinese card game he had discovered called Khanhoo, persuaded Messrs Goodall (UK) to publish an adaptation of it for western cards. The 62-card pack, reflecting the Chinese original, comprises two packs of 31, each consisting of numerals Ace to Nine in three suits, plus Jack, Queen, King, and Joker of no suit. Each receives fifteen cards, the aim is to go out by melding them into sequences and triplets, and the mechanism is precisely that of Rummy, even to turning the waste-pile to form a new stock.

A similar Chinese card game is reported by Andrew Pennycook[3] under the name Kon Khin, which sounds sufficiently like Conquian or Coon-Can to give much food for thought. One possibility is that such a game first reached the south-western states in the hands of Chinese immigrants. Another is that something of this sort under something like this name was transmitted first to the Portuguese (via Macao?) and from them to Mexico perhaps via the Philippines. In this connection we can't ignore the popular Spanish game of Chinchón, which is virtually Gin played with the Spanish pack of 40 or 48 cards. Whether this relates to the Spanish town of that name, or is the original name of the game, or is cognate with Kon Khin or Coon-Can, or even influenced the choice of 'Gin' as a name, are questions in search of an answer.

From Rum to Gin

Hardly less tantalizing is the word 'Rum', which first appears as 'Rhum, or Rhummy' in a Hoyle published by Donohue of Chicago not later than 1905. It may be named after the drink by analogy with Whisky Poker, but this does not force a derivation from the actual game: the connecting link need only be that both are appropriately named because they are drinking games. There are other possibilities to consider. One is the cluster of ancient card-playing terms including *ronfle*, *rompha*, and the like, which denote scoring combinations and may themselves derive from some form of *triomphe* or 'triumph'.[4] But this is too old and distant to be a likely source; and we must also regretfully dismiss, as an attractive red herring, the eighteenth-century French writer Bullet's proposed derivation of *ronfle* from Celtic *rum*, 'a gathering together', and *fell*, 'combat'.[5] More serious reference may be made to the later German game Rum (und) Stich, French Romestecq, whose scoring combination called *rum* or *rome* probably reflects the German word now spelt 'Ruhm'. This literally means 'fame' or 'glory', but in card-playing terminology corresponds exactly to *honneur* or 'honour' in Whist and Bridge. The Dutch equivalent, *roem*, is the usual word for a meld in the Dutch game Klaverjass. Some such word could have influenced the initial choice and spelling of 'Rhum', leading to 'Rum' as a more intelligible rationalization.

Whatever its name, the game itself underwent rapid evolution on both sides of the Atlantic between 1900 and 1910. Rhum, so spelt, was played with a 52-card pack by up to six players receiving from seven to nine cards each. In its original form the discards were displayed separately on the table and a player could take any one of them quite freely. Modern players will think this makes the game too easy, and will therefore not be surprised to read the following variation: 'The game is sometimes rendered more difficult by having only one card face up, each discard being placed on top of the original faced card, so that there are two piles to draw from [and] only the top card may be taken from either . . . This makes the game much longer, but adds to the skill demanded.'

The anonymous text of 'Rhum, or Rhummy', appears word for word in subsequent editions of the US Playing Card Company's annually revised *Official Rules of Card Games*, edited by R. F. Foster. By 1912 he is spelling it 'Rum' and describing it as a combination of 'Conquain' [*sic*] and Whisky Poker. By 1919 it is headed 'Poker Rum'.

Another version was played at this time with a double 53-card pack, Jokers wild. Known simply as 'Double Rum' in America, it became popular in English card clubs under a confusing transformation of its original title into 'Khun Khan'. Later English books complicate matters even further by reverting to 'Coon-Can' and renaming the two-hand game 'Colonel'.

Also dating from this period is the many-handed version of Conquian known as Panguingue (three syllables). Pan, a popular gambling game, makes do with at least five and preferably eight 40-card packs shuffled together. It remains much played as a house game in the Nevada casinos and western states. Perhaps also relating to Conquian is the Spanish game of Ramy, which uses two or more 40-card packs shuffled together, features Deuces wild, and deals a nine-card hand which must be formed into three-card melds to entitle its holder to go out. Some claim this to be the ultimate ancestor, but it looks more like an offshoot of the Contract branch, and the name itself, meaningless in Spanish, is clearly a Spanish spelling of 'Rummy'.

Basic 40-card Conquian for two players must have experienced its 52-card conversion shortly after 1900. Reading between the lines of recorded history suggests that it may first have been played as 'Poker Rum' or 'Rum Poker', and differed from Conquian in these distinctive ways: Melds were not made piecemeal; instead, drawn cards could be added to the hand so that melds were built up in secret, the game ending when one player 'knocked' and showed his hand. With cards counting at face value (Ace 1, courts 10), it was permissible to knock with deadwood totalling 15 or less. The winner scored the combined face value of cards left in his opponent's hand, doubled if he 'went rummy' by melding every card. Note that the 52-card version now enabled a player to go out with a single long sequence—an impossibility in 40-card Conquian, which requires eleven cards to be melded but contains only ten in each suit.

This game was also known as Knock Poker, and, with the knocking requirement reduced to 10, as Poker Gin or Gin Poker. Gin is said to have been perfected in 1909 by Elwood T. Baker, a Whist teacher, at the Knickerbocker Whist Club, New York. Be this as it may, the game is not recorded as 'Gin Rummy' much before 1940, when it suddenly swept Hollywood and, as 'the game of the stars', went into a 'nova' state—appropriately enough—almost comparable to that of Contract Bridge. An elegant feature of the later game is that the minimum requirement for knocking is determined by the face value of the current upcard. If it is an Ace, you need a 'gin' hand (fully melded) to go out. Another is the so-called Hollywood scoring schedule, which has the effect of enabling three games to be played simultaneously.

Branch-line to Michigan

Gin is the most sophisticated representative of the oldest branch of Rummy games, i.e. those in which the object is simply to go out first. Further developments of the Rummy principle got under way after the First World War. A new but inevitable idea was to credit players with plus-scores for the melds they actually make, instead of just penalizing them for the cards they fail to meld. This novelty was accompanied by another evolutionary advance, that of increasing the number of cards which may be taken from the waste-pile. The discards are now spread slightly so that all are visible, and players may take any visible card provided that they (1) meld or lay it off immediately and (2) also take and add to their hand all those lying above it. The result is that hands are now alternately increasing and decreasing, the game lasts longer, and the emphasis is transferred from going out to making lots of melds. This line culminates in Canasta—the classic point-scoring game as opposed to the classic out-going game of Gin.

In Michigan Rum, apparently the first of its type, each deal was complete in itself. Michigan was succeeded by Pinochle Rum, also called 500 Rum from its target score. Later developments included the neat partnership game of Persian Rummy, and Oklahoma Rummy, or Arlington. Parallel developments took place in inter-war Europe. Remigio, or Rabino, a multiple 52-card game of Spanish provenance with ten cards dealt to each of any number of players, still emphasizes going out but increases the losers' penalties if the winner can exhibit certain special melds. A fully melded 'clean' hand (i.e. without wild cards) is paid double, a ten-card flush (not necessarily in sequence) is paid four times if clean or five times if 'mixed' (containing a wild card), and a ten-card sequence (not necessarily in suit) is worth five or six times. When enough packs are in use, the maximum hand is ten of a kind, called *remigio* and counting 10 times the value of opponents' penalties. The equivalent Italian game of Ramino supplanted the more primitive Scala Quaranta of reportedly Hungarian origin. This also featured extra pay-offs for special hands, including most of those listed above plus another consisting entirely of court cards—a 'blaze', as it used to be called at Poker.[6]

Inter-war experimentation also resulted in a curious Italian hybrid called Ramino Pokerato, in which the cards were dealt as for Ramino but players opened a pot by betting, raising, equalizing, and, if desired, dropping out, before drawing and discarding began. The same idea cropped up in South America under the name Pif-Paf, a Brazilian game which enjoyed a popularity of near-epidemic proportions around 1940 and soon began to make headway in the United States.

Both, however, were superseded in the 1940s by a game played under the name Pináculo or Pinaclo in Spain and Pinaccolo in Italy. It worked best for four as partners and contained embryonic ideas which would later mature into the main features of Canasta. Although its name might suggest some origin in Pinochle Rummy, it also happens to be the word for 'summit' or 'pinnacle' in both languages, and denotes a high-scoring combination in both games.

Contract games

Even Rummy, though not a trick-taking game, failed to remain uninfluenced by the 1930s craze for Contract Bridge. 'Contract Rummy' is said to have been prefigured in a game called Zioncheck invented by Ruth Armson. Contract is played over seven deals, four of ten cards each and three of twelve. In each hand, players may not meld or lay off until they can start by melding a minimum contract requirement. The respective contracts are: two sets, a set and a sequence, two sequences, three sets, two sets and a sequence, one set and two sequences, and, in the last hand, three sequences. Contract is recorded under a variety of names: Liverpool Rummy, Progressive Rummy, Shanghai Rummy, and many others.

An offshoot of the contract principle appears in several games, including Canasta, as the rule that a player or partnership's first meld must be of a certain minimum value, which increases on subsequent deals according to the score so far accumulated—the more you have, the more you must make to start with. A variation occurs in Czech Rummy, where there is no score for melds and players drop out as and when they reach 300 penalty points. A novel feature is that the minimum initial meld varies according to players' current positions, being lowest for the player who is losing most and highest for the player with the lowest current score. Possibly related to this idea is that of Continental Rummy, popular in the 1940s, in which players start with fifteen cards and have to meld them all in one of three patterns: five three-card sequences; three of four and one of three; or a five, a four, and a three. Sets are not allowed.

The Vatican connection

An early Rummy development was the possibility of getting rid of unwanted cards by laying them off to other players' melds as well as to your own. By a later extension of this theme it became possible to appropriate cards from other players' melds and attach them to yours. A yet further extension has produced a branch with the unusual feature that melds are not personally owned: as community property they are constantly being broken up and re-formed, and the object remains the old one of simply going out first. Hence there is no discarding and no waste-pile.

Such games seem to have proliferated in Europe, and their development is not easy to follow. By far the best is Vatican, which Andrew Pennycook collected from a Czech player, though it does not appear in *Hrácy Karty, Karetní Hry*. As this has the rare merit of being a game of skill for any number of players, it is well worth knowing.

Vatican (twentieth century, Czech?). Two to five players, best for three or four. Use a double 52 pack plus two Jokers, 106 cards in all. Deal thirteen cards each and stack the rest face down. The object is to go out first by getting all one's cards into melds. Jokers are wild.

Each in turn may draw one card from stock or make an initial meld (or both), which must be a sequence of at least three cards. There is no discard. Having made an initial meld, a player may on future turns do one or more of the following: (1) draw the top card of stock, (2) make one or more melds from hand, (3) break up and re-form any meld or melds on the table, provided that he also adds to one or more of them from his own hand on the same turn. A player who starts by rearranging melds on the table must complete his turn by either playing a card from hand or drawing from stock.

Every meld, both when made initially and when robbed or re-formed, must consist of either (*a*) at least three cards in suit and sequence (Ace high or low), or (*b*) three or four cards of the same rank. More than four of a kind is not allowed, and a recommended optional rule is that four of a kind must contain one card of each suit.

A Joker cannot be moved from one meld to another unless it is first replaced by the card it represents. Neither it nor any other card may be taken from a meld back into hand. When no cards remain in stock the player in turn may pass if he can find no way of playing from hand, but if he starts rearranging cards and then finds himself unable to play from hand he loses the game. The winner is the first out of cards. There is no official scoring system.

Pennycook also describes, as a possible forerunner of Vatican, a German game called Krambambuli, which involves robbing melds but has not yet dispensed with the waste-pile. Another early game of this type appears in *Culbertson's Card Games Complete* under the name Carousel. Two play with a single pack plus Joker: each in turn must draw at least one card and meld if possible, otherwise he must draw a second, and a third if necessary; but if unable to meld after drawing three cards he ends his turn. A player with a count of 5 or less after drawing the first or second card may end the game by knocking.

Canasta

All these inter-war experiments in the realm of Rum were bound to result in a major game of universal appeal, probably of Spanish or South American origin. So it proved. The product was Canasta and its point of departure Uruguay. It became a world-wide craze in the early 1950s, eclipsing for a while even Contract Bridge in its hold on the card-playing public's attention. At time of writing, Canasta remains the last natural card game to have achieved this distinction, even though every so often journalists primed by commercial interests claim that some new craze is sweeping the United States and threatening to replace Canasta and Bridge as the greatest card game in the world. They are invariably wrong. (Who remembers 'Onze' from the early 1970s?)

By general agreement, Canasta was first played at Montevideo in about 1940, slipped naturally over the Plate into Buenos Aires, spread throughout Argentina, engulfed the whole of South America, and was attracting attention in the United States by the end of the war. It arrived too late to make the first edition of Albert Ostrow's *Complete Card Player* (1945), but appears as an appendix to the 1949 edition with the remark: 'It is said to have been invented by the ladies of Montevideo as a counter attraction to Poker which, in their opinion, took up far too much of their menfolk's time.' Jaime Poniachik, of Buenos Aires, assures me that its place of birth was the Punta del Este beach-club.

Canasta swept the States in 1949, and within a year addicts were on their knees begging Bridge-guru Ely Culbertson for advice on how to play it properly. 'From the very start', writes the author of *Culbertson on Canasta*,

Canasta writers and enthusiasts urged me to join the Canasta movement. 'Your authority, your science of card games, publicity outlets and organization of three thousand Bridge teachers would give the needed push to make Canasta permanent,' Jesse C. Beesley, himself the widely known author of *Canasta Up-to-Date*, who helped launch Canasta with his articles in *Vogue*, said to me.

Culbertson's fortunately inimitable style may be savoured from his opening paragraph under the heading 'What I think of Canasta (in lieu of an Introduction)':

Canasta is a bizarre, exciting and charmingly exasperating game. It is simple enough for a child, deep enough for an expert. It can be learned in thirty minutes, but forgotten never. It is as modern as an atomic bomb; and yet it is as old as the first embryonic melding games of three centuries ago. It is a true partnership game, like Contract Bridge, and it has bluff, as in Poker. It looks like Persian Rummy, has the flavor of Pinochle, and barks wildly like Oklahoma. It cribs from Cribbage. And withal, it has an inner world and logic of its own, taxing the capacity of the scientific mind. It has methods all its own. The only thing it needs is a Culbertson method to be added to its madness. If the game can be stabilized, if the chaotic flood of variations, contradictory laws, multiple revisions, can be channeled, we will have a great game for the enjoyment of millions.

Happily, the enjoyment of millions was secured by the inclusion, in this literary milestone, of the Official Laws of Canasta—drawn up in 1950 by the Canasta Committee of New York's Regency Club, pronounced 'Effective Immediately', and graciously endorsed by Culbertson with only marginally less than whole-hearted enthusiasm.

'It might', he concedes, 'have been tempting for me to join with some other writers and publish a better version of the Official Laws. But I believe that one imperfect code is far superior, for the good of the game, to two "perfect" codes. The Official Laws as they stand today are adequate, and I am sure they will bring peace on the Canasta front.'

Canasta is a highly elaborate game, complicated rather than deep, and decorated, like Bridge, with a scoring system characterized by lots of noughts, so that when points do come, they come not single spies but in battalions. It is played with a double pack including four Jokers, and the main object is to score for melding sets of three or more cards of a kind (no sequences). Melds may be increased by the addition of further cards, the really big scores accruing when they are thereby extended into *canastas*. A canasta is seven cards of the same rank, carrying a large bonus if consisting entirely of natural cards or a slightly smaller one if containing one or more wild cards. An attractive feature of the game is that natural canastas are stacked face up with a red card on top, mixed ones with a black card. Canasta is the Spanish for 'basket'. By way of explanation, Culbertson points to the Spanish term for building up a meld, namely 'tejiendo las cartas', literally 'weaving the cards' together. The end product of such weaving is, naturally enough, a basket.

The idea of drawing more than one discard, started in games of the Michigan branch, is perpetuated in Canasta with a novel twist. Now the player must take the whole waste-pile, not just part of it, and then only if the upcard can be used at once in a new or existing meld—it may not be taken into hand. Further restrictions apply if the pile is 'frozen', which it is to (*a*) *all* players whenever it contains a Joker, (*b*) *a partnership* that has not yet made an initial meld, and (*c*) *one player* when the upcard is a black Three. A frozen pack may only be taken if the upcard is immediately melded with two or more natural cards from hand.

Various cards are used in various inventive ways. Jokers and Deuces are wild, but they cannot be melded together and a new meld may not contain more than one or a new canasta more than three of them. Black Threes may only be melded in the same turn as going out. Red Threes are never melded but laid face up on the table as and when acquired, where, at end of play, they attract a separate score—or penalty, if their holders have not melded.

Structurally, a game is played up to 5,000 points over several deals, with the minimum value of an initial meld increasing with a partnership's current score. Going out is never the main object of play and carries only a small bonus, though on occasions it may be employed as a tactical device.

All in all, Canasta's popularity is justly merited for its visual attractiveness, balanced structure, and variety of strategic eventualities.

The Canasta craze was established in Britain by 1952, achieving social prominence through its espousal by Princess Margaret, the then most popular member of the royal family. Peaking in the mid-1950s, it settled down to a more proportioned lifestyle as a classic game of comparable status to Bridge but with less demanding attributes. Though challenged by a number of extensions and variations, none of them effectively displaced the parent game, any more than the proper pack was ousted by so-called 'Real Canasta' cards, with red and black blobs instead of traditional suitmarks. Melds of wild cards had been a feature of Uruguay, the name under which Canasta was originally played, and re-emerged in such variations as Bolivian, Brazilian, Chilean, and Cuban Canasta. The sequence was reintroduced into several games, most notably Samba—Canasta's most successful offshoot—under its usual Spanish name escalera, or 'ladder'. Other variants include Combo, Hollywood, Imperial, Italian, Joker, Mexicana, Pennies from Heaven, Quinella, Racehorse Canasta, and Tampa.

Calypso

An irresistible postscript to the Canasta story is provided by a hybrid game of tricks and melds invented by R. B. Willis of Trinidad and promoted by two major card companies in 1954. Calypso is a partnership game played with four 52-card packs over four deals of thirteen each. Each side's aim is to make calypsos, a calypso being a full thirteen-card suit sequence. There are, theoretically, four available in each suit, making sixteen in all, though a partnership does pretty well if it succeeds in assembling more than two or three of the eight available to it. The real novelty of the game lies in the way it is played, which is not by draw-and-discard but by trick-and-trump. Each player has his own personal trump suit and compiles calypsos in that suit only from cards taken in tricks, being, however, at liberty to pass required cards over to his partner.

A fascinating if long-winded game, Calypso's interests were perhaps not best served by its being launched right in the middle of the Canasta boom.

13

The patient pursuit

Games for one player are childish and simple, and not worth learning. When a man is reduced to such a pass as playing cards by himself, he had better give up . . .

'Captain Crawley', *The Card Players Manual* (1876)

Patience is the mental equivalent of jogging: its purpose is to tone the brain up and get rid of unsociable mental flabbiness.

David Parlett, *The Penguin Book of Card Games* (1979)

Is Patience really a game or merely a glorified puzzle? 'Game' normally implies some form of competition between players, which of course is absent from a solitary pursuit. Yet Patience involves more physical activity than is normally associated with 'puzzle', and actually feels more like a game than the so-called game of Solitaire in which you gradually eliminate thirty-six marbles from a pattern of holes by jump and capture. Like other one-player games, this type of Solitaire is better counted as a puzzle, since it has just one solution (or set of solutions), which only has to be memorized or written down to render future playings pointless—except perhaps as a form of therapy, or as a true test of 'patience' in the virtuous sense of the word. Like other puzzles, it ceases to be a puzzle once solved.

Card Solitaire, on the other hand, is open-ended. It has no general solution, for the fact that cards are shuffled before play makes each new deal a different puzzle from what it was before. Solving or not solving it feels just like winning or losing a game. Moreover, there are nearly as many different Patiences as there are competitive card games, the best of which can be won by strategic skill. Where there is strategy, there is a game by definition. Finally, there exist competitive varieties of Patience for two or more players, and these unquestionably count as games. We therefore have to admit Patience as a category of game, and must accordingly revise our understanding of 'competition'. Perhaps we may expand it to include a contest between, on one hand, the lone player, and, on the other, the shuffled pack, or the same player on different occasions, or Fate, according to taste.

In a typical Patience game the player starts by shuffling the pack very thoroughly and then aims to get the cards back in order by following certain rules of play. The successful end-product will normally be four piles of thirteen cards (or eight in a double-pack game), each pile consisting of all the cards of a suit in numerical order from Ace low to King high. There are obvious variations, of course—the piles may or may not have to follow suit within themselves, or sequences may be built in reverse numerical order, and so on; but the principle is generally the same. What gives many Patience games their individual flavour and delight is the imaginative layouts or *tableaux* which act as a workspace for partial arrangements of cards before they can be correctly shifted on to their final sequences.

There are other sorts of Patience, but fewer of them. In 'elimination' games, such as Pairs, Fourteens, Accordion, etc., the aim is not to arrange cards in order but merely to eliminate them from the intermediate layout in matching pairs or similar patterns. In Poker Patience, points are scored for arranging cards into Poker combinations as they are turned from the pack, a 'win' being defined as reaching a particular target score.[1] Older Patience books often include exercises that hardly count as games. 'Caesar', for example, merely requires you to arrange the numerals Ace to Nine in a 'magic square' so that all rows and columns total fifteen. This is not a game but a puzzle. Once you have done it, you can do it.

The excitement of a given Patience lies in whether or not it will 'come out': it would be dull and boring if you knew you could always reach the required finishing position regardless of the lie of cards or of how well or badly you play. Whether or not it is likely to come out depends on the degree of choice and information it displays:

Choice. Patiences vary in the degree of choice they offer as to the placing or movement of cards within the workspace. Many older specimens give no choice whatsoever. Whether or not they come out at all depends on the order in which cards happen to emerge from the shuffled pack, and whether they do so more or less often depends on the particular mechanism of play. They are therefore games of chance and thus true tests of patience. Modern games usually offer a fair degree of choice, and are therefore games of strategy. It is important to get the balance right. A game affording too much choice will always come out and so remain unsatisfying. Ideally, there should be just enough choice to ensure that making too many wrong decisions will result in failure.

Information. Games also vary in the extent to which the positions occupied by cards are open to view. Information is irrelevant in games denying any choice of play. In strategic games of imperfect information the player typically draws cards one by one from the shuffled pack and must base decisions on the likelihood of certain other cards turning up sooner or later in the deal. As Cavendish puts it,[2] they present 'indefinite problems for solution', and call upon one's powers of judgement and intuition. In those of perfect information all cards are dealt face up before the opening move is made: they present 'definite problems for solution', and are solved (if the lie of cards allows) by analysis and calculation. Between these two extremes lie games of 'increasing' information, in which the cards are not all visible to start with, but become so in time to be of use.

Perhaps I should illustrate these generalizations by describing some particular games.

1. *Quadrille* (*traditional*). Arrange four Queens in a cross, and around them deal all Fives and Sixes in a circle. Turn cards from the pack one by one. A Seven turned up may be built on the Six of the same suit; on that will go the Eight when it appears, and so on, until the Sixes have been built up in suit as far as the Jacks. Similarly, a Four turned up goes on the Five of the same suit, and is to be followed (when possible) by the Three, Two, Ace and King. Any unplayable card is added face up to a single waste-pile. The top card of the waste-pile may always be played on a building pile whenever it fits. When no cards remain in hand, turn the waste-pile upside down and go through it again. You may make up to three turns and redeals, and, if successful, will finish with a pretty pattern of Queens surrounded by Kings and Jacks in the dance formation appropriate to a quadrille.

This is a game of chance, requiring no skill or judgement beyond keeping your eyes open. The redealing rule is traditional but entirely arbitrary: Quadrille would hardly ever come out if you allowed no redeal at all, but is bound to come out eventually if you redeal often enough. Three redeals sets the game to succeed about fifty per cent of the time. Despite its intellectual limitations, Quadrille is a pleasing exercise. Its dance-based theme (further illustrated in such games as Cotillion, Virginia Reel, Cock o' the North, Pas Seul, etc.) makes a pretty pattern whichever way you look at it.

2. *Black Hole* (*by David Parlett*). Set a black Ace at the centre of the board. Holding the pack face up, deal the next 51 off in sweeps or fans of three at a time, arranging the seventeen fans in an orbit

around the central Ace. Your aim is to get all 51 cards built up in a pile on top of the black hole. They needn't follow suit, and the sequence may go up or down ad lib, changing direction as necessary. (For example, the Ace might be followed by 2-3-4-3-2-A-K . . . etc., or by K-Q-J-10-9-10-9-8 . . . etc., or even by 2 to K, then Ace again, and so on all the way up without any change of direction.) For this purpose only the uncovered card of each fan may be taken and built in the centre. As each is taken, of course, it releases the one below it for subsequent play.

Black Hole is a game of perfect information and therefore pure calculation. Theoretically, you can win in either of two ways: (1) by working out all 51 moves before touching a card, and then making them in the right order, or (2) by proving—also before touching a card—that the order in which the cards have come out renders no solution possible. Traditional games of perfect information include Belle Lucie, Baker's Dozen, and Fourteen Out.

3. *Strategy (by Morehead and Mott-Smith)*. Turn cards one by one from the pack. As each Ace appears, place it at the head of the board. Play every other face up to any one of eight waste-piles. You may spread these piles in columns towards you to see what's gone. When all 48 have been dealt, your aim is to build on each Ace the Two of the same suit, then the Three, and so on up to the King, finishing with four thirteen-card suit-sequences. For this purpose only the top card of each waste-pile (the one at the uncovered end of a column) may be taken and built at each move.

This is essentially a game of judgement. Success depends almost entirely on placing turned cards in the appropriate column in such a way as to avoid impossible blocks and entanglements from upsetting the play-off. For instance, it is obvious that you mustn't deal (say) the ♣7 to the pile already containing the ♣6. At the next level, you must also avoid such cross-blocks as placing ♣7 before ♥6 on one pile if ♥5 was placed before ♣8 on another. Although the inventors estimate the probability of success as one in five, I have never (when in practice) failed to get it out with a properly shuffled pack, except by demonstrable mistake. However, just as the rules of Quadrille can be varied to make it come out more or less often by varying the number of redeals allowed, so Strategy can be made harder or easier by varying the number of waste-piles to which turned cards are dealt. For more of a challenge, try six, and don't set the Aces up as they appear but play them to the waste-piles as well.

4. *Klondike, or Canfield (traditional)*. Deal seven piles of cards face

down in a row, with one in the first pile, two in the second, and so on up to seven in the seventh. Turn the top card of each pile face up. Aim to place the four Aces at the top of the board as and when they become available, and to build each one up into a thirteen-card suit-sequence headed by the King. Turning cards from the pack one at a time, play each one face up either to (*a*) one of the Ace-piles, provided that it goes on the next lower card of the same suit, or (*b*) one of the seven processing columns, provided that it goes on a next higher card of the opposite colour (e.g. red Nine on black Ten), or (*c*) a rubbish heap. Throughout play, the top card of the rubbish heap may be played to an Ace-pile in ascending sequence of suit, or to one of the central columns in descending sequence of alternating colour. The topmost (uncovered) card of a central column may also be so played in accordance with the same rules of following. A whole sequence of properly ordered cards in alternating colour may be shifted from one central column to another provided that the join follows the rule. Whenever a face-down card is exposed, turn it face up. Whenever the last card is played from a central column, the space it leaves may be filled only with a King, or with a proper sequence from another column headed by a King. Having run out of cards from the main pack, you may not (as in other patiences) turn the rubbish heap and go through it again. It is therefore vital to play off the topmost rubbish card at every available opportunity.

This game is so widely played that many people just call it 'Patience'. In fact it has several names, being known in Britain as Canfield—a title which in America attaches to the patience known in Britain as Demon—and previously as Small Triangle, to distinguish it from the two-pack version called Large Triangle. It is a test of patience and attention rather than deep skill, and rarely comes out.

Names and origins

'Patience' is only one of several words used to denote one-player card games: it is the earliest recorded of them, is evidently French, and also denotes one-player games in general.[3] In modern French the card game is more often referred to as *réussite*, meaning 'success', or 'favourable outcome', to distinguish it from *patience*, now meaning 'jigsaw puzzle'. The practice of any form of solitaire was once regarded as an exercise of 'patience' in its literal sense as a virtue. Thus in modern Italian *pazienzia* applies to such activities as building card houses, while card solitaire is usually known as *solitario*. The French use of *réussite* is explained in Littré as 'a combination of cards [by] which superstitious persons try . . . to divine the success of an undertaking, a vow, etc.' If this suggests an origin in fortune-telling, the theory is reinforced by the name of the game in Danish, Norwegian, and Icelandic, namely *kabal(e)*, or 'secret knowledge'. In Poland, where Patience is called *pasjans*, the word *kabała* also occurs with the specific meaning of 'fortune-telling with cards'. Perhaps, then, the original purpose of a Patience game was light-heartedly to 'divine the success of an undertaking, a vow, etc.', as Littré suggests. If the game 'succeeds' (*réussit*), the answer is favourable, otherwise not.

The same idea emerges from the *Fortune-Telling Patience* described as follows by Mary Whitmore-Jones in about 1895:[4]

This is a game for three or more players, and is a favourite with young ladies, as being supposed to afford them a glimpse of their future destiny. The four aces are laid in the middle of the board, their significations being: hearts, loved; diamonds, courted; clubs, married; and spades, single blessedness. . . . If you finish off all your cards on one of the ace packets, it shows what your fate will be; but if your cards work off on your neighbours' packets, the oracle is veiled, and your fortune remains untold.

The theory is further supported by the fact that the earliest description of Patience occurs within a few years of the invention of card layouts for cartomancy (fortune-telling), which, contrary to popular belief, is not reliably reported before about 1765.[5]

As so often in the history of card games, the fact that 'patience' is a French word does not necessarily make France its place of origin. As Ross and Healey show,[6] it is more probably of German or Scandinavian provenance. The earliest reference I know of occurs in the 1783 edition of the German game anthology *Das neue Königliche L'Hombre-Spiel* as both 'Patience' and 'Cabale'. In *Das neue Spiel-almanach für 1798* 'Patiencespiel' is represented as a contest between two players, each of whom in turn plays a game of Patience while bystanders, and presumably the players themselves, lay bets on the outcome. Single and double-pack versions of the game are given, their description being consistent with that later recorded in English books under the title 'Grandfather's Patience'. There follow two references in the *Journal of a Swedish Girl during Captivity in Russia 1808–9*, by Adelaide von Hauswolff, who kept company with her father during his apparently not very onerous internment as a prisoner of war in St Petersburg and elsewhere. One quotation reads (in

Swedish) 'Major Hjärne played patience with my father', the other 'In the afternoon . . . the Major practised patience.' A third reference occurs in a Swedish poem by J. D. Valerius published in 1809, entitled *Mitt spel*, 'My game', and ending: 'I play *Tok* against girls and, in sorrows and distress, Patience against my Fate.' (Tok is a card game whose title means 'fool', cf. Russian Durak.)

I quote these references in detail because, as Ross and Healey point out, it is unclear whether Patience was primarily regarded as a solitaire or a two-hander. A solitaire is suggested by 'The Major *practised* Patience' and by an implicit contrast between Tok and Patience in Valerius; but when the Major is described as playing Patience 'with' Adelaide's father, it is uncertain whether they are playing against each other alternately or with each other cooperatively towards the solution of a single game—or, indeed, are playing a two-hand competitive Patience. It may well be that Patience was originally devised as a two-handed contest with separate packs of cards, and that players first played it solitaire by way of practice for the real thing, only later discovering that it offered rewards of its own to those of a solitary disposition.

Whether that disposition was shared by Napoleon Bonaparte is extremely unlikely, even though such titles as Emperor, Napoleon at St Helena, Napoleon's Favourite, Napoleon's Flank, Napoleon's Heart, Napoleon's Square, Napoleon's Tomb, St Helena, seem to assert that the retired emperor whiled his exiled hours away by means of Patience cards. Unfortunately for the story-books, those days on St Helena are well enough documented to negate the assertion. Napoleon is known to have played Vingt-Un, Piquet, and Whist; but Ross and Healey have closely examined the Patience story and shown it to be based on the misinterpretation of an incident that took place at the Whist table. In fact, the person reported to have been seen 'playing this solitary game of patience' was Las Cases, who had been sent to a corner of the room and instructed to keep shuffling a sticky pack of cards until they ran more easily. The patience in question here was thus not so much a game as a virtue.

The oldest known book of Patience games was published in Moscow, 1826, as *Sobranie kartochnykh raskladok, izvestnykh pod nazvaniem Grand-pasiansov*—'A collection of the card layouts usually known as Grand-patiences'. At least six more collections were published in Sweden before 1850, three of them before 1840. Scandinavian and Polish references from the 1830s add weight to the apparent Baltic origin of Patience games, and Ross–Healey argue for Sweden as the likeliest ultimate source. They also quote a nice additional back-reference from the 1889 *Notes and Reminiscences* of H. G. Trolle-Wachtmeister, in the form of an anecdote about Charles XIII of Sweden which concludes 'Old Charles listened carefully to this, then put aside his Patience-cards . . .'. 'This' refers to the pilgrimage of Gustav Adolf to Jerusalem, which took place in June 1815.

The first French collection appeared in 1842, entitled *Le Livre des patiences, par Mmede F****, whom Ross-Healey identify as the Marquise de Fortia. That Patience was now current in upper French society is indicated by a letter from the Danish dramatist Oehlenschläger, who visited Louis-Philippe at Paris in 1845 and reports: 'Here there was sitting the noble old queen, with white hair, at a big table; she was playing Patience with two packs of cards. The King's sister, Mme Adelaide, was also playing Patience, with smaller cards.' Another nineteenth-century French collection was published in Brussels as *Le Livre illustré des patiences* and credited to the Comtesse de Blanccœur, who claims to have based it on her own researches. The same text later appears in English, however, as *The Illustrated Book of Patience* (1920), translated by 'Professor Hoffmann' (Angelo Lewis) not from Blanccœur, of whom he appears unaware, but from a German-language edition, leaving unclear whether the French or the German edition came first.

Patience did not penetrate English society much before the second half of the nineteenth century, if the date of the first English-language collection is anything to go by—and since all its contents have French titles, even that may have been a translation. This was *Illustrated Games of Patience*, written by yet a third Adelaide in the Patience saga, namely Lady Adelaide Cadogan, daughter of the 1st Marquess of Anglesey. Copies of the second edition of 1874 still find their way into specialist bookshops, but the date of the first remains unknown, thanks to a wartime incendiary at the British Museum library. The only previous reference to the game recorded by the *OED* occurs in *Great Expectations*, in which Dickens represents Magwitch as playing 'a complicated kind of Patience with a ragged pack of cards'. Coincidentally, the novel first appeared in 1861, the year of the death of an illustrious player in the form of Albert, Prince Consort. Biographical reminiscences published a few years later by Queen Victoria reveal Albert to have been a devotee of the patient pursuit, presumably from his youth in Saxe-Coburg. Whether this actually enhanced the popularity of the game, as has been claimed,[7] is doubtful, in view of the Queen's relative unpopularity in early widowhood.

Lady Cadogan published a second collection in 1883, this time cribbing from an unspecified German anthology, and in 1890 the ubiquitous Henry 'Cavendish' Jones applied his usual intellectual rigour to the exercise in a perceptive but boring volume simply entitled *Patience*. He it was who first drew a clear distinction between games presenting 'definite' and those presenting 'indefinite' problems—in other words between games of calculation (as in Black Hole) and games of judgement (as in Strategy), to the exclusion of games of pure chance (as in Quadrille), which played no part in Jones's ordered world. Shortly afterwards appeared the first of seven volumes of Patience games compiled by, and, I suspect, largely invented by, the indefatigable Mary Whitmore-Jones—inventor of the 'Chastleton' portable Patience-board for long-distance travellers—whose comprehensiveness and genial description counterbalance Cavendish's somewhat spartan approach. Few twentieth-century Patience collections are worthy of note, most being repetitive hack-work. Not until the late 1940s was a thorough reappraisal of the subject made, when Albert Morehead and Geoffrey Mott-Smith published their rather generously titled *The Complete Book of Patience*. My contribution, *The Penguin Book of Patience* (1979) follows similar principles but in greater depth.

Competitive Patience

A notable twentieth-century development of Patience has been the continuing evolution of a two-player folk game which crops up in books in a variety of guises. Any form of Patience can, of course, be played competitively by two or more players (which is a good reason for preferring the word 'Patience' to 'Solitaire'): we have already seen that the earliest recorded Patience was played by two. The oldest method is for players to play the same game separately with their own individual packs and treat it as a race, the winner being the first to succeed. There are also two-handed co-operative games in which each plays alternately towards a solution of the same game: examples include 'Sympathie' in Blanccœur's book and Mary Whitmore-Jones's 'Conjugal' Patience. The method employed in Racing Demon, which may be applied to any other game, is for each to play individually in race fashion, but with an element of interaction, in that players may off-load cards from their own layouts to those of others in order to hold them up. There are two versions of this approach: the hilarious racing version, in which all play simultaneously as fast as possible (Grabbage, Racing Demon, Spit), and the comparatively intellectual version in which two players play alternately, progressing the game as far as they can before getting blocked and so having to cede the turn to play. A particular game of the latter type has been widespread since at least the mid-nineteenth century in a variety of incarnations. It first appears as Rabouge or Robuse; by the end of the nineteenth century it was also known as Crapette or Crippette.[8] Just after the First World War it became something of a fad in the United States, encouraging R. F. Foster to publish a mini-treatise on *Foster's Russian Bank*. It later resurfaced as 'Spite & Malice' in a book by Easley Blackwood (1970).

14

Simple tricksters

Of shoes—and ships—and sealing wax—
Of cabbages—and kings—

Lewis Carroll, *Through the Looking-Glass*

Of cows—and popes—and kaisers too—
And tricks and trumps and things . . .

D.P.

The rest of this book deals with trick-taking games—'tricksters', for short—which are by far the most varied and widespread forms of card-play in the west. The basic idea was outlined in Chapter 6, where we suggested that it probably entered Europe with the pack itself. We also saw that tricksters may be subdivided into (1) *plain-trick* games, in which all that counts towards winning is the number of tricks taken, and (2) *point-trick* games, in which the win is determined by the total value of point-scoring cards ('counters') contained in the tricks taken. These will be covered systematically in due course. Here, however, we start with some quaint and mostly ancient tricksters of both sorts which exhibit a curious habit in regard to trumps, in that they either lack them completely, or, at least, embody them in strange and extravagant forms.

A trick, it will be remembered, is normally won by the highest card of the suit led to it. Trumps or 'triumphs' are cards with special powers which break this rule by capturing the trick they are played to regardless of the suit led. Usually, trumps are all the cards of a given suit, which is chosen at start of play by turning a card or by bidding for the privilege of naming it. Since the earliest games of this type—appropriately called Triomphe, Triumph, Trump, and suchlike—do not appear before the late fifteenth century,[1] over 100 years after cards first entered Europe, trumps may be suspected of being a European invention. Suspicion is reinforced by their absence from eastern card-playing traditions, and by the fact that some ancient

European games (notably Trappola) started life without trumps and only acquired them later. On the other hand, no known game started with trumps and later dropped them, except as an optional 'no-trump' bid.

What evidence survives of fifteenth-century card games shows three approaches to the idea of trumps, which may correspond to the way in which they evolved.[2] The first appears in Kaiserspiel, which, under the name Karnöffel, is the oldest known trickster (1426). Here, certain cards possess limited trumping powers over certain others, and are given special names such as Pope, Kaiser, Devil, etc.; but although such trumps belong to a given suit, not all cards of that suit are trumps. Furthermore, the word 'trump' seems never to have been applied either to the trumping cards, which are known simply as 'beaters' (*Stecher*), or to the suit they belong to, which is just called the 'elect' or 'chosen' suit (*gewählte Farbe*). Thus stage one in the evolution of trumps may have been that of according special powers to certain named cards.

The second is represented by the invention of Tarots, which took place in Italy shortly before 1440. Tarots, at first called *trionfi* or 'triumphs', are a series of elaborate picture cards constituting in effect a special fifth suit, any of which will beat an ordinary suit-card led to a trick, and all of which beat one another in a specified order despite their original lack of numbering. These appear to be the first true trumps. They also bear, and indeed depict, such names as Pope, Emperor, Devil, etc., but there is no evidence to suggest that the idea of trumps was inspired by the 'elect' cards of Karnöffel or the like.[3]

Stage three was to replicate the effect of a trump suit without going to the expense of producing such large and elaborate packs, by simply making one of the ordinary suits trump. From the way in which trumps are almost invariably selected in games without bidding, this must originally have been done by turning a card from stock or the last card dealt (as in Triomphe and Trump), and entrumping the suit it displays.

The following games, though dissimilar in many ways, have in common that they are very old and seem to reflect a pre-trump tradition. The oldest, Karnöffel, exhibits partial trumps and 'elected' cards with special powers. The group involving Put, Truco, and Aluette, certainly sixteenth century and probably earlier, variously exhibit either a few 'elected' cards or no trumps at all. As for Piquet, its remarkable non-trump status has remained virginally intact for at least 500 years. They also share some other features of probable antiquity. All are plain-trick games, and all except Piquet exhibit 'lax' rules of trick-play, in that players are not obliged to follow suit to the card led.

It is possible that the ancestral European trickster was a trumpless plain-trick game in which, though suit need not be followed, the trick could only be won by a card of the suit led. This still obtains in the Indian game of Ganjifa,[4] and may suggest a common origin. We may further speculate that an obligation to follow suit naturally followed the introduction of trumps as a way of keeping their trick-taking power under control. Half-way house would then be represented by the All Fours rule whereby one may freely follow suit or trump, but may not renounce if able to follow.

Karnöffel—The Kaiser game

Long thought extinct, like the Coelacanth, Karnöffel has recently been discovered alive and well and living in remote valleys of Switzerland under the name Kaiserspiel or Kaiserjass. Its previous obscurity may be explained by this modern alias and the fact that it is played with traditional Swiss cards, both of which disguise it as one of the Jass games to which the nation has been addicted since the end of the eighteenth century. Its true nature was not revealed until the 1970s, when Rudolph von Leyden showed that Kaiserspiel was the barely changed descendant of Europe's oldest card game.[5]

Karnöffel first appears in 1426 in a town ordinance of Nördlingen, Bavaria, permitting the game to be played in public. From this and similar references—forbidden at Augsburg in 1446, permitted at Balgau in 1448, etc.—Schreiber identified it as a trick-taking game played by soldiers and peasants rather than by the upper crust.[6] That it was not just lower-class but positively bolshie is suggested by its violent title; for Karnöffel—denoting the highest trump (a Jack)—literally means 'hernia'. Civic and ecclesiastical authorities often objected to it. Bishop Geiler, preaching in 1496, saw Karnöffel as the embodiment of that medieval nightmare 'the world turned upside down'. Ordinary card games, whatever their demerits, at least reflect a sensible social order, with the King superior to the Ober (or Queen), the Ober to the Unter (Jack), and so on. 'But now', he complains, 'we have a game called Karniffelspiel in which everything is turned upside down: the 3s beat an Ober, the 4 beats the Unter, the 2 and the 6 beat a King; and a card is turned over, so that now one is Kaiser, now another becomes Kaiser, as luck will have it.' He would like to burn them all, including 'the King, the Kaiser, the Ober, the Banner and the Devil'.[7]

Later references to named cards and disturbed ranking include a satirical work of 1546 in the form of a dialogue between the Pope and the Devil, from which, as Dummett puts it, 'We learn that neither of the Devil and the Pope beats the other; that the Pope beats all the cards, including the Kaiser and the Kings, with the exception of the Karnöffel; that the Karnöffel beats the Pope, the Devil and all other cards; that the Karnöffel is an Unter . . . the 2 beats the King, the Obers and the other Kaisers; and that the 5 is beaten by all other Kaisers, and by the King, Ober, Pope and Karnöffel, but beats only the 10, 9, 8, etc.' Karnöffel was evidently enjoyed as a substitute for anarchy, and whether it was forbidden or permitted in various fifteenth-century ordinances obviously hinged more on political perceptions than on the ethics of gambling.

References to the game, both literal and allegorical, are common in sixteenth-century Germany but absent by the seventeenth, causing Schreiber to regret that rules for the game were 'probably no longer recoverable'. Thanks to the late von Leyden's researches, however, we now know how it works and how it has survived. It was being played in Switzerland by 1620, Berlin and Lübeck soon after, Thuringia in the eighteenth century, Westphalia in the nineteenth, and Friesland in the twentieth. Some occurrences are supported by detailed rules of play, which, together with those of the game as now practised at several localities in Nidwalden, south of Lake Lucerne, enable us to give the following generalized description.[8]

Karnöffel is a four-hand partnership game played with a 48-card German-suited pack lacking Aces. Five cards are dealt to each player and each side's object is to win most tricks. Each player's first card is dealt face up, and the suit of the lowest-ranking of them—or the first dealt of equally lowest—establishes a quasi-trump suit. For this purpose cards follow natural ranking order: K-O-U-10–9-8–7-6–5-4–3-2. (Ober and Unter are equivalent to Queen and Jack.)

The eldest hand leads to the first trick and the winner of each trick leads to the next. Players need not follow suit and partners may discuss between them what to play. Play continues until either side has won three tricks. A trick is taken by the highest card of the suit led, or by the highest trump if any are played. In plain suits, cards rank in natural order from King high to Daus (Deuce) low. In 'trumps' the situation is quite complicated, and herein lies the game's distinctive character.

Certain cards of the so-called trump suit have varying degrees of power over plain-suit leads, as follows.

trump Unter	(*Karnöffel*)	beats all plain-suit cards
trump Seven	(the Devil)	beats all, but only if led
trump Six	(the Pope)	beats all
trump Two	(the Kaiser)	beats all
trump Three	(the Overtaker)	beats all but King
trump Four	(the Undertaker)	beats all but King and Ober
trump Five	(the Suit-taker)	beats all but King, Ober, and Unter

It will be seen that Karnöffel, Pope, and Kaiser are the only universal trumps. Since they beat any lead, even a King, they are collectively known as 'King-takers' (*Königstecher*). The Seven, or 'Devil', is also a King-taker if led to a trick, beating all cards in the pack except Karnöffel. However, it wins only when led, and may not be led to the first trick.

The next three cards are partial trumps. The Three is an *Oberstecher* ('Overtaker') because it beats any plain card from the Ober down, but not a King. Similarly, the Four is an *Unterstecher* ('Under-taker'), because the highest card it beats is an Unter, and the Five a *Farbenstecher* ('suit-taker') because it beats plain-suit cards other than courts.

The remaining cards of the elected suit have no trumping powers, and count, when led, as simple plain-suit leads. When the suit is led, its cards beat one another in the following order from high to low: U-(7)-6–2-K-3-O-4–5-10–9-8-(7). This odd-looking sequence follows logically from the rules above: the Three ranks between King and Ober because it is an Overtaker but not a King-taker; and so for the others, depending on their special trumping powers.

Modern Kaiserspiel is played without Nines and Eights, and incorporates a novel feature whereby any player holding one or more Banners (Tens) may declare it before play begins, in which case it becomes a trump. The Banner of roses, if declared, is called *Blass* and acts as a King-taker ranking immediately below the trump Two. That of acorns (*Grün*) is an Overtaker ranking below the Three; that of shields (*Tätsch*) an Under-taker ranking below Four; that of bells (*Fugel*) a suit-taker ranking below Five. All declared Banners are called Kaisers, while the top trump is *Jos*. The trump Seven was known as *Sibille* or *Babeli* in nineteenth-century Swiss play, but has since dropped this title.

Other variations occur in other descriptions of the game from various parts of northern Europe, but its peculiar essence has remained unchanged and undoubtedly dates back to its earliest report. Karnöffel is remarkable for its early display of features common to many later games of different types. The superiority of the Jack of trumps appears in later games like All Fours and Loo, while the aim of winning at least three tricks out of five underlies the whole family of five-card games covered in the following chapter. Other curiosities that may be derived from, related to, or at least influenced by, Karnöffel include the Bavarian game of Watten and the Danish game of Brus.

Watten[9] is an eccentric gambling game of unknown origin but with features reminiscent not only of Karnöffel but also of the Put-and-Truco family yet to be described. It uses a 32-card German-suited pack and works best for four in partnerships. Each receives five cards (3 + 2) and the aim is to win three of the five tricks, play ceasing as soon as one side takes its third. Its greatest peculiarity lies in trumps, of which there are three sorts.

1. The top three trumps, or 'Criticals' (*Kritische*), are the King of hearts (*Maxi*), the Seven of bells (*Belli* or *Welli*, cf. *Sibille*, above), and the Seven of acorns (*Spitz*).
2. These are followed by the 'Strikers' (*Schläge*), which are all the cards of a given rank selected by the opponent at the dealer's left before the first trick is played. If he chooses Nines, for example, then the fourth highest trump, or Chief Striker, is the Nine of trumps, followed by the other three Nines. The later are equal: if more than one is played to a trick, the first played is best.
3. These are followed by the remaining cards of the trump suit, which is chosen and announced by dealer as soon as the eldest hand has declared Strikers. They rank Deuce, King, Ober, Unter, 10–7.

Not all suit-trumps will be present, as one will be a Striker and another may be a Critical. Similarly, if Kings or Sevens are the nominated rank, Strikers will be short by one or two because they are Criticals. Further, there will be no Chief Striker if the selected trumps are Kings and hearts, or Sevens and either bells or acorns. To compound the volatility of trumps, some may lie out of play among the undealt cards.

A trick is taken by the highest card of the suit led or by the highest trump if any are played. Players need not follow suit or trump unless the Chief Striker (*Hauptschlag*) is led, when they must play a trump and head the trick if possible. The first player or side to win three tricks scores at least 1 game point, and the first to 15 wins the game.

What makes Watten a gambling game—it is already a game of chance, with so many cards out of play—is that the value of each deal can be increased by challenging and won by bluffing, a feature also present in modern Kaiserspiel. At any stage in the proceedings a player may challenge his opponent(s) by saying 'Go!' If they concede, the challenger wins the current value of the game without further play (even if he or his side has yet to take a trick) and the cards are thrown in without being revealed. If they accept, the value of the round is increased by one and play continues. They may even counter the challenge by replying 'Go!' themselves, which again threatens to increase the value. A player or side at 12 or 14 points may not challenge. Amongst other refinements is the fact that partners may communicate the holding of key cards to each other by a code of facial signals such as winks and lip movements.

Brus, an equally eccentric Danish game from Jutland,[10] is played by three or four with 36 cards lacking Twos, Threes, Fours, Fives, and Tens. Exactly half its 36 cards are 'trick-takers' or quasi-trumps, the other eighteen being ordinary cards or 'trick-fillers' with no competitive power at all, even over one another. (A trick consisting entirely of fillers is 'won' by nobody.) The three top trick-takers are the club Jack, known as *Spids* (cf. *Spitz* in Watten), the heart King, or *Brus* ('fizz'), and the spade Eight, or *Galhund* ('mad dog'). These are followed by the Nines, Aces, the three remaining Jacks, and Sixes. As between cards of equal rank, club beats spade beats heart beats diamond. Sevens play a peculiar role, having no trick-taking power over other cards but beating one another in the suit-order quoted above. The club King beats any Seven, but can itself then be beaten by the spade King—which in itself has no power over Sevens unless the club King is played to the same trick! As a further peculiarity, two or three cards of the same rank may be led to a trick simultaneously, thereby drawing the same number from other players' hands. Cards are not played to a communal pile, but left on the table in front of each player, with a winning card indicated by being turned face down. Three cards each are dealt and a replacement drawn from stock after each trick. A deal is won by the first player or side to win five tricks.

Put and Truco

If you want to be robbed, my son, play Put in a tavern.[11]

The strange old game of Put represents a family in which suits are virtually irrelevant to trick-play: there is no requirement to follow suit, and the trick is simply taken by the highest card played to it. An odd but logical consequence is that in the event of a tie the trick is either ignored from the account or is held in abeyance pending some other determining factor.

Its lowly status is well attested. Cotton (1674) describes it as 'the ordinary rooking game of every place', and Barrington (1787) consigns it to the servants' quarters together with Loo, Whist, and All Fours. Unlike Loo and Whist, it never rose above stairs, and unlike All Fours, whose descendants still flourish in alehouses, it seems to have died out in the nineteenth century just when Hoyle-compilers were plucking up the social courage to describe it. One element it might have bequeathed to posterity is that feature of Brag whereby the best hand is three Threes and the highest run is not A-K-Q but 3–2–A.

Put is a basically two-player game of tricks, bluff, and highly organized cheating, to which Cotton devotes more attention than to the play. Cards rank Three, Two, Ace, King, and so on down to Four. Three cards each are dealt and the object is to win a majority of tricks. This may sound trivial, but there is a catch. With no trumps and no obligation to follow suit, the fall of equally high cards to the same trick leaves it 'spoiled' and belonging to no one. You can therefore win by taking three or two tricks, or even one if the other two are spoiled; but a commoner result is that each player wins one trick and the third is spoiled, producing a draw by 'trick and tie'. The game is nominally five points up, but is won outright if all three tricks are played and either player wins two. The hand can be abandoned before completion, and single points are then scored as follows: either player, before playing to the first trick, may concede for one point by simply throwing in his hand; alternatively, he may challenge his opponent to concede by saying 'I put'. If the opponent concedes, the putter scores a point; otherwise, the hand is played out.

Similar to Put is the French game of Truc, Truka, or Tru, played respectively in Roussillon, Pays Basque, and Poitou,[12] originally with a 36-card pack ranking 7–6–A-K-Q-J-10–9-8. Note that the two nominally lowest cards are promoted to top position, as in Put. Since modern French packs lack Sixes, the Six is now replaced by the Eight. One would logically expect the top cards to rank Eight, Seven; in fact, they rank Seven, Eight, and the Eight is actually called the 'Six'! This curiosity perpetuates a tradition antedating the time (around 1700) when Sixes were dropped from the French pack, the game itself being recorded from 1583.

Truc has a more interesting structure than the Put described by Cotton. Non-dealer, if not satisfied with his hand, may propose an exchange of cards, which the dealer may accept or reject. If he accepts, the next cards are dealt three to each player and play must then begin. Game is 12 points. Each deal is worth a nominal point to start with, but either player, when about to play to any of the three tricks, may offer to double its value so far or throw the hand in. If the other agrees to throw it in, the double does not take effect and the proposer scores what it was worth before he proposed. If doubling would give a player what he needs for game, he instead offers to play for 'my remainder'; but his opponent may then counter with '*my* remainder', even if this amounts to more than a double. A spoiled trick is described as 'pourrie', literally 'rotten'.

In the four-hand partnership version, only eldest can propose an exchange of cards. Eldest and dealer each act as governor for their respective partnerships, each instructing their partner in general terms what to play. In the Catalan and Basque (but not Poitevin) forms, partners may also convey to each other the holding of certain high cards by means of such conventional signals as nods, winks, and so on, preferably without the other side seeing—a feature shared by such disparate games as Mus, Aluette, Watten, and Flüsslen. Structural similarities to the Triomphe family will not go unremarked: notably, there is a small number of tricks, the aim is to win a simple majority, and the non-dealer may propose (once) an exchange of cards before the game begins.

The Spanish equivalent of Truc is Truque or Truco, whose interest has been extended by the promotion of four specific cards to the post of top trumps, or *cartas bravas*, namely the Aces of swords and batons, Sevens of swords and cups. In South America, Truque evolved further and now lays claim to counting as the national card game of both Uruguay and Argentina.[13] In Truquiflor a score accrues for holding a three-card flush, or *flor* ('flower'). The feature is also present in Argentinian Truco, otherwise called either Hasta la siete because the top card is a Seven, or Truco ciego, 'Blind Truco', because there is no trump turn-up. (Some serious-minded players eschew the chance element and play Truco *sin flor*, 'without flushes'.) In Uruguay it has produced an even more complicated game played not only with *flores* but also with a trump suit and top cards called *matas*—compare the matadors of Hombre and the *cartas bravas* of Spanish Truco. This game is known as el Oriental (Eastern Truco) or Hasta el dos, the highest card being a Deuce. Some flavour of this extraordinary game may be released by simply recording the ranking order and names of cards from the top down. The top trumps or *piezas* are the Two, Four, Five, Caballo, Sota, and King of trumps, Caballo and Sota being known respectively as 'Perico' and 'Perica'. These beat the *matas*, which are Ace of swords (*espadilla*), Ace of clubs (*bastillo*), Seven of swords, and Seven of coins. These are followed by the *figuras* or *negras*, which are the non-trump courts, and these in turn by the *blancas*, or remaining non-trump Sevens and so on down to Deuces.

Both forms of Truco are played by four in partnerships, with one member of each side acting as governor and all employing the usual range of facial signals customary in Hispanic partnership games. There are three possible parts to the play, though a hand may be won on any one of them. In the first, players sing out their *flores*, if held, and score according to the outcome. The second is the *envido* or betting on who holds the highest-valued two-card flush. For both these purposes the cards carry idiosyncratic point-scores reminiscent of those in the Basque game of Mus—in Oriental the trump Deuce counts 30, Four 29, Five 28, Caballo and Sota 27 each, and so on, with two *blancas* or *negras* together counting face value plus twenty.

There follows the *truco* or trick-play itself, with the possibility of doubling and redoubling and of one player's throwing his hand in so that his partner may play alone. Although tricks may be tied (*empardadas*), as in most members of the Put family, the round itself is always won, if necessary by ascribing extra value to the first trick— 'la primera vale dos' ('the first one counts two').

Reference to 'singing out' one's *flores* was quite intentional, for an essential feature of Truco—'el alegre juego que se canta' (the happy singing game)—is the repertoire of traditional verses which players recite or sing in making their bids. For instance, *flor* itself may be announced in song as follows:

> Para pintar a mi chines
> no hay pinceles ni pintor,
> ni flores en las jardines
> comparadas a mi flor.

Which may be loosely rendered:

> To paint the pretty hand I've got
> you'll neither artist find, nor brush:
> nor flowers to grace your garden plot
> so lovely as my flowery flush!

Other verses may be used to suggest strategies of play or to show the holding of a key card. As players are encouraged to improvise new verses on the spot, Truco must be the only card game in the world designed to be won by poets.

No account of Truco would be complete without this plea of Enrique de Maria made in 1937 against the threat of Official Rules to render el Truco suitable for play in national tournaments:

> Que un juego tan oriental
> como es el Truco hasta el Dos
> no tenga, !válgame Dios!
> un reglamento oficial.

Or, even more loosely:

> May God forbid that such a game
> of eastern origin and name—
> so favoured by card-playing schools—
> be blighted with official rules!

A *Reglamento General del Truco Oriental* did appear shortly afterwards, but its unpoetic compilers were sufficiently tactful to remain anonymous.

Aluette—the Cow Game

This ancient and curious game is played by sailors and fisherfolk in various coastal regions of western France stretching roughly from Vannes to the mouth of the Gironde. Schools may also be traced patchily along the Loire almost as far as Orléans, and others occur along the north coast from about Paimpol to Cherbourg.

Its nickname 'le jeu de vache'—'the Cow Game'—is explained by the fact that one of its top trumps bears the picture of a cow and is known by that name. Aluette, however, is less easy. It is not to be confused with *alouette*, 'lark', despite the birds depicted on several of its cards, nor with *lutte*, 'battle', even though its top trumps are known as *luettes*. Its true name is in fact la Luette, of which l'Aluette is a hypercorrection or refined corruption. Of all the suggestions enumerated by Alain Borvo in his pioneering study of the game, the least implausible is that relating it to the old French form of *l'œillet*, 'eyelet', perhaps in allusion to the facial signalling which takes place between partners.[14]

The distinctive Aluette pack, produced by several manufacturers in slightly varying designs, is basically the old Spanish 48-card pack with suits of cups, coins, clubs, and swords. There are no Tens, the numerals from Ace to Nine being followed by Valet, Cavalier, and King. One odd feature is that the cavaliers are actually cavalières, the viewer being left in no doubt as to their femininity. Other design oddities include the eponymous cow on the Two of cups, a female bust about to be crowned by two birds on the Three of cups, and a babe on a swing hanging from the Two of clubs, whose symbols look more like oak trees.

Most of these images make sense when the top trumps are examined. Aluette lacks a trump suit, as do Put and el Truco, but, like the latter, promotes certain cards to the status of quasi-trumps. The top four are known as *luettes* and the next four as *doubles*. These cards and their nicknames are listed from the top down.

Luettes:	Three of coins	*monsieur*
	Three of cups	*madame*
	Two of coins	*le borgne* (blind man)
	Two of cups	*la vache* (cow)
Doubles:	Nine of cups	*grand neuf*
	Nine of coins	*petit neuf*
	Two of clubs	*deux de chêne* (two of oaks)
	Two of swords	*deux d'écrit* (two of writing)

The 'Two of oaks' is so called from the way the clubs are drawn, the 'two of writing' from the fact that it traditionally bears the manufacturer's name and place of origin. These are followed by the *moyennes* or middling cards (Ace, King, Cavalier, Valet) and the *inférieures*, the remaining numerals from non-trump Nines to non-trump Threes. As in Truco, two non-trump cards of equally high rank spoil the trick, which belongs to no one.

Nine cards are dealt to each of four players and the undealt twelve remain untouched. There is no obligation to follow suit or head the trick. Aluette has an unusual object, in that it is won by the partnership of the player who takes the greatest number of tricks individually, or, if equal, who takes that number first. The only other major game in which this occurs is Hombre, which may suggest a Spanish connection, perhaps through Triumphus Hispanicus.

Another peculiarity is the bid of *mordienne* or *morguenne* (an interjection vaguely equivalent to English 'gadzooks'), by which one player contracts to take his winning margin of tricks in unbroken succession up to the ninth, having previously taken none. This could be done, for example, by losing the first five and winning the last four, provided that no other player—including his partner—wins more than three.

The origins of Aluette are uncertain. Early references to 'les luettes', said to have been played by Anne de Bretagne and Archduke Philip the Fair in 1503, and by Gargantua in 1534, seem to suggest a game of the Nim family (removing numbers of objects from rows and columns). Dummett explains Borvo's failure to trace it convincingly to Spain by pointing out that the supposedly Spanish suitmarks must have been indigenous to France before the invention of the French system of spades, clubs, hearts, and diamonds. Though evidently related to Put and Truc, Aluette is more highly developed, and it is not until the eighteenth century that 'cartes aluettes' are attested as such.[15]

Piquet (Picket)

From the early sixteenth century Piquet has been widely regarded as the best card game for two. In 1534 Rabelais placed it high on the list of games played by Gargantua, and in 1892 (according to *Le Guide Marabout*) the delegates to a card congress held at Vienna voted it the most 'classic' of all card games. It was also regarded as the most aristocratic of games, being the favoured pastime of those whose favourite reading was the *Almanach de Gotha*. Perhaps for this reason, and because it is excessively complicated by comparison with such twentieth-century games as Rummy, it died out of everyday play by the end of the First World War, and now survives as a game for connoisseurs.

Piquet has always been regarded as the national game of France, even as an emblem of French patriotism. As Chatto says, 'It would seem that the French consider the invention of Piquet as a national point of honour, and that the native author who should call it into question would render himself liable to a suspicion of incivism.' Stories invented to account for its origin and significance range from the picturesque to the ludicrous. Positively simple-minded is the belief that it was invented by Picquet, the seventeenth-century mathematician of Troyes. More picturesque was the theory that it was inspired by a ballet performed at the court of Charles VI (d. 1422) or, by another account, of Charles VII (d. 1461)—a fairy-tale event sometimes confounded with the *Ballet du Jeu de Piquet* forming an interlude to Thomas Corneille's *Le Triomphe des Dames* (1676).

Bordering on the ludicrous is the oft-quoted *Mémoire sur l'origine du jeu de piquet* by Père Daniel, published in 1720, in which (as Cavendish puts it) 'Piquet is credited with being a symbolic, allegorical, military, political, and historical game. From the names of the personages on the court cards of early French packs, and from the marks of the suits, the Père believed . . . Piquet . . . to have been devised about 1430.' Some flavour of Daniel's original is conveyed by Chatto's account of his explanation of how the French suits came into being:

The Ace is the Latin *As*, a piece of money, which also signifies wealth; and as money is the sinews of war, the Ace has for this reason the precedence at Piquet. The *trèfle*, or clover plant, which abounds in the meadows of France, denotes that the general ought always to encamp his army in a place where he may obtain forage for his cavalry. *Piques* and *carreaux* signify magazines of arms, which ought always to be well stored. [*Carreaux* = 'quarrels' = square-headed crossbow bolts.] *Cœurs*—hearts—signfied the courage of the commanders and the soldiers. David, Alexandre, Caesar and Charlemagne are at the head of the four suits at Piquet, because troops, however brave and numerous, yet require prudent and experienced leaders . . .

And so on. Later clerics who devoted attention to the origins of Piquet include the Abbé Bullet, a Celtic scholar who delighted in deriving every unexplained technical term in the game (and a few explained ones) from Celtic roots, and Père Menestrier, who relates suit symbols to social stratification. Court cards, he says, represent the nobility, hearts the ecclesiastics, their place being in the *c(h)œur*, ('choir'). Pikes (spades) represent the nobility, *carreaux* (paving-tiles) the bourgeoisie, and trefoils the peasantry.

The name of the game may relate in some way to the suit of *pique* or spades—not because they play a more notable role than any other suit, but because they are more characteristic of the French as opposed to the German or Latin suit-systems, and so identify the nationality of the game with that of the pack used for playing it. Yet Piquet does not seem to have been so called until the seventeenth century. To Rabelais and his contemporaries it was known as Cent, from its target score of 100 points. Whether it can be traced back any earlier depends on what similarity it may have borne to the fifteenth-century Italian game of Ronfa, also listed by Rabelais under the name Ronfle. That feature of Piquet now known as 'the point', and signifying the greatest number and value of cards in any one suit, was formerly known in French as 'la ronfle' and in English as 'the ruff'. In some contexts it implies the point itself (as in *The Compleat Gamester*, under Piquet and Gleek) and in others the act of exchanging cards with a view to improving one's best suit (ditto, under Ruff and Honours, or Whist). Possibly, Ronfa was a simpler forerunner of Cent, providing the basis for a newer game comprising several parts. Since shortened packs are particularly characteristic of the sixteenth century, one might assume that Ronfa was played with the full 52-card pack and that the reduction to 36 cards was a distinctive feature of the new game.

Piquet has been played in England long enough to have become thoroughly naturalized. For most of its English history its vocabulary has been either replaced by equivalent English terms or at least pronounced as if of English origin. The use of French terminology such as carte blanche for 'blank', and of pseudo-French pronunciation such as 'P.K.' for 'Picket', is a nineteenth-century reversion. Cavendish's researches[16] discover its earliest mention in a tract of 1532: 'We fell to Saunt, five games a crown.' It is often portrayed not just as for two but for couples. 'Husband, shall we play at Saint?' asks a character in Heywood's *A Woman kilde with Kindnesse*, and Markham's *Famous Whore or Noble Curtezan* (1609) declares:

> Were it Mount-cent, primero, or at chesse,
> I wan with most, and lost still with the lesse.

A game of 'Mount-Saint' depicted in Machin's *The Dumb Knight* (1608) mingles technical terminology with the language of love in such passages as:

> QUEEN. What are you, my Lord?
> PHYLOCLES. Your Highness' servant, but misfortune's slave.
> Q. Your game, I mean.
> P. Nothing in show, yet somewhat in account:
>   Madam, I am blank.

The name 'Picquet' (older spelling) must have been replacing 'Cent' before 1600, as the *Dizionario Etimologico della Lingua Italiana* records it as early as 1607. Cavendish dates its English adoption from the marriage of Charles I to Henrietta of France in 1625. Piquet's popularity among the literate is suggested by its prominence in the earliest books of instruction in card-playing, an activity which had hitherto been regarded as something one just picked up, like the common cold. It retained pride of place for three centuries in various editions of *The Compleat Gamester* and the *Académie des jeux*, formed the subject of a treatise by the real Edmond Hoyle in 1744, and has never been dropped from serious card-game compendia to the present day. In the eighteenth and nineteenth centuries the home of intensive Piquet play for real money was at Bath, along with Whist.

In the late nineteenth century the game of Piquet au Cent, or Hundred Up Piquet, was replaced by a new structure under the name Rubicon Piquet. In the old game play continued until one player reached 100 points. This won a single game, or a double if the loser failed to reach 50, and the session or *partie* was carried by the first to win five games. Rubicon Piquet consists of exactly six deals, at the end of which the loser is penalized for failing to reach 100 points.

Like Cribbage, Piquet is a game of almost continuous point-scoring: traditionally, you recite your score as you go along and only write down the result at the end of each round. As this tradition is now lost, and special Piquet markers are a thing of the past, it may be better to use a Cribbage board.

Piquet (generalized). Two players use 32 cards ranking A-K-Q-J-10– 9-8–7 in each suit. A game is either played up to 100 points (Piquet au Cent), or consists of exactly six deals (Rubicon Piquet, there being a penalty if the loser fails to 'cross the Rubicon' of 100 points).

Deal. Deal in turns. At each turn dealer is 'younger hand', non-dealer is 'elder'. Deal twelve each in twos or threes and spread the last eight face down to form a stock.

Blank. A player whose hand contains no court card may score 10 for 'blank' by declaring and showing it, but it need not be shown until the opponent has exchanged.

Exchange. The aim of exchanging is to improve the hands. Elder discards from one to five cards face down and draws replacements from the top of the stock. Younger then discards and draws up to as many as remain. (Elder must exchange at least one; younger need not exchange any. If elder draws less than his entitlement of five, he may privately peep at those of the five which he leaves behind. If younger takes less than his entitlement, it is up to him whether to reveal those untaken to both players or to leave them turned face down. If elder declares a blank, he draws his extra cards without looking at them, waits for younger to exchange, then shows the blank hand and discards before seeing their replacements. The purpose of this rigmarole is to give players as much information as is consistent with the fairness of their relative positions.) Players may subsequently refer to their own discards but not to their opponents'.

Point. Whoever declares the greater number of cards in any one suit scores for point at the rate of 1 per card. Elder declares first. If both have suits of equal length, that of greater value wins, counting Ace 11, courts 10, numerals face value. If still equal, neither scores for point. The winning point must be specified or shown on request; the losing point may remain unspecified.

Sequence. Whoever declares the longest sequence of three or more cards in any one suit scores for it and for any other sequences that may be declared in the same hand, at the rate of 3 for each sequence of three (*tierce*), 4 for four (*quart*), and 15 to 18 for

King of bundles of cord, Queen of dog collars, Valet of double nooses, Ten of hunting horns, from a complete 52-card French Hunting Pack of about 1470. Portrayal of Valet (Jack) as Jester underlines true origin of Joker.

'Cupid and my Campaspe play'd
At cards for kisses; Cupid paid . . .'

Lines from John Lyly (1554–1606) and this detail from a fifteenth-century tapestry at Basle demonstrate the
traditional popularity of cards with couples.

The Card Players (c.1520) by Lucas van Leyden. It is evidently a trick-taking game played counter-clockwise (from left to right), with a card turned for trump and placed under the stock.

Illustration from Ingold's anti-gaming tract *Das Güldin Spil* (The Golden Game), mid-fifteenth century.

The Ace and Ten of polo-sticks, from a fifteenth-century pack of Mameluke playing-cards in the Topkapi Museum, Istanbul. Polo being then unknown in Europe, the suit was translated into staffs or batons.

Woodblock-printed cards from a late fifteenth-century Viennese *Hofämterspiel*, or 'court personnel pack'. It contains 48 cards, consisting of ten numerals plus King and Queen in each of four suits associated with the coats of arms of Germany, France, Bohemia, and Hungary. German suit (yellow): I Fool, II Messenger, III Courier, IIII Barber. French suit (blue): V Cook, VI Maiden, VII Cup-bearer, VIII Stewardess.

A good hand for a bid of *voltereta* at Hombre. On Spanish cards, the number of breaks in the shorter edge of the frame surrounding the design is an aid to suit identification.

sequences of five to eight respectively. Elder declares first by length, and, if younger can match it, then specifies its top card. If both tie for length and height, neither scores for any sequence—second-bests are not considered. All sequences scored must be specified or shown on request.

Set. A set is three or four cards of the same rank, Tens or higher. A trio scores 3, a quartet (*quatorze*) 14. Elder declares his best set first, which younger either concedes or denies. Whoever has the best set, if any, scores for it and any others sets declared from the same hand. Sets are not shown, and only the rank of a trio need be specified—i.e., its holder need not state which suit is missing.

Repique. A bonus of 60 for *repique* is credited to either player who scores at least 30 in declarations before the other has scored any at all. For this purpose, note that scores accrue strictly in order blank, point, sequence, set, and that equality is no defence. (Example: if both tie for point with six cards worth 57, after which younger counts sequences of six and five, and elder finally declares 'fourteen Aces', then younger gains the repique for making 31 on sequences before elder's 14 became countable, giving him 91 in all.)

Pique. A bonus of 30 for *pique* is credited to elder if he reaches 30 for combinations and tricks before younger has made anything at all. (Younger cannot score *pique* because elder scores 1 for the opening lead. Note also that if elder makes 29 to 0 on combinations, his 1 for leading gives him only 30 for *pique*, not 60 for *repique*.)

Tricks. Elder leads; tricks are played at no trump; and the winner of each one leads to the next. Score 1 point for leading to a trick, 1 for winning a trick led to by the opponent, and 1 for winning the last trick. For winning seven or more tricks, score a bonus of 10. For winning all twelve, score an additional bonus of 30 (making 40, in all, for *capot*).

Game. At Rubicon Piquet, the winner's recorded game score is 100 plus the difference between the two player's end-scores. If, however, the loser fails to reach 100, he is 'rubiconed', and the winner counts 100 plus the total of both end-scores. (Example: For finishing at 123:103, count $100 + (123 - 103) = 120$; for 123:93, count $100 + (123 + 93) = 316$ for game.)

Optional extra. In some traditions a bonus accrues for a hand in which every card counts towards a scoring combination. It is variously known as 'carte rouge' or 'full house', and variously scores either 20 or 50.

Piquet is particularly interesting for two respects in which it aspires to the condition of Chess. In the first place it is asymmetric, in that elder and younger are confronted with strategic requirements as different as those between white and black. As at Chess, the player who moves first has a strong advantage. Elder's five-card exchange improves his chances of making combinations compared with younger's three, and having the first lead usually enables him to bring home all the cards in his point suit. Experience confirms that, between experienced players, elder can expect to make an average of about 28 points to younger's 14, counting combinations and tricks. In the second place, it is almost a game of perfect information. Because each player knows all the cards of which the adversary's twelve are a selection, and because almost everything declared must be shown before it can be scored, each one often enters the play knowing most of the other's hand, and can complete that knowledge within the space of a few tricks. One of the subtleties of the game is 'sinking'— that is, refraining from declaring (and therefore scoring) the whole or part of a combination actually held, in order not to release information that might enable the other to score 10 for cards or 40 for capot.

Piquet is remarkable for having resisted the introduction of trumps for so long. Not only does it not need them: it is actually spoilt by trumps if they are introduced by way of experiment. This is because the primary purpose of trumps in most games is not so much to win tricks as to gain the lead by ruffing or 'trumping in'. The more players there are, the less chance each one has of gaining the lead by any other means. In a two-player game this is of no importance. Guarding one's suits, knowing which to discard from, gaining the lead at a judicious time, are all respects in which the experienced Piquet player will earn '10 for cards' where only average players will divide them. It is not true, as sometimes asserted, that the play for tricks yields 'no surprises'.

But surprises of a different kind are occasioned by sudden reversals of fortune. Elder can win a single hand by a margin of no less than 170—thus: After the discard, he holds A-K-Q in each suit and counts 3 for point (rather improbably). Four tierces add 12 for 15, three quatorzes add 42 for 57, and repique makes it 117. One for leading each of twelve tricks, plus 1 for last and 40 for capot, makes 170 in all. An even higher-scoring hand can be concocted, though winning every trick would require younger's co-operation. Counting 10 for blank, Elder exchanges to four Aces, four Tens, and King, Queen, Jack, Nine of a suit. Point and sequence of six adds 22 for 32, repique makes it 92, and two quatorzes bring him to 120. If permitted to win every trick, he finishes with 173.

Piquet has changed little through the centuries and has generally resisted the temptation to engender deviant offspring. Older French books include adaptations for three (Piquet Normand) and four in partnerships (Piquet Voleur). Auction Piquet, perfected by some English prisoners of (First World) war, has some interesting points. Players can bid for the right to become Elder hand and exchange five cards, which seems sensible enough, though the introduction of negative bids seems to complicate matters unnecessarily. I have experimented with Contract Piquet, in which combinations are scored above and tricks below the line, and winning exactly the number of tricks bid attracts a bonus of 30 for 'counterpique'. Another perversion involves scoring for a point and sequence of nought: a void suit after the exchange counts as a point of 50 for 5, and as a quint ranking between Ace-high and King-high, scoring 10. A way of simplifying and enlivening the play is to score a flat 1 per trick and to award the bonus of 10, not for winning most tricks, but for winning the last one.

Imperial

Although we are supposed to be looking at trumpless games, Piquet must be followed by Imperial, or Piquet with Trumps. A hybrid of Piquet and Triomphe, it is known from the mid-sixteenth century[17] and appears in books of the *Maison académique* tradition from 1659. In 1718 it is described as 'bien en usage encore aujourd'hui', suggesting some surprise at the fact; but Gerver, in *Le Guide Marabout*, expresses no trace of surprise in asserting that it is still (1966) played in the Midi. Vingt-Quatre, an apparent relative of Imperial, can be disregarded as a separate game: the *Maison académique* refers to it as the old name for Imperial, and the only real difference seems to be that it is scored in fours instead of ones.

Imperial resembles Piquet is being primarily for two and played with a 32-card pack (formerly 36), each receiving twelve. Scores are made for point (Ace 11, courts 10, etc.), sequences, and fours-of-a-kind, the holder of the best in each class scoring for it and any others held. There are also bonuses for taking most tricks, for capot, and for a blank, and scoring combinations must be shown to the other player. The differences, however, are quite substantial. There is a trump suit, established by turning the top card of the stock; but there is no exchange, the stock being left face down and out of play.

Four Sevens count, but not Eights or Nines. Ace ranks medially, between Ten and Jack, as at Ecarté. The most fascinating feature of the game is its scoring system. Certain items are scored in single points, others in imperials, one of which is equivalent to six points. (Compare *piedras* and *amarracos* in the game of Mus.) Each player starts with five white counters (points) and five red (imperials) on his left, passing them from left to right as they are scored. Whenever one player makes an imperial, either by adding one point to five already held, or by scoring an imperial feature, his opponent's odd points are all thereby cancelled, any whites on his right being transferred to his left. Part of the skill of the game lies in delaying the announcement of an imperial-scoring feature, as long as may be permitted by the rules, until the opponent has scored sufficient points to make it worth while cancelling them out. The winner is the first to make six imperials.

Rumstick

It's a pity there is no such thing as Rumstick, as it sounds a good name for a game. Its appearance on p. 306 of Taylor's 1865 translation of Boiteau d'Ambly amounts to a misspelling of Rumstich, the German version of a game recorded as Romestecq in French and Roemstek in the Low Countries, to which it seems to have been indigenous. It first appears towards the end of the sixteenth century, notably as Rum und Stich in Fischart's translation of Rabelais.

It was a five-card game for four in partnerships using a 36-card pack—Ace high, no trumps. Before play, stakes were won for declaring various quartets, triplets, and double or single pairs, the combinations bearing such quaint names as *virlicque*, *double ningre*, *triche*, and *village*. There was also a point for winning the last trick, or *stecque* (cf. *stich*, the German for 'trick'). Rausch[18] explains the *rum* element as short for *herum*, 'around'. 'To this day in Alsace', he says, 'the passionate player will accompany his vigorous thumping down of card with a menacing "rum", in expectation that his adversary will not win the trick.'

The *Maison des jeux* ascribes the game to Holland and notes that it is played from left to right (Spanish fashion), besides informing us that the Parisians play it somewhat differently from the inhabitants of Rouen, who more closely follow Dutch procedure. The general feel of the game—declare combinations, play at no trump, score one for last—is reminiscent of Piquet.

15

Five fingers make a hand

To win two tricks signifies nothing, to win three or four signifies one, but to win five is the winning of five.

Cotton, *The Compleat Gamester* (1674)

From primitive games in which trumps are absent, undeveloped, or aberrant, we pass to an ancient and distinctive family of games that may have been the first to feature trumps in the fully fledged sense of the word. Typically, five cards are dealt to each player, the next is turned for trump, and the aim is either, in two-sided games, to win a majority of tricks, or, in round games, to win at least one. Though some of the former give significant scope for the exercise of strategic skill, many of the latter afford so little information as to which cards are in play and where they lie as to be largely games of chance. They therefore tend to be pursued either as gambling games with a positive objective, i.e. to win, or as drinking games with a negative objective, i.e. to avoid being the loser and so having to pay for the next round.

The fact that most European countries exhibit some national or regional folk game based on this pattern, and that such primitive games as Karnöffel, Watten, and Brus are essentially five-card or five-trick games, may suggest that the present family arose from a combination of this idea with that of nominating a whole suit as trumps. Because the family includes the classic game of Ecarté, formerly called Triomphe, it is tempting to trace it back to the Triomphe mentioned frequently in France from the late fifteenth century, notably by Villon and Rabelais. But it would be rash to press this conclusion. For one thing, we have no detailed description of the early French game, and, for another, 'Triomphe' must have referred to a variety of games in those days of pre-standardization. Indeed, some such name—Trump, Triunfo, Triumphus, etc.—also applied in the sixteenth century both to the English ancestor of Whist and to the Spanish ancestor of Solo Whist (Ombre), neither of which is a five-card game. (That the winning of five tricks is significant in Solo and Hombre is probably coincidental.)

Triomphe, Ecarté

The earliest description of a game called Triomphe occurs in the *Maison académique* of 1659, where it is apologetically described, in a passage recalling Cotton on Whist, as so well known as to be hardly worth mentioning.[1] It is played by four with a 52-card pack and includes the device known as 'robbing the pack'—i.e. the holder of the Ace of trumps, or the dealer upon turning it up, may *piller*, literally 'pillage', by exchanging any unwanted card for the turn-up, and may keep doing so for as many successive cards beneath it as may also belong to that suit.

In the eighteenth century Triomphe increasingly came to denote a short-pack two-hander which, in the nineteenth, developed into the following classic that should be known to all well-educated players:

Ecarté (French, nineteenth century). Two players, 32-card pack ranking K-Q-J-A-10-9-8-7 in each suit. Game is five points up, requiring several deals to reach. Deal five each in twos and threes. Turn the next card for trumps, placing it at the bottom of the undealt pack. If it is a King, dealer scores 1 point for it; if not, whoever has or gets the King of trumps scores 1 for declaring it before playing to the first trick. If this brings his total to 5, he wins without further play.

Starting with elder, each in turn may pass or play. If both pass, each discards any number of cards face down and receives a like number from stock. This continues until either player, satisfied with his hand, undertakes to play, thereby prohibiting any further exchanges. The turn-up may not be taken, and if the stock runs out then younger is obliged to play.

Elder starts and the winner of each trick leads to the next. The rules of trick-taking are *F,T,r* (follow suit and head the trick if possible; if unable to follow, trump if possible).

If cards were exchanged, the winner scores 1 point for taking three or four tricks, or 2 for the *vole* (all five). If not, whoever wins three or more scores 2 points regardless.

Ecarté, though highly skilled, became a popular gambling game of Parisian society under the restoration, partly because it was sufficiently fast, exciting, and interesting for kibitzers to place bets on the outcome. It remained popular in French casinos until well into the twentieth century, but has since fallen to Blackjack and Baccara. It also achieved international repute and is still perpetuated in the everyday card-game compendia of the west. Late nineteenth-century card experts such as 'Cavendish' rather spoilt the fun by subjecting Ecarté to gruelling analysis and providing it with a set of *jeux de règle* or optimum procedures—specimen hands on which it was right or wrong to bid depending on the state of the score.

The earliest recorded multi-player version of Triomphe is a seventeenth-century game known originally as l'Homme ('Man'), later as la Bête ('Beast').[2] Anyone who undertook to win three tricks thereby became 'the Man' or lone bidder (cf. Spanish 'Hombre'). He could be challenged by the announcement 'contre', and in the event of failure was then no longer a 'man' but a 'beast', and, being beasted, had to pay a double stake or *bête*, whence the name of the game. (Labet, in German.)

Beastly descendants and relatives cropped up everywhere. Homme d'Auvergne was a simpler variety, Bête Ombrée a more complex one with features relating to Hombre. In Sixte and its partnership version Sizette (*Académie universelle des jeux*, 1718), six players receive six each from a 36 or sometimes 52-card pack and a point is scored for being the first to win three tricks, or for taking the first if everybody wins exactly one. In Guimbarde, a 32 or 52-card curiosity possibly influenced by Poque, and named after a courtly dance, cards rank King high to Seven low except in trumps, which are headed by Guimbarde (♥Q), Roi (♥K), and Fou (♦J). Stakes are won for holding any of these cards, for *mariage* if King and Queen of a suit are held or captured in a trick, for drawing to a flush of three or more cards, for winning a trick with the Fool, and for winning a majority of the five tricks played. In the German Kontraspiel the Unters of acorns and leaves—equivalent to the two black Jacks—count as permanent top trumps, a device ancestral to the 'right and left bowers' of Euchre, and shared by its non-bidding relative *Bester Bube* ('Top Jack', literally 'Best Boy').[3]

The likes of Loo

Ev'n mighty Pam, that kings and queens o'erthrew,
And mow'd down armies in the fights of Loo . . .

Alexander Pope, *The Rape of the Lock* (1711)

In the round-game branch of the five-card family, as opposed to contract games like Homme and Ecarté, once a trump is turned players may either throw the hand in or elect to play, in which case they oblige themselves to win at least one trick. Its classic English representative is Loo, a potentially vicious gambling game first described by Cotton in 1674 and widely played until the late nineteenth century, when it was ousted by the more intelligent contract game of Nap.

Loo—which 'may be plaid several ways', as Cotton himself says, in a rare fit of understatement—is complicated in the description by its extreme variability of rules and formats. Basically these amount to several three-card and several five-card varieties, the latter resembling such Triomphe derivatives as Mouche and Pamphile, the former being more reminiscent of Put and Truco. In three-card Loo (lacking from Cotton's text, but noted by Pepys in the margin of his own copy of it) a spare hand is dealt face down for 'miss', and each in turn may pass, play, or exchange his hand for 'miss' if no one has already done so. Trumps must be led, suit followed, and the trick headed if possible, leaving virtually no choice of play. Each trick won earns a third of the pool, while a player taking none is 'loo'ed' and increases it. In 'Limited Loo' the increment is fixed; in 'Unlimited' it is the size of the existing pool—a device that can cause rapid ruin and did considerable damage to the game's reputation. In some versions a trump is not turned until someone has failed to follow suit and the trick has been quitted; in some, a three-card flush sweeps the pool. Apparent relatives of three-card Loo appear in various guises. Irish Loo is a three-card version without a miss. In the popular Spanish game of Tomate, anyone who fails to take a trick is 'a tomato'—perhaps because its figurative meaning, 'a hole in a stocking', symbolizes zero.[4] In the Uruguayan game of Porrete, which is actually a point-trick hybrid (with Ace 11, Trey 10, etc.), a player taking all three tricks is said to make his opponents *porrete*, 'rotten'. The German Dreiblatt, Zwicken, or Tippen may also be related.[5]

In five-card Loo each won trick earns one fifth of the pool. The game also comes with optional extras, of which the three most significant are (1) robbing the pack; (2) sweeping the pool with a five-card flush; and (3) appointing ♣J as permanent top trump under the name 'Pam'—from the medieval comico-erotic character Pamphilus, literally 'loved by all'. Pam and a four-card flush beats a natural five-flush. It became customary for the holder of Pam to withhold it from the trick, being allowed to renege if necessary, if the Ace of trumps was led and its player remembered to say 'Pam, be civil!' As we shall see later, Pam is the real ancestor of the modern Joker.

Lanterloo, to give it its full name, is described by Cotton in 1674 as a five-card form with flushes but without Pam—perhaps by oversight, as the *OED* quotes a 1685 reference to 'The very Pam at Lanterloo, the name that picks up all.'[6] In terminology it recalls French varieties of Triomphe, from which it may be derived, although the most relevant of them, Mouche, does not appear in an *Académie des jeux* before 1718. Described as a provincial game that has yet to catch on in Paris, Mouche is essentially five-card Loo without Pam but with the five-card flush. This last is known as 'lanterlu', a meaningless cooing refrain used in lullabies. Later versions include the ♣J as top trump and wild card under several names which also designate the game itself, notably Pamphile, whom we have already met, and Mistigris, from Mistigouri, first recorded in the late sixteenth century as a pet-name for cats and sweethearts. 'Mistigris' was later to designate the wild card of Bouillotte and Poker, showing again that the modern Joker is a highly evolved Jack. Whether it was first invented as top trump in a trick-game like Mouche, or as wild card in a vying game like Brelan, remains an open question. I suspect the former, and believe English Loo to reflect seventeenth-century French games possibly deriving from Bête. This is supported by Chatto's quotation (*Facts and Speculations*, p. 138) of a Dutch pamphlet of 1648, in which a game called Labate is positively equated with Lanterluy.

Related to Loo is a very loose-knit group of gambling and drinking games typified by the nineteenth-century French, Alsatian, and Belgian Rams (also spelt Rammes or Rems, German Ramsch, American Rounce). Everyone starts with five counters and pays one into a pool for each trick won. Players withdraw from the game as they run out of counters, and the last one in is the loser. A player who fails to take a trick in any deal has five counters added to his pile. Real excitement comes with the bid of *Rams Général*, which is an undertaking to win every trick. Many varieties of the game[7] include a spare hand equivalent to the 'miss' of Loo, variously known as *la demoiselle, la fille,* or *le mort*. The members of this group range widely, from Spanish Julepe to Czech Pêt Navíc to Sweden's Norrlandsknack. In Swedish Femkort, 'Five-Cards', there is no trump and the aim is simply to win the last trick.[8] The German Mauscheln, Danish Mausel or Mousel, is a four-hand, four-card game with trump turn-up, in which, if no one will bid two tricks, the eldest must win at least two and the others at least one each.[9]

Five Fingers (Spoil Five, Twenty-Five, Forty-Fives, and Maw)

They young lads
So conceity-like and fly with all yon play
Of euchre and such foolish Yankee fads,
And their chat of girls and money all the day
And their dandy pipes with silver on the stem—
Aru! Twenty-five's not good enough for them! . . .

'Dermot O'Byrne' (Arnold Bax)[10]

English-language Hoyles still record an old round game of apparently Gaelic origin called Spoil Five. Whether anyone still plays it as such seems doubtful; but its venerable ancestor, Maw, was a favourite of James VI of Scotland, and its modern cousins include the Irish national game of Twenty-Five and the Canadian game of Forty-Fives. That the Irish word for 'five', *cúig*, also means 'trick' is a curious coincidence whose implications remain to be explored.

Briefly, from two to ten players each pay one chip to a pool and receive five cards. Their aim is either to sweep the pool by winning three or more tricks, or, at least, to prevent anybody else from winning three, thereby 'spoiling' the division of the five tricks and carrying the pool forward to the next round. A player winning the first three may claim the pool without further play, but if he leads to the fourth he is said to 'jink' it, thereby undertaking to win all five, with appropriate rewards or penalties.

This simple idea is decorated with complications of historical interest, including the upside-down ranking of two suits and the attachment of reneging privileges to the three top trumps. These are headed by trump Five—the 'Five card' or 'Five Fingers'—followed by the trump Jack and the Ace of hearts, regardless of the current trump suit. These act like 'matadors' in Hombre, in that they cannot be forced out by the lead of lower trumps. Also suggestive of Spanish origin is the 'jinking' feature, which reflects the Hombre rule whereby the player who does not claim the pool upon winning a majority of tricks obligates himself, by leading to the next, to win the remainder. Certain differences from Hombre are interesting, even puzzling, but do not cast doubt on a relationship between the two. For instance, it is the reverse of Hombre in that the black suits rank upside down rather than the red—as the saying goes, 'highest in red, lowest in black' takes the trick. Again, the rules of trick-play are not those of Hombre or Whist but basically those of All Fours—*ft,tr*—with special rules as to matadors.[11]

Maw is frequently referred to from 1548 onwards, often by means of the distinctive phrase 'heaving at the Maw'. It soon became an upper-class game, being described in 1576 as 'a playe at cardes grown out of the country, from the meanest, into credit at court with the greatest'.[12] This status is affirmed by its further distinction of being the earliest game for which a set of laws survive, namely 'The Groom-porters lawes at Mawe, to be obserued in fulfilling the due orders of the game',[13] a document spoilt for us only by the fact that it does not explicitly describe the rules as opposed to the laws. Only the Ace of hearts is mentioned here as being of any significance, but from a text of 1593[14] we learn that 'Although the knave of trumpes be the seconde carde at Mawe, yet the five-finger may commaunde both him & all the rest of the pack.' Its association with James I (VI of Scotland) is well attested. Weldon's *Court and Character of King James* refers to 'the king's card-holder' at Maw, provoking Chatto into the observation 'His Majesty appears to have played at cards just as he played with affairs of State—in an indolent manner, requiring in both cases someone to hold his cards, if not to prompt him what to play.'[15] In satirical vein, an engraving of 1626 depicts James at Maw with the kings of Denmark and Sweden. The caption includes these lines:

> Denmarke being bold
> Deales freely round; and the first card he showes
> Is the five finger, which, being turn'd up, goes
> Cold to the Muncke's heart; the next Denmarke sees
> Is the ace of hearts . . .
> The Muncke could shew him nothing but the Knave.[16]

The apparently reduced position of the trump Jack is confirmed in Cotton's *The Compleat Gamester* of 1674, where 'Five Cards' is described as 'an Irish game, much play'd in that Kingdom . . . The five fingers (*alias*, five of trumps) is the best Card in the pack; the Ace of Hearts is next to that, and the next is the Ace of trumps, then the Knave . . .'. By this time Maw was *passé* and evidently dropping out of English consciousness. It does not return to print before Pardon's 'Hoyle' of 1863, now under the name Spoil Five (first recorded 1839)[17] and with the Jack restored to his former glory.

When Spoil Five is played by two individuals or partnerships, one side is bound to take a majority of tricks. In these circumstances the pool is replaced by a soft score of five points for taking three or four tricks or ten for taking all five, and the game is known either as Five and Ten, or as Twenty-Five or Forty-Five depending on the agreed target. Twenty-Five remains the target of the Irish game. Forty-Five was carried to or evolved in Canada and (especially) Nova Scotia, of which it may now be described as the national card game. Under the influence of Bridge, it later developed into the partnership game of Auction Forty-Fives—in which the forty-five ceases to bear any literal significance, as the basic scores are five per trick and five for the highest trump in play, and the game target is 120.

Jucker, Euchre, and Joker

'Those who are familiar with life in the United States', wrote R. F. Foster[18] in 1909, 'must be aware of the enormous popularity that the game of Euchre enjoys, in one form and another. Before the advent of Bridge it was the national game if we omit Poker . . . Even now, it is not uncommon for thousands of Euchre players to assemble at any of the games given in aid of various charities. There were 1260 players at the Hotel Astor last March, in that year of Bridge, 1908, all playing Euchre.'

Euchre has since been thoroughly eclipsed by Bridge and seems now to be confined to the north-eastern states of America, where it probably originated. Its introduction is generally attributed to the 'Pennsylvanian Dutch' (German immigrants), though the earliest American account I know of it (Boston, 1857) says 'Formerly it was but little known except in the West and South.' An earlier date is suggested, albeit humorously, by a correspondent to *The Westminster Papers* of 1 June 1875, who says of 'Yewker': 'This ill-bred game ov kards is about twenty-seven years old. It was first diskovered by the deck hands on a Lake Erie steamboat, and handed down by them tew posterity in awl its juvenile beauty. It is generally played by four persons, and owes mutch ov its absorbingness to the fackt that you kan talk, and drink, and chaw and cheat while the game is advancing.' Earlier still, however, 'Uker', together with Seven Up and Poker, is the subject of an incident described by Joe Cowell as taking place on a steamboat trip from Louisville to New Orleans in 1829.[19]

Underlying Euchre is the Alsatian game of Jucker or Juckerspiel.[20] Modern Euchre is characterized by the fact that its top cards are (1) the Joker, or Best Bower, (2) the trump Jack, or Right Bower, (3) the other Jack of the same colour as trumps, or Left Bower. 'Bower', rhyming with 'flower', represents German *Bauer*, Dutch *boer*, both meaning primarily 'farmer' and secondarily 'Jack'. Before the Joker was introduced, the top Jack was also known as the Best Bower. Proto-Euchre, or Jucker, evidently equates with the German Bester

Bube recorded in 1808 and the Dutch 'Beste Boeren or Lanterlui' (1828),[21] and therefore ultimately derives from a variety of Loo.

Euchre is thus the game for which the Joker was invented, probably in the 1850s. This honour is sometimes claimed for Poker; but 53-card Poker is, I believe, only first recorded in *The American Hoyle* of 1875, where the 'blank card accompanying every pack' is referred to not as 'Joker' but as 'Mistigris'. The same volume, however, is apparently the first to describe a game called 'Railway Euchre', which

is played with a pack of thirty-three cards, consisting of a regular Euchre pack, and an additional blank card, which is usually called the Joker, or imperial trump. Instead of the blank or specimen card, there will be found in some packs an extra card, printed with a suitable device, and intended expressly for use in this game.

Although the spare card originally bore a variety of devices, there can be no doubt from surviving packs that it was associated with Euchre from the first. Hargrave[22] describes a card from a pack of 1862 depicting a Tiger and labelled 'Highest Trump', and another from 1865 inscribed 'This card takes either Bower', followed by a device and the further explanation 'Imperial Bower, or Highest Trump Card'. Although she does not state whether these were 33 or 53-card packs, the 1865 card is elsewhere confirmed as belonging to the short (Euchre) pack.[23] Western manufacturers generally began to incorporate a spare card in the 1880s, still under a variety of names and designs, and it was presumably only when they were customary in full-length packs that Poker-players started using them as wild cards. It was not until the end of the century that the depiction of Joker as a kind of court jester became widespread. We may therefore surmise that the visual image was inspired by what the card was already called, and suppose that the name itself was suggested by the title Euchre, especially under its German spelling 'Jucker'.

Euchre does not appear in English Hoyles before that edited by Pardon in 1863, to which it is briefly appended along with the newly discovered games of Bezique and Spoil Five, and the Joker variation first appears in the anonymous *Euchre: How to Play it* of 1886. It is still played in the south of England, the Channel Islands, and especially in Cornwall. Jono Wardle, my Cornish correspondent, describes a 25- or 21-card form with Nine or Ten low, the spade Two as top trump or 'Benny', and tricks played as at All Fours—*ft, tr.*

Classic four-hand partnership Euchre runs as follows:

Euchre (USA, nineteenth–twentieth century). Deal five each from a 32-card pack and turn the next for trumps. Each in turn may pass or accept the trump, thereby obligating his side to win at least three tricks. If the first suit is accepted, dealer may exchange the turn-up for any card in his hand before play begins. If not, it is turned down, and each in turn may pass or offer to play in another suit with the same obligation. If all pass again, the cards are shuffled and dealt anew. Whoever initiates the game by accepting or nominating trumps may offer to play alone for a higher score, in which case his partner lays his cards face down without playing and the bidder must take at least three tricks alone.

The first trick is led to from the dealer's left, or, in a lone game, from the soloist's left. Whist rules apply, i.e. follow suit if possible, otherwise play any card. The best card wins and the winner of each trick leads to the next. Cards rank A-K-Q-J-10-9-8-7 in each suit except as modified by trumps. In trumps the top cards are the Jack (Right Bower), followed by the other Jack of the same colour (Left Bower), followed by Ace etc.

The *point* is three or four tricks, the *march* all five. If successful, the bidding side scores 1 for the point, 2 for the march if played in partnership, or 4 for the march if played alone. If not, it is *euchred* and the other side scores 2. Game is normally 5 up (sometimes 7, sometimes 10).

Of many variants, Hasenpfeffer ('Jugged Hare') is a particularly interesting partnership game played with 25 cards including the Best Bower but lacking Sevens and Eights. Each receives six and the last is left face down. Players in turn bid and overbid without naming a suit until a contract is established. If all pass, the holder of the Best Bower must bid three. The bidding side scores 1 per trick actually taken if it makes its contract, otherwise it loses the value of its bid. The other side scores 1 per trick taken in any case. In some accounts the declarer may pick up the odd card in exchange for a discard. That this can hardly be the original idea of the game is suggested by its title, for 'Hasenpfeffer' presumably relates to the German expression 'Da liegt der Hase im Pfeffer'—literally, 'There lies the hare in the hotpot', a phrase that rises naturally to the lips when the identity of the undealt card is finally revealed.

Call-Ace Euchre is a good alliance game for four to seven players, in which the bidder, besides nominating trumps, names another suit the holder of whose highest card will be his partner. The partner may only reveal himself by playing that card when legally able. As some cards are out of play, the bidder occasionally gets to the end of a deal only to find that he has been partnering himself all the time.

In his 1904 treatise on the game, R. F. Foster specifies Australia as its country of origin. This connection requires further exploration, for the popularity of Euchre in Australia persists to this day in an advanced form of the game entitled, from its target score, Five Hundred.

Five Hundred

Five Hundred, also known as Bid Euchre, was copyrighted by the US Playing Card Company in the 1890s. Whoever devised it—and Foster is a likely suspect—seems to have taken his inspiration from the contemporary ousting of Whist by Bridge. Five Hundred was designed to be a sociable game for two to six players, in character more advanced than Euchre but less intellectual than Bridge. It retains the bowers of Euchre, including Joker as best, but, like Bridge, puts all the cards into play and varies the value of game contracts according to the suit selected as trumps. The actual suit order is that of original Bridge—spades, clubs, diamonds, hearts, and no trump, with a nullo or misère bid later added as an optional extra. The original schedule had the demerit that a bid of a smaller number of tricks in a higher suit could overcall one of a higher number in a lower suit, some contracts having the same value as others. An improved schedule, the Avondale, was copyrighted in 1906. Five Hundred enjoyed considerable success at this time, many Euchre-players going over to it in much the same way that Whist-players were going over to Bridge.

A distinctive feature of the game is that each receives ten cards, no matter how many are playing, and three are laid aside as a widow through which the declarer may exchange. Three therefore play with the original 33-card Euchre pack, four with 43, and five with 53 cards. For six players, the Australians manufacture a special 63-card pack, which includes—besides a Joker in the form of a kookaburra or laughing jackass—four Elevens, four Twelves, and two red Thirteens. (Great fun may be had in carrying one of these cards around and suddenly plonking down a Thirteen of hearts in the middle of a game of Bridge.)

Five Hundred is a good three-hander, though my Australian correspondents insist that it is at its best in four-hand partnership play.

Nap

We played penny Nap after supper. We played for about an hour and a half, after which time George had won fourpence and Harris and I had lost exactly twopence each. We thought we would give up gambling then . . . It breeds an unhealthy excitement when carried too far. (J. K. Jerome, *Three Men in a Boat* (1889).)

Widely recorded in European gamebooks as a simplification of Euchre—though 'an elaboration of Rams' would be more like it— Napoleon has long enjoyed particular social status as Britain's national five-card game, though never under its full name but always shortened to 'Nap'. In 1890 Baxter-Wray wrote[24] 'It was introduced into this country from the United States . . . about 1865, although it is recorded that the game had previously been played for high stakes at some of the more notorious gambling clubs.' He may, however, be confusing Nap with Euchre, or possibly Cinch, with which it shares the feature of declaring trumps by 'pitching' one to the first trick. I don't think Nap has ever been current in America, or that it appears in American Hoyles before those of the twentieth century produced with an eye to the British market. The timing may be more accurate. Nap is noted as 'comparatively new' in 1881,[25] and evidently commemorates Napoleon III, who retired to Britain after losing the Franco-Prussian War in 1870, and has since been described as 'the nearest thing Europe ever produced to a Mississippi river-boat gambler'.[26]

> *Nap* (*English, late nineteenth century*). Two to seven players use a 52-card pack ranking Ace high, Two low. Deal five each. Each in turn may pass or raise the bidding in the following series: one, two, three, miz, four, five (= 'Nap'). The highest bidder shows trumps by leading one to the first trick and must take at least as many tricks as bid. From one to four tricks win or lose the same number of pence. Miz, a no-trump misère, wins or loses three pence, and Nap wins 10 from, or loses five to, each opponent.
>
> As optional extras not suitable for less than five players, Nap may be overcalled by 'Wellington', a five-trick bid that pays 10 each if lost, and Wellington by 'Blücher', also a five-trick bid but paying out 20 each if lost.

Nap has engendered inevitable variants. In Peep Nap one or more players may, for a price, peep at the top card of stock and exchange it for an unwanted card from hand. In Widow Nap, or Sir Garnet, a spare hand is dealt from which a player bidding five may draw good cards in exchange for bad ones. In Purchase or Ecarté Nap players may purchase fresh cards in exchange for discards. In Seven and Nine-card Nap either the hand is stripped to five before play begins or the range of bids is extended to Naps of seven or nine. The purpose of Pool Nap is self-explanatory. Dedicated Nap-players nowadays play with a pack stripped of sufficient lower numerals to reduce the undealt cards to about five, thus augmenting the skill factor by diminishing the element of uncertainty. In French, Dutch, and Scandinavian Hoyles Napoleon is normally described as played with a stripped pack unless seven or more take part.

An unusual cross between Nap and Rams is represented by the Swedish game of Rödskägg, i.e. 'Redbeard', or 'Barbarossa'. Six cards each are dealt from a 52-card pack; everyone may bid, with 'Redbeard' equivalent to 'Wellington' in Nap; and those who do so will all score if successful. But pressure is exerted to bid high by virtue of the fact that the highest bidder has the opening lead—a distinct advantage, since, like so many Scandinavian tricksters, Redbeard is played at no trump. Each starts with ten counters and pays one to a pool for each won trick, the winner being the first out of counters. All penalties— including one for picking cards up before the dealer knocks to announce completion of the deal—count five against, whence its alternative title Fem Opp, 'Five Up'.

16

From Hombre to Solo

Think not when Woman's transient breath is fled,
That all her vanities at once are dead:
Succeeding vanities she still regards,
And tho' she plays no more, o'erlooks the cards.
Her joy in gilded chariots when alive,
And love of *Ombre* after death survive.

Alexander Pope, *The Rape of the Lock* (1711)

I don't go a bundle on that.

Unenthusiastic response of Solo Whist players

Various nations play a game called Solo, though the games so called
are as varied as the nations that play them. English Solo is more
widely but less accurately known as Solo Whist; American Solo, also
called Slough, or Sluff, goes back to German Tarock; German Solo
comes from French Quadrille; and Spanish Solo is a cross between
Hombre and Manille. But for all their apparent differences they share
a common base, and this, when reached, reveals a number of other
games conforming to it which are *not* called Solo—notably the
ancestral Spanish game of Hombre, and its immediate but now extinct
descendants Quadrille and Boston Whist.

The underlying format is as follows. Instead of turning a card for
trump and leaving everyone to battle for as many tricks as they can
make, players 'bid' for the right to nominate the trump best suited
to the hand they have been dealt. The highest bidder, in return for
that privilege, contracts to win a minimum number of tricks by
playing against the combined forces of the other players, usually
alone, but sometimes with the assistance of a temporary partner, or
ally.

It helps to refer to the lone player as the 'soloist' and to describe
games of this sort as 'Solo' (although, strictly speaking, 'solo' is a
technical term for playing with one's hand of cards as dealt, without

first trying to improve it by an exchange of cards). Alternatively, they might be described as 'alliance games', since, although everyone plays for himself in the long run, at each deal two or more will be playing co-operatively together as temporary allies. This puts them half-way between 'cut-throat' games like Hearts or Loo, where players only play for themselves, and fixed-partnership games like Whist and Bridge, where partners are determined at start of play and remain constant throughout. I believe it is because alliance and partnership games appeal to different temperaments that Solo players tend not to be Bridge players, and why Foster's attempt to turn Bridge into an alliance game ('Pirate Bridge') was stillborn. Charles Lamb, in a humorous essay of 1830 entitled *Sarah Battle's Opinions on Whist*, gives eloquent expression to a preference for the partnership nature of Whist over the alliance principle of Quadrille:

Whist . . . was a long meal; not like Quadrille, a feast of snatches . . . The skirmishes of Quadrille, she would say, reminded her of the petty ephemeral embroilments of the little Italian states, depicted by Machiavel; perpetually changing postures and connections; bitter foes today, sugared darlings tomorrow; kissing and scratching in a breath;—but the wars of Whist were comparable to the long, steady, deep-rooted, rational, antipathies of the great French and English nations.

As we shall see, the idea of bidding to establish a contract involving one's own choice of trumps, now associated chiefly with Bridge, was first invented and explored in the realm of solo or alliance games, and has subsequently spread to every type of trickster from Whist to Tarot. Here we concentrate on the original family ranging from ancestral Hombre to modern Solo Whist. They are typically plain-trick games, in which most of the pack, if not all, is dealt out amongst the players, thereby leaving little to chance, and enhancing the element of skill.

Hombre (Ombre)

A game of cards that the better sort of people play three together at . . .
> Vanbrugh, *The Provok'd Husband* (1727)

A game for card gourmets and snobs . . .
> Grupp, *Kartenspiele* (1975)

Ombre, originally pronounced 'umber', is an anglicization of *Hombre*, which in turn is the Spanish for 'man' and denotes the highest bidder or lone player. Equally peculiar is the German equivalent Lomber, from the French form l'Hombre. The game in general is best referred to as Hombre, with other spellings reserved for particular national varieties of it. Towards the end of the seventeenth century it became the greatest card game of the western world, remaining so until well into the nineteenth, when it found itself whittled away by Whist and ultimately buried by Bridge.

Hombre originated in sixteenth-century Spain as a four-player game. By the mid-seventeenth century Spanish players were forsaking the original for a three-player adaptation called Renegado ('traitor') and its five-hand equivalent Cinquillo. It was just at this period that the game spread to France, Italy, and England, doing so in its three-handed form but under its four-handed title, Hombre. In the following description, based on various sources including an invaluable study of the game and its history by Thierry Depaulis,[1] I use the traditional English terms of the game, which are corrupt versions of the French forms of the original Spanish.

Hombre (Renegado), (Spanish French English, late seventeenth century). Three players contribute equally to a pool and receive nine cards each from a 40-card pack (lacking Eights, Nines, and Tens). The undealt thirteen form a face-down stock.

From high to low, black-suit cards rank K-Q-J-7-6-5-4-3-2, red-suit cards K-Q-J-(A)-2-3-4-5-6-7. The three highest trumps are always:

(1) *Spadille*, the Ace of spades;
(2) *Manille*, the nominally lowest trump (Two in black, Seven in red);
(3) *Basto*, the Ace of clubs.

These are called *matadors*, and have special powers in play. If a red suit is trump, the fourth best card is its Ace, called *Punto*, but it is not a matador.

Each in turn may pass or declare himself 'hombre', thereby undertaking to win an individual majority of tricks in return for choosing trumps. He may play either a simple game, in which case he announces trumps, makes any number of discards, and draws replacements from the top of the stock; or a 'solo', in which case he announces trumps and plays the hand as dealt. A bid of solo overcalls a simple game. If all pass, anyone holding ♠A is obliged to play a simple game (*spadille forcée*).

Players must follow suit if possible, otherwise may play any card. The privilege of matadors is that they cannot be forced out by the lead of lower trumps. If a lower trump is led, a player holding no trumps but matadors may 'renege' by playing any suit. Only if a higher matador is led must he play a lower matador if he has no other trump.

Hombre wins by taking more tricks than either opponent individually—i.e. five tricks always wins, and four wins if the others split three–two. (In play, therefore, an opponent who plays a potentially winning card may instruct his partner not to cap it, as it is only necessary for one of them to beat the soloist.) If *hombre* takes the first five tricks straight off he may claim the pool without further play, but if instead he leads to the sixth, he thereby undertakes to win all nine ('the vole').

If *hombre* loses he is 'beasted'. If tricks are tied (4–4-1 or 3–3-3) he loses by *puesta* and doubles the pool, but if either opponent wins a majority he loses by *codille* and pays that stake to the winner. Individual payments are also made, one way or the other, in respect of special feats or outcomes such as playing solo or winning the vole.

Hombre entered England with the return of king and cavaliers from foreign parts in 1660, as suggested by a political tract of that year metaphorically entitled *The Royal Game of Ombre*.[2] Catherine of Bragança, Charles II's wife from 1662, was a keen player, as were so many denizens of high society that by the end of that year Parliament had proposed to pass an Act against the playing of Ombre, or at least to limit the stakes to £5, a proposition 'received with ridicule'.[3] In 1665 Pepys remarked 'If [my Lord Treasurer] can have his £8000 per annum and a game at l'ombre he is well.' The year 1662 also sees the first published description in English of 'The Noble Spanish Game, called l'Ombre' in Cotgrave's *The Wits Interpreter*, later plagiarized in Cotton's *Compleat Gamester*. Hombre is well known in English literature from Pope's description of a game played by Belinda, the heroine of *The Rape of the Lock*, which provides an authentic card-by-card account of the play of the hands. The reference is of further interest for confirming that Hombre, like its successor Quadrille (and, indeed, Bridge), was especially popular with women. But the Hombre bubble, like the South Sea Bubble, was not to last. Though still accounted 'a royal game' in Seymour's *Court Gamester*, published in 1719 'for the use of the young princesses', Hombre was already being challenged in both England and France by its French four-player development Quadrille. Hoyle's 1745 treatise on Quadrille ignores Hombre, which Barrington declares 'almost forgotten' in 1787; and its absence from scores of nineteenth-century pseudo-Hoyles makes

Lord Aldenham's privately printed treatise of 1874 read like the work of a lovable old eccentric.

Elsewhere, Hombre is first recorded in Italy in 1671 and forms the subject of a treatise published at Rome in 1674.[4] This year also sees the first French account of the game, entitled *Le Jeu de l'Hombre* and generally attributed to de Méré, in a text which finds itself reprinted, plagiarized, and translated throughout Europe for many years to come. De Méré confirms the Spanish origin and remarks that its popularity in Paris is assured, Maria Theresa being clearly smitten by the new game, even if Louis XIV finds it tedious.

In Spain itself three-hand Renegado is first described in 1663 (Madrid), four-hand Hombre in 1669 (Saragossa), and five-hand Cinquillo some twenty years later. The author of the four-hand description—an improbable 'Dr Franco-Furt'—claims to have based his text on a now-lost treatise published at Barcelona in 1631. It certainly appears consistent with such details as may be gleaned from a variety of earlier sources, including Lope de Vega (1618, 1625), and, also in 1625, a remarkably detailed *auto sacramental*, or mystery play, in which Christ and the World play against Death and the Devil. The players, in fixed partnerships, are dealt nine cards each, the last four forming a face-down stock of which the top is turned for trump. A player declares himself *hombre* in the turned suit by inviting whoever has the trump Ace to 'rob', i.e. to exchange an unwanted card for the trump turn-up. Partners keep their tricks separately, the object of *hombre*'s partner being to ensure (in his own interests) that *hombre* wins an individual majority of them. Although this game includes top-trump matadors, either 'Franco-Furt' in 1669, or his source of 1631, disdainfully observes that ill-bred folk still play without them, implying that they are of fairly recent origin.

Depaulis[5] derives four-hand Hombre from Triumphus Hispanicus, or Spanish Trump, as described in the *Dialogues* of Juan-Luis Vives in 1539. This was played with a 48-card pack, with nine cards each, a stock of twelve and a trump turn-up. There are no matadors, but the 'robbing' feature is foreshadowed by the fact that if the turn-up is an Ace or a face it reverts to the dealer. It bears resemblances both to Triomphe or 'French Ruff', and to Cotton's 'English Ruff-and-Honours, *alias* Slamm' (52 cards, 12 each, 4-card stock, trump turn-up, and 'ruff' or 'rob the pack').

Why was the game that swept seventeenth-century Europe under the name Hombre not the four-handed original but its three-handed adaptation, Renegado? Dummett[6] ascribes the latter's success to its introduction of an entirely novel and captivating feature: that of bidding for the right to name the suit, an evolutionary step which he places on a par with that of the invention of trumps. Hitherto, players could only either accept or refuse the turned suit. Now, they were required to assess the hand before deciding whether and what to entrump, a requirement that opened up new realms of skill and judgement.

At first, the purpose of bidding was to choose between variable conditions under which the soloist was to achieve the invariable objective of winning most tricks. A player could only overcall or outbid another by making the conditions more difficult for himself. Hombre-players were quick to explore this idea by ingeniously extending the range of conditions to choose from. In *gascarille*, described by Seymour in 1719 as a bid admitted when all have passed, the soloist discards all but one from the hand, draws eight replacements from stock, and then announces trumps. Variations on this theme, including the retention of two cards or none, reappear throughout European card literature under a variety of names.[7] In *tourné*, *voltereta*, *vuelta*, or English 'whim' (Seymour, 1719), the soloist turns the top card of stock and accepts its suit as trump.

Later, the concept was expanded to vary the objective of play, as well as or instead of the conditions. Players could then overcall by offering to take a greater number of tricks, or to perform special feats such as taking none at all, or exactly one. Best known is the bid of *devole*, *contrabola*, or 'countervole', an undertaking to lose every trick, and the original of misère in Solo Whist and null in Skat. Its first recorded appearance is traced by Dummett to the 1757 edition of *Das Neue königliche l'Hombre*.[8]

All these variations led, of course, to the development of new and distinctive games, leaving three-handed Hombre soon to fall out of favour, at least in France and England. It retained, however, a patchy following in Germany throughout the nineteenth century and in the Netherlands until perhaps the Second World War, and is still played in Denmark. In Spain itself, Renegado survived under the name Tresillo (emphasizing three-handedness, cf. Italian Terziglio), until perhaps the Civil War. In Portugal it survived into the twentieth century under the name Voltarete. Da Silva, in *Tratado do Jôgo de Boston* (1942), explains that it reached Portugal in 1780–90, when the Spanish game was currently known as Tresillo de voltereta ('somersault'), following the introduction of the *tourné* contract. Latin Americans from Mexico to Patagonia played it throughout the nineteenth century under the names Tresillo and Rocambor. It has since been displaced by Spanish Solo, a hybrid of Tresillo and the point-trick game of Malilla, which we shall come to in due course.

Quadrille

It will not be unnecessary to acquaint the Reader, that the following Game of QUADRILLE has been about two years, and is at present, the favourite game at the French Court . . . QUADRILLE is more amusing and entertaining than OMBRE, or any other Game on the Cards; either because ev'ry Deal is play'd out, or that it better suits the Genius of the Ladies, to whom Complaisance and good Manners must Prejudice the Gentlemen in its favour. (Anon., *The Game of Quadrille, or Ombre by Four* (1726).)

Triangular tables specially designed for the play of Hombre may still be found lurking in dark corners of obscure museums, but they evidently proved insufficient to fix the game in its three-handed form. In France, Hombre soon found itself swept aside by an adaptation for four, thus enabling more people to share in the enjoyment at any one time, and increasing a strong player's potential winnings by up to fifty per cent.

One might expect the new four-hander to represent a reversion to Spain's original form of Hombre. In fact, the Spanish dimension had long since been forgotten, and 'Quadrille' was modelled on the earlier five-hand game of Quintille, first mentioned by Mme de Sévigné in 1680[9] and itself based on Spanish Cinquillo, or Cinqueño. There was a technical reason for this. In a three-hander, the player of a simple game could first improve the hand by drawing from stock, and such a bid could be overcalled by offering to play 'solo', or *sans prendre*— 'without exchanging'. But Quadrille left no stock to draw from, all forty cards being now dealt out, and this considerably reduced the chances of anyone's receiving a hand strong enough to play alone against the other three. The answer was to borrow a lower bid, one that had already been developed for the old five-hander, whereby the soloist played with the assistance of an ally, which she found by calling for a King not in her own hand. Its holder became the soloist's partner, sharing in her gain or loss, but was not allowed to reveal herself except by playing the King when the opportunity arose. This new bid—*demande* or 'ask-leave' (sc. 'to play', because the bidder could be overcalled by a solo)—is the ultimate origin of 'prop and cop' in Solo Whist, and was to engender a whole family of Tarot games typified by Austria's Königsrufen.

Later, perhaps by 1735, two other significant features were added. The first was the bid of *médiateur*, ranking between a *demande* and a *sans prendre*, whereby the soloist played alone after nominating a King (or a Queen if she held all four), and taking it in exchange for an unwanted card from her own hand. The other was the appointment of a *couleur favorite*, or suit of preference, established either for each deal by revealing the last card dealt, or for the whole session by cutting before play. Any given bid 'in ordinary' could be overcalled by the same bid 'in preference', and would then be played for double stakes. Herein lie the origins of auction by suit hierarchy as subsequently developed in Boston, Skat, and Bridge.

The new game became known as Médiateur in France. The English continued to call it Quadrille, under which name it remained popular with Englishwomen until the end of the century, when revolutionary francophobia combined with the assault of Whist to drive it into limbo. In 1822 the author of *Quadrille Elucidated*—an unlikely sounding 'Q. Quanti'—wrote 'though in England it is not at present so much in vogue as Whist . . . yet with many it continues to be decidedly a favourite'. By 1858 Thackeray observes, in *The Virginians*: 'Card-playing is greatly out of mode: very likely there are not six ladies of fashion in London who know the difference between Spadille and Manille.' Like so many once fashionable games, it lingered longer in the provinces than in the metropolis, as suggested by Lord Aldenham in 1874: 'Quadrille . . . blooms only in Holland and in some old-fashioned nooks of England (I played it at Oxford in 1840).'

French Quadrille, or Médiateur, underwent a variety of developments in its native country. One lot took the form of adaptations for different numbers of players. Piquemedrille was a two-player version hybridized with elements of Piquet. Five indulged in 'Quintille nouveau', as opposed to the 'ancien' variety, while Sextille, needless to say, was for six. Three players might have been expected to stick to original Hombre. But no—they now invented Trédrille. As Seymour explains in *The Court Gamester*:

There are some people who will play at this branch of Ombre by dealing out *Ten* cards apiece between *Three*, and this, in downright *Irish* phraseology, they call *Three-handed Quadrille*; which in plain English is *Four-handed Ombre* played by *Three* persons. But this silly manner rather deserves our ridicule than any other notice.

One is inclined to agree. It was played with a 30-card pack made by stripping out ♥6 and all diamonds but the King—diamonds then being appointed the suit of preference. A bid in preference, naturally, overbids anything, since it contains only three trumps: *spadille*, *manille* (♦K), and *basto*.

Further development lay in the proliferation of highly imaginative bids, including some borrowed or adapted from Hombre. 'Quanti' enumerates: (1) Forced spadille; (2) Alliance ('ask-leave'); (3) Dimidiator (*médiateur*); (4) Casco, or Respect, whereby a player holding Spadille and Basto could call a partner by means of a King, that partner nominating trumps; (5) Grandissimo, with Spadille and Basto the only trumps; and (6) Nemo—a misère with only Spadille and Basto as trumps. Each was separately biddable in or out of the preferred suit, and there existed also a complicated series of side-payments for special holdings of trumps. The interaction of all these features required the learner to master (or mistress) such everyday rules of the road as 'A beast in grandissimo is always codille: it admits of the vole; and in its rank can only be superseded by a vole announced, or a nemo.'

German Solo and French Alliance

German Solo is a neat little descendant of Quadrille forming a pleasant introduction to games of the stock of Hombre.

Four players use a 32-card pack basically ranking A-K-Q-J-10–9-8– 7, except that the top trump is ♣Q (*spadille*), followed by trump Seven (*manille*) and ♠Q (*baste*). The aim is to win at least five of the eight tricks played. The bids are: (1) *Frage* (*demande*), in which the soloist announces trumps and calls for a partner by naming an Ace not in his own hand, the partner revealing himself only by playing it at the earliest opportunity; (2) *Großfrage*, the same, except that the partner chooses the trump suit, which may not be that of the called Ace; and (3) Solo, a self-explanatory bid which is obligatory for anyone holding both black Queens and all four Aces, and optional otherwise. If all pass, the Spadille holder must play *Großfrage*. As in the old game, the bidding side either stops after winning the first five tricks straight off, or leads to the sixth as an undertaking to win all eight (*Allstich*, or *tout*). The suit entrumped at first deal remains the suit of preference for the rest of the session. Strict rules of trick-taking apply—*F,T,r*—but the top trumps do not have matador status. *Frage* and enforced *Großfrage* win 2, *Großfrage* and Solo win 4, *Allstich* is worth 8, or 16 if bid before the opening lead. All these values are doubled if made in the favourite suit. (From Grupp, *Kartenspiele*, 1975. Older versions are more elaborate and varied.)

German Solo may derive from a form of 40-card Quadrille played in eighteenth-century Germany under the name Kaufquadrille, or 'Purchase Quadrille', in which each received eight cards and there was a stock of eight for the soloist to exchange through ('purchase' from). A curiosity of German Solo is that nineteenth-century reports exist of a special 40-card Solo pack containing eight cards in each of the traditional German suits plus a fifth one of 'flowers', though no record exists of how it was used. It may have been devised for a five-handed version of the game.

Alliance, a 52-card modification of Médiateur, is more obscure. It is described in several nineteenth-century German compendia as an old French game, but is not actually attested in French sources. Four players (five and six-hand versions are also described) receive twelve cards each, leaving a stock of four, of which the topmost is turned for 'preference'. The aim is to win at least seven tricks; or, in case of a six-all tie, either (*a*) to have captured the *Fahne* ('Banner'), i.e. the Three of trumps if black or Nine if red; or, should it lie in the stock, (*b*) to have captured the majority of honours, i.e. King, Queen, and Jack of trumps.[10]

The bids are (1) *alliance*, same as *médiateur*; (2) *couleur*, the same but 'in preference'; (3) *levée*; (4) solo. In *levée*, the soloist turns up a card of stock to determine trumps, may then discard and draw from stock to improve the hand, and finally calls a King to partner. Solo can be overcalled by a solo in preference. In the unlikely event of two players' bidding solo in the same suit, the second bidder announces *résistance*, whereupon the game is played all against all and determined by a majority of tricks, or, if equal, by capturing the banner. A successful *alliance* wins 2 units, *levée* or solo 4 units, doubled in case of *résistance*. Winning the first seven tricks earns a bonus of 2, winning all twelve earns six. There are side-payments of 1 for capturing the King of trumps, 2 for the Queen, 3 for the Jack, and 4 for the Banner.

The peculiar definition of the Banner, plus the fact that Ace is high only in trumps, seem to imply the upside-down ranking of two suits as at Hombre–Quadrille; but this is nowhere explicitly stated. Hoffmann, in *Der Meister in allen Kartenspielen*, says 'The order of cards is King, Queen, Jack, Ten, Nine, Eight, Seven, Six, etc., and the Ace—except in trumps—counts only as 1 and comes in red suits after the Jacks, in black ones after the 2; but in trumps it is the highest and beats the King.' If this means red suits rank upside-down, then the Banner is always the second-lowest trump.

Boston Whist

By the late eighteenth century English players were forsaking Quadrille for partnership Whist. In France, Quadrille-playing society was finding itself rapidly decimated by the guillotine. This left room for the development of a new game of the same 'alliance' genre as Quadrille but of simpler, more populist structure and free from what must have been regarded as the effete associations of an aristocratic women's game. Such was Boston Whist, 'le whist bostonien', which became the great nineteenth-century alternative to Quadrille almost everywhere in the western world except Britain—where, however, it eventually emerged as Solo Whist, a somewhat simplified descendant.

Boston is usually, but misleadingly, represented as a variation of classical partnership Whist made by abandoning the fixed-partnership principle. It is better regarded as a solo or alliance game created by grafting the simpler mechanics of Whist on to the structural stock of Quadrille. Whist provided the 52-card pack, with natural ranking from Ace high to Two low throughout, uncomplicated by the existence of top-trump matadors with special powers, and possibly the trump turn-up. These are all superficialities. The essence of the game is its solo/alliance nature and varied range of bids, in which respect Boston retains rather the thrill of Quadrille than the twist of Whist.

The origins of Boston are shrouded in dubious legend. It is claimed that Bostonians under siege in 1775 sought to relieve their tedium and political frustrations by divorcing English Whist from fixed partnerships and stressing the solo or 'independence' element—a claim supported by reference to additional bids under such names as Philadelphia, Souveraine, and Concordia. A survey of nineteenth-century game compendia, however, shows that most of them were introduced long after the event in question. Another view credits the game to officers of the allied French fleet then lying off Marblehead. Two little islands in the harbour are known as Little Misery and Big Misery, by which, it is said, the bids of *petite misère* and *grande misère* were inspired; but these, too, prove under examination to be later additions. Yet another claim is that Benjamin Franklin, who was a keen player and is even said to have invented the game, introduced it to the court of Louis XVI on a trip to Versailles in 1767.[11] More likely than any of these romantic flights of fancy is that it developed in France and took its name and inspiration from current events in America, to which it had become a welcome export before the signing of the Franco-American alliance of 1778. (In this connection it is perhaps only an attractive red herring to note that Trappola cards were known in parts of Europe as 'Boston-Karten', from the suit of *bastoni*, or clubs.)[12]

Two early forms of Boston are described in the *Almanach des jeux* of 1783. In *le whischt bostonien* the last card is turned for trump and no other suit can be nominated. The lowest bid is a *demande* or 'ask-leave' to win five tricks solo. To this, any other player can call 'je soutiens' ('I support'), thereby allying himself with the asker and contracting to win at least eight between them. The higher bid of *indépendance* offers to win at least eight tricks playing solo. In either event there is a bonus for winning all thirteen tricks, formerly called *la vole* but now *le chelem*, from English 'slam'. (Resemblances to modern English Solo, or Solo Whist, are remarkable.) The other variety, Mariland, is more elaborate. All bids are solos, the lowest being for four tricks in any suit. Each can be overcalled by bidding a higher number of tricks or the same number in a better suit. For this purpose a better suit is that of *préférence*, previously determined by turning the last card of the deal, and best of all is *surpréférence*, which for the whole session remains the suit turned for *préférence* on the first deal.

An apparent compound of Mariland and original Boston appeared around 1800[13] under the name Boston de Nantes. This also has two preferred suits (*belle* for permanent, *petite* for each deal); in addition, ♦ J is a permanent top trump, known as the 'carte de Boston', or simply 'Boston'. It also has bids of 'proposal', which may be accepted by another player, and solo, for playing alone.

The ultimate game of this family, Boston de Fontainebleau (*c*.1810),[14] carries the principle of suit preference to its logical conclusion by specifying a fixed and permanent hierarchy, namely (from low to high): spades, clubs, diamonds, hearts—a sequence which reappears in a variety of nineteenth-century Whist-derivatives including Cayenne, Vint, Bid-Whist, and the earliest form of Bridge. It also extends the range of bidding possibilities by recapitulating features from the Hombre–Quadrille tradition, with no fewer than sixteen bids:

Cinq levées (= Mariland's *demande*): declare trumps, take five tricks alone, or, if accepted, eight with ally;

Six levées: six alone or ten with ally;

Petite misère: all discard one, lose all twelve tricks at no trump;

Sept levées: seven alone or eleven with ally;

Piccolissimo: at no trump, win exactly one trick;

Indépendance: eight alone or twelve with ally;

Grande misère: no trump, take none of thirteen tricks;

Neuf levées: nine-trick solo;

Misère des quatre as: the soloist has four Aces but offers to lose every trick at no trump (being, however, allowed to renege once in the first ten played);

Dix levées: ten-trick solo;
Petite misère sur table: as before, but with soloist's hand revealed;
Onze levées: eleven-trick solo;
Grande misère sur table: as before, but with soloist's hand revealed;
Douze levées: twelve-trick solo;
Boston seul: take all thirteen tricks;
Boston sur table: the same, with cards revealed.

The bids increased in pay-off value, each being further augmented
by the holding of three or four honours, by the entrumpment of a
preferred suit, and by overtricks. About the only thing it does not
include is a positive no-trump bid, whose first appearance is traced
by Thierry Depaulis to about 1818 in Boston de Lorient under the
bid-name 'quatre couleurs'.

Boston's popularity spread fast and wide throughout the west,
giving rise to countless variations under a variety of names. It would
be tedious to trace them all, especially as they do not all include
'Boston' in the title. Boston remained essentially a nineteenth-century
game, and was largely trampled under the march of Bridge. Its
importance lay in the two invaluable legacies it left to all serious
trick-taking games of the future: (1) the evolution of a permanent
suit hierarchy from the idea of suit preference, and (2) that of using
bids to vary the objective of the game as well as the conditions of
play.

Préférence and others

Préférence—better called by its English name Preference—is not the
French game it is often guessed to be from its title, which merely
derives from the technical term which we have already encountered
in Boston as denoting the preferred trump suit. It has a distinctly
Germanic feel about it, and Dummett traces its earliest known
description to *Das neuestes Spielbuch* of 1802. It is particularly
associated with eastern Europe. 'Russia, when at home, in dressing
gown and slippers, plays chiefly at Preference', says Taylor (1865)
in translation of Boiteau d'Ambly. Whether the Russians still play it,
or even still wear dressing-gowns, I do not know; but it certainly
flourishes in Austria, mostly in full dress.

Three play with 32 cards ranking normally (Ace high, Seven low).
Ten cards each are dealt, the other two forming a *skat* or blind.
Starting with the eldest, each in turn bids or passes. The aim is to
win at least six tricks after exchanging two cards with the blind and

then naming trumps. The basic bids run from 'one' to 'four', each being made strictly in turn (no 'jump-bidding'). A bid of 'one', if accepted, permits the bidder to name any suit; 'two' restricts him to spades, diamonds, or hearts; 'three' to diamonds or hearts; 'four' to hearts only. An earlier bidder who has not passed may 'hold' the higher bid of a later player, thus forcing the latter to bid higher or pass. Any of these may be overcalled by offering to play from the hand (i.e. without exchanging). A hand bid may be overcalled by the same in a higher suit, the bid of 'preference' denoting specifically hearts from the hand. Higher bids include *Bettel* (misère), *Durchmarsch* (slam), and each of these played *ouvert*.

A peculiarity of the game is that each opponent then declares whether he will play, thereby undertaking to win at least two tricks, or drop out. If one drops, the soloist plays against one partner; if both drop, he wins without playing at all. Assuming both play, a further peculiarity concerns the rules of following. Basically, 'strict' rules apply—head the trick if possible, trump if unable to follow suit: *F,T,r*. If, however, all three are playing and the soloist leads to a trick, the second player must, given a choice, play the lowest card necessary to beat the lead, so as not to hinder his partner from winning his two requisite tricks. This may have begun as a convention, but has since become a definitive rule.

Amongst several variations may be mentioned one in which, after the bidder has exchanged, an opponent may take the discards and declare a higher game—a feature resembling one characteristic of the Hungarian game of Ulti.

Vira, Sweden's national card game, is a cross between Hombre and Boston. It spread through the country in the early years of the nineteenth century, being first mentioned in 1818.[15] Like Hombre, it is played by three and there is a stock of thirteen cards from which to draw replacements or turn a card for trumps, though, as the full 52-card pack is used, each player receives 13 cards instead of nine. The schedule of bids and payments drawn up towards the end of the nineteenth century draws heavily on Boston, with suits of first and second preference, and contracts of from six to thirteen tricks interleaved with various negative bids. A Danish relative, Ligeud, is played in several varieties by differing numbers of players.[16]

Brandeln is an early nineteenth-century four-handed cross between Nap and German Solo played with a 28-card pack lacking Eights. Cards rank normally in plain suits but in trumps are J-7-A-K-Q-10–9. With seven cards each, players may bid from three (*Brandel*) to seven tricks. Six is overcalled by *Bettel* (misère), and that by *Mord* (seven). Seven can be played at no trump (*Herrenmord*), which wins more but cannot be used to overcall a *Mord*. The contracts are worth from one to seven units respectively. The soloist names trumps and leads to the first trick, and suit must be followed and headed if possible: *F,tr.*

Solo Whist

Solo reached Britain towards the end of the nineteenth century and soon established itself as a family favourite in preference to the more formal and upmarket Bridge. It has long held sway as a commuter game and is still vigorously pursued in pubs, often in forms found disconcerting by those brought up on books.

It is not a simplification of Boston de Fontainebleau, as sometimes claimed, but clearly derives from an earlier, unelaborated form of Boston still popular in the Low Countries under the name Whist de Gand, or 'Ghent Whist'.[17] Nor should it be regarded as a variant of Whist—in fact, I would rather speak of it as English Solo than as Solo Whist, which makes it sound like a poor relation.

Of its introduction into Britain Abraham Wilks writes:

In its present form [1898] Solo Whist was first played in England somewhere about the year 1852 by a family of Dutch Jews, and for the following fifteen or sixteen years it was practically unknown outside Jewish circles. From 1870 to 1872 it began in the London sporting clubs to supplant the card games formerly in vogue, and has since then enjoyed an unbroken record of ever-widening popularity, until now . . . it is as well known, and certainly much more generally liked, than its great congener Whist.

'More generally liked' was a dig at the Whist-playing establishment of London's clubland, for, as the game gains ground, we find Wilks more boldly jibing at 'a certain section of the conservative adherents of Whist proper who have hitherto tabooed the newcomer'.[18] Cavendish and his friends had been accused of killing ordinary mortals' enjoyment of partnership Whist by their increasing obsession with playing the game 'scientifically'. Solo enthusiasts such as Wilks were looking for some equally intelligent and respectable alternative to the then king of card games, and hoped that Solo might fulfil this desirable role. A similar feeling emerges from an in-depth study of the game brought out in 1899 by C. J. Melrose, author of *Scientific Whist*. 'Portland', in his introduction to *The Whist Table* (*c.*1895) more non-committally describes Solo as:

a variety of the game which seems to have fascinated our younger generation of players. The 'Old School' look at it somewhat askance as a dangerous hybrid—a game with pitfalls for the impetuous or unwary 'plunger', and one which does not exhibit the calm, refined science of the ancient 'noble game'. Mr Wilks, who may be regarded as the authoritative exponent . . . has here added every safeguard which his expedience can suggest . . . to reduce to a minimum any tendency to irregularity or temptation to excessive speculation . . .

If 'Portland' hoped that Whist would soon reassert its nobility over the upstart Solo, and Wilks that Solo would prove the equal of scientific Whist, both were about to be severely disappointed, for Bridge was then just entering the clubs, and within a few years neither Whist nor Solo would hold any further attraction for the serious player or social climber. (By 1901 C. J. Melrose—the author of *Scientific Whist*—had seen the writing on the wall and brought out a new in-depth study entitled *Bridge Whist*.) At a stroke, the future of Solo was shifted to the dining-room table, the 7.15 to London Bridge, and the public bar of the Rose and Crown.

By 1920 Solo had developed into Auction Solo, with a wider range of bids inspired by Auction Bridge. The indefatigable Wilks brought out his *Solo Whist and Auction Solo* in 1924, as did Basil Dalton his, under the same title, in 1929. In the event, Auction Solo failed to displant the original game, and by modern writers is relegated to a postscript. The game bequeathed to twentieth-century Hoyles is thus more like its nineteenth-century original—regrettably under-developed, I feel, through its restricted range of bids and lack of a challenging point-score schedule. The vigorous evolution of Bridge between 1900 and 1930 demonstrates how the strategy of a game may be shaped by its scoring method, and tempts speculation as to what a great game Solo might have become had it ever been accorded the attention it deserves.

Solo Whist (English, current). Four players; 52 cards; deal thirteen each in batches of three, the last four singly, the last one turned for trumps. Eldest bids first and always leads. From lowest to highest, the bids are as follows.

Prop and Cop: a proposal to accept the turned suit as trump and win eight tricks in partnership with anyone who accepts the proposal (by announcing 'Cop'). A proposal may not be accepted once a higher call is made. This is the only partnership bid.

Solo: to win at least five tricks, playing alone in the turned suit.

Misère ('miz'): to lose every trick, playing at no trump.

Abondance ('a bundle'): to win nine tricks alone in a suit other than that turned.

Royal abondance: the same, but in the turned suit.

Misère ouverte: ('spread misère'): as misère, but with the soloist's cards spread face up on the table.

Abondance déclarée ('slam'): to win all thirteen tricks, playing at no trump but with the advantage of leading to the first trick.

A player having once passed may not rebid, apart from the eldest, who is allowed to accept a proposal. Anyone who proposes without being accepted or overcalled may pass or make a higher bid. If all pass, the hands are thrown in and the next in turn deals.

Tricks are played as at Whist *f,tr*. Each deal is complete in itself and settled in hard-score, typically as follows: For a prop and cop, 10 for game plus 2 per over/under-trick, paid as between each partner and one opponent. Solo: the same, but as between the soloist and each opponent. A bundle: 30 for game plus 3 per over/under-trick, as between the soloist and each opponent. Other pay-offs are fixed, e.g. misère 20, spread misère, and slam, 40 each.

One problem with the game is that proper shuffling produces many indifferent hands which have to be thrown in, causing hold-ups and wasting time and energy. Some seek to overcome this by playing without shuffling until (say) a bundle has been played, which may be acceptable to gamblers but produces too many freak hands to engage the attention of serious players. Alternative devices current in the 1890s are still encountered. For example, players may agree to a 'general misère' or 'misery', in which there are no trumps and no winner, but whoever takes the last trick pays an agreed amount to each of the others. Alternatively, the winner is the player who takes fewest tricks, or the loser the one who takes most, or (my variation) the first to take four. A different approach, originally known as Kimberley or Flying colours, is to recognize a solo of six tricks in a suit other than that of the turned card, biddable only if all have passed or no proposal has been accepted. This still leaves a gap in the range of non-misère bids lower than a bundle, which Auction Solo plugged by recognizing the whole gamut from five to thirteen tricks. I have experimented with other gap-filling possibilities, of which two worth mentioning are (1) *reversis*, a no-trump bid ranking below a solo, in which declarer undertakes to capture no cards of the turned suit, after the manner of Hearts or Black Maria; and (2) *shorthouse*, a bid of seven no trump, ranking between a solo and a misère.

Higher up the scale, there has long been confusion as to whether or not a slam can be played with a trump suit. The trump slam is absent from original Solo, but crept so logically into the Auction game as to meet with the approval of Wilks himself. With the demise of Auction, some schools continue to recognize it as overcalling the no-trump equivalent. As both bids occur so rarely, even without shuffling, it seems pointless to admit both in the same game. If they are admitted, the no-trumper should be led by declarer and the trump slam by eldest hand regardless of declarer's position.

People who do not like playing for money either ignore the game because it looks like gambling, which gets it a bad name, or else keep quasi-payment records on paper, which look more like balance-sheets than scoresheets and are unnecessarily cumbersome, since it is quite easy to record single scores and convert them into zero-sum payments afterwards. At the very mention of scoring for Solo one hears Wilks turning in his grave and muttering it 'deprives Solo and Auction Solo of one of their chief attractions, the possibility of rising from the table at a few minutes' notice, neither owing nor being owed'. But then, as Dalton counters, 'The reader, if unconvinced and clinging to the old, familiar method, is urged to give the score-sheet an impartial trial . . . The game is not affected, whichever method you adopt. You might as reasonably quarrel over the colour of the cards' backs'. I use the following soft-score system for Solo. At Prop and Cop, each partner scores 1 point per trick taken if successful (range: 8–13). Solo scores a basic 10, plus 1 per overtrick (10–18). Bundles score a basic 20, plus 5 per overtrick (20–40). For losing any of these games, deduct 10 per undertrick. Fixed scores (win or lose): misère 20, spread misère 40, slam 50.

It is also interesting to revive the original Hombre rule defining 'solo' as an individual majority of tricks, i.e. to take more than any single opponent. By this rule seven tricks wins always, six tricks almost invariably, five tricks usually, and four tricks if no one else takes more than three.

In Nomination Whist—much played in the Royal Navy, according to my correspondent Rodney Jones—whoever bids the highest number of tricks announces trumps and names a card, the holder of which becomes his partner in the contract but may not reveal himself except by means of play. The bidder may alternatively play a secret solo by naming a card held in his own hand. A nice touch is the exaction of a penalty for taking all 13 tricks if a smaller number was bid. Nomination may be a spin-off from prop-and-cop in English Solo, but it is amusing to be able to trace it back to the bid of *médiateur* in 18th-century Quadrille.

17

From Whist to Bridge

Ruff and Honours (*alias* Slamm) and Whist, are games so commonly known in England, in all parts thereof, that every child almost of Eight years old hath a competent knowledg in that recreation . . .

Cotton, *The Compleat Gamester* (1674)

Whist . . . is now the King of Card Games, and seems destined, for many a long year, to retain that distinction.

'Cavendish', *Card Essays* (1879)

A generation is rapidly arising, which, though passably proficient at Bridge, is entirely ignorant of Whist . . .

'John Doe', *The Bridge Manual* (1900)

How England's national card game developed into the most illustrious card game of the western world is a story that takes us from London to New York via Paris and Constantinople, passing through Shakespearian alehouses, Johnsonian coffee-houses, and an exotic variety of exclusive clubs and rural retreats.

Whist is a deceptively simple game. Four players in two partnerships receive 13 cards each from a 52-card pack, the last being turned for trump. Players must follow suit if possible, otherwise may play any card, and the side taking most tricks scores a point for every trick taken over and above six. A game is won by the first side to reach five points—or seven, in American Whist—over as many deals as it takes. A rubber is won by the first side to win two games. And that's all, unless you count 'scoring for honours', which nobody now does. (A side scores an additional 4 for having been dealt all four top trumps, or 2 if dealt any three of them; but this swamps the skill factor and only appeals to gamblers.) For all its simplicity, Whist plumbs the depths of intelligent card-play. Considerable skill is exercised in so playing each card, whether or not with a view to trick-winning, as to convey information to your partner about the lie of your remaining cards. In the long run, the winning partners are those who consistently acquire reliable information early enough in the game to be able to play the rest of the hand to most advantageous effect.

Bridge is Whist with bidding, a feature whose invention and development were traced from Hombre to Solo in the preceding chapter. Instead of turning a card for trump, players bid for the right to nominate a trump suit or to play at no trump. Instead of aiming to take a simple majority of tricks, players bid against their opponents by raising the number of odd tricks they are offering to win in order to advance their score. (Odd tricks are tricks above six. The lowest bid, 'one', is therefore an undertaking to win at least seven tricks, and a bid of 'seven' an undertaking to win all thirteen.) Instead of playing with all hands concealed, the partner of the declarer or principal bidder lays his hand of cards face up on the table as a 'dummy', leaving declarer to play from both hands according to his own judgement. Instead of lumping all scores together, only those made for a successful contract count 'below the line', i.e. towards winning the game and rubber, whereas bonuses for tricks made in excess of the contract, for defeating an opponents' contract, and suchlike, are kept in a separate account 'above the line'—a device ingeniously devised to reward and so encourage accurate bidding.

The point of Bridge is quite different from that of Whist. At least half the game is played in the preliminary auction, many bids being made not as serious suggestions for a contract but as a means of conveying information about one's hand in accordance with standard bidding conventions—Acol, Goren, Two-Club, and so on. By the time play begins, both sides should have learned as much about the lie of unseen cards as would take about seven or eight tricks to discover at Whist. This degree of information is even further increased by the fact that each of the three active players can see twenty-six cards, including those of the dummy, instead of the mere thirteen of his or her own hand. Given that there still remains some mystery as to the lie of particular cards, trick-play at Bridge may be nearly 100 per cent strategic manœuvring and a few per cent information discovery, whereas that of Whist is at least fifty per cent groping for information.

Trump, Ruff, and Whist and Swabbers

Whist is first described by Charles Cotton in 1674 with the oft-quoted but indispensable introduction heading this chapter. In fact he describes two related games, both ancestral to the classic form.

In the first, 'English Ruff and Honours, or Slamm', each receives twelve cards from a full pack and four are dealt face down to one side as a stock, the topmost being turned for trump. Whoever holds the Ace of trump may 'ruff'—i.e. take these four into hand and discard any four in their place. With 'ruffing' equivalent to 'robbing', this game is remarkably similar to Triumphus Hispanicus, or Spanish Trump, which we encountered in the preceding chapter as ancestral to Hombre and Solo. The description 'English' differentiates this game from French Ruff, a five-card game ancestral to Ecarté.

Various references show that English Ruff was previously known as Trump, and under that name goes back to the early sixteenth century. One of 1688 speaks of 'Ruff, vulgarly called Trump'; Cotgrave's French–English Dictionary of 1611 equates Triomphe with 'Ruffe, or Trump'; and an earlier one still, of 1589, may imply a slight distinction between the two.[1] A round of Trump is sketchily depicted in the 1551 comedy *Gammer Gurton's Needle*, and Eliot describes it, in *Fruites for the French* (1593), as 'a verie common alehouse game'. Of the original game we know only that it was one of tricks and trumps played with French-suited cards as early as 1522, when we find 'ye Tryumphe' listed in a translation of a sermon by Bernadine of Sienna (along with Momon, Gleke, Flusshe, Torment, Regnet, and One-and-Thyrty).[2] Its nature is apparent from a sermon preached 'On the Card' by Hugh Latimer, Bishop of Worcester, on the Sunday before Christmas, 1529:

And whereas you are about to celebrate Christmas in playing at cards, I intend, by God's grace, to deal unto you Christ's cards, wherein you shall perceive Christ's rule. The game that we shall play at shall be called the triumph, which, if it be well played at, he that dealeth shall win; the players shall likewise win; and the standers and lookers upon shall do the same, insomuch that there is no man willing to play at this triumph with these cards but they shall be all winners and no losers.

Latimer was burnt at the stake in 1555.

The other game described by Cotton is almost Ruff, but without the ruffing. There is no stock of four: instead, the Deuces are stripped out, the other 48 cards are evenly divided, the last is faced for trump, and twelve tricks are played. It first appears under the alternative name 'Whisk' in *Taylor's Motto* of 1621, in the same breath as Ruff, Slam, and Trump. Whist with a 't' is first recorded in 1663. Both names remained current until the latter part of the eighteenth century, when 'Whisk' died out.[3]

At some stage in its development the game acquired an additional feature called 'swabbers', being then known as 'Whisk and Swabbers' as if in jocular parallel to 'Ruff and Honours'. Swabbers are first defined in 1700 as certain cards whose declaration entitles their holder(s) to a share of the stake, namely the heart Ace, club Jack, trump Ace, and trump Deuce.[4] Their apparent absence from the written record before 1700, and particularly from Cotton's account of 1674, suggests that swabbers may have been a late seventeenth-century addition. Whisk and Swabbers is mentioned throughout the eighteenth century despite its social eclipse by classical Whist from 1730 on. Well worth repetition is a passage from Swift's *Essay on the Fates of Clergymen* (1728), in which Archbishop Tenison—'a dull man'—demurs as follows at the recommendation of a certain clergyman for preferment:

His Grace had heard that the clergyman used to play at Whist and Swobbers; that as to playing now and then a sober game at Whist for a pastime, it might be pardoned, but he could not digest those wicked swobbers.

That swabbers persisted into the nineteenth century is shown by a story in *Cavendish on Whist* derived from R. B. Wormald in 1873:

Being driven by stress of weather to take shelter in a sequestered hostelry on the Berkshire bank of the Thames, he [Wormald] found four persons immersed in the game of Whist. 'In the middle of the hand, one of the players, with a grin that almost mounted to a chuckle, and a vast display of moistened thumb, spread out upon the table the ace of trumps; whereupon the other three laid down their hands, and forthwith severally handed over the sum of one penny to the fortunate holder of the card in question. On enquiry, we were informed that the process was technically known as a 'swap' (qy swab or swabber), and was *de rigueur* in all properly constituted Whist circles.'

Since writing this, and while researching illustrations for the present work, I found in the Victoria and Albert Museum a satirical print of 1807 (Woodward, *Mrs Fig's Card Party Disturbed*) bearing the caption 'Indeed, gentlemen, we were only playing at Wisk and Swabs' [*sic*].

The name of the game opens up some interesting blind alleys. Cotton, making an obvious guess, says Whist is so called 'from the silence that is to be observed in the play'—i.e. from 'whist!', now obsolete, meaning 'hush!' This piece of folk etymology is sufficiently suspect for Dr Johnson later to hedge his bets by non-committally defining Whist as 'A game at cards, requiring close attention and silence'. Not that such derivations are without parallel: modern games named from appropriate interjections include 'Oh Hell', 'Bastard', and 'Spit'. The problem is that 'whist' evidently derives from 'whisk', which has never been an exclamation. William Pole[5] suggests that 'whisk' became assimilated to 'whist' by association, accompanying a gradual recognition of the game's more intellectual possibilities and hence of the increasing appropriateness of the customary call for silence.

But this still leaves the original 'Whisk' unexplained. Some lexicographers allude to cards being whisked off the table as a by-product of rapid play. Chatto approaches the problem by way of a pun.[6] Since both ruff and whisk are terms for an ornament of dress made of lawn or cambric, 'Whisk' (he says) may have arisen as a jocular alternative to 'Ruff' and eventually replaced it as a matter of course. He goes a stage further by similarly relating 'Whisk and Swabbers' to 'Ruff and Honours':

It would seem that the two former terms were merely the ludicrous synonyms of the latter—introduced perhaps about the time that ruffs were going out of fashion, and when the honours represented by the coat cards were at a discount. Swabbers . . . were possibly so termed because they who had certain cards in their hand were entitled to take up a share of the stake, independent of the general event of the game. The fortunate, therefore, clearing of the board by this extraordinary stake, might be compared by seamen to the *swabbers* (or cleaners of the deck), in which sense the term is still used.

A problem with Chatto's pretty word-play is that it only works if the 'swabbers' feature antedates 1650, whereas we have no evidence for it earlier than 1700. In this connection it is interesting, though not very helpful, to note that in Pandoer, a nineteenth-century Dutch game, 'zwabber' is a bid to win every trick, playing at no trump.

The character of Whist as a low-class game, even as something wicked by association with cheating, goes back to Trump itself and persisted until the early eighteenth century. Old Dame Chat, in *Gammer Gurton's Needle*, warns 'Take heed of Sim Glover's wife, she hath an eie behind her.' Cotton, following Cotgrave, offers such useful hints as 'There is a way to discover to their partners what Honours they have; as by the wink of one eye, or putting one finger to the nose or table, it signifies one honour; shutting both the eyes, two; placing three fingers or four on the table, three or four honours.' Seymour, in his 1734 edition of Cotton's work, devotes a chapter to 'Piping at Whisk'. By this he does not mean playing the flute, but:

When one of the company that does not play . . . sits down in a convenient place to smoke a pipe and so look on, pretending to amuse himself that way. Now the disposing of his fingers on the pipe, whilst smoking, discovers the principal cards that are in the person's hand he overlooks, which was always esteemed a sufficient advantage to win a game. This may also be done by another way, i.e. by common conversation. 'Indeed' signifies diamonds; 'truly', hearts; 'Upon my word', clubs; 'I assure you', spades.

Classical Whist: from Bedford Row to Bath

When Seymour's *Court Gamester* first appeared in 1719, it would appear that the only games considered suitable for the edification of its princessly dedicatees were Ombre, Piquet, and Chess. Although Whist is notable by its absence, its star by this time had risen at least to the social heights of country squires and clergy. Swift's clerical reference we have already noted. In Farquar's *The Beaux' Stratagem* of 1707, Mrs Sullen deprecates country 'pleasures' as 'Racks and torments! Dost think, child, that . . . my parents, wisely foreseeing my future happiness in country pleasures, had early instructed me in the rural accomplishments of drinking fat ale, playing at whisk, and smoking tobacco with my husband?' Similar status is accorded the game by Pope in a couplet from his *Epistle to Mrs Teresa Blount* (1715):

> Some Squire, perhaps, you take delight to rack,
> Whose game is Whisk, whose treat a toast in sack . . .

By now the Age of Reason was at hand, and Whist was about to come of age. Its initiation was set in the genteel surroundings of 'The Crown' coffee-house, Bedford Row, a then aristocratic neighbourhood of London. Coffee-houses—a cut above the 'ordinaries' which, since Pepys's day, had virtually degenerated into gambling dens—were used by lords and professionals as everyday social centres, the forerunners of gentlemen's clubs of the Victorian era. Here, around 1728, a group of gentlemen including the first Lord Folkestone turned their attention to the humble game of Whist and began to develop its potential for serious play. We may suppose that, as reasonable men, they were looking for a game of skill free from all the unreasonable disadvantages of Quadrille: its irregular 40-card pack, its irrelevant complications, its cultural associations, and, perhaps above all, its shifting alliances. For the first principle they discovered was the need to concentrate on co-operative play, which could only be fully explored in fixed-partnership format. 'They laid down the following rules', wrote Daines Barrington in 1786, apparently from the reminiscences of a first-hand source: 'To play from the strongest suit, to study your partner's hand as much as your own, never to force your partner unnecessarily, and to attend to the score.'[7] In other words, as later commentators put it, they began to play 'scientifically', and 'on principles', rather than haphazardly and *ad hoc*. This is not to say that no one had ever thought intelligently about the game before. Cotton had already observed 'You ought to have a special eye to what Cards are play'd out, that you may know by that means what to play if you lead, or how to trump securely and advantageously.' But Cotton was speaking to individuals. The brilliance of Lord Folkestone's party lay in exploring the partnership element.

The subsequent spread of Whist was largely due to the promotional talents of Edmond Hoyle, whose tutoring in the game helped it become a social accomplishment, and whose *Short Treatise on the Game of Whist*—published, sold out, and reissued in 1742—saw to its widespread circulation. It penetrated the royal household, as indicated by its transfer from the 'city' to the 'court' section of *The Compleat Gamester* in 1754, and soon graduated to academic circles. Pole cites a 1758 issue of the *Tatler* in which 'the senior fellow of a college at Cambridge represents himself and his party as "sitting late at Whist in the evening"'. That year also yields reports of Whist parties of fashionable people at Bath, which was to remain a major centre of Whist-playing until well into the nineteenth century. In 1804, Thomas Matthews published at Bath the first edition of his *Advice to the Young Whist Player*, with some rather unkind words about the late Mr Hoyle. ('So far from being able to teach the game, [he would be] not fit to sit down even with the third-rate players of the present day.') Adulation of the game reached new heights of fatuity with the publication, in 1791, of Alexander Thomson's epic *Whist: a poem in twelve Cantos*.

As often happens with classic games, the recognition of Whist as a social accomplishment meant that many people who would really have been more at ease with something else felt morally obliged to subordinate their taste to that of the prevailing fashion, with unhappy and counter-productive results. We have already met the young lady whose papa made her 'drudge at Whist' till she was tired of it (Chapter 5). In 1772 Mrs Boscowan describes the not unmixed delights of a family evening's activities:

The whole concluding with one game of Whist *en famille*, at which I am a mere goose; for 'tis a great science, and requires, too, a degree of memory which I am not possessed of. Quadrille was much better suited to my capacity; but that is out of fashion, it seems, which will cost me many a sixpence.

Later, she cattily refers to a ladyship friend as 'falling a victim to Whist in her old age'.[8] Not all women found the game difficult or unbearable. It was a well-kept secret of the time that *Bob Short's Rules*, which first appeared about 1792 and remained a classic for many decades thereafter, actually emanated from the pen of one Anne Lætitia Aikin—'authoress of the famous *Evenings at Home* and *Early Lessons for Children*, etc.'. Her original rules, twenty-eight in number, are followed by appendices entitled *Twelve Short Standing Rules for Ladies with Short Memories*. (Rule 12 reads: 'When in doubt, win the trick. Note: The maid who hesitated was undone!')

The format of partnership Whist has changed little since 1730. Early in the nineteenth century the points for game, variously nine in Cotton's day and ten in Hoyle's, found themselves drastically cut to five. This variety, 'Short Whist', is said to have arisen from an incident at Bath.[9] Lord Peterborough lost a large stake, and his friends offered him the chance of a speedy revenge by halving the target score. Whether he actually recouped his loss is unrecorded; but the shorter game proved so exciting that its players adopted it permanently and successfully introduced it to their clubs. Long and Short Whist tussled for perhaps half a century before the latter finally won out. In 1864 *The Laws of Short Whist* were published, drafted by J. L. Baldwin on his model of several years previously, and agreed by the Portland and other leading clubs. It has been observed[10] that the distinctively British concept of official rules dates back to the nineteenth-century gentlemen's club's view of itself as an instrument of state. If they could rule India, they could rule Whist too . . .

Philosophical Whist: from Portland to Limbo

The object of their rule was now proudly described as 'philosophical Whist', an esoteric exercise of such science and logic as to render the game virtually unplayable by ordinary mortals. It was based on the discovery that successful play required each partner to regard his hand not just as thirteen cards, but as the visible half of the partnership's 26-card hand. The discovery seems first to have been published abroad. In a work entitled *Le Génie du Whist* . . . (Paris, 1839) the Baron Victor de Vautré undertook to teach 'the mode of playing with twenty-six cards . . . and not with thirteen like everybody else'. At about the same time there appeared in Vienna the dispiritingly entitled *Das rationelle Whist*, by the Ritter Ludwig von Coeckelbergle-Dützele. Under the heading 'Verständigungspiel', the Ritter declares:

To make the best and most advantageous use of your own as well as your partner's hand, you must endeavour to find out what his cards are, and to afford him similar information as to your own. Both these objectives are effected by what is called *Kartensprache* (card language), or *Signalkunst* (the art of signalling). The cards selected to be played serve, by their relative values, as telegraphic signs, by which the two partners carry on a reciprocal communication, and convey indications as to what cards they hold, as well as suggestions of their respective views and wishes.

According to William Pole, on whose *Evolution of Whist* I deeply draw, only in its native soil did Whist produce its finest flower. The particular flower-bed Pole had in mind was one started by a group of Cambridge students in the 1850s under the unimaginative title 'The Little Whist School'. When Pole suggested in a magazine article that Whist might prove as worthy of scientific analysis as Chess if only the data existed on which to effect it, he promptly received from a member of this circle the good news that he had built up just such a collection of data on real-life Whist games, with analyses and principles of play, which might help establish Whist upon this novel footing. That student was the young Henry Jones, who, under Pole's encouragement, published in 1862 the first edition of *The Principles of Whist*, by 'Cavendish'—a work that would run to over twenty editions in the space of thirty years. Other notable tomes of the times included *A Treatise on Short Whist* by James Clay, widely acknowledged the finest practical player then living, and Pole's *The Philosophy of Whist: An Essay on the Scientific and Intellectual Aspects of the Modern Game.*

Within the constraints of following suit and needing to win tricks there were still many occasions on which players would have a wide choice of cards to play, and it was in this factor that scope existed for the development of meaningful conventions. 'Philosophical Whist' involved the extensive use of signalling systems whereby partners could communicate their forces and desires to one another by the significant play of cards. 'Whist is a language', Clay declared (echoing Ludwig von Coeckelbergle-Dützele), 'and every card played an intelligible sentence.' In this respect Cavendish, Pole, and others were aided and abetted by American players, who were even more enthusiastic about systematic play. They had also gone further in their formal development of the game. Under the name 'straight Whist' they slightly lengthened the 'short' game to a logical seven points—the most that can be made on a single deal—and eliminated the ridiculous feature of scoring for honours. Having devised so perfect a game structure, it is hardly surprising that American players should prove more amenable than their transatlantic counterparts to the development of correspondingly intelligent modes of play. As Pole admits in 1895, 'The new system has not, as a whole, been yet adopted largely in England; but, to make amends, it has been received with remarkable earnestness and enthusiasm by the United States of America, where it may indeed be said to have become the standard form of the game.'

Many basic techniques of strategic card-play first identified and developed by nineteenth-century Whist experts remain fundamental to the repertoire of Bridge and other games of comparable depth. The *OED* definition of 'finesse' is word-for-word 'Cavendish', and 'petering' (requesting a trump lead by playing an unnecessarily high card to a trick) goes back to a Whist convention, the Blue Peter, named after a naval flag signal. Leading fourth best from a long suit is another Whist invention, enabling the leader's partner to gain useful information by applying Foster's 'Rule of Eleven'—i.e. deduct from eleven the numerical value of the card led to discover how many higher cards of that suit are lacking from the leader's hand, from which even more useful deductions can be made.

Simpler conventions of this type are merely the codified recognition of techniques arising naturally from the practice of expert players. The trouble with codes and conventions is that they tend to become more and more refined, until they refine themselves right past the stage of general intelligibility, eventually becoming an end in themselves. 'The new list of leads in the 21st edition of Cavendish, 1893', Pole proudly declares, 'contains some sixty rules, occupying seven pages!'

Some flavour of these rules may be gained from Pole's commentary on just one of them:

Suppose I hold King, Knave, Nine, Eight, and Two, and lead the Eight. Considering the Eight as a *penultimate lead*, my partner, when I drop the Two, will know I had five cards originally. But considering it as the lead of the 'fourth best', he may gain much more valuable information. Suppose he himself holds Queen, Ten, and a small one, and that when he plays the Queen it is taken by the Ace. Then, when he considers that I must hold three cards higher than the Eight, and that Ace, Queen, and Ten are not among them, he knows, on completion of this very first round, just as positively as if he looked over my hand, that I hold the King, Knave, and Nine. This seems very obvious and simple . . .

It was the thought behind 'just as positively as if he looked over my hand' that gave rise to such controversy in English club circles, leading, in some quarters, to the castigation of 'artificial leads' as no better than cheating. 'Unless players make a determined stand against such absurdities,' warned a critic of the time, 'the day is near when there will be rival systems of signals, some players adopting one and other players others, and the game be turned absolutely topsy-turvy.' That critic, 'Mogul', was nearly right. Whist was just about to be turned topsy-turvy, though not quite in the way that anyone foresaw. By 1900 it had been replaced by a game called Bridge, leaving 'Cavendish' forlornly signalling to himself for a few lingering years over a card-table in some dark corner of the Portland Club. He eventually succumbed to the new game, but died almost immediately.

Partnership Whist has since been handed back to the descendants of Gammer Gurton, and is today alive and well and living in drives. The form most often played is Progressive Whist, in which players proceed from table to table allying themselves with different partners in order to produce an ultimate individual winner. As may be inferred from the printed Progressive score-pads obtainable from any stationer, the trump suit also follows a regular progression from one to another, in place of being determined by the turn of the dealer's last card.

All great games engender illicit progeny, and Whist is no exception. Many of its nineteenth-century variants may be seen as steps along the road to Bridge. Perhaps the most significant was Dummy Whist, which may have started life as a means of indulgence when two or three players were gathered together but unable to find a fourth. An obvious approach is to deal four hands, the one at the unoccupied side of the table going face up as a dummy whose live partner plays from it as well as from his own hand. As this increases the information available and therefore the degree of skill involved, many players found it preferable to the real thing, and persisted in playing that way even when the table was quorate. Double Dummy was the equivalent two-hand version, with each player facing and playing from an exposed hand. A similar principle was followed in so-called Chinese Whist, playable by two to four. Each receives six cards face down in a row, another six face up in a row across them, and one card to the hand. Whenever a faced card is played, the one beneath it is turned up. In 'Norwegian Whist' the only possible bids are 'grand' and 'nullo', i.e. to win and lose, respectively, a majority of tricks at no trump. 'German Whist' is another attempt to render Whist playable by two, this time on the play-and-draw basis of Bezique, each receiving thirteen cards and drawing from stock after playing to a trick. 'Dutch Whist' is a compound game with different objects in each succeeding deal; others of that type include Bismarck and Sergeant Major. 'Scotch Whist' is a point-trick game, and nothing to do with Whist at all.

Most of these are fossils. The commonest variation played today is the rather juvenile gambling game of Knockout Whist. Any reasonable number take part. The number of cards dealt at each round, normally starting at seven, is reduced by one in each succeeding deal, for each of which a fresh trump is turned. Anyone failing to take a trick drops out of the game; those who remain add to their stakes before continuing. The fact that only one card is dealt on the last round makes Knockout a gambling game *par excellence*—or *par décadence*, as the case may be.

From Biritch to Bridge-Whist

One autumn day at the Portland in 1894, so legend tells, Lord Brougham dealt for Whist and forgot to turn a trump. 'Sorry,' he explained, 'I thought I was playing Bridge.' True or not, it has never been disputed that the new game's invasion of the Portland Whist tables was due to Lord Brougham, and that it enjoyed immediate victory. Portland players dropped Whist almost overnight; the Turf Club turfed it out soon after; and other major clubs fell over themselves to follow suit. In December, three Portland members were appointed to draw up an official code of laws, which later appeared as an adjunct to the second 1895 edition of *The Pocket Guide to Bridge*, by 'Boaz'.

But Bridge had been in the air, and even in the clubs, for several years before. In Paris, it had been the subject of an article in *Le Figaro* of 26 November 1893. At this time, according to Dalton,[11] Henry I. Barbey of New York wintered there and returned home in April fired with enthusiasm for the new game. Later that year he introduced it to the New York Whist Club, and his publication of the rules led to the hiving off of a separate Bridge club meeting at a different venue from the Whist players. American visitors to the Portland in 1893 and 1894 expressed surprise at the absence of Bridge. Had they visited St George's Club in Hanover Square, they might have found tables set aside for Bridge since 1892, according to Frank Nathan, who claimed to be one of the first to play it there.[12]

Bridge was evidently known in England before it reached the clubs. In 1886 an unidentified 'John Collinson' published a four-page leaflet entitled *Biritch, or Russian Whist*, from which the Bridge of 'Boaz' differs only in minor details.[13] In his history of Bridge,[14] Rex Mackey mistakenly asserts that the pamphlet derives it from the genuinely

Russian game Vint, and continues 'The Russian attribution would be more plausible if there were a word Biritch in that language, but there is not. Possibly it was a Slavonic mode of address to a female partner.' This joke is spoiled by the fact that there is in fact a Russian word *biritch*, meaning 'herald' or 'town-crier'.[15] However, as it is not recorded with any gaming association, this discovery takes us no further. For all anyone knows, the mysterious Collinson could have taken a game already called 'Bridge' and invented the Russian spelling.

Biritch (after Collinson, 1886). Play like Whist, but without a trump turn-up and with these modifications:

Dealer must either announce trumps or pass this privilege to his partner, who must then exercise it. Whichever of them declares may either nominate a suit or announce *biritch*, making it no trump. Either opponent may double (*contre*); declarer or partner may redouble (*surcontre*), and such doubling and redoubling can go on indefinitely. The player at dealer's left leads; dealer's partner then lays his hand face up on the table, and dealer plays from both hands throughout. Consultation is not allowed.

A rubber is the best of three games. A game is won by the first side to reach 30 points in play, irrespective of honours. Each trick taken over six scores, according to the trump suit: spades 2, clubs 4, diamonds 6, hearts 8, biritch 10. There is a bonus of 40 for 'grand slam' (taking every trick), or 20 for 'petit slam' (taking all but one). Winning the rubber carries a bonus of 40 for 'consolation'. All but the rubber scores are affected by any doubling that took place.

Points not scored towards game, but recorded separately and contributing to the final margin of victory, are made for 'honours' and various other features as follows. All remain unaffected by doubling.

At *biritch* the only honours are Aces. Three held score the equivalent of 3 tricks, four of 4 tricks, four in one hand of 8 tricks. In trumps, the honours are A, K, Q, J, 10. Three held ('simple honours') score as for 2 tricks; four as for 4, or, in one hand, 8; five as for 5, or, in one hand, 10. A hand without trumps when any are declared is called *chicane*. It entitles the holder to add the value of simple honours to any other honour score his side may make—or, if none, to deduct it from the opponents' honour score.

Bridge is no exception to the rule that anything of unknown origin emanates from the east. A. G. Hulme-Beaman, in *Pons Asinorum*

(*Bridge for Beginners*), 1899, claims many years' personal experience of the game as played in Eastern Europe. 'Slam', writing in 1901, declares Bridge to be 'known in Turkey as Biritch . . . though more resembling the Russian *Vint*, perhaps, than any other game. It has been played in South Eastern Europe, in its present form, ever since the early 60's, and from there travelled firstly to France . . .' Foster, writing in 1901,[16] states (without references) 'A hybrid form of it has been played for the past 30 years or more in Constantinople, and later in Alexandria and the Riviera, under the name *Khedive*. Another variation has long been popular in Holland, and something very much like it is known in Russia under the name *Yeralash*.'

Of these, the only first-hand source seems to be Hulme-Beaman; but two alleged eye-witness accounts of the game's introduction to England also assert Balkan and Levantine associations. Dalton received a letter from 'a well-known Greek gentleman' assuring him 'that the writer can remember the game of Bridge, very much in its present form, being regularly played among a colony of Greeks, settled in Manchester, of whom his own father was one, as far back as the seventies'. (Not to be confused with the colony of Dutch Jews whom Wilks cites as having been the first in Britain to practise Solo Whist.) And Frank Nathan, in his letter to the *Bridge Magazine*, quotes one of the first four St George's players as saying that it was of Levantine origin, and that he had learnt it at the trenches at Plevna during the Russo-Turkish war of 1877–8. A score for authenticity may be credited to Hulme-Beaman, and to the Greek gentleman whom Dalton deems too well known to be worth identifying, for noting that the original no-trump trick value was 10 points rather than the 12 specified by Brougham and 'Boaz'. In this they accord with Collinson— presumably by coincidence, since they seem unaware of the Russian connection.

A Turkish origin for proto-Bridge seems unlikely. Turkey does not figure prominently in the world of card games, and 'biritch', though complying with Turkish vowel harmony and looking like a word beginning with the prefix *bir-* ('a' or 'one') does not belong to the native lexicon. It could be a phonetically felicitous loan-word, in which case we might postulate a Russian game—not necessarily called Biritch, 'Herald', in allusion to the declarer's role—entering Turkey as a by-product of Russian activities in the Balkans.

As Russia seems a more plausible source than Turkey, it may be worth examining some of her relevant Whist-like games. One of the earliest, Yeralash ('Medley'), is described by Dalton as virtually Short Whist played without trumps.[17] (Interestingly, if not helpfully, trumpless trick-games are characteristic of Scandinavia.) By the 1870s a more advanced Whist variant was being played at St Petersburg under the name Siberia, in which the dealer declared trumps and stated how many tricks his side undertook to win.[18] In a later version, the partner could raise the bid to a higher suit or a greater number of tricks. Later still the no-trump feature was introduced and all four players were allowed to bid.

This new game became known as Vint, i.e. 'Screw', allegedly because players raise or screw up their adversaries to the highest pitch in the game they declare, thus rendering them vulnerable to a higher penalty for failure. Contracts are graded, from low to high, spades, clubs, diamonds, hearts, no trump, but this relates only to bidding power, as Vint scoring is the same in all suits and varies only with the number of tricks contracted. The suit order will be recognized as that deriving ultimately from Boston or Preference, while the no-trump bid may have been suggested by Yeralash or Biritch. Vint is still popular in Scandinavia under various national forms of the name Screw, e.g. Swedish Skruv. It differs somewhat from the Russian Vint described in English in 1900. Twelve cards are dealt and there are bids of null, suit, and no trump or 'grand'. Declarer then reveals the four undealt cards and distributes one to each player at his discretion.[19] As Vint is more advanced than Biritch and was practically unknown in the west before 1900, it can hardly have influenced Bridge except in the later direction of Auction. But it was a brilliant game for its time, and it is only by chance that the niche now occupied by Contract Bridge houses a game of American rather than Russian development.

In attempting to draw these threads together we may find it misleading to seek a single line of development towards Bridge, which is perhaps better regarded as an accretion of features already well known in the latter half of the nineteenth century. Four-handed Dummy Whist was favoured by the French, who were to figure prominently in the creative evolution of Bridge. Trump selection by the dealer, variable suit values, and a no-trump bid were all present in Cayenne Whist (c.1860) though it was not played with a dummy. The same elements, together with dummy play and a primitive form of above and below-line scoring, are found in a game described by Anton under the title 'Sturmwhist', or Storm-Whist.

One gaming feature which Bridge brought back into play, following its notable absence from sociable foursomes since the demise of Quadrille, was that of sex appeal. Unlike Whist, Bridge immediately attracted women. Male mythology might relate this to the fact that, whereas Whist is by tradition synonymous with 'silence', Bridge involves bidding, and bidding involves talking. Mackey asserts that the average female Bridge-player is better at the game than the average male, but that men tend to excel at the highest levels of proficiency. Or, to put it another way, men are more inclined to intellectualize their pleasures by pursuing them to the remotest realms of mental abstraction. Women were writing on Bridge as early as 1901, when Mrs J. R. Tennant brought out her *ABC of Bridge*. From articles by three writers on the topic 'Is Bridge Immoral?' in the November 1904 issue of the *Lady's Realm*, we learn, amongst other things, that Bridge was now raging furiously in country houses, and that 'The gentlemen do not linger long in the dining room, but join the ladies with alacrity, longing for the fray.' Other early textbooks ranged in approach from C. J. Melrose's *Scientific Bridge* to *Bridge over a Sandwich* by R. J. Lloyd Price. (Gastronomic note: The sandwich was invented by Lord Sandwich over Whist at Bath, perhaps in a fit of protest against Bath buns. Later, it was itself to be ousted by the Bridge roll.)

Auction Bridge: from Allahabad to Philadelphia

Even as men and women happily frayed over a sandwich at country houses the length and breadth of Britain, Bridge in the first decade of the twentieth century was being taken apart by more adventurous minds and put together again in a revised version known as Auction Bridge. Auction was devised to overcome the obvious flaw of Bridge-Whist that it may not have suited either member of the dealer's side to nominate trumps, while their opponents might be sitting on excellent hands which the rules of the game prevented them from doing anything about. The basic idea of Auction was that each of the four players in turn could bid for the right to nominate trumps, that privilege devolving upon the player offering to play the game of highest value.

Credit for the invention of Auction is usually accorded to Francis Roe, an Indian army officer who wrote under the transparent pen-name 'John Doe'. Some, including Charles Goren in the *Encyclopaedia Britannica*, trace it back to *The Bridge Manual*, by *John Doe* (Allahabad, 1899; London, 1900). In fact there is nothing like it here: Roe merely remarks, in a chapter on variations, 'Cut-Throat Bridge, which, I may say, is a game of my own invention, is not bad fun for three players if you cannot get four.' The game is not described, but, as there are only three players, it presumably enabled everyone

230 Whist to Bridge

to bid. Roe only describes an equivalent four-hander late in 1903, in a series of articles in the *Pioneer*, later incorporated into his second book, *Auction Bridge*, in 1904. But Roe himself does not claim credit for this version, saying that he developed it 'from a chance reference to the possibilities of such a game in a magazine article'. It is possible that he was referring to a primitive form of Auction first described in *The Times* of 16 and 25 January 1903 (not 1905, *pace* Goren) in correspondence initiated by Oswald Crawfurd. 'Auction Bridge,' says Crawfurd, 'which I have seen much played and much liked this winter, is more lively than dummy Bridge, and is free from some of the objectionable flaws of that game.' Again, however, what he is discussing is an adaptation of Bridge-Whist for three players, and not a true Auction for four.

The earliest description I know of four-hand Auction appears in *Foster's Bridge Tactics* (London and New York, 1903), to which are appended chapters on both three and four-handed forms of Auction. The former, here called 'Dummy Bridge', is essentially Crawfurd's game with some novel features. Suit values are spades 2, clubs 4, diamonds 6, hearts 8, no trump 12, misery 14—the last being (in effect) a bid to win not more than four tricks—and honours score only as captured in tricks, not as dealt. A game is three deals, with no target score. Such rationalization might point in Foster's direction; but he gives no clue as to authorship one way or the other, and years later, in *Foster on Auction*, himself endorses Roe's reputation as its inventor.

Auction Bridge, minus the misery bid, was codified by the Bath Club in 1908 and the Portland in 1909. The latter retains the 2–4-6–8-12 scoring system, but adds penalties of 50 per undertrick and increases the rubber bonus from 100 to 250, probably to obviate the chance of a technical win on points scored above the line. By 1910 Auction had superseded Bridge-Whist as thoroughly as Bridge-Whist had supplanted Whist only fifteen years before—certainly so in America, though as late as 1916 Dalton could describe Bridge-Whist as not quite defunct, only 'dying a slow and lingering death'.

But the game was still not right. Many players were grumbling about its unsatisfactory scale of values, which led (wrote Bergholt in 1918) to a ridiculous preponderance of no-trumpers and an equally ridiculous outlawry of spade calls. The fault lay in the system of value overcall, if not in the actual scale of values itself. With hearts worth 8 per trick and spades only 2, it may be logical for a bid of two hearts (16) to overcall one of seven spades (14), but it is also absurd.

Experimentation forged ahead on both sides of the Atlantic.

Bostonians in 1910 introduced an extra bid of 'royal spades' for a value of 10 each—later reduced to 9 so that no-trump might retain its unique ability to yield game with three odd tricks, a feature surviving in modern Bridge. This became known as 'Lily Bridge' by the unpredictable sort of process which makes research into card-game history such exasperating fun. Someone, somewhere, renamed royal spades 'lillianos' after a former Queen Liluiokalani of the Sandwich Islands. 'Lillianos' were promptly shortened to 'lillies', which in turn was taken as a misspelling for 'lilies'.

In 1912 Milton Work, of Philadelphia's Racquet Club, was inspired by a Bostonian visitor to devise a new scale of values running spades 2, clubs 6, diamonds 7, hearts 8, royal spades 9, no trump 10. This was soon adopted by the New York Bridge Club, and by the end of the year had become popular throughout the country. Some expressed reservations about spades' two-faced value as trumps, but the Philadelphian school clung to it with enthusiasm, using it as a convenient washing-line on which to hang a complicated series of signalling devices based on all low spade bids up to seven.

In 1913, New York abolished the score for chicane. No tears were shed. 'It was a puerile sort of thing anyhow', wrote Florence Irwin, 'and its existence, or non-existence, is unimportant.'

If the Americans had been making all the running for a few years, it was now up to the Portland Club to make some kind of mark. This it did by publishing in 1914 its Laws of '(Royal) Auction Bridge'. The vestigial score of 2 for low spades was surgically removed, leaving the rational score series 6, 7, 8, 9, 10, corresponding to the modern suit-order of clubs, diamonds, hearts, spades, and no-trump. Portlanders followed New Yorkers in scrapping chicane and curtailing the infinite doubling system inherited from Bridge-Whist, and made some further revisions of their own: slam premiums were raised from 20/40 to 50/100, and dealer was no longer obliged to bid on the first round.

America rapidly capitulated to Britain's courageous initiative on the spade front, but, not to be outdone, in 1915 abandoned the whole system of value overcall and went over instead to majority overcall. Now any given bid could be beaten by simply raising the number of tricks, regardless of their actual suit value. 'There is something to be said for the system . . .', admitted Dalton in 1916. 'I have never tried it myself, and I have never heard of it being played on this side of the Atlantic, but there are certainly possibilities in it, and it is quite on the cards that we may adopt it later on.'

But we never did; and value overcall remained a backward feature of British Auction Bridge right up to the last revision of its Portland Laws in 1933.

From Jokers to Pirates

Auction Bridge proved no exception to the rule that those whom the gods would destroy they first make mad. Many variations on a theme of Bridge had been essayed and abandoned almost before the ink was dry on the Treaty of Versailles.

In Joker Bridge the Deuce of clubs was replaced by a Joker, which acted as the permanent highest trump and produced a game richly deserving of neglect. Bolshevik was Auction with the addition of an un-overcallable personal misère bid played one against three. Equality Bridge basically consisted in stacking the pack before dealing—an idea which, if it did not exist, it was unnecessary to invent. Reverse Bridge, by R. F. Foster, offered hope to bad hands by recognizing an alternative bid of any suit 'reversed', with Ace the lowest-ranking card and Deuce the highest. Cairo Bridge, Standard Bridge, and Compound Bridge offered various complicated ways of attacking the value-overcall problem of ordinary Auction, their remedies being mostly more debilitating than the illness. 'The main defect of Compound Bridge', wrote Manning Foster in *Auction Bridge Variations*, 1923, 'is that if you have a good hand it doesn't much matter what you do.'

Other variations, if not necessarily mad in principle, in practice failed to scrape through the sanity test. From about 1914 onwards Florence Irwin tried to promote some form of Nullo-Auction, apparently unaware of Foster's 'misery' bid of 1903. A bid of *n* nullos is an undertaking to lose at least *n* odd tricks, playing at no trump.

Some players developed an aversion to the dummy feature, and adapted Auction to the Whist-like practice of playing with all four hands concealed. 'It is astonishing how much difference the elimination of dummy makes in both calling and play', remarks Manning Foster. 'Take away the dummy and the faults of many so-called good Bridge players become ruthlessly exposed.' A superior version of this game later devised by Hubert Phillips under the name Contract Whist is recommended to anyone whose dislike of Bridge centres on the dummy feature.

Various attempts have been made to adapt Bridge for other numbers of players, or at least to apply Bridge principles to previously existing Whist variations. What makes them varieties of Bridge is little more than the fact that some cards are exposed and Bridge scoring is used (whether Auction or Contract). But the essential feature of Bridge, i.e. partnership play, is necessarily absent. The simplest and least satisfactory form of Bridge for three players is Cut-Throat. A dummy hand is dealt face down as partner to the dealer and is not revealed until a contract is declared. Dealer's opponents bid as normal, while dealer bids on the basis of the only hand he can see. If East-West become the declarers, they still play with hands concealed. Trio Bridge (George Coffin, 1932) is a more playable version of the same thing. In Towie (Replogle and Fosdick, 1931), half the dummy is exposed before the auction, and if the final bid is not enough for game, the cards are carefully stacked and redealt in such a way as to produce more biddable hands for a second auction. The most intelligent three-hander of its type is Hubert Phillips's 'Booby', dating from World War II. One card is dealt face down to the dummy and seventeen each to the three live players. Each then reduces his hand to thirteen by making any four discards to the dummy, from which the eventual declarer plays.

Bridge for two seems even more futile than Bridge for three. Several variations are based on the trick-and-draw principle of German Whist, as in the appropriately named Draw-Bridge and Honeymoon Bridge (also called Strip Bridge). As Andrew Pennycook observes in *The Book of Card Games* (Granada, 1982) 'Either there is too much information, and the game becomes an exercise in logic, or there is too little and chance plays a dominant role.'

Perhaps the most interesting unsuccessful variation on Auction was Pirate Bridge. Here each plays for himself in the long run, but at each deal bids for a temporary alliance with any one of the other three players, as in Quadrille or Solo. It was tested at the Knickerbocker Whist Club in 1916 by a company including Foster, who published a book on it in 1919. 'Auction as now played', he later remarks (in *Foster on Auction*) seems to have reached the end of its evolution. Pirate will probably replace it.' He was wrong. Critics attributed its failure to the fact that success was a foregone conclusion for the players with the two best hands.

He was right, however, when in the 1921 edition of that work he opened a new chapter on yet another Bridge variation with the words 'Among the recent suggestions for novelties in the way of variations from the standard game of auction . . . there is one which seems to promise a more permanent following than any of its predecessors, and that is Contract Bridge.'

From Plafond to Contract

At first sight, the jump from Auction to Contract looks smaller than that from Bridge-Whist to Auction. In Contract, any tricks taken by Declarer in excess of the number contracted do not directly count towards winning the game but are only added to bonuses scored above the line. This increases the pressure on partners to reach the highest contract they can safely make, which in turn places considerably more emphasis on more accurate and highly communicative bidding. As Rex Mackey characteristically remarks, 'Auction demanded no such accuracy. If the bidding died at, say, One Spade and the Declarer proceeded to make Four, he scored his game just as if he had bid them; this was naïve and pleasant for sweet old ladies and retired warriors at the nineteenth hole, who found it difficult to add up to four anyway.' The new game did not at once take fire. Many considered it too advanced or scientific for ordinary players, chiefly because the effect of this new rule was to transfer the game's centre of gravity from skill at play to skill at bidding, and suitably ingenious bidding systems had yet to be devised. The most distinctive feature of modern Contract Bridge is that half the game is over before the first card has been played.

The idea of Contract is generally credited to the French, but its true history is complicated by the later efforts of British players to denigrate the Americans' success in popularizing their version of the game. According to Manning Foster, Contract was first played in France under the name Plafond, and the term 'contract' was introduced by Pierre Bellanger. Bellanger, in his introduction to Manning Foster's *Bridge-Plafond* (1933), affirms that Plafond was invented in France in 1917–18. Culbertson and Morehead, in the *Encyclopaedia Britannica*, say it was played in the United States as early as 1915 but rejected from the 1917 and 1920 revisions of Auction Bridge Laws because the committee thought such a difficult game would forfeit the popularity of Auction. Dalton says, 'Few in England even knew of it . . . in 1919 and 1920 I played it on the long voyage to and from Japan, and it made some progress in Paris and on the Riviera.'[20] Buller says, 'It was I who, in 1919, endeavoured to introduce Contract ("Plafond") into the Portland. I ploughed a lonely furrow. They would not look at it.'[21] Manning Foster adds: 'It was introduced into England in 1919. In 1919, 1920 and 1921 I wrote enthusiastically about it in the press, and brought out a brochure on it under the title Contract Bridge, now out of print . . . It was considered too difficult for the ordinary player . . . At only one

London club, the Cleveland, did it persist for several years until the American form of the game came along in 1925–26 and swamped it.'[22]

If Plafond was played as early as 1915, as suggested by Culbertson and Morehead, it seems odd that it should have escaped R. F. Foster's pen before 1921. The earliest English description of Contract I can vouch for actually appears in *How to Win at Royal Auction Bridge*, by 'Cut-Cavendish' (Edwin Anthony), London, 1920. In 1923 Manning Foster put Contract first in his book entitled *Auction Bridge Variations*, adding 'There was a time when I thought that Contract Bridge might prove a serious rival to Auction. It has practically superseded it amongst French and Belgian players. But . . . it has never been adopted by the chief card-playing clubs and has never achieved official recognition.'

Two years later, in November 1925, Harold S. Vanderbilt boarded the SS *Finlandia* for a Caribbean winter cruise. Docking again early in 1926, he brought back with him a game that was shortly to sweep the world.

Basically, it was the same Contract Bridge he had started out with. But Vanderbilt had wrought some changes on it. Being a millionaire, he found the scoring system rather tame and decided to make it more exciting by throwing in lots of noughts. He correspondingly raised the game target from 30 points to 100—much easier to remember—and adjusted basic trick values to 20 in clubs and diamonds, 30 in a major suit, and 35 at no trump. The purpose of this odd figure was to perpetuate the feature whereby attainment of the game target in one deal required a successful bid of five in a minor suit ($5 \times 20 = 100$), four in a major ($4 \times 30 = 120$), or three at no trump ($3 \times 35 = 105$). Later, when players were even having difficulty in adding up numbers ending in 5, some mathematical genius discovered that the same effect could be achieved by scoring 40 for the first no-trump trick and 30 thereafter.

Next, Vanderbilt scrapped the bonus for making an accidental slam of 12 or 13 tricks. To score it, you had to bid it. By way of compensation, he doubled the bonus to 500 and 1,000 respectively. The effect of this huge increase was to make slam-bidding a key feature of the new-found game.

These innovative scores were rendered even more excitingly complicated by the addition of vulnerability. A side is 'vulnerable' when it has won a single game and so requires just one to win the rubber. All right-thinking people will agree that a partnership finding itself in this situation is bound to indulge in reckless bidding, in an attempt to shut their opponents out of a winnable game by themselves entering into an impossible contract whose loss will only affect scores made above the line. The temptation must therefore be overcome by increasing the penalties imposed on a side prepared to go down waving the flag. But that gives rise to another problem. Increasing the penalties for entering into a deliberately unwinnable contract may render the vulnerable side more nervous about its bidding, and so liable to miss the best game for its pair of hands. Obviously, increased penalties for failure must be matched by correspondingly increased scores and bonuses for success. And so they were, thus leading to the lunatic scoring schedule of the modern game, and allowing Bellanger to describe Bridge as 'no longer a game of tricks but a game of points'.

As vulnerability was a controversial feature, it should be added that Vanderbilt did not invent it. The word 'vulnerable', he later wrote, apparently in all seriousness, 'was originally suggested by a young lady passenger on board, whose name I cannot remember, but she had played some other game in which the term was used'.[23] Manning Foster observed that it had already been adopted by such world-famed establishments as the Jockey Club (Vienna), the Casino (Budapest), and other watering-places of Italy, Germany, Yugoslavia, and Czechoslovakia. R. F. Foster, in a hasty appendix to the 1926 edition of his Auction Bridge classic, slighted vulnerability and faulted the game for going on too long. Bellanger, predictably, was against it. 'Do not let anyone accuse us of Chauvinism', he nobly pleads, preparing us for a logical *tour de force* equivalent to not eating his cake and regurgitating it. 'The "vulnerable" against which we fight is, alas, a French invention.'[24]

In the summer of 1926, reports Milton Work, 'Contract broke out in Newport and Southampton and virtually eliminated all other card games . . . In the ensuing autumn it appeared in New York City and became immensely popular in certain rather restricted circles.' In 1927 the Knickerbocker grudgingly accepted a watered-down version of the new game, withal retaining Auction scores and relegating vulnerability to optional status. The New York Whist Club, however, swallowed Vanderbilt's game whole. Contract soon conquered all the clubs and upper reaches of card-playing society on both sides of the Atlantic, leaving Auction to wither quietly away. It was then ready to make that truly significant conquest which had hitherto eluded Auction, Bridge-Whist, and even Whist itself since the latter first donned a wig and stepped through the portals of the Crown coffee-house into the fashionable world. Bridge was about to step back out again, disguised as Contract, and become the property of the person in the street. All it needed was a more demotic Edmond Hoyle, with an intuitive appreciation of human psychology, ready access to the forces of mid-twentieth-century technology, a large quantity of cheek, and a modicum of ability at the game. Such a man was currently living in New York. He was a well-educated but underemployed Russian émigré, who had modified his name to Ely Culbertson and married an Auction Bridge teacher called Josephine Dillon.

How Culbertson came to convert all the world and his wife to Contract Bridge is too well documented to need repetition. 'Culbertson rightly felt', says Rex Mackey, referring to a game fad of the twenties, 'that people who would play Mah Jongg would play anything. He made them play Contract Bridge. If comparatively few of them have ever succeeded in playing it particularly well, largely thanks to him, they have played it in their millions ever since.'

18

Tarot games

> . . . it seems to me reasonable to feel that, once you have experienced the subtlety and variety of games played with one or other form of the Tarot pack, you will see little point in going back to games played with so dull a piece of equipment as the ordinary regular pack of playing cards.
>
> Michael Dummett, *Twelve Tarot Games* (1980)

Tarot cards, once little known in English-speaking countries outside the specialist world of T. S. Eliot's 'Madame Sosostris, famous clairvoyante', are now almost commonplace. Whether or not this reflects a populist quest for spiritual values in an increasingly materialistic society, it certainly reflects an increase in the quantity, quality, and variety of modern Tarot packs, many of which are works of art and, literally, collectors' items. What it evidently does not reflect is any significant move towards the playing of Tarot games in countries which lack that tradition. Which is rather ironic, when you consider that Tarots were originally invented for playing games with (their occultic and fortune-telling functions date from the late eighteenth century)[1] and that, having now been played for over 500 years, Tarot is still the everyday card game for thousands, perhaps millions, of European players.

Tarot games are still played in Italy, where they originated: in Austria and Hungary, where they have long flourished: in France, where they are on the increase: and to some extent in Switzerland, Sicily, Yugoslavia, Czechoslovakia, and parts of Germany. Players are still said to be found in Denmark, and I can vouch for Romania. The tradition was also once enjoyed, but has since been lost, in the Netherlands, Poland, Sweden, and Russia. The only areas it never effectively penetrated are the British Isles, the Iberian peninsula, and the Balkans.

Modern Tarots are of three functional types: those produced for playing games, those intended for fortune-telling, and those designed for collectors. The lines between them are not too sharply drawn, for almost any pack produced for one purpose can be used equally well for another. Fortune-telling cards have developed design traditions of their own, though even the best known of them, the Tarot de Marseille, was originally designed for play, and in France remained so used until well into the twentieth century. Designers' and collectors' cards, though not governed by any particular discipline of content, tend to refer back to the occultist tradition. As we are only interested in games, neither category need detain us further.

Cards for playing

Cards produced for Tarot players exhibit a wide variety of designs and constitutions, as befits a range of folk games practised for centuries over a large and mountainous area culturally characterized by a diversity of traditions, each tenaciously held.

The Tarot pack consists of two parts. One is an almost orthodox four-suited pack with numerals Ace to Ten, but with four court cards instead of three, the additional one being a Knight, or Cavalier, ranking between Queen and Jack.[2] To this is added a fifth 'suit' of colourful picture cards, normally twenty-two in number, of which twenty-one are trumps. There is no particular symbol for this suit. Instead, the trumps bear individual illustrations, sometimes with explanatory names or labels, and are usually numbered from 1 to 21. The twenty-second is generally known as 'the Fool', and in some traditions has come to act as the highest trump. Any similarity between the Fool and the modern Joker is purely coincidental.[3]

Tarot playing packs are broadly divisible into an older and a younger tradition. The older, formerly universal but now restricted to Italy and Switzerland, is characterized by the 'Latin' suit-system of cups, coins, swords, and batons. There are ten numerals, which in cups and coins often rank upside down from Ace high to Ten low. The Fool is not a trump but an 'excuse' for not following suit. The twenty-one trumps bear Roman numerals and are known as *atouts* in French and *trionfi* in Italian. Differing slightly from pack to pack, they are typified by the series represented in the Tarot de Marseille, namely: (1) the Juggler, (2) the Popess, (3) the Empress, (4) the Emperor, (5) the Pope, (6) the Lovers, (7) the Chariot, (8) Justice, (9) the Hermit, (10) Fortune's Wheel, (11) Fortitude, (12) the Hanged Man, (13) Death, (14) Temperance, (15) the Devil, (16) the Tower, (17) the Star, (18) the Moon (19) the Sun, (20) Judgement, (21) the World. Hence there are 78 cards to a pack: 4 × 14 suit-cards, 21 trumps, and the Fool.[4]

The younger tradition, dating from the eighteenth century, uses the French system of spades, clubs, hearts, and diamonds. In the 78-card French and Swiss branch there are ten numerals in each suit, the twenty-one trumps bear Arabic numerals, and each one has two illustrations of various nineteenth-century scenes of people at work and play. In the 54-card Austro-Hungarian branch there are only four numerals in each suit, running 7–8–9–10 upwards in black suits and A–2–3–4 downwards in red. The twenty-one trumps, called Tarocks, have Roman numerals. Each bears two nineteenth-century illustrations of scenes from the folklore of countries associated with the old empire. A similar 54-card French-suited pack is used in Germany for the game of Cego. Cego trumps have Arabic numerals and, in one of two major designs, depict animals instead of country folk.

In all Tarot games three of the picture cards are particularly significant to the play and tend to retain their original names even when divorced from their original designs. They are the Fool and the highest and lowest trumps.

1. The Fool (Italian *il Matto*, French *le Mat* or *le Fou*). In the older tradition of France and Italy the Fool is not normally a trump: it is an odd card that may be played as an 'excuse' for not following suit to the card led, to protect a high card from being lost, or to avoid spending a trump. It is therefore known in modern French as 'l'Excuse'. In the younger, central European tradition it has been transformed into the highest trump, but retains a Germanicized form of the word 'Excuse', variously spelt *Sküs*, *Skys*, *Skiss*, *Stiess*, etc.

2. The top trump, No. 21, usually represents 'the World'—Italian *il Mondo*, French *le Monde*. In German it is *der Mond*, literally 'the Moon', but obviously a corruption of *Monde*. In France, where the traditional pictures have been dropped, it is now just called 'le 21'.

3. The lowest trump, normally No. 1, is the Juggler or Mountebank (*il Bagatto* or *Bagatello*). Again, modern French Tarot has discarded the equivalent character (*le Bateleur*), and the card is now called 'le Petit'. In central Europe the Italian word has become *Pagat*.

The word 'Tarot' is of unknown origin, which is not to deny that many different origins have been proposed for it, some highly imaginative. The special cards—and, by extension, the whole pack containing them—were originally known as *trionfi* or *triumphi*, 'Triumphs', perhaps inviting reference to characters in medieval re-enactments of Roman triumphal processions. It was not until the early sixteenth century, when the idea of trumps and triumphs had been adopted into games played with the ordinary pack, that the special cards reasserted their distinction by adopting the name *tarocchi* (singular form *tarocco*), from which derive French *Tarot*, German *Tarock*, and related words.[5]

Playing with Tarots

Tarot games are more remarkable for their similarities than for their differences: they feel like regional dialects of one and the same language of play. They are essentially trick-and-trump games, and trumps are always the illustrated cards, never one of the conventional suits. Play invariably proceeds from left to right, the opposite of Bridge. Players must follow suit if possible, otherwise are obliged to trump (except for the holder of the Excuse in games where it is recognized).

The most remarkable common feature is their distinctive scoring system. They are essentially point-trick games, in that the object of play is to win a majority of card-points rather than a minimum number of tricks. Different cards have different values, the commonest schedule being usually expressed as follows.

trump 21 (XXI)	5 points
trump 1 (I)	5
the Fool	5
each King	5
each Queen	4
each Cavalier	3
each Jack	2

But the actual counting takes place in a special way. During play, all cards won by a given player or partnership are not separated into tricks but are thrown to a single pile. After play, scores are usually reckoned by counting won cards off in batches of two, three, or four, depending on the particular rules of the game. Each batch should, so far as possible, consist of one counter and the rest blanks (non-scoring cards). The scoring value of each batch depends on the number of counters it contains, as follows.

0 counters	1 point
1 counter	face value
2 counters	face value minus 1
3 counters	face value minus 2
4 counters	face value minus 3

(Face value means the total value of any counter(s) contained in the batch.)

The rule of one counter to a batch is designed for convenience, as no subtraction has to be made. In fact, for any given batch number, it doesn't matter how the cards are arranged for counting. For example, suppose you finish up with two fives, two fours, three threes, a two, and ten blanks, and cards are to be counted off in threes. Two possible ways of calculating the score are shown in Table 3.

TABLE 3

5–3–0→7	5–5–4→12
5–2–0→6	4–3–3→ 8
4–0–0→4	3–2–0→ 4
4–0–0→4	0–0–0→ 1
3–0–0→3	0–0–0→ 1
3–0–0→3	0–0–0→ 1
27	27

This bizarre procedure is easily explained if it is assumed to derive from a basically three-handed game. The score of 27 would then be obtained if (*a*) each trick counted 1 point regardless of content, and (*b*) the counting-cards bore the more logical values 1–2–3–4 instead of the actual 2–3–4–5. In the example quoted above there would be six for tricks and 21 for counters, making 27 in all.

That this more 'logical' method was the original one can hardly be doubted. It explains, for instance, why a game originally designed for *p* players should specify counting in batches of *p* cards, even if it happens to be played by some other number. Again, suppose we experiment with the example above by assuming that exactly the same cards were won in a four-player game and counted off in batches of four. Counting the odd half-trick as a whole one, we find that by any of the methods and arrangements described the final score is always 26, there being (nominally) five tricks instead of six. More telling is the fact that the total score available in a three-hand game fully employing the 78-card pack always totals, by any of the systems described above, exactly 78 points.

What this does not explain is why such a basically simple scoring system should have been universally replaced by one that sounds so complicated in the telling. Dummett makes the following suggestion:[6]

Presumably . . . players found it tedious to carry out two operations, one of counting the number of tricks and one of adding up the point-values of the

French court cards have always borne individual names, though not always the same ones,
nor invariably attached to the same figures. (Mid-nineteenth century.)

Mrs Fig's Card Party Disturbed (1809) by Woodward. The caption balloon at top right suggests that 'Whisk and Swob' was still in use but may have been regarded as vulgar.

Twopenny Whist (1796) by Gillray. Full-length courts and lack of indices on cards necessitated their being held in both hands to aid identification.

(*Left*) King from a nineteenth-century American Indian pack, hand-painted on deerskin, based on a 40-card Spanish original.

(*Below*) Pope Joan in progress, using nineteenth-century Pope Joan board with modern counters and Waddingtons Poker cards.

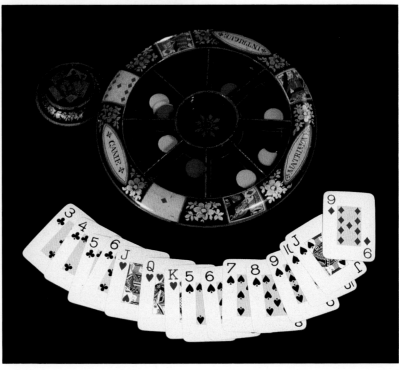

Eighteenth-century staking board for Poch, under its dialectal name *Boekel*. Reading clockwise from bottom left, the compartments are labelled *Sau* (lowest card), *Unter*, *Ober*, *Braut* (Marriage), *König* (King), *Zehn* (Ten), *Seq.* (sequence), and *Bock*, which is the German for 'goat' and a pun on the word *Poch*.

Card table decorated with laburnum parquetry. English, *c*.1715.

French-suited cards of a distinctive pattern are used for Skat and other German card games.

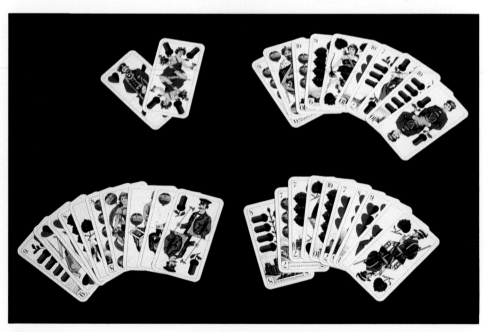

The same hands are here laid out with traditional German-suited cards (acorns, leaves, hearts, bells) of the Prussian pattern.

The 'Triestine' pattern of Italian playing-cards is characterized by Aces bearing humorously apt mottoes in Venetian dialect. That surrounding the Ace of coins (bottom right) translates as 'Friends are mighty rare / When you've no cash to spare.'

Playing-cards with traditional suits of acorns, escutcheons, roses, and bells, are used for Switzerland's national card game, Jass.

Austrian Tarock players. Tarot games are widely played in France and across Central Europe.

Publicity shot representing casino Blackjack as fun for all the family.

counting cards, and fused the two together . . . At first, the combined operation would be thought of as consisting of adding 1 to the sum of the point-values of the counting cards in each trick. But, in the course of time, since there would most often be at most one counting card in a trick, and since it might, in any case, be easiest to count by rearranging the counting cards so that no more than one card was included in a trick, the point-values associated with the counting cards must have come to be increased by one; and thus the method of counting that has been described would have been arrived at.

One wonders whether there must not have been some additional inducement to complicate matters. Perhaps fifteenth-century players were not so accustomed as we are to follow Cotton's advice to 'Lay your tricks angle-wise, that you may the more facilely compute them.' Tarot cards were as large as they were numerous, and on a modest-sized table cluttered up with drinks and coins it may have been practically impossible to lay one's tricks sufficiently angle-wise to compute them facilely and at a glance. The fact that won cards were thrown together in a heap may have provided that additional inducement. Newcomers to Tarot games might be forgiven for ignoring the complications and reverting to the presumed original system.

In the simplest game the cards are evenly divided amongst three players and the winner is the player taking most card-points. A commoner format is for the dealer to receive more cards than his opponents and to discard the excess before play. With the introduction of bidding games inspired by Hombre a 'solo' format was devised, whereby players bid for the right to take the stock of excess (undealt) cards and played against the combined forces of the opponents. The further influence of Quadrille inaugurated four-handed 'alliance' games in which the soloist could either play alone or seek as ally the holder of a nominated card.

Many games include scores for declaring card-combinations. Apart from increasing the interest, this also increases the skill factor by affording information as to the lie of significant cards. There are also partnership versions in which partners are provided with various conventional means of conveying useful information to each another. Central European games are further characterized by a range of additional 'announcements' that may be made, such as undertaking to play without exchanging any cards, to win the last trick with the lowest trump, to capture all the trump counters, to win every trick, and so on. Such announcements are often of greater strategic and scoring significance than the bids themselves.

Games ancient and modern

Tarot games were first played in Italy in the 1430s.[7] As they were fairly sophisticated even in principle, and the necessarily hand-painted cards expensive in practice, they must have been invented in noble or aristocratic circles and at first restricted to these levels of society. By the end of the century, when cards were more readily produced and knowledge of the game had filtered down through the social strata, several traditions had become established in different localities, probably all using seventy-eight cards but each with a characteristic order or constitution of the trump suit.

The principal centres were at Ferrara, Bologna, Florence, and Milan. Practical details are lacking of the first of these, which is not known to have left descendants. That of Bologna survives in modern Tarocco Bolognese, formerly known as Tarocchino (Little Tarot) from its having been played with a stripped pack since about the 1520s. The early Florentine game is uncertain, but Florence gave birth to the later game of Minchiate, played with a pack enlarged to ninety-seven cards from perhaps the 1530s. Minchiate later spread to other parts of Italy, notably Rome in the seventeenth century; it seems to have been played by a dwindling band of aficionados until well into the twentieth century, but is now extinct. The early Milanese game, though also unrecorded, may have been ancestral to all Tarot games subsequently played outside Italy.

Tarot games had spread to Switzerland and France by the early sixteenth century. Significantly, Rabelais includes 'le tarau' in his 1534 list of Gargantuan games, but no equivalent appears in the even longer list of his German translator Fischart, which was last extended towards the end of the century. They do not seem to have reached German-speaking regions until the early seventeenth century.

The period from about 1650 to 1750 saw the greatest expansion in the popularity of Tarot games, chiefly in that form developed in the east of France and played there with the pack now known as Tarot de Marseille. 'Classic Tarot', as Dummett terms it, spread as far west as Normandy, north as Sweden, and east as Russia. It may or may not be significant that the beginning of this period coincides with the earliest records we have of actual rules of play. Unfortunately, the tradition soon died out in Paris, where the gamebooks were mostly published, so that for much of the eighteenth century no record remains of the game's continued development in eastern France. Classic Tarot persisted in nineteenth-century Germany under the generic title Grosstarock ('Great Tarock'), from which derive versions of the game played formerly in the Netherlands and still in Denmark.

In the late eighteenth century a form known as Tarok l'Hombre became popular in Lombardy, characterized by the incorporation of bidding features borrowed from Hombre/Quadrille. This novelty, though failing to survive in Italy, soon reached Austria and became one of three principal features distinguishing the whole range of games subsequently played in Austria, Hungary, Czechoslovakia, Trieste, and Slovenia. A second major feature was the abandonment, by 1800, of the 78-card Italian-suited Tarot and its replacement by the 54-card French-suited Tarock now current in central and eastern Europe. A third distinctive feature of these games was the universal promotion of the Fool to the position of topmost trump.

Modern French Tarot, the only tradition which actually seems to be on the increase, developed from forms of the game played in nineteenth-century France, notably at Besançon and Dijon. These do not appear continuous with those played in the days before a blanket of silence descended on the editors of eighteenth-century *Académies des jeux*. The pack is still 78 cards and the Fool an Excuse, but the games are played with a French-suited pack (the French being, paradoxically, the last to abandon Italian-suited tarots) and incorporate bidding features seemingly derived from some form of Tarok l'Hombre.

The Swiss, described by some seventeenth-century travellers as almost entirely given over to Tarot games, have since abandoned them in favour of Jass, and are no longer a numerically significant Tarot-playing nation. The tradition lingers on in the Graubünden (Grisons), Wallis (Valais), and some villages in the Jura (Vaud and Neuchâtel). It is not vigorous in the last two areas, which use French-suited cards and may be classed as minor appendages to the modern French tradition. In parts of the Graubünden and Wallis, however, enthusiasm flourishes for games played with the Italian-suited pack—variously called Tarock, Troccas, Troggen, etc.—which have probably changed little since the seventeenth century, or even the sixteenth in the Graubünden.

In Italy, the Tarot-players of Piedmont and Lombardy use a distinctive Italian-suited pack, the Tarocco Piemontese, apparently derived from the French Tarot de Marseille. The games generically known as Permesso in Piedmont and Tarocc'Ombre in Lombardy are remarkable for incorporating a primitive form of bidding borrowed from Hombre in the eighteenth century—remarkable, that is, in that most Italian Tarot games have tended to resist this practice.

Bologna remains the home of a unique 62-card pack, formerly known as Tarocchino, with which an equally distinctive and challenging game is played. The plain suits are shortened by the omission of Twos to Fives, while the trump series, headed by the Angel, includes four Moors of equal rank in place of trumps 1 to 4. (The last played to a trick ranks highest.) Most of the games, notably Ottocento, are for four in partnerships. Points are scored for tricks and counters, as usual; for various combinations declarable before play begins, as is not unusual; and also for combinations which partners can make from the cards they have captured in tricks, which is distinctly unusual. 'It can be shown', says Dummett, 'to have remained nearly unchanged since the beginning of the eighteenth century . . . Although even in Bologna it is probably known only to a minority of card players, it is still played there with enthusiasm by people of all ages and social classes.' And the fact that it remains unique to Bologna makes it 'a symbol of local patriotism'. Bologna and surrounds also enjoy a three-hander called Terziglio, remarkable in its own way for its possession of a rudimentary form of bidding.

Hardly less remarkable than the Tarocco of Bologna is that of Sicily, played in four out-of-the way localities which, prior to fieldwork carried out by Dummett in the 1970s, remained practically unknown to the world—one of them, indeed, unknown to the other three. At the north-eastern towns of Tortorici and Barcellona Pozzo di Gotto, and at Mineo in the province of Catania,[8] a fairly basic game with simple bids is played by (usually) three players with a distinctive 64-card Sicilian pack. The pack is remarkable in several respects. The highest trumps are (20) Jupiter and (19) Atlas; the Devil is replaced by a Ship, and, ranking beneath what is elsewhere the lowest trump (1, *Bagatto*) is an even lower, unnumbered trump representing Poverty (*Miseria*). The Fool is called the Fugitive (*il Fuggitivo*). The design of suit symbols is that now classified as Italo-Portuguese, long thought extinct in Europe. The pack is shortened by the omission of numerals Ace to Four in three suits (no suit ranks upside down) and the Two and Three of Coins; furthermore, in practice, the Ace (or Four) of coins is also discarded before play, which normally takes place with only 63 cards.

The current Central European games of Austria, Hungary, Czechoslovakia, Slovenia, Trieste, and Baden (Germany) form a fairly coherent group, characterized by the use of a French-suited pack not exceeding 54 cards. The Fool—*Sküs, Skiss*, etc.—is normally the highest trump, and (except in Cego) significance attaches to attempting to win the last trick with the lowest trump, or *Pagat*. All are bidding

games, and many incorporate it as an additional side-bid known as
Pagat ultimo, which may be won or lost independently of the main
bid. Many can be traced back to the late eighteenth-century game of
Tappen. Tapp Tarock and its more advanced derivative Point Tarock
are still played in Austria, as is the distinctive Badenese game of Cego
in Germany. Most of these are basically for three players. Another
branch is represented by various four-hand 'Rufer' games, so called
because the bidder may call (*rufen*) for an ally by naming a card
lacking from his own hand. In Königsrufen, Austria's principal Tarot
game, the called card is a King. In others it may be a high trump,
the appropriate games being known as Zwanziger-Rufen (trump XX)
and Neunzehner-Rufen (trump XIX). Czech and Hungarian games are
chiefly of this type. Hungarian Tarokk, dating from about 1870 and
formerly known as Paskiewitsch, is a game of remarkable skill and
subtlety played with a pack further shortened to 42 cards by the
removal of all plain-suit numerals except black Tens and red Aces.
So-called 'Bavarian Tarock', although derived from a Tarot game, is
now played with an ordinary German-suited 36-card pack. We shall
come to it later.

Tarot games are a fascinating family and are well worth exploring.[9]
To overcome initial strangeness it is probably best to start off with
modern French Tarot, for which instructions are not hard to come
by. Tapp Tarock makes a good introduction to central European
games, the highest reaches of which are attained in Austria's
Königsrufen and Hungarian Tarokk. The Tarocco games of Italy are
more idiosyncratic, but may appeal to bolder explorers.

19

Primitive pointers

> When I had settled in the town of Sacco, I used to delight in this game [Trappola] to a marvellous degree; it was from that that all my good fortune began . . .
>
> Cardano, *The Book on Games of Chance* (1564)

Many other European card games besides Tarot are of the point-trick type, in which certain cards have counting-values, and a game is won not on the number of tricks taken but on the total value of counters taken in tricks. Britain is about the only western country from whose native repertoire such games are virtually absent. (The system is only partially developed in All Fours, and survives only vestigially in Bezique.) Anybody unacquainted with the principle can imagine its effect by supposing a version of Whist in which, at end of play, each side sorts through its won tricks and counts 1 for each Jack taken, 2 per Queen, 3 per King, and 4 per Ace. As there are 10 possible points in each suit, making 40 in all, the winning partners will be those whose tricks contain cards totalling at least 21 points— even if they have won only two of the thirteen tricks played.

The point-trick principle is of uncertain origin. Absent from Karnöffel, the oldest known trickster (1420s), but central to Tarot, the second oldest (1430s), the question is whether it should be credited to the inventors of Tarot together with the idea of a fully developed trump suit. Dummett doubts whether it should, remarking 'One radically new and fundamental idea is as much as we can expect at one time.' Yet the invention of trumps may be less radical than it might appear, since they are already prefigured to some extent in Karnöffel. And the idea of giving different values to individual cards is by no means as revolutionary as the invention of trumps. It may be that what we now interpret as playing to win tricks was originally regarded as merely playing to win cards, as suggested by the ancient lack of a suitable word for 'trick';[1] in which case the characteristic of plain-trick games is not that cards have no values but that they all have identical values. In other words, plain-trick games are merely point-trick games in which each card counts 1 point, or 1/nth of a point, where *n* is the number of cards in a trick. Such is suggested by the fact that cards in the game of Tressette are mostly valued at one-third of a point each, perhaps reflecting a three-player original. Varying the values of individual cards requires no great leap of creative imagination: it could have arisen naturally from the common practice of according side-payments for the possession or capture of premium cards, as suggested by the fact that Tarot games award points for tricks as well as counters.

Another reason for doubting that card-points originated with Tarot is the existence of various other point-trick schedules not easily derivable from it. Some, like Tressette, do not even incorporate trumps. Yet trumps so obviously enhance the depth, variety, and interest of trick-play that it is hard to imagine the inventors of any game borrowing the point-trick principle of Tarot while at the same time eschewing that of trumps. Then there is the case of Trappola. From its earliest known appearance (1520s) it has always been a point-trick game with a counting schedule strongly reminiscent of Tarot. Nevertheless, it was originally played without trumps, and, as it seems unlikely that such a game can have been directly modelled on Tarot, it may be thought to perpetuate a point-trick tradition parallel to that of Tarot, if not older.

Beyond this we cannot go. It would be too fanciful to speculate that an increase in the number of court cards from two to three, which certainly occurred before cards reached Europe, was linked to a differentiation of high-card values. The possibility of western origin seems supported by the absence of point-tricks from the known games of Persia and India. Their absence from English tradition further suggests that its long-standing preference for plain-trick games took root before point-tricks developed elsewhere in Europe.

We can expand on this last point by noting that all point-trick games are played with shortened packs, typically of 40 or 36 cards, more recently of 32 or 24. Trappola, the oldest non-Tarot example, uses 36. Early records and surviving cards show stripped packs becoming the norm in several countries by the end of the sixteenth century, though they are not attested much earlier. Fifteenth-century packs were commonly reduced from 52 to 48 cards by the omission of Tens or Aces, but this was probably initiated by card-makers for technical reasons, 48 being a more convenient production number than 52. Practical card-players, possibly grumbling, presumably acquiesced on finding most 52-card games just as playable with 48.

A more radical reduction to 36 cards, however, would hardly have been accepted by players on grounds of manufacturing economics. It seems more likely that they would have initiated the practice themselves. If we ask what gaming principle might have led to the suppression of lower ranks, we find an obvious answer in the development of point-trick games. Since only the higher ranks bore card-points, the lower numerals were correspondingly less interesting, and the fewer there were of them, the more quickly the counters were brought into play. The absence from English card-playing tradition of both point-trick and short-pack games strongly suggests a connection between the two ideas, and raises the possibility that first the point-trick principle and then the shortened pack developed in a period when England was relatively unreceptive to continental ideas.

Point-trick games are dominated by those of the 'Ace-11, Ten-10' family, which is so large and distinctive as to require extended treatment (Chapters 20–22). This chapter covers certain games which are not of this tradition, are not demonstrably related to one another, and are of uncertain or varying ages. We start with the oldest, Trappola, and continue with Italian games of the Tressette family, which, though not recorded before the seventeenth century, exhibit ancient features such as an absence of trumps. There follow the family represented by French Manille and Spanish Malilla, and finally games of a more northerly flavour, including All Fours and Pitch.

Trappola, Bulka, Hundertspiel, Spady

Playing-card enthusiasts have long been fascinated by a distinctive pack of cards known as Trappola. One peculiarity is that, although bearing Italian suitmarks and courtly figures, it is mainly associated with central Europe and disappeared from its Italian homeland centuries ago. Another is that it distinguishes itself not only from the normal Italian pack in being stripped down to 36 cards, but also from other 36-card packs in the selection of ranks stripped out. A comparison of different packs in Table 4 points these peculiarities out.

Early researchers found Trappola something of a mystery. Examples of the pack kept turning up from different parts of Europe at different periods of time, suggesting various lines of cultural continuity which no one was able to disentangle convincingly. Understandably, Trappola was often assumed to be the oldest European card game, perhaps even ancestral to the Tarot. But recent researches carried out by members of the International Playing-Card Society[2] now enable

TABLE 4

Italian 40		K	C	F	.	.	.	7	6	5	4	3	2	1
Trappola 36	1	K	C	F	10	9	8	7	.	.	.	.	2	
Swiss 36	2	K	O	U	10	9	8	7	6	.	.	.	.	
Old French 36	1	K	Q	J	10	9	8	7	6	.	.	.	.	

Note: C = Cavalier, F = Footsoldier, O = Over, U = Under. Ace and Deuce appear as 1 and 2 for clarity.

us to date the earliest appearance of Trappola and to chart its persistence, under various names, into the twentieth century, as well as to appraise its distinctive character and assess its influence on other games.

The truth proves no less fascinating than the mystery that preceded it. We know from Cardano that Trappola was played in Venice as early as 1524, and can take it to be a Venetian invention. If the flow of Italian references to it accurately reflects the position, it had dropped out of Italian consciousness by the end of the sixteenth century. By the seventeenth, however, it was fanning outwards. It continued in Bohemia and Moravia at first under the name Trappola, later as Trapulka, shortened to Bulka, and as Šestadvacet ('Twenty-Six', from a significant score), certainly until the nineteenth century and perhaps into the twentieth.[3] In the eighteenth and nineteenth centuries it flourished in Austria and southern Germany under the alias Hundertspiel, from its target score of 100 points,[4] while the closely related Špády persisted in Silesia and Czechoslovakia into the twentieth century. The last known production of Trappola cards took place at Prague in 1944.[5] A Greek dimension also remains to be explored, since the demotic Greek word for any pack of cards is *trapoula*.

Throughout these periods and differing circumstances Trappola has undergone many formal changes but has not lost sight of its most characteristic features. Basically, it is a point-trick game with a distinctive counting schedule. Cards contained in tricks count to their winners as follows: each Ace 6 points, King (*Re*) 5, Cavalier (*Cavall*) 4, Footsoldier (*Fante*) 3, making 18 in each suit and 72 in all. An additional 6 for winning the last trick makes the total 78 (a number particularly associated with Tarot games, suggesting perhaps that the bonus was deliberately introduced to yield that more significant number). Even more distinctive is a scoring feature which gives the game its strategic point and explains its long-standing popularity.

This is the feat of winning a trick with the lowest card of a suit ('The Deuce take it!') which, of course, can only be done by leading it at a late stage of play when no one else can follow suit.

The version Cardano describes is for two. Each receives a hand of nine cards, and, if dissatisfied, may discard it face down and take the next nine from the stock of eighteen. As at Piquet, points are then scored for declaring combinations. Three or four courts count 6 or 12 respectively, Deuces 10 or 20, Aces 12 or 24. Nine tricks are played at no trump, and points scored according to the counters captured in them. Leading a *Do* (Deuce) and winning the trick with it scores a bonus of 10. This is doubled to 20 if effected on the last trick, which, with 6 for last, makes 26. Winning the last two tricks with *Dos* earns 52 points, and the last three, in succession, 78 points—or, in some circles, 104, which Cardano castigates as illogical.

While the original two-handed, no-trump game described by Cardano survived as Bulka in nineteenth-century Czechoslovakia, the German Hundertspiel and Czech Špády were both four-hand partnership games with trumps, though with markedly different rules of following. (Špády exhibits the 'strict' rules of Ecarté, i.e. *F,T,r*, whereas Hundertspiel follows the 'lax' rules of Pitch, i.e. *ft,tr*.) This innovation had interesting repercussions on the play. It now became possible to lead a *Do* when no others of its suit remained, and yet lose it to a trump. Further developments included special scores for winning a plain-suit lead with the trump *Do*, for winning the first trick with it, and for successfully announcing one's intention of winning with one or more *Dos* before play beings. Herein may lie the origin of the scoring feature of winning the last trick with the lowest trump, as exemplified by the 'Pagat ultimo' announcement of Tarock and the unorthodox 'mit Spitze' of Skat.

Besides being the first demonstrable example of a point-trick game played with non-Tarot cards, Trappola is also the earliest known trickster both using a stripped pack and promoting the Ace to topmost position. Unfortunately, a shortage of comparative data on contemporary games prevents us from drawing any useful conclusions from this. The unusual pack-shape suggests either that the idea of playing with stripped packs was still at an experimental stage at the beginning of the sixteenth century, or that Trappola reflects a much older tradition; but the latter seems negated by lack of earlier references and by the high position of the Ace, which also is not demonstrable from the fifteenth century. (It is high in Piquet and ranks between Ten and Jack in Triomphe, two contemporary plain-trick games.) The fact that Threes to Sixes have been removed, leaving Deuces low, suggests that Trappola was originally played with the full 52-card pack, though Dummett doubts this for lack of evidence.[6] Had it been invented as a short-pack game, one might expect the suppression of Twos to Fives, leaving Six the rank of special significance. Perhaps this was the case, the Sixes being later replaced by Deuces in order to make the key cards more striking in appearance and so easier to keep track of. It may also be significant that the missing numerals, 3-4-5-6, correspond precisely to the point-values of the topmost cards, thus appealing to that same sense of card-players' neatness already gratified by bringing the total of points up to 78. However much we know now about the subsequent development of the game, its origins still remain mysterious.

Tressette, Terziglio, Calabresella

See, those priests enter a café . . . They call for cards, and sit down to their national game. The glassy eyes become bright, and the dull countenances full of life. They are playing Calabrasella [*sic*] which we mentioned last month, and which we now proceed to explain. ('Cavendish', *The Westminster Papers*, 1 Nov. 1870.)

If we ask what trick-taking game replaced Trappola in sixteenth-century Italy and helped, with Primiera, establish the supremacy of the now standard 40-card Italian pack, the likeliest contender would be some early form of Tressette. First mentioned in 1631, it achieved 'nova' proportions in the mid-eighteenth century and remains one of Italy's major national card games to this day.

Tressette and Calabresella (the latter so spelt, and more properly called Terziglio) so resemble each other and differ from non-Italian games as to suggest a common parentage within the peninsula. One marked feature is their complete absence of trumps, implying an antiquity perhaps comparable to that of Trappola and Piquet. Another is that not only the Ace but also the Deuce and Trey are promoted to high position, so that cards rank in trick-taking power 3, 2, A, Re, Cavallo, Fante, 7, 6, 5, 4. Both features are shared with the ancient Put/Truco family of plain-trick games.

The Italian games also share a distinctive card-point system. The 20 Threes, Twos, and court cards are called *figure*, 'honours'. At end of play each player or side scores 1 point for winning the last trick, 1 point for each Ace captured in tricks, and 1 point for every three honours in tricks. In other words, honours count $\frac{1}{3}$ of a point each and fractions are disregarded from the total—'fractions fall to the floor', as the saying goes. The total available is therefore 11, and in Tressette (literally 'three sevens') the target score is normally 21. This method of counting reflects traditional Tarot practice and may imply an original three-player format.

Tressette is a four-player non-bidding partnership game in which all the cards are dealt out, as opposed to other games of the family, in which there is a *monte* or stock of undealt cards through which exchanges can be made. To overcome the obvious restrictions of no-trump play the partners of each side are allowed to give each other information or instructions within certain well-defined limits. For example, the play of a card with the announcement 'volo' means it was the last one of its suit which that player held. To add to the interest of play points are scorable for certain *accuse*, or combinations declarable before play begins. Three or four cards of the same rank higher than Seven score 3 or 4 points respectively, and another 3 is awarded for a *napoletana*, i.e. 3–2-A of one suit. When combinations are counted, as they usually are, the game is played up to 31 instead of 21 points. A game can also be won outright, for example by winning every trick.

In three-hand Terziglio each receives nine cards, there is a *monte* of four, and players bid for the right to play solo against the other two with the aim of taking more card-points. A *chiamo* or 'call' bid undertakes to win after (*a*) calling for a card, which its holder gives the soloist in return for any discard, and (*b*) taking the *monte* and discarding four in its place. In *solo*, the soloist uses the *monte* but does not call, and in *solissimo* he does neither. In *solissimo aggravato* he even allows his opponents to use the *monte* themselves.

Mediatore and Quadrigliati (or Quadriglio) are four-hand non-partnership games best characterized as a cross between Terziglio and Quadrille. Quadrigliati is relatively tame, with all cards dealt out; the more varied and exciting Mediatore features a four-card *monte* and a wide range of possible bids. Readers acquainted with the progeny of Quadrille will not be surprised to learn the existence of Quintiglio or Tressette for five players, Sestiglio for six, and Ottigliati for eight. There also exist a two-hand relative, Tressette a Pizzichino, and a wide variety of 'negative' or trick-avoidance games. Giampaolo Dossena characterizes Terziglio as the neatest member of the Tressette family,[7] the negative Rovescino as a classic, Mediatore as 'fascinating', and Quintiglio or Bellora as 'not without interest'. Sestiglia and other multi-player games he dismisses as 'the inventions of desperate men, only worth considering for people shipwrecked on a desert island'.

Whatever the early history of this family, we know it only

from the time it went into nova state under the influence of eighteenth-century games headed by Hombre/Quadrille. Tressette is first mentioned at Naples in 1631 and 1632, and referred to by De Luca in his treatise on Hombre in 1674.[8] A spate of references in the 1750s at Bologna, Naples, and Milan suggests that it was expanding its borders and entering a vogue period, a suggestion strengthened by the high status accorded it in literature of the time. In 1756 the Venetian patrician Lodovici Morelli published a mock heroic poem entitled *Il Trionfo del Tressette*, and an enquiry into the game's origins appeared at Naples in 1777. Terziglio or Tersilio, a title implying three-handed play and clearly cognate with Spanish Tresillo (Hombre), is first mentioned at Florence in 1822 under the name Calabresella. Relations between the two names are suggested by an 1845 reference to 'Terziglio, denominato volgarmente Calabresella'.[9] If 'Calabresella' and the less common alternative 'Calabrese' for Tressette allude to the province of Calabria, this may, in conjunction with the nominal similarity of 'Terziglio' to 'Tresillo' and the use of a 40-card pack, suggest a possible origin in the formerly Spanish-dominated part of Italy, if not in Spain itself. In this connection the resemblances to Truco assume an added significance.

Manille and Spanish Solo

Of Spanish origin, and once widespread in the Languedoc, Manille was being played around Bordeaux in 1845 and by the end of the nineteenth century had achieved considerable currency in France as a sociable and family trick-taking game roughly equivalent in status to (though quite different in kind from) Solo Whist in Britain. Whether or not it might have conquered the whole of France became an academic question from about 1920, when the introduction and rapid rise in popularity of Belote completely eclipsed any inroads it might have been making in Paris and the north. Between the two world wars a balance hung between Belote in the north and Manille in the south, but after the second of them Belote began to advance vigorously in the south and has since firmly established its position as France's major national card game. Though Manille still has its followers, they are now restricted to the south-west and isolated patches elsewhere in the south.[10]

Manille forms perhaps the simplest introduction to games of the point-trick variety. It is played with the 32-card French pack (Seven low). In the partnership game each receives eight cards and the last is turned for trumps. Each suit is headed by its Ten or *manille*, followed by Ace or *manillon*, then K-Q-J-9-8-7. 'Strict' rules of trick-taking apply (follow suit and head the trick if possible; if unable to follow then trump and overtrump if possible), but with the unusual variation that a player who cannot follow or overtrump need not play a lower trump but may renounce (*F, T, tr*). Each trick taken scores 1; in addition, any Ten contained in a trick counts 5 points, any Ace 4, King 3, Queen 2, and Jack 1. This makes 68 in all and a winning target of 35.

The usual range of formal variants made their appearance before the end of the nineteenth century. One of the most interesting was Manille Parlée, 'Manille with talking', in which partners could communicate information or instructions to each other in accordance with a strictly controlled code of announcements. (Contrary to some reports, this was not the original form of the game.)[11] Others include a non-partnership version, Dix-Sept, in which each tries to take at least 17 points; a three-player version with an eight-card dummy; a highly contrived two-player exercise with two dummies; and the inevitable, if little played, negative version known as Manille à l'envers, or 'Manille upside down'. Equally inevitable was the subsequent introduction of bidding under the influence of Bridge, although, surprisingly, Manille aux Enchères (Auction Manille) is not mainly regarded as a partnership game but is playable by any number from three to seven on a solo basis. Players bid to take a minimum number of points; the highest bidder nominates trumps and seeks to improve his hand by taking up a talon of undealt cards and making appropriate discards; and the soloist wins or loses according to the value of his bid, so it actually resembles Contract rather than Auction. The partnership equivalent is Manille Contrée, or Manille Coinchée.

The equivalent Spanish game—Malilla in Castilian, Manilla in Catalan—is played with the 48-card pack lacking Tens, suggesting either considerable antiquity or a Catalan origin, and the eponymous card is therefore the Nine of each suit. Spanish Solo, much played in South America, is a neat little cross between Malilla and Tresillo (Hombre). Three play with a 36-card pack ranking Seven (*Malilla*) worth 5, Ace 4, King 3, Cavalier 2, Valet 1, 9-8-6-5 (or 6-5-4-3) zero. The soloist plays to take at least 36 points, there being 60 in the pack plus one per trick. A bid of *juego* ('play') is overcalled by *bola* (to win every trick after receiving a specified card in exchange for an unwanted one), and that by *bola sin pedir* ('without exchanging'). Each can also be overcalled by the same bid in coins (diamonds), the suit of preference. There is also an optional misère bid, *bola pobre*. If no one bids, eldest nominates trumps and the game is played all against all.

Manille is first described in *Le Jeu de la Malille*, published in 1776, perhaps at Amsterdam. The text is translated from a Spanish publication of some ten years earlier and the game is said to have been long popular in Spain. Beyond that it is hard to go. A scoring system combining card-points with trick-points immediately brings Tarot to mind, as does the requirement to trump when unable to follow suit. Perhaps the forerunners of both Manille and Tressette, like such Germanic games as Bavarian Tarock, arose from the translation of Tarot features into standard card games. It would be interesting to learn whether Manille was always played with trumps or, like Trappola, only acquired them later.

All Fours

All-Fours is a Game very much play'd in Kent, and very well it may, since from thence it drew its first original . . . (Charles Cotton, *The Compleat Gamester* (1674).)

Though no longer played in its original form, All Fours is ancestral to many games still current in England, the United States, and former British colonies—especially the West Indies, according to my Trinidadian informant. Its progeny includes such games as California Jack, Auction Pitch, and Cinch, and its great mark of distinction lies in having bequeathed us the homely name 'Jack' for the card previously known as 'Knave'.

All Fours is named from its four main scoring points, namely High, Low, Jack, and Game. The point for High goes to the player dealt the highest trump in play (not all cards being dealt out), and that for Low to the player dealt the lowest, though in later derivatives this is scored for winning it in a trick. 'Jack', the Knave of trumps, yields a point to the player capturing it in a trick, or to the dealer if it is turned for trumps. If undealt or unturned, it goes unscored. Though unlikely, it is possible for Jack to be the only trump in play, in which case it scores one point each for High, Low, and Jack. The fourth point, Game, goes to the player capturing the greatest value of counting-cards in tricks.

With gaps repaired from later accounts, Cotton's description is as follows:

All Fours (*English*, 1674). Two players; 52 cards; deal six each in threes and turn the next for trumps. If it is a Jack, and its suit is accepted as trump, dealer scores 1 for it.

Non-dealer may either 'Stand', thereby accepting the turned suit as trump and initiating play, or 'Beg' a point. If he begs, dealer may either 'stand' himself—in which case non-dealer scores a point for 'Gift' and play begins—or else 'run the cards' in quest of a different trump. He does this by turning the trump-card down, dealing three more cards each and turning the next card up for trumps. If this turn-up is of the same suit as the first, he runs the cards again, extending each player's hand by three cards as long as necessary until a different suit appears or not enough cards remain. In the latter case the cards are thrown in and the same dealer deals again. Otherwise, the new suit is taken as trump without question and play begins. The dealer scores 1 if this new turn-up is the Jack.

If cards have been run, both now reduce their hands to six by discarding the appropriate number face down.

Non-dealer leads to the first trick and the winner of each trick leads to the next. Lax rules of following apply, i.e. follow suit or trump as preferred, but renounce only if unable to follow suit: *ft,tr*.

One point each is scored for being dealt the highest trump in play; being dealt the lowest trump in play; capturing the trump Jack; and taking a majority of card-points in tricks (A = 4, K = 3, Q = 2, J = 1, Ten = 10). Game is any agreed target. Cotton says 11, later accounts say 10, and nineteenth-century American players made it 7, whence the alternative title 'Seven Up'.

All Fours is also playable by any number up to seven, but only eldest hand may 'beg'.

It is hard to know whether to class All Fours with short-hand games like Triomphe and Euchre or with point-trick games such as Manille, as it feels like an exact mixture of the two. Unlike Tressette and Manille it is essentially played with short hands so that there is an element of uncertainty as to the cards in and out of play. Like Triomphe, it is basically a two-player game with scope for others to join in. As in Ecarté, the non-dealer may propose an exchange of cards, which the dealer need not accept, and, as in two-handed Triomphe, one player can earn a point for conceding. Its unusual rules of trick-play reflect those of Spoil Five. On the other hand, it differs from the Triomphe and Euchre family in being played for card-points rather than plain tricks; furthermore, the basic card-point system of Ace 4 to Jack 1 is identical with that of Manille.

As it is not mentioned before 1674 and is conspicuously absent from *Taylor's Motto* of 1621, we might guess All Fours to be one of the games which reached England from the continent in Charles II's train, and suspect a possible Dutch origin. It remained a low-class gambling game throughout the eighteenth and nineteenth centuries, as witness a tract of 1754 entitled *Serious Reflections on the Dangerous Tendency of the Common Practice of Card-Playing, especially the Game of All Four.* (Other serious reflections might be prompted by the singling out of a working-class game rather than, say, Piquet or Faro.) In 1890 the studious Dr Pole omits it from his *Handbook of Games* on the grounds that it is 'seldom played now-a-days', while the more egregious 'Captain Crawley', in *The Card-Player's Manual* of 1876, asserts 'Among the minor games at cards, All-Fours holds a deservedly high place', and introduces it with lines attributed to Martin Tupper:

> We have played together,
> Many a time and oft, at Put and Crib;
> And at All-Fours have cheated with the best.
> How can we reconcile such conduct with our honest seeming,
> Or bear our heads so proudly in the world?

It was in the United States that All Fours underwent its greatest expansion, becoming the foremost card game by the beginning of the nineteenth century.[12] By the middle of the century it was being challenged by Poker as a gambling game and by Euchre as a more thoughtful trick-taking game, and responded not by disappearing but by developing new points of interest to compete with both—chiefly by introducing new scoring features and raising the target score. In All Fives, the trump counters were individually scored as and when taken, with an additional 5 for the trump Five. California Jack, or French Fours, was played by 'trick-and-draw', like Bezique, with the stock lying face up in California Jack and down in Shasta Sam. In Commercial Pitch, later called Auction Pitch or Sell-Out, there was no turn-up. Instead, eldest either declared trumps by 'pitching' a card of the desired suit as his opening lead, or sold this birthright, for a pottage of game-points, to the highest bidder. Pitch remains in many ways the most classic member of the whole family and will probably appeal to modern players more than the next line of development about to be described.

The trump Five at All Fives came to be known as Pedro, and, in a later version called Pedro Sancho, the Nine of trumps ('Sancho') attracted a further score of 9 points. In Double Pedro, or High Five, scores were attached both to the trump Five or Right Pedro and to the other Five of the same colour or Left Pedro—an obvious borrowing from the Right and Left Bowers of Euchre. Another Euchre borrowing was the Joker, which counted 15 and was known as Dom in the game of Dom Pedro. By this time the point for Low was being awarded for capturing the lowest trump in play rather than for having been dealt it, and the point for 'game' being won for capturing the Ten of trumps. Ensuring the capture of a Pedro by playing a pre-emptive high trump became known as 'cinching' it, and the game itself was then called Cinch. Cinch apparently originated in Denver, Colorado, round about 1885, and for ten years or so enjoyed a highly organized popularity on the club circuit.[13] It eventually succumbed to the challenge of Auction Bridge, and a perusal of twentieth-century American Hoyles shows the All Fours family settling down into quiet retirement.

All Fours might have been thought dead at this point were it not for the researches of Arthur Taylor, who showed it to be flourishing in and around Blackburn, Lancashire.[14] Whether it was traditional All Fours, with (for example) the point for Low going to the holder of the lowest trump in play rather than its winner, or a modern derivative based on Pitch, is not stated. This lapse is compensated by the further description of two close relatives. Nine-card Don is a four-player partnership game in which each receives nine cards and the first one pitched determines trumps. The rules of following are those of Whist or Nap—*f,tr*—rather than of ancestral All Fours—*ft,tr*. Certain cards captured in play are scored immediately on a Crib board, namely trump Nine for 9, trump Five 10, trumps Ace to Jack 4–1 respectively, and 5 for any other Five. After play, all cards from Ace to Ten are reckoned up as at traditional All Fours, and the side with the greater total pegs another eight towards game. Substantially similar is Phat, said to be played 'on a highly organised league basis in and around Norwich'. In this version, trump Nine counts 18 instead of 9 and non-trump Nines count 9 each.

These games are clearly extensions of Pedro Sancho or Dom Pedro, with loss of the special points for High, Low, and Jack. Don, which I have heard spoken of as an Irish game, may relate to the 'Dom' of Pedro. The relation of Don and Phat to mid-nineteenth-century American games is obscure. Even the direction of transatlantic travel is not beyond question.

Postscripts: Zwikken, Penneech

Zwikken—unrelated, except by name, to German Zwickern—is an old gambling game of the Dutch soldiery.[15] It uses 20 cards, Ten low, and works best for three. Up to three cards are turned for trumps until someone elects to play by bidding the whole or a proportion of the pot. A part-bid can be overcalled by a larger part, or the whole. Once a bid is made, anyone holding the trump Ten may exchange it for the turn-up. The bidder wins by (*a*) declaring a *zwik*, i.e. three cards of the same rank, unless someone holds a higher-ranking *zwik*; or (*b*) winning two tricks; or (*c*) winning one trick if it contains more card-points than the other two combined, counting each Ace 4, King 3, Queen 2, Jack 1.

As English point-trick games are rare, it is worth mentioning one known only from Cotton's *Compleat Gamester*, under the inexplicable name 'Penneech'. Two players each receive seven from a (probably) 52-card pack; the next is turned for trump, and tricks are played, presumably to Whist rules. The winner of each trick covers the trump card with the next one turned from stock, 'and so every trick produceth a fresh Trump, till all the seven be played'. For turning an Ace the player scores 5, for a King 4, a Queen 3, a Jack 2, and for the Seven of diamonds 14. The winner of the seventh and last trick makes a final turn-up and possible score. As Cotton explains,

If the Seven of diamonds be turn'd up . . . That is *Penneech*, and is reckon'd fourteen turn'd up, but it is but seven in hand, and not that neither unless Diamonds be Trumps; if it be Trump it is the highest Card and wins all the others; if it be not Trump, it wins all Diamonds . . . Lastly, having play'd out all the fourteen cards betwixt ye, count how many Cards you have more than your own seven at first dealt you, and for every Card reckon one, and so you must reckon the value of your Coat-Card trumps, with *Penneech* turn'd up or in hand, till you come to sixty one, which is the game . . .

Here note, if you have neither Ace nor face, you may throw up your Game and deal again.

20

Ace 11, Ten 10

Scat, du bist die große Kette,
Die die Spielerwelt umfängt:
Sieh, wie Alles um die Wette
Sich zu deinem Freuden drängt.
Deinem Zauber weicht die Mauer,
Die der Castengeist ersann:
Scat spielt Pastor mit dem Bauer,
Bürger mit dem Edelmann.

Hempel, *Das Scatspiel* (1848) (to Beethoven's
melody for 'An die Freude')

(Skat, who hold the gamesters' world in one great all-embracing chain,
See how to your joyous pleasures people throng with might and main:
Yours the spell that crumbles walls of class and social disaccord:
Skat plays pastor with the farmer, townsman with the noble lord.)

Many of Europe's most popular card games are point-trick games
with cards counting Ace 11, Ten 10, King 4, Queen 3, Jack 2. Lower
numerals usually have no value, and tricks as such are pointless in
themselves. There being a total of 120 card-points in the pack, games
are typically won by capturing more than half that total (at least
61), doubly for taking three-quarters (at least 90), and trebly for
winning every trick. This may be described as the 'Skat schedule',
from its most illustrious manifestation in Germany's national card
game.

Many other members of the 'Ace-11, Ten-10' family enjoy the
status of national or regional games and are played with the short
pack associated with the area in which they are practised. The French
Belote, Dutch Klaverjass, Franconian Binokel, Bavarian Sixty-Six, and
Austrian Schnapsen are played with packs stripped to 32, 24, and
even 20 cards. German Tarock and the Jass games of Switzerland use
36-card packs. Italy's Briscola, Spain's Tute, and Portugal's Sueca
use the Latin-suited 40-card pack lacking Eights, Nines, and Tens,

with the 10-point value variously ascribed to the Three or the Seven. Some relatives emigrated in the nineteenth century and are now firmly rooted in American soil. Pinochle, especially, has developed into an American classic in its own right. Ironically, the only one to reach the English card-table—Bezique—had dropped the card-point feature before finding its way across the Channel. British card-players are therefore often surprised at how mathematical continental card games seem to be, and even more surprised to find that in many countries point-trick games are the rule rather than the exception.

Three extensions of the family may be distinguished.

In the Skat/Schafkopf branch the trump suit is lengthened by the promotion of all Unters or Obers (Jacks or Queens)—or both—to permanent top trumps, in addition to those of the actual trump suit. Hence at least a third and up to half the cards in play are trumps, as opposed to the mere quarter of Whist or Bridge.

In the Marriage/Sixty-Six branch there is a bonus of 10 for winning the last trick, bringing the total to 130 and the consequent target to 66, and another for declaring a 'marriage', i.e. King–Queen of the same suit. In its Bezique/Pinochle offshoot, scores attach to additional combinations such as quartets and sequences.

In the Jass branch, which also includes these features, the two top trumps are always the Jack and Nine of the trump suit, known respectively as *Jass* and *Nel* (for *Menel*, cf. *manille*).

The origin of the point-schedule is uncertain. Games of this family can hardly have arisen in countries using Latin-suited packs, as these lack Tens, making the ascription of that value to Threes and Sevens somewhat artificial. A Dutch origin is widely favoured, on grounds argued by Dummett as follows.[1] It must have been invented by users of French cards, as it is more logical to attach the value 11 to an Ace than to its German equivalent, the Deuce. It can hardly have been France itself, where Ace-11 games have never predominated. Netherlands fits the bill, and the choice is supported by such other factors as the well-attested Dutch origin of Jass.

As to how it arose, Dummett suggests a possible development via some non-trick game akin to Thirty-One or Pontoon, in which cards counted face value, with courts 10 each and Ace 11. When packs were increasingly produced without lower numerals in the late sixteenth century, the missing values 2 to 5 may have been restored by attaching them to the courts, i.e. Jack 2, Queen 3, King 4, Ace 5 or 11. The scheme might then have been transferred to trick-games with loss of value from cards ranking below Ten. This makes sense, though it is questionable whether non-trick games need be brought into the process. Pontoon-like games seem to have counted Ace 1 rather than 11 before the eighteenth century, and there is no shortage of models within the trick-taking field itself, from Tarot, Trappola, and Reversis onwards. The very scheme proposed as a possible forerunner is strongly suggested by Piquet, in which, although it is a plain-trick game, cards bear face values for the purpose of establishing who has the better 'point', with Ace 11 and Ten 10. There is even an early version of Schafkopf in which cards exhibit Skat values when captured in tricks but Piquet values for the purpose of bidding.[2]

As to when it arose, the question does not admit of a precise answer. Games of this family became prominent and profuse in the eighteenth century, but some of their characteristics are discernible much earlier and may be more coincidental than ancestral. A Latin dialogue printed at Anvers in 1526[3] sketches a trick-and-trump game called Monomachia in which the top cards count, and seem to be ranked, King 4, Queen 3, Jack 2, Ace 11, Ten 10. What Rabelais shortly afterwards refers to as 'le Mariaige' or 'la Mariée' do not necessarily correspond to the 'Mariage' of considerably later date. Bazzica, the Italian form of Bezique, appears as early as 1532,[4] but, as described in the eighteenth century, it proves to be a gambling game with features reminiscent of Brelan and Trente-et-Un, and is not positively equated with Bezique before the nineteenth century. The equivalent Spanish name Baciga applies to a Cassino-type game.

It may help to view the seventeenth century as a period of point-trick experimentation, with a forerunner of the Skat schedule crystallizing by the beginning of the eighteenth. It is at least interesting to tabulate certain recorded schedules in a more or less chronological sequence (see Table 5), though we must remember that many recorded games are of unknown date and provenance, that many variations may have been lost from the record, and that others may not have been recorded until long after their origination.

The sixteenth-century Monomachia looks remarkably ancestral to the earliest forms of Jass, which were Dutch; but its Latin title ('Battle') gives no clue to its native original.

The point-schedule of Reversis, a sixteenth-century trick-avoidance game without trumps, also appears in Trümpfspiel, 'The Trump Game', which is represented as the German equivalent of French Triomphe in a French–German reader of 1637.[5] This schedule (d) transforms easily into those of All Fours (e) and Manille (f) by additional treatment of the Ten. All Fours, perhaps of Dutch origin,

TABLE 5

(a)		K–5	Q–4	C–3	J–2				Tarot games
(b)	A–6	K–5	C–4	J–3					Trappola
(c)				K–3	Q–2	J–1	A–11	T–10	Monomachia
(d)			A–4	K–3	Q–2	J–1			Reversis, Trümpfspiel
(e)			A–4	K–3	Q–2	J–1	T–10		All Fours
(f)		T–5	A–4	K–3	Q–2	J–1			Manille
(g)		K–5	Q–4	J–3					Quarante de Roi
(h)		A–5	K–4	Q–3	J–2	T–1			Fünfzehnern
(i)		A–5	K–4	Q–3	J–2		T–10		Bassadewitz
(j)	A–11			K–3	Q–2	J–1	T–10		Smoojas, Dutch Jass
(k)	A–11		K–4	Q–3	J–2		T–10		Schafkopf, Swiss Jass
(l)	A–11	T–10	K–4	Q–3	J–2				Brusquembille, Skat, Klaverjass

Note: T = Ten, C = Cavalier, and the Daus, Ober, and Unter of German packs are translated respectively into Ace, Queen, Jack.

and Manille, certainly of Spanish, first appear in the late seventeenth century.

Quarante de Roi (German Vierzig vom König) is a partnership game with cards ranking K-Q-J-A-T-etc., and scores for melds or cliques. The highest clique is four Kings for 40, whence the name of the game. I believe it first appears in the *Encyclopédie Méthodique* of 1792, but the fact that players need not follow suit suggests greater antiquity. Fünfzehnern ('Fifteening') is a traditional German game of unknown date, though its trumplessness may be an ancient feature.[6] A similar schedule, but with Ten = 10, obtains in Bassadewitz, a trumpless trick-avoidance game first recorded in the nineteenth century.

Nothing in Table 5 forces the conclusion that all these point-trick games represent a single evolutionary family. The idea of winning by card-points rather than plain tricks looks more like an additional feature sometimes grafted on to a plain-trick original. Thus All Fours and Smoojas (proto-Belote) feel like card-point elaborations of Triomphe, as do Fünfzehnern of Elfern and Jass of Hombre. Spanish Solo is basically Tresillo decorated with the card-point system of Malilla. What is interesting is the way in which the Ace and Ten have gradually worked their way up from their 'illogical' counting positions in early games such as Monomachia to the 'logical' one of Skat, via an intermediate stage with Ace-11 high and Ten-10 low.

Einwerfen, Sueca

A simple introduction to the 'Ace-11, Ten-10' family is afforded by a German game recorded in nineteenth-century collections as

Einwerfen or Zählspiel.[7] Earlier dating may be inferred from its card-ranking, elemental structure and alternative titles, which both suggest an air of novelty about the idea of playing for card-points rather than tricks. *Einwerfen*, literally 'in-throw', means to play high-counting cards to a trick won by a partner (also called *wimmeln*, 'swarm', or *schmieren*, 'fatten')—this being the essence of point-trick strategy. *Zählspiel*, 'the counting game', speaks for itself.

Four playing in partnerships receive eight each from a 32-card pack ranking Ace 11, King 4, Queen 3, Jack 2, Ten 10, 9–7 nil. If the dealer forgets to turn the last for trumps, a suit may be nominated by the eldest hand. Tricks are played as at Whist: *f,tr*. A side taking 61+ card-points wins a single game, doubled for 90+ or trebled for winning every trick. A 60–60 tie doubles the value of the following deal. The trump of the first deal remains 'favourite' throughout play, doubling the value of any subsequent deal played in it.

Remarkable similarity to Einwerfen is exhibited by the unexpected Portuguese game of Sueca, which I know only from a little monograph long on style but short on detail as to rules and background.[8] ('Sueca' means 'Swedish', for what that may be worth.) Four play in partnerships, or three with a dummy (*manca*), receiving ten each from the 40-card Spanish pack ranking Ace 11, Seven (*Manilha*) 10, King 4, Queen 3, Jack 2, and 6–5–4–3–2 nil. The last is turned for trump and tricks are played as at Whist. The winning side marks 1 game point for 61-plus, 2 for 91-plus ('capote'), or 3 for winning every trick. A 60–60 tie doubles the following round, quadrupling it in the unlikely event of two tied rounds. Game is 4 points.

Six-Bid and German Tarock

Six-Bid Solo is a modern American game which, in a nice piece of detective work constituting the final chapter of *The Game of Tarot*, Dummett traces back to a form of 54-card Tarock played in eighteenth-century Austria.

Three players each receive eleven cards from a 36-card pack. The odd three go face down to form a *skat* which counts (if relevant) to the soloist at end of play. Cards rank Ace 11, Ten 10 etc. down to Six. The six bids are:

Solo in a named suit other than hearts: the soloist scores twice the number of card-points taken in tricks above 60, or loses twice the difference between it and 60 if unsuccessful;

Heart solo, worth three times the difference above or below 60;

Misère (no trump), worth a flat 30: the soloist may take a trick, provided it contains no card-points;

Guarantee solo, worth 40: the soloist must take at least 80 card-points, or 74 if playing in hearts;

Spread misère, worth 60, with the solo hand exposed;

Call solo, worth 150 in hearts or 100 in another suit: this is a bid to capture all 120 card-points—not necessarily to win every trick—after first calling for a desired card and giving its holder any unwanted card in exchange. (Another may be called if the desired card is out of play.)

Six-Bid derives from various games played in southern Germany under the name Tarock—misleadingly, as Tarock cards are not actually used for them. German Tarock may have arisen from an attempt to simulate real Tarock with ordinary cards. So may Schafkopf: but whereas Schafkopf paralleled the Tarock feature by elevating certain ranks to trumphood, German Tarock did so by restricting trumps to one suit, hearts. This remains the case in Bauerntarock, still played in the Brixental, though in later derivatives hearts has become a preference rather than a compulsion.

Many forms of German Tarock are called Tapp, indicating Tapp Tarock as their point of reference. Dummett dates their original to (at latest) the early nineteenth century and describes it under the name Württemberg Tarock. This was played with German-suited cards, as is its modern derivative Bavarian Tarock or Haferltarock, known from about the 1930s. Tapp itself became attached to a form of the game played with French-suited cards, and to the cards themselves, which appeared in the mid-nineteenth century. The 36-card French pack is also used in Berliner Tarock, another modern form of the game. German Tarock has spread to Switzerland, where it is played with Jass cards in two main versions, Zuger Tapp and Schellen Tapp.

Tapp also spread to the United States in the nineteenth century and there gave rise to a number of varieties in the south-western states. It first appears as Frog (a corruption of the lowest bid, *Frage*), later as Solo, Slough, Sluff, Sixty Solo, Heart Solo, etc., from which Six-Bid evolved as a uniquely American contribution to the genre. It was first described in 1920–4 by R. F. Foster, who traces its origin to Salt Lake City, Utah.[9] Frog penetrated Mexico in the early years of the twentieth century, where it was translated into 'Rana'—the Spanish for 'frog'.

Two relatively primitive features of the game are the use of the

36-card pack and the fact that 'call solo' and misère are defined as taking, respectively, all and none of the card-points rather than all or none of the tricks as in Skat and Schafkopf. It's a pity no eighteenth-century game description survives to show whether it exhibited the pre-Skat schedule with Ace high, Ten low.

Distant relations

Several black sheep of the 'Ace-11, Ten-10' family may be mentioned in passing. (Negative members, such as Bassadewitz, will be found in Chapter 22.)

In Bohemian Schneider, a nineteenth-century two-hander, each receives six cards from a 32-card pack and plays by trick-and-draw as at Bezique or Sixty-Six. Cards rank normally, with Ten low, and the object is to capture a majority of honours (Tens or higher). Suit need not be followed, but a led card can only be captured by the next-higher card of the same suit. Andrew Pennycook reports a variation[10] in which cards bear their Skat values and the winner scores a single game for 61 +, double for *schneider* and treble for *schwarz*.

In the related Czech game of Sedma,[11] played by two or four with four cards each from a 32-card pack, there is no obligation to follow suit and the led card can be beaten only by one of equal rank or any Seven. If it is beaten, the leader may either concede it or, if possible, contest it further by matching ranks again. A trick therefore contains either two or four cards. Cards are then drawn to restore the hand and play continues. The aim is to win a majority of points at the rate of 10 per Ace and Ten and 10 for last, total 90.[12] A substantially similar game is played in Finland under the title Ristiklappi, or 'Cross-clap'.[13]

Catch-the-Ten, or Scotch Whist, is a round game played with thirty-six cards ranking as at Whist except in trumps, whose top cards are Jack 11, Ace 4, King 3, Queen 2, Ten 10. First described in the 'Excelsior' Hoyle (New York) of 1887, it has the look of a traditional game that has been surreptitiously interfered with.

Yukon is first described by Ostrow in 1945 (I believe) with the revelation, as unstartling as it is unsupported, that it dates from the days of the Yukon gold rush. (It appears in Scandinavian books under the name Guldgravere, 'Gold-Digger'.) The only trumps are all four Jacks, known as 'Yukons'. The spade Jack, or Grand Yukon, is highest and counts 15 in play, the others being of equal rank and worth 10 each. In each suit, cards rank Ten 10, Ace 5, King 3, Queen 2. The game looks as if inspired by an ignorance of Skat.

In Réunion, 'a Rhenish game',[14] the upward sequence Ten 10, Ace 11 is followed by two Jacks worth 12 each, the highest being the Jack of trumps and the second highest that of the same colour as trumps (cf. right and left bowers in Euchre). The Norwegian Harjan is substantially similar.[15]

Schafkopf, Doppelkopf

Schafkopf—'Sheepshead'—is the original folk game from which sprang Germany's national card game Skat. It is so called because each side's game-points were originally recorded as lines gradually building up into the nine-line caricature of a sheep's head. Many different varieties of the game are known, no fewer than eight being described when it first appeared in print, in 1811, suggesting that its roots go well back into the eighteenth century.[16]

Its essential features can be appreciated from a description of Wendish Schafkopf, of which a modern derivative is still widely played in Bavaria.[17] Four players each receive eight cards from the 32-card pack, usually German-suited. There are fourteen permanent trumps, namely (from highest to lowest) the Obers of acorns, leaves, hearts, bells, then the Unters of acorns, leaves, hearts, bells, followed by the A-T-K-9-8-7 of bells. In acorns, leaves, and hearts all cards rank A-T-K-9-8-7. (If French cards are used the trumps are ♣Q-♠Q-♥Q-♦Q-♣J-♠J-♥J-♦J followed by the remaining diamonds.) Tricks are played as at Whist and Bridge: *f,tr*.

The two top trumps are known as *die Alten* (the Old ones). If they are in different hands, their two holders automatically become partners, but this fact is not revealed until the defining cards are played to tricks. If they are both in one hand, their holder has the option of (*a*) calling as his ally the holder of a particular Ace, or the winner of the first trick not won by himself; or (*b*) playing a 'secret solo' by leaving bells as trump and letting the others believe (for as long as they can) that he is playing an ordinary alliance game; or (*c*) declaring acorns, leaves, or hearts as trump and playing solo against the other three. This option may in fact be declared by anyone. If more than one bid it, priority goes to the elder hand.

The soloist, or each ally, scores 1 game point for taking at least 61 card-points in tricks (counting Ace 11, Ten 10, etc.), or 2 for making the opponents *schneider* by taking at least 90 card-points, or 3 for making them *schwarz* by winning every trick. No one scores for a 60–60 tie. Game points are usually translated into immediate hard-score, e.g. 10, 20, 30 Pfennig won or lost.

Modern Bavarian Schafkopf has lost the 'secret' bids so characteristic of this family and probably unique to it. Other varieties of Wendish Schafkopf include Dreiwendsch, a three-hander evidently based on the format of Skat; its American equivalent known as Sheepshead or Shep; and Doppelkopf, a four-handed alliance game very popular in the German north and west. This is played with a double 24-card French pack (Nine low) ranking as described above, with all Queens, Jacks, and diamonds as trumps and the first of two identical cards played to a trick beating the second. The holders of the club Queens become 'secret' partners, or the holder of both may exercise options similar to those described above. The soloist or allies must take at least 121 card-points to win, and there are bonuses for taking 150, 180, 210, and all twelve tricks. Doppelkopf also enjoys a wide range of decorative features, such as ranking both heart Tens above the club Queens as top trumps, and awarding bonuses for capturing an opponent's trump Ace, or winning the last trick with a club Jack (known as 'Karlchen Müller').

The defining characteristic of the Schafkopf group is its promotion of Obers, Unters, or both to permanent top trumps, in which capacity they are called 'wenzels'. The earliest recorded varieties include forms with four, eight, and sometimes six wenzels (four Unters, plus the Obers of acorns and leaves). Most of these were fixed-partnership games, some with bells as permanent trumps, some with a trump nominated by a player holding at least five trumps, or, if no one did, by the holder of the top wenzel. In these varieties, still played—patchily—under the heading German Schafkopf, the Ten ranks low, between King and Nine. Its promotion in Wendish forms may reflect the influence of Skat.

Because Schafkopf is not described before 1811, and then appears in various forms, its pre-nineteenth-century origins are obscure. A possible clue to them may be sought in the name 'wenzel', which some derive from *Scharwenzel*—an intensive form of Latin *serviens*, and meaning an excessively devoted servant, perhaps 'lickspittle'. Now a 32-card game is recorded in Germany in 1715[18] under the name Scharwentzeln, and later in the Netherlands as Scharwensleven, variously spelt. The name, and perhaps the game it refers to, survives (at least in books) as Skærvindsel, a Danish 36-card game played by four in fixed partnerships.[19] Though not a point-trick game, its trump suit is headed by seven 'matadors', namely ♣Q, trump-7, ♠Q, ♣J-♠J-♥J-♦J, followed by A-K-(Q)-T-9-8-(7)-6. If this bears obvious material resemblances to Schafkopf, its plain-trick nature and trump Seven feature (compare German Solo) make it an equally obvious derivative of Hombre. Perhaps, then, Schafkopf represents the trick-point embellishment of an Hombre-derivative with a distinctive promotion of the Unters (Jacks) to the role of 'excessively devoted servants' to the original three Matadors or top trumps.

Skat

To describe Skat as Germany's national card game is to damn it with faint praise—it is more of a national institution. Though comparable to Bridge in depth and variety, it is an essentially classless game, being played as enthusiastically in homes and hostelries as it is played seriously in clubs and tournaments under the aegis of the Deutscher SkatVerband. Elsewhere, the game is also current in surrounding countries, notably Poland, Czechoslovakia, and the Netherlands, and in North and South America, though the North American standard game now differs significantly from its modern German cousin.

Skat (*German, current*). There are three active players: if four play, the dealer sits out. Each receives 10 cards from a 32-card pack, dealt 3-(2)-4-3, the odd (2) forming a face-down *skat*. Whoever bids to play the highest-valued game becomes the soloist and plays alone against the other two. His aim is normally to take at least 61 card-points in tricks, counting each Ace 11, Ten 10, King 4, Queen 3, Jack 2. The possible games are:

1. *Suit.* The soloist names a suit as trump. The top four trumps are always ♣J- ♠J- ♥J- ♦J, followed by A-T-K-Q-9-8-7 of the trump suit, making 11 trumps in all. In plain suits, cards rank A-T-K-Q-9-8-7.

2. *Grand.* If he announces 'grand', only the four Jacks are trumps, ranking as above. In the other four suits, cards rank A-T-K-Q-9-8-7.

3. *Null.* There are no trumps and the soloist aims to lose every trick. Null may be played with the skat or from the hand, and with or without the soloist's hand of cards exposed (*ouvert*). Cards rank A-K-Q-J-T-9-8-7 in every suit.

Suit or grand may be played *with skat-exchange* or *from the hand*. In the former, the soloist takes the skat and discards any two cards in its place before announcing his game. In the latter, he leaves the skat untouched and plays with the cards as dealt. In either

case, any card-points contained within the skat count in his favour
at the end of play.

In suit or grand the soloist wins by taking at least 61 card-points
in tricks. His game value is increased for making his opponents
schneider (they take 30 or fewer), and further for making them
schwarz (they lose every trick). If the soloist wins, he scores the
value of his game plus any applicable bonus; if not, he loses that
value, plus any applicable penalties.

For bidding purposes, each player must determine the prospective
value of the highest-valued game he is prepared to undertake. Null
games have fixed and invariable values (below, right). Suit and
grand games have base values (below, left), which are increased
by multiplication according to the contingencies of the game:

diamonds	9	null (skat)	23
hearts	10	null hand	35
spades	11	null ouvert	46
clubs	12	null hand ouvert	59
grand	24		
grand ouvert	36		

Game value at suit and grand is found by multiplying the base
value by a number of playing factors. All applicable playing factors
from the following list are added together first, and the base value
is then multiplied by their total.

(*a*) 1 per matador. 'Matadors' means an unbroken sequence of
trumps from ♣J downwards, whether held in the soloist's hand
(and skat) or missing from it. Thus, if the soloist holds ♣J but
not ♠J, he is with 1 matador; if he has ♣J- ♠J but not ♥J, he is
with 2; if he has four Jacks and trump Ace but not Ten, he is with
5; and so on. Alternatively, if his highest trump is ♠J, then he is
playing without 1; if ♥J, he is without 2; if the trump Ten, he is
without 5, and so on. Only the number of matadors counts: it
makes no scoring difference whether he is with or without them.
The highest possible number is 11 in a suit game or 4 at grand.

(*b*) 1 for game, i.e. for taking at least 61 card-points. (Since this
is assumed by the very fact of bidding, this multiplier is always
counted.)

(*c*) 1 for schneider. (To count this, the bidder must be confident
of taking at least 90 card-points—roughly speaking, nine tricks.)

(*d*) 1 for schwarz. (To count this, the bidder must be confident
of winning every trick.)

(*e*) 1 for playing from the hand.

The next three factors can only be applied if the bidder plays from the hand:

(*f*) 1 for schneider declared. (The soloist declares in advance that he will win schneider. This point is additional to that for actually making it.)

(*g*) 1 for schwarz declared. (Additional to the points for schneider, schneider declared, and actually making schwarz, all of which are implicit in the declaration.)

(*h*) 1 for playing a suit game ouvert, i.e. with all one's cards exposed before the play. (This factor includes all those up to and including schwarz declared, since the game may only be played ouvert if the bidder undertakes to win every trick. It does not apply to a bid of grand ouvert, which instead has a greater base value.)

The lowest possible game value, and hence the lowest possible bid, is 18 (diamonds: with or without 1 matador, game 2, times base 9 = 18). The highest possible suit game is theoretically 216 (clubs: with 11, game 12, hand 13, schneider 14, declared 15, schwarz 16, declared 17, ouvert 18, times base 12 = 216. In practice, this hand would be played at grand ouvert, worth 360.) The lowest grand is 48 (with or without 1, game 2, times base 24 = 48), and the highest 360 (grand ouvert: with 4, game 5, hand 6, schneider 7, declared 8, schwarz 9, declared 10, times base 36 = 360).

The player at dealer's left is Forehand, at his left Middlehand, and at his left Rearhand (dealer himself, if three play). Bidding is based on the principle that Forehand has a prior right to become the soloist, which can only be wrested from him by offering to play a higher-valued game. Middlehand therefore, if not prepared to pass immediately, starts raising Forehand by announcing all possible game values from the lowest upwards (18, 20, 22, 23, 24, 27, 30, 33, 35, 36, 40, 44, 45, 46, 48, etc.). To each of these, Forehand says 'Yes' if prepared to play a game of equal or higher value. When one of them passes, Rearhand may either pass or continue bidding against the survivor, until one of them passes. Whoever remains is the soloist, and must play a game worth at least the amount of the last bid made or accepted. If everyone passes, the cards are thrown in and the deal passes to the left. (But see Ramsch, below.)

The soloist then either (*a*) takes the skat, discards two cards, and announces a trump suit or grand or null; or (*b*) announces a game from the hand, declares a suit, grand or null, and adds any declarations that may apply (schneider or schwarz declared; or ouvert, in which case he immediately exposes all his cards).

Forehand always leads to the first trick. Tricks are played as at Whist or Bridge: *f,tr.* In a suit game, the lead of any trump (Jack or otherwise) calls for the play of any other trump (Jack or otherwise). At grand, the lead of a Jack calls for the play of a Jack (if possible).

At null, play ceases if and when the soloist takes a trick. All other games are played out, and, at end of play, the skat is turned up and counted towards the soloist's game. To win, he needs at least 61 card-points in tricks and skat, or 90 if he declared schneider, or every trick if he declared schwarz. He then recalculates the value of his game, taking into account any extra multipliers that may be due for schneider or schwarz. If this value equals or exceeds his bid, it is added to his score.

The game is lost if he gets less than 61 card-points, or fails to make a declared schneider or schwarz, or wins a game worth less than his bid. Before being deducted from his score, the value of a lost game is increased by one multiplier if the soloist was schneidered (taking less than 31 card-points), and by as many more multipliers as are necessary to make it equal or exceed the amount he bid. The final amount is then doubled if he played with the skat, but not if he played from the hand.

An unexpected loss may occur if the bidder plays from the hand without two or more matadors. Suppose, for instance, he takes the bid at 40, reckoning without 3, game 4, hand 5, times clubs 12 = 60. He apparently wins his game, but at end of play finds ♠J in the skat. His game now proves to have been: with 1, game 2, hand 3, times clubs 12 = 36. This being less than his bid of 40, he is obliged to lose the next higher multiple, i.e. 48—unless, that is, he made schneider, which increases his game value to 48 and so justifies his bid. In practice, experienced players are rarely caught out by this apparently unfair trap: they are aware of the danger, and can judge the probable lie of Jacks by the bidding.

A game may be of any length so long as every player has dealt the same number of times.

Ramsch. It may be agreed to play Ramsch in the event that no one bids 18. Jacks are trumps (as at grand), each plays for himself, and the aim is to avoid taking the greatest number of card-points. There are several varieties. In Augenramsch, whoever takes most card-points has their total deducted from his score, doubled in the event that either opponent does not win a single trick.

Primitive Skat was developed from around 1810 by members of the Brommesche Tarock Club at Altenburg, some twenty-six miles south of Leipzig. Their basis was either a now lost three-handed Schafkopf, or, more probably, ordinary Schafkopf converted by them to the three-handedness to which they were more accustomed by their attachment to Tarock. This fact is embellished by a not necessarily untrue legend to the effect that Schafkopf, then unknown in Altenburg, was introduced to one of them—Advocate F. F. Hempel—by his coachman, who had picked it up while travelling in the Erzgebirge. It was a four-wenzel version, all Unters (Jacks) being top trumps, and Ten ranking low between Ober (Queen) and Nine. An article by Hempel in an issue of the *Osterländische Blätter*, 1818, and later accounts by Professor J. F. Hempel in 1833 and 1848,[20] show the principal stages of development. At first, the dealer received 12 cards to the others' 10, discarded two (*skat* = 'discard') and played to take 61 + card-points in a trump suit previously cut from the pack. This risky business was soon changed by dealing the last two cards to the table and allowing each player an opportunity to become the soloist by picking up the skat. In another version, bells (diamonds) were made permanent trumps, as in many forms of Schafkopf. In another, bells could be overcalled by hearts, which won or lost double, hearts by leaves (quadruple), and leaves by acorns (octuple). By 1820 a major innovation had been made, credited to Carl Adam Neefe, in that a simple skat-exchange bid (*Frage*) could be overcalled by a 'solo' or 'hand' game. Game values were now 1–2–3–4 for *Frage* in bells, hearts, leaves, and acorns respectively, and 5–6–7–8 for the same played solo. There was no grand or null, and bids were made by suit, not by value.

At the time of the 1833 description Skat was spreading throughout Thuringia, having by 1826 reached Leipzig University and thus entered the circulation of the nineteenth-century equivalent of 'wandering scholars'. Tens now ranked high, and in some unorthodox circles extra payments were being made for 'matadors' (consecutive top trumps). At first, such payments were end-of-play extras and had no effect on the bidding, which was still carried out by suit—i.e. a bid in a higher suit beat an equivalent bid in a lower suit regardless of the number of matadors involved. Some players, however, especially students, replaced simple suit-bidding with that of raising according to the value of the game they expected to win with the eventual score for matadors included. This meant that a bid in a given suit could now be overcalled by an equivalent bid in a lower suit played with or without a greater number of matadors. The traditionalists referred disparagingly to this practice as *Räuber-Skat*, 'Robber Skat', because a player with a promising game in a high-valued suit could be 'robbed' of his due by an upstart low suit more strongly supported by matadors. The struggle between suit valuation and game valuation would remain a contentious feature of the game for many years to come.

By 1848, a number of variations were being introduced from other games—Hombre, Tarock, Boston, etc.—probably independently in a variety of places. These included grand and null, both originally playable only from the hand, and both castigated as unnatural by the purists. Both also had variants. Däuserspiel was a grand in which Unters (Jacks) were not trumps but ranked in each suit between Ober (Queen) and Nine, thus making *Däuser* (Aces) invincible. Nullogrand was a null played in grand format, i.e. with Unters (Jacks) as trump.

By 1867 some circles had borrowed from Hombre the bid of *tourné* (German *Wende*), whereby the highest bidder undertook to turn the top card of the skat and accept its suit as trump. At a later date he could play 'second turn' if the first did not suit him (Paßt mir nicht'). Several varieties of Ramsch are recorded by Hertefeld in his classic work of 1884,[21] as well as such aberrations as Uno and Duo— both played as at grand, with the object of taking, respectively, exactly one trick or exactly two. Other peculiarities included the announcement 'mit Spitze', whereby the soloist undertakes to win the last trick with the lowest trump, and the rather jolly bid of 'Spitzengrand', in which cards retain their point-values but rank upside down in each suit, from Seven high to Ace low.

Native Thuringian Skat-players objected to such fripperies for the difficulty of deciding and remembering whereabouts they all fitted into the bidding schedule, a problem less acute in Leipzig, Berlin, and the north, where players preferred to bid by game value rather than suit value. If no form of Skat could yet be rightly designated 'standard', that described by Hertefeld in 1884 is at least typical of its time. The base values for diamonds, hearts, spades, and clubs, respectively, were, in *Frage* 1–2–3–4, *Tourné* 5–6–7–8, solo 9–10–11–12. Grands counted tourné 12, solo 16, ouvert 24; and nulls had fixed values tourné 16, solo 24, both doubled if played ouvert, and 'revolution' 72—the latter a null ouvert so invincible that the opponents were invited to show their hands, discuss the position, and exchange as many cards as they liked before playing! Like most experts, Hertefeld countenanced neither null nor grand played with simple skat exchange, though both were practised—the former under the name Kauf-or 'Purchase' null, the latter as Gucki or 'Peep' grand.

But stronger and more widespread objections stemmed from the fact that two players from different circles, let alone different parts of the country, could hardly sit down for a bout of Skat-bashing (*Skat dreschen*) without first going through a lengthy check-list of mutually acceptable games, values, bidding procedures, and pay-offs, with the risk of total dissatisfaction with the resultant compromise. Thus arose, in the wake of German unification and the founding of the First Reich in 1871, an equally patriotic move towards the unification of the new state's national game, culminating in the first National Skat Congress at Altenburg in 1886, and the promulgation of—if not exactly the widespread acceptance of—the first *Allgemeine Deutsche Skatordnung* (General Rules of German Skat). A second soon followed at Leipzig, and the third, at Halle-Saale in 1899, saw the founding of the Deutscher Skatverband, whose West German descendant subsequently moved to Bielefeld.

Whether these early congresses actually achieved unity is questionable. Delegates and officials made such a claim, but perhaps only amongst themselves, and because it made them feel their efforts had been worth while. How attuned they were to general practice may be gauged from the official insistence on playing with German-suited cards, when sales of French-suited Skat cards were three times as great, and on the Altenburg practice of bidding by suits when most of the population followed the Leipziger practice of bidding by game valuation. Ramsch was not admitted as part of the official game, a ruling that 'officially' applies today, even though everyone still plays it, except in tournaments. Subsequent congresses continued to endorse the original *Skatordnung* until the 1920s, by which time it had fallen even further out of step with everyday practice. During the First World War, Skat had undergone considerable levelling at the hands of soldiers constantly on the move and mingling. The distinguishing features of what was now called Leipziger Skat were bidding by game valuation and the admission of a grand played with skat-exchange, whence the alternative name Gucki-Skat. The eleventh Congress (Altenburg, 1927) agreed to adopt for a one-year experimental period the *Leipziger Skatordnung* first published in 1923, and its ratification in 1928 established the main lines of the modern German game. Tourné was abolished, as were differing suit-game values in favour of the universal 9–10–11–12 with an extra multiplier for hand-play. Grand and grand ouvert were respectively valued 20–30, and the fixed nulls 23–25–46–50. In 1932 these were revised to 24–36 and 23–35–46–59, and in 1937 the system was completed by the admission of suit games 'ouvert, with Schwarz declared'.

It would be idle to pretend that everyone follows the official *Skatordnung* in domestic and informal play, especially in northern Germany, Berlin being a particular hotbed of heresy. Writing in 1969, the Berliner politician Ernst Lemmer[22] offered the following check-list of points to be agreed when members of different Skat circles get together. 'Uncertainties may still exist', he says, as to whether:

Grand counts 20 or 24
Doubling and redoubling are permitted
If so, whether nulls may be doubled
Null hand is an acceptable bid
Null hand ouvert counts 59 or 69
Revolution may be bid
Hand games count double if lost
Ramsch or Schieberamsch shall be played
Bock rounds are played, and, if so, when
Mit Spitze(n) may be bid, and, if so, when
Stakes are played for, and, if so, how high.

(Revolution scores 92. 'Bock', a round of deals on which all scores are doubled, even if doubled or redoubled already, is often imposed after a specified event, such as a lost grand, or any game lost 60–60. If a foreign Skat enthusiast may be allowed an impertinence, I concur with Lemmer in regretting that grand was raised from 20 to 24. Grands are about two-thirds as frequent as suit games, but are worth more than twice as much, and are considerably less interesting to play. If the purpose is to ensure that the lowest grand (formerly 40) cannot be overcalled by null ouvert (46), it would seem preferable to abolish nulls played with skat-exchange.)

American Skat, as promoted by the North American Skat League,[23] may be described as a streamlining of the German game as it existed before the revisions of 1927–8. The simple suit-game with skat-exchange does not exist, base-values being tourné 5–6–7–8 and solo 9–10–11–12, making the lowest possible bid 10 (diamond tourné with or without one). Grands are valued at 12 for tourné (optional if a Jack is turned, the other choice being to play in the suit it belongs to), 16 guckser (with the skat), 20 solo (hand), 24 ouvert. Null and null ouvert, playable only from the hand, count 20–40 respectively. Players acquainted only with the German game will find the American one rather stimulating. Properly approached, tourné is not as chancy a bid as it may at first appear. It sometimes forces the bidder into playing with only four trumps, which, though something of a challenge, is by no means unwinnable, and is very rewarding to win. Grands have more sensible values, and the rejection of nulls with the skat has much to commend it. Ramsch, played when no one is prepared to bid, is an integral part of the official rules.

The American Skat League was founded in 1898 at the fourth of a series of Skat Congresses beginning at Brooklyn in 1887. A Texas Skat League, established 1924, favours a form of the game still called Robber Skat.[24] It shares the streamlined values of the North American game, but, as in Germany, retains the simple exchange game (Frage) in place of tourné.

That Skat has attracted no significant following in Britain is regrettable, not least because this makes proper Skat cards difficult to obtain. For all the complexity and illogicality of the German game, it rates as one of the world's great card games and is undoubtedly the best for three players. And there can surely be no other in which you can successfully entrump a suit of which you hold not a single card! As witness:

On taking the skat you hold ♣A-9–8-7, ♥A-T-8–7, ♦A-T-8–7. If you declare clubs trump, discard the red Aces, and successfully lead the other Ace and both Tens, you are bound to take in at least 66 card-points. Your actual score (without 11, game 12, times clubs 12) will be 144. You could declare Grand, but then the game would be 'without 4, game 5, times grand 24'—a mere 120.

21

Marriage lines

He . . . with a shamed and crimson cheek
Moaned 'This is harder than Bezique'.
Lewis Carroll, *The Three Voices* (1869)

Many games of the 'Ace-11, Ten-10' family award points to a player
holding the King and Queen of the same suit, appropriately known
as a 'marriage'. From American Pinochle to French Bezique, Spanish
Tute, Italian Briscola, German Sixty-Six, Austrian Schnapsen, Czech
Mariáš, and Hungarian Ulti—to name but a few—all give the
impression of being variants on one basic game, whose essentials are
as follows. Two players each receive a small number of cards. Each
in turn plays a card to a trick and draws a replacement from the
undealt stock. When the stock is empty the hands are played out.
Points accrue for winning counters in tricks and for declaring
marriages, whether dealt originally or made by drawing from the
stock a King or Queen marriable to a partner already in the hand.

In countries where the two top figures of the native pack are both
male, the term 'marriage' is often dropped in favour of something
less incongruous, such as German *Paar* (pair), Swiss *Stöcke* (branch,
genealogically speaking), Dutch *Stuk* (piece), Hungarian *Béla* (from
belle, 'trump suit'), Spanish *acuse* (declaration), or, more colourfully,
cántico (something to sing out); and so on. But this is an historically
recent development, the original and classic term having always been
'marriage' (German *Braut*, Dutch *bruid*, etc.) despite the masculinity
of the cards concerned.

The members of this family (which are, of course, all related by
marriage) are so prolific and interbred that it is very hard to
disentangle their ancestral lines and ramifications. It may therefore
help our survey to start with games not embodying all three essential
features—trick-and-draw format, the 'Ace-11, Ten-10' schedule, the
marriage—with a view to suggesting, tentatively, a way in which
they could have come together.

Elfern, Brusquembille, Briscola

The trick-and-draw principle is one of several devices enabling two people to play trick games without either's knowing exactly what the other holds. (Any resemblance to the draw-and-discard principle of Rummy is entirely coincidental, besides misleading.) As it does not seem older than the Marriage family as a whole, it may perhaps be original to them.[1] Although many have since given rise to games for three or more, in which case the trick-and-draw format is usually dropped, I feel sure that these derive from a two-handed original and not vice versa.

A possible ancestor might be sought in something resembling a simple game still played by German children under the name Elfern ('Eleven-ing') or Figurenspiel ('Honours Game'). Two players receive six cards each from a 32-card pack and play at trick-and-draw without trumps. A win consists in capturing 11 or more of the 20 'honours', namely, Aces, Kings, Queens, Jacks, and Tens. Taking 15 or more scores double, all 20 treble. Although Elfern is not recorded before the nineteenth century, its non-trump nature may suggest greater age.

It is easy to imagine steps by which such a game could have evolved into the ancestor of Marriage games. The first would be the introduction of trumps and the attachment of more interesting scores to the honours. An early game exhibiting both these features is Brusquembille, which first appears in the 1718 (Paris) edition of the *Académie universelle des jeux*. This game affords, I believe, the earliest explicit record of the Ace-11, Ten-10 schedule with both cards highest in their suit. It doesn't include marriages, but does award on-the-spot side-payments for the capture of Aces and Tens, which are known as *brusquembilles*, a feature surviving in the *brisques* of Bezique. ('Brusquembille' is said[2] to perpetuate the stage name of the actor Deslaurier, an enthusiastic player who allegedly codified its rules. This is about as likely as the story deriving Piquet from the mathematician of that name and *naipes* from the initials of their supposed inventor Nicolas Pépin.)

Clearly related to Brusquembille is Briscola, first mentioned in 1828 and currently one of Italy's most popular national card games. It is played throughout the country in several distinct varieties, each with fairly constant rules. It has also hybridized with Tressette to produce Briscolone and the peculiarly Venetian game of Madrasso. Two-handed Briscola is virtually Brusquembille but without the brusquembilles. Each receives three cards from the Italian 40-card pack ranking Ace

11, Trey 10, King 4, Cavalier 3, Fante 2, 7–6–5–4–2 zero. A card is turned for trump and laid face up half-covered by the stock. Suit need not be followed, a trick being taken by the higher trump, if any, otherwise by the higher card of the suit led. The winner of each trick draws the next card from stock and leads to the next when the other has also drawn. When the stock is empty, suit must be followed in the last three tricks. Whoever takes over 60 of the 120 card-points wins, the hands being fully played out. A 60–60 tie annuls the game.

Relations between Brusquembille and Briscola are unclear, not to say confusing. That *briscola* is the normal Italian word for 'trump' suggests that trumps were seen as the most characteristic feature of the game when it first appeared; but this does not help determine whether trumps were added to a game originally played in Italy without them, or whether the game only received its name after entering the country—where, it may be noted, the other national game of Tressette significantly lacks them. If the game and the name are of Italian origin, the word may derive from the long-established term for a scoring sequence at Tarocco variously appearing as *versigole*, *versicole*, *bresigola*, etc.[3] But an Italian origin for a game in which the Trey ranks second highest and counts 10 seems most unlikely. Even when we assume, as we surely must, that this oddity was occasioned by adapting to the Italian pack lacking Tens a game designed for the French or German pack containing them, it is hard to explain their replacement by the Trey. Why not the Deuce?—or, if originally copied from a German game involving Deuces instead of Aces, the Ace?

Mariage

The oldest known game of the family incorporating marriages first appears in a German book of 1715[4] and is called, not surprisingly, Mariagen-Spiel. As is so often the case, its French element does not entail an origin in France, as French was the language of upper-class society in seventeenth to eighteenth-century Germany. Mariage (for short) is played like Briscola, but with six cards each dealt from the 32-card German pack (Seven low). With 10 for the last trick, the game-winning target is not 61 but 66 points. In addition, either player, provided he has already won a trick, may declare a marriage for 20 points, or 40 in trumps, making the target more easily reached, not to say sometimes more dramatically. The 1715 description notes a variation in which marriages do not score points but instead attract on-the-spot side-payments. This brings *brusquembilles* to mind, and, if it represents an earlier form, may suggest that the family was created by first attaching the marriage feature as an external extra to a game resembling Brusquembille, and subsequently incorporating it into the scoring structure. Of course, marriages may have come in before card-points; but I am not aware of any plain-trick member of the family, living or dead, that combines marriages with play by trick-and-draw.

When and where marriages were first incorporated remains open to question. No earlier game description is known, and none of the few other references to a game called Mariage can be attached to one of this type with any degree of certainty. Nothing is known of the 'Mariaige' appearing in Rabelais's list of Gargantuan games (1534). Cotgrave, in his French–English Dictionary of 1611, explains Mariage as 'a game at cards, resembling (somewhat) our Saint'; but 'Saint' is Piquet, and its resemblance to what we know as Mariage more than justifies that cautious 'somewhat'. There is a German tradition to the effect that Mariage—or Sixty-Six, as now called—was invented at Paderborn, Westphalia, in 1652; but my attempts to check its credentials have not met with success.[5]

Marriages were almost certainly borrowed from older card games not involving tricks. In French Glic and German Poch, the fifteenth to sixteenth-century ancestors of Poker, a stake is won by the holder of a *mariage* or *Braut*, respectively. In Guimbarde, marriages figure both in the luck of the draw and in the play for tricks. Although this game is described as 'new' in the 1718 *Académie universelle des jeux*, its tripartite structure plainly derives from Poch or Poque, perhaps via the German 'Brautt Spil', for which a gaming-board of around 1700 is illustrated in Hargrave's *History of Playing-Cards* (p. 150). 'Matrimony' also features in games of the Stops family, which first appear in the seventeenth century and may themselves be an offshoot of the Poch branch.

Marriages presumably arose in a card-tradition involving courts headed by a King and Queen. Queens first appear on early fifteenth-century German cards, but marriages are not recorded before the late fifteenth-century French game of Glic, by which time they were characteristic of French cards. The equivalent German game of Poch also features the marriage, still called 'Braut' despite the self-evident masculinity of the relevant German cards, either as a translation of the French term, or through the survival of an earlier tradition. I think it likely that the marriage was transferred to the trick-taking field, specifically into a point-trick game of the incipient Ace-11,

Ten-10 family, not greatly before 1700, and probably in a German rather than French-card milieu.

Sixty-Six

The fast and challenging two-hander known as Sixty-Six, still widely played today, has changed little from the Mariage game as first described in 1715. It is my belief that Sechsundsechzig was the original name of the game (from its target score, of course); that it was renamed Mariage when the marriage feature was added; and that the original title reasserted itself in a period of German nationalism.

Sixty-Six (German, traditional). Two players; 24 cards ranking Ace 11, Ten 10, King 4, Queen 3, Jack 2, Nine 0. Deal six each in threes and turn the next for trumps. Whoever holds or later draws the trump Nine may exchange it for the turn-up, subject to the requirement of having won a trick. With 120 card-points in play and 10 for winning the last trick, making 130, the target is 66 and play ceases as soon as either player correctly claims to have reached it. A trump marriage counts 40, a plain one 20. To score, its holder must show both cards upon leading either of them to a trick.

Non-dealer leads first and the winner of each trick leads to the next. After each trick both players draw a card from stock, the trick-winner first. The follower to a trick may play any card until the end-game is reached, after which 'strict' rules apply—i.e. follow suit and head the trick if possible, otherwise trump if possible: *F,t,r.* End-play normally begins as soon as the last card of stock has been drawn. It may, however, be forced by either player's announcing 'I close' and turning the trump-card down before the stock is emptied—thereby undertaking to reach 66 from the five or six cards remaining in hand. In a forced game the score of '10 for last' does not apply.

Game is seven game points. Score one for reaching 66 first, two for *schneider* (opponent fails to reach 33), or three for *schwarz* (opponent takes no trick). If a player is discovered to have reached 66 without announcing it, the deal is drawn and the following deal carries an additional game point. Claiming 66 incorrectly, or failing to reach 66 after closing, gives the opponent two game points, or three if he has not yet won a trick.

Sixty-Six is a fast and challenging two-hander which should be in a card-player's repertoire. Its whole point lies in knowing exactly when to force an early closure of the stock. Lacking the experience of foresight, novices tend to play each deal through to its bitter end and then reproach the game for reaching a foregone conclusion.

Versions and derivatives of Mariage are popular throughout Europe. The reduction of the pack from 32 to 24 cards, which tightens the game up by omitting some of the non-counters, has been carried to its logical conclusion in its even snappier Austrian relative, Schnapsen, from which the Nines are also gone. A partnership version known as Gaigel or Kreuzmariage appeared in the nineteenth century and is much played, with varying rules, in northern Württemberg.[6] It uses a double 24-card German-suited pack lacking Eights and Nines, and features a 'sudden death' win for acquiring five Sevens in one hand.

Czechoslovakia's national card game Mariáš, played by three with a German-suited 32-card pack, seems to have hybridized with bidding games reminiscent of Tarock, Skat, and Jass. There is a deal of ten cards and a skat of two, followed by three possible bids: one to win a majority of card-points with a trump suit (hearts being 'favourite' and counting double), and no-trump bids of null (lose every trick) and slam (win every trick). The only counters are Daus (or Ace) and Ten, worth 10 each, a parallel development to that of brisques in Bezique. Also applicable are 40 and 20 for marriages, 10 for last, and a bonus for winning the last trick with the lowest trump, a feat that may also be used as a bid-raiser. This feat, borrowed from the *Pagat ultimo* of Tarock, may be the origin of '10 for last' in games of this family. It has certainly become the principal feature of Hungary's national card game, a highly sophisticated development of Mariáš known as Ulti. Ulti is a three-player game, with hands of ten cards each and a skat of two, but to this common central European format a novel twist has been added. Each time a player bids, he first picks up the skat cards or talon, adds them to his hand, and discards any two in their place before making his announcement. As John McLeod observes:[7] 'Because the talon is exchanged every time a bid is made, players participating in the auction get to see and even use each other's discards, and genuine or misleading information can be passed in this way.'

An apparently recent member of the Marriage branch is that which seems to have replaced Tresillo as Spain's national card game. Tute, pronounced like and said to derive from Italian Tutti,[8] is played in a variety of formats for different numbers of players. It uses the Spanish 40-card pack ranking Ace 11, Three 10, etc., and has scores of 40 and 20 for the King–Caballo equivalent of a marriage. In addition, the game can be won outright by declaring a *tute*, which is a quartet of Kings or Caballos. Tute most resembles Sixty-Six in its 'memory' factor whereby a player wins not just by reaching a target number of points (100) but by correctly claiming to have done so.

An interesting development of marriage games is that of declaring a marriage to establish a trump suit. Most old accounts of almost every game in the series give alternative methods of establishing trumps: one by upturning the top card of stock, the other by playing at no trump until a marriage is declared. If the first perpetuates an old idea deriving from Triomphe/Trump etc., the second is evidently a later development unique to games with marriages. By extension, in some games the trump suit changes every time a new marriage is declared. This feature appears, for instance, in a round game described in early twentieth-century English books under the title 'Pip-Pip', which, having no known antecedents, was probably born out of cultural wedlock. A further development is the crediting of increasing scores to successive marriages. In a 24-card two-hander called Mariage in Switzerland and Tausendeins in Austria, the first marriage declared scores 20, the second 40, the third 60, and the fourth—if it gets that far—80. The equivalent 32-card Czech game of Tisíc a jedna, also played in the Ukraine under the name Tyzicha Odin ('Thousand-and-One'), varies the principle by attaching specific scores to specific suits: 40 for a marriage in diamonds, 60 in hearts, 80 in spades, and 100 in clubs. Progressive marriage scores also occur in Italian 40-card relatives variously known as Mariaccia, Mariaschia, Marianna, etc., which appear to be forms of Briscola influenced by Mariage.[9]

Varieties of Sixty-Six are also played in Scandinavia. They include Danish Seksogtres, Norwegian Hundreogen, and the more aberrant Swedish Bondtolva. The Danish game is preferred with trump-changes induced by marriage declarations, that particular version being known as Deliriumseksogtres.

Briscan, Bezique

Brusquembille remains prominent in French gamebooks of the eighteenth century, but by the end of that period is challenged by Briscan, or Brisque, a related game of almost hysterical excitement and complication. This Gothic extravaganza squeezed a truly phenomenal range of scores and melds from the deal of five each from the 32-card pack. Besides the Ace-11 card count and additional scores for *brisques* (trump Ace 30, other Aces and Tens 10 each), Briscan also counted 10 for a hand containing no courts cards (carte blanche), 20 for a hand containing nothing but court cards; 10 for turning up a counter for trumps; from 10 to 300 for no fewer than fourteen different sequences, and doubled in trumps; quartets of high cards; marriages scorable not only from hand but also by capture in a trick; 10 for taking the last card of stock, 30 for then holding five trumps, 20 for winning all five last tricks, and 10 for taking the majority. Its 600-point game target must have been very quickly reached!

Bezique (Bésigue), the more sober relative of Briscan, must have been evolving in western France in the early nineteenth century. It was not until the 1840s that it took the Paris casinos by storm in the classic double-pack version which was soon to become one of the most illustrious games of European high society. French researchers traced it back to the old province of Limousin, where it was originally played with the single 32-card pack under the name Besi or Besit, or as Cinq Cents from its target score of 500. Each player received six cards and played at trick-and-draw for the following melds: trump sequence 250; plain sequence 125; four Aces 100, Tens 80, Kings 60, Queens 40, Jacks 30; marriages 40 and 20, and *mariage de besi* 40. Old accounts differ, as the game was never standardized; but common to all was the addition of scores at end of play for counters taken in tricks, following the usual Ace-11, Ten-10 schedule. A partnership equivalent first appears in the 1802 *Académie des jeux* under the name 'Homme de Brou'.

The distinguishing feature of this game, as of the whole of the Bezique/Pinochle branch of the Marriage family to which it gave rise, was that peculiar meld first recorded as *mariage de besi*, and consisting of the spade Queen and diamond Jack, evidently symbolizing an illicit liaison in parody of the true marriage of King and Queen in the same suit. The origin of this feature can only be guessed at by reference to related themes. The Jack of diamonds has significance as a wild figure or 'joker' in many traditional games—as the *quinola* in Reversis, as the top trump in original Boston, as the third best (*le fou*) in Guimbarde, and so on. It may be of Germanic origin, as the German equivalent of diamonds is bells, and bells are traditionally associated with fools. ('Pull the other one . . .') Less universal significance seems to attach to the Queen of spades, apart from those of cartomancy and her role as Black Maria. It is at least interesting that ♠Q and ♦J find themselves thrown together as a winning combination in Hoc, the French equivalent of Poch, as early as the 1654 edition of the *Maison académique des jeux*. In Marjolet, played in south-western

France and said (by Gerver) to be of Spanish provenance, *Marjolet* denotes the Jack of trumps, who may be married to a plain Queen for 20, or to the Queen of trumps for 40, provided that she has already been married to the King. Whether this feature is ancestral or derivative depends on the age of the game, which we are not told. Some, recalling the Italian word *bàzzica*, 'companion', relate Bezique to the card game Bàzzica recorded in Italy as early as 1532.[10] This, however, is an entirely unrelated game which must have fallen out of use by 1800, leaving its name free for attachment to the new French game when it later entered Italy. Similarly, the Spanish Baciga is a game of the Fishing variety, while the attempted etymology based on *besico*, 'a little kiss', is as misleading as it is pretty.

In Paris the game emerged as Bésigue (in various spellings, not always with the accent) after undergoing substantial modifications. The pack and target score were doubled to 64 cards and 1,000 points respectively, and the Ace-11 schedule dropped in favour of 10 each for *brisques*, i.e. Aces and Tens.

The introduction of Bezique into Britain is unusually well documented. William Pole first published an account of the game in the December 1861 edition of *Macmillans Magazine* as the last of three 'Games at Cards for the Coming Winter'. After describing Quadrille and Piquet as out of mode but eminently worthy of revival, he introduces 'Bazique', somewhat unhelpfully, as 'probably of late invention and of quite a novel kind', and, later, as 'an unwritten game'. Bezique (with an 'e') next occurs as a one-page afterthought in Pardon's 1863 edition of *Hoyle's Games Modernized*, whose sketchy rules contain the gratuitous assertion that in the play of the last eight tricks the cards revert to Whist order, with Ten low. Later that year appeared a booklet on Bésique (with an accent) by 'J.R.W',[11] who repeats Pardon's Whist rule and wrongly attributes '10 for last' to the 24th trick, i.e. that which exhausts the stock. More interesting is the following extract from the author's introduction:

It is somewhat strange that exactly as the Queen's statement [about Albert] with regard to the royal game of Patience brought that almost forgotten entertainment into something like fashionable vogue, so the game of Bésique has been rebrought, it is said, into fashion here in England through the patronage bestowed upon it during his voyages by H.R.H. the Duke of Edinburgh [Victoria's second son, Alfred]. The game is now most fashionable and is daily spreading in popularity . . .

'Berkeley', writing in 1901,[12] says that the game caught on in 1869. That it was not to everyone's taste is suggested by the Lewis Carroll quotation heading this chapter and, in 1870, by a writer in the *Westminster Papers*, who in seeking to extol the virtues and revive the practice of Ombre dismisses Bezique as 'that slowest of slow games'. This did not prevent Henry ('Cavendish') Jones from jumping on the bandwagon and producing his 1870 monograph on the game, with such speed that a new and much-corrected edition was rapidly called for.

The popularity of Bezique is shown by the number of extensions and imitations to which it rapidly gave rise. In 1880 the Paris card clubs agreed rules for a four-pack version of the game called Rubicon Bezique, and the English Portland Club followed suit in 1887. Chinese or six-pack Bezique just antedates 1900, and rules for an eight-pack version followed a little later. A fascinating feature of multi-pack versions is the redefinition of bezique itself. Typically, play proceeds at no trump until a marriage is melded; its suit is thereby entrumped, and bezique is then the Queen of trumps and a Jack of opposite colour, spades linking with diamonds, hearts with clubs. In the early 1870s Messrs Geo. Hunt sought to popularize a peculiar game called Zetema: it requires five suits and can be described as a cross between Bezique and Poker.[13] One of the more subtle variations on the basic games is that known as Fildinski, or Polish Bezique, in which melds are formed not from the hand but only from cards won in tricks.

Bezique survives today as a classic well known to card-game connoisseurs. The simplest variety (from which you may progress as you become more experienced) is:

Two-Pack Bezique (English rules, nineteenth century-current). Two players each receive eight cards (3 + 2 + 3) from two 32-card packs shuffled together. The next is turned for trump and the rest laid face down as a stock partly covering the trump card.

Cards rank A-T-K-Q-J-9-8-7 in each suit. Aces and Tens, or *brisques*, score 10 each when counted in won tricks at end of play.

Each in turn plays any desired card to a trick—*ftr*—which is taken by the higher card of the suit led, or the higher trump if any are played, or by the first played of two identical cards. The trick-winner is thereby entitled to declare and score for a meld by laying its constituent cards face up on the table, where they remain available for play to subsequent tricks.

The declarations are, from high to low: a *sequence* (A-T-K-Q-J of trumps) for 250; a *quartet* of Aces for 100, Kings 80, Queens 60, or Jacks 40; a *marriage* of K–Q of a suit, worth 40 in trumps or 20 in plain; *bezique*, consisting of the Queen of spades and Jack of diamonds, for 40, or *double bezique* (both of each card) for 500; and the Seven of trumps, which scores 10 and may be exchanged for the turn-up.

Only one meld may be declared when a trick is won; a declaration once made and broken up by the play of a card may not be reformed; and an unplayed card declared in one scoring meld may later be used in the formation of a higher-scoring meld but not a lower one of the same type. (For example, you may declare a trump marriage and later incorporate either card in a sequence, but you may not declare a sequence and claim for the included marriage.)

Having (optionally) declared, the trick-winner draws the top card of stock, waits for the other to draw, then leads to the next trick.

When the last card of stock has been taken—i.e. the faced trump-card—and any final declaration made, any declared cards are taken into hand and the last eight tricks are played. Strict rules now apply: the follower must head the trick if possible, otherwise follow suit if possible, otherwise trump if possible: *F,T,r*. Winning the last trick scores 10.

Game is 1,000 up. If neither has reached 1,000, the brisques are counted, and if still neither has won, the next deal is played.

Binocle, Binokel, Pinochle

Across the Atlantic, Bezique took sufficient hold to reach the pages of Dick and Fitzgerald's *Modern Pocket Hoyle* of 1868. It was, however, very soon eclipsed by its more down-to-earth German cousin, and that cousin was eventually to become one of America's most illustrious contributions to the world of card games.

Binokel, still widely played as a family game in Württemberg,[14] is of the usual 'origin obscure'. The game itself is virtually identical with Besi, the forerunner of Bezique; indeed, stripping out the Sevens and Eights to produce a 48-card pack, and then following the rules for Bezique given above, produces a fair approximation of original Binocle/Pinochle, which was essentially a two-hander. Its name, which also applies to the characteristic Queen–Jack meld, evidently derives from the French word *binocle*, 'pince-nez'. A fanciful explanation has it that the appropriate Queen and Jack in certain standard card patterns are each distinguished by being depicted in profile, thereby displaying only one eye each but two when lying together. The fact that Binokel is played with the 24-card pack

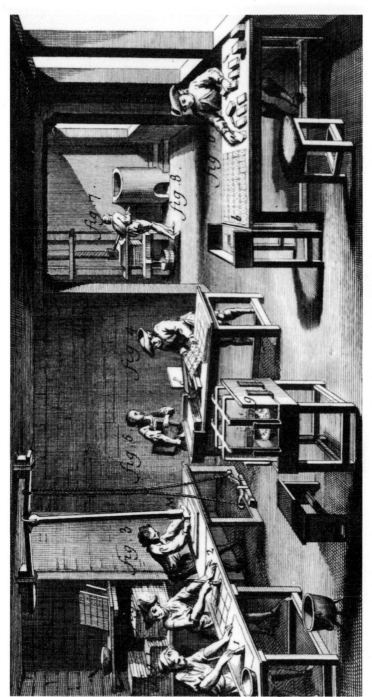

A playing-card manufactory: engraving from Diderot and d'Alembert's *Dictionnaire raisonné* of 1751–2.

Geo March 1770

Mr. *HOYLE*'s
GAMES
OF

𝔚𝔥𝔦𝔰𝔱,	ℭ𝔥𝔢𝔰𝔰,
𝔔𝔲𝔞𝔡𝔯𝔦𝔩𝔩𝔢,	A N D
𝔓𝔦𝔮𝔲𝔢𝔱,	𝔅𝔞𝔠𝔨-𝔊𝔞𝔪𝔪𝔬𝔫.

COMPLETE.

In which are contained,

The Method of PLAYING and BETTING,
at THOSE GAMES, upon equal, or advantageous Terms.

INCLUDING

The LAWS of the feveral GAMES.

The THIRTEENTH EDITION.
To which is now firft added,
Two *New Cafes* at *Whift*, never before printed;
ALSO,
The *New Laws* of the Game at *Whift*,
As played at
White's and *Saunders*'s Chocolate-Houfes.

LONDON:
Printed for THOMAS OSBORNE, in Gray's-Inn;
HENRY WOODFALL,
And RICHARD BALDWIN, both in Pater-nofter-Row.
[Price Three Shillings, neatly bound.]

Edmond Hoyle
Tho: Osborne

Hoyle on troubled waters: none genuine without this signature.

(*Left*) This illustration from the 1930 edition of Charles Lamb's *Mrs Battle's Opinions on Whist* demonstrates her opinion of Cribbage.

(*Below*) That Bridge has always been popular with women largely accounts for its worldwide social success. These Parisians, snapped in 1922, are playing Auction, or perhaps Plafond, the earliest form of Contract.

SHE WAS NEVER GREATLY TAKEN WITH CRIBBAGE

English bliss is a round of Whist before the rain comes down.

Film Poker is a game on its own. Here, the Kid (Steve McQueen) takes on the Man (Edward G. Robinson), while Shooter (Karl Malden) looks as if he'd rather be somewhere else. (*The Cincinnati Kid*, MGM, 1965.)

normally associated with Sixty-Six adds another tantalizing strand to the web of intermarital relationships exhibited by the far-flung Marriage family.

It first appears in American Hoyles of the 1880s under the spelling Penuchle—the closest to its actual pronunciation—later as Pinocle, and eventually as that cross between the two which is now the standard spelling. (R. F. Foster at first complained about the intrusive 'h' and defiantly published his *Complete Pinocle* in 1907. His less defiantly spelt *Laws of Pocket Pinochle* followed in 1908.) Finding itself, with Bezique, soon threatened by various forms of Rummy, Pinochle promptly demonstrated its greater vitality by developing more interesting versions for three or more players. Of these, Auction Pinochle counts by any reckoning as one of the world's great three-handers. Here is one of several varieties. It will be noted that, in common with most forms of American Pinochle, the original card-point system of 11–10–4–3–2 has been simplified.

Auction Pinochle with Widow (US, current). Three active players; if four, each in turn deals and sits out. Use a double 24 pack, 48 cards in all, ranking and counting Ace 10, Ten 10, King 5, Queen 5, Jack 0, Nine 0. Deal fifteen cards each in batches of three. After the first three, lay three aside, face down, as a *widow*.

Players bid to become the Bidder, whose aim is to make at least as many points as he bid by (*a*) scoring for melds after exchanging any three cards for the widow, declaring trumps, and then, if necessary, (*b*) clearing the deficit by winning counters in tricks. Eldest bids first; the minimum bid is 300 (variable by agreement); each in turn must raise by a multiple of 10 or else pass, and, having passed, may not come in again.

The Bidder turns the widow face up and then announces trumps. From the eighteen cards in his possession he shows and scores for as many as possible of the following melds:

Flush (A–T–K–Q–J in trumps)	150
Royal marriage (K–Q in trumps)	40
Plain marriage (K–Q in non-trump suit)	20
Hundred Aces (four Aces, one per suit)	100
Eighty Kings (four Kings, likewise)	80
Sixty Queens (four Queens, likewise)	60
Forty Jacks (four Jacks, likewise)	40
Pinochle (♠Q–♦J)	40
Dix (pronounced 'deece': trump Nine)	10

(If any of these appear twice—the pack being doubled—both count. If a flush is declared, the royal marriage it contains may not be scored separately.)

If he has already scored the amount he bid, there is no play and the Bidder wins the value of his game (see below). If not, and he thinks he cannot do so, he may concede without playing, and loses only his game value (*single bate*), as opposed to twice that value (*double bate*) if he should play and still fail.

To play, the Bidder takes all eighteen cards into hand, discards any three face down to count in his favour at end of play, and leads to the first trick. On a plain-suit lead, it is obligatory to follow suit if possible, otherwise to play a trump if possible: *f,t,r*. When a trump is led, it is obligatory to follow suit and head the trick if possible: *F,r*. A trick is won by the highest card of the suit led, the highest trump if any are played, or the first played of two identical winning cards. The winner of each trick leads to the next. The last trick scores 10 to the side that wins it.

If the Bidder has made his bid, he scores or receives from each opponent an agreed game value related to the size of the bid; if not, he loses or pays double that amount. A game valuation scheme might be 1 unit or game point for a bid of 300–40, 2 for 350+, 3 for 400+, 5 for 450+, 7 for 500+, and so on.

All scores are doubled when spades are trump; many schools also rate hearts triple. Some also award side-payments for special melds, such as 5 for a 'roundhouse' (four marriages, one in each suit), flush 4, double pinochle 2, hundred Aces 2, four different Kings 1, likewise Queens or Jacks.

As befits one of America's most popular card games, Pinochle is played in a wide variety of shapes and sizes, and by any number of active players from two to eight.

Jass

Jass (pronounced like Londoners' 'yus' for 'yes') is a distinctive branch of the Marriage family. Because it is the national card game of Switzerland, 'Jass' has also come to denote the traditional Swiss 36-card pack described in Chapter 3. By an even further and confusing extension, it is often applied to all games customarily played with Jass cards, including some from entirely unrelated families which have been adapted to the Swiss pack but ignore the distinctive features of Jass itself. So-called Schellen-Jass is actually a variety of Hearts,

Tschausepp of Crazy Eights, Zuger-Tapp of Bavarian Tarock, and so on.

True Jass games are uniquely identifiable by their top trumps. The highest is the Jack, usually called 'Jass' and always worth 20. The second-highest is the trump Nine, variously known as *Menel*, *Nel*, *Näll*, etc., and counting 14. These are normally followed by Ace 11, King 4, Queen 3, non-trump Jack 2, Ten 10, and others zero, though not without variation. Most games also award points for melds similar to those of Bezique, including a suit-sequence of three or more cards, a quartet of counting-cards, and a marriage of King and Queen in the same suit. Jass games are not restricted to Switzerland, being Dutch in origin and also very largely Jewish by adoption. They also include the Dutch national card game Klaverjas, French Belote, Hungarian Alsós, the Yiddish Klaberjass, and the American Klob so favoured by Damon Runyon.[15]

When Jass was first mentioned in Switzerland, in 1796, it was described as 'new' and said to have been imported by Dutch mercenaries.[16] Its presumed parent is recorded in the Netherlands as Jasspel from the 1720s and is preceded by several references to a game called Belle-Bruid, a term used in Jass to denote a marriage in trumps.[17] 'Jas' is a personal name, short for Jasper. The naming of Jacks is a well-known card feature: compare 'Jos' in Kaiserspiel, 'Wenzel' in Schafkopf, 'Pam(philus)' in Loo, etc. 'Jack' itself, of course, derives from the name of the knave in All Fours, which I believe to be of Dutch origin and not too distantly related to the marriage family.

The choice of rank and value for the two top trumps is not entirely clear, but may be guessed at. The pattern itself reflects the top trumps of Hombre, as indicated by the term '(me)nel' derived obviously from 'manille'. The substitution, as top trump, of the impish figure of the Jack for the relatively colourless Ace is a widespread phenomenon (cf. Euchre, Skat, etc.), and in this instance is perhaps influenced by games of the Loo family. Its face value, 20, relates easily to 10 for the Ten and 2 for an ordinary Jack. The value 14 for the Nine is more peculiar: it would more naturally attach to the Seven. One possible explanation, unsupported by any evidence, is that the second trump originally was the Seven; that the game went through a phase of being played with a 24-card pack stripped of Sevens and Eights, leaving Nine the most logical replacement;[18] and that the Nine then stuck, regardless of the pack subsequently used. The position of the Ten is worth an incidental note. Almost universally in Jass games, Ten ranks low for the purpose of making sequences (J-T-9-etc.) but high for that of trick-taking (A-T-K-etc.). In Switzerland, however, it continues to rank low for all purposes, suggesting that this was its original position.

The following Dutch game forms a simple and pleasant introduction to the Jass branch of the family.

Klaverjas (*Dutch, current*). Four players; fixed partnerships; 32 cards; deal eight each in fours. Each in turn has one chance to declare trumps; if three pass, the dealer must declare. Whoever declares thereby obligates his side to win a majority of the points available, which are 152 for cards, 10 for the last trick, and extras for melds made in tricks.

Cards rank Ace 11, Ten 10, King 4, Queen 3, Jack 2, 9–8–7 zero, except in trumps, which are headed by Jack (*Jas*) 20, Nine (*Nel*) 14.

Melds are: sequence of four 50; of three 20; a quartet of any rank 100; a marriage in any suit 20. (For sequences only, trumps rank in plain-suit order.)

Eldest leads to the first trick and the winner of each trick leads to the next. Players must follow suit if possible; if unable, they must, if possible, not only trump but also play a higher trump than any so far played to the trick. (This rule is followed strictly in Rotterdam. In Amsterdam it is not obligatory to overtrump if one's partner is winning the trick.)[19]

Any meld formed by cards contained within a trick counts to the side winning it. If a sequence includes a marriage, both count.

At end of play each side totals its points for tricks and melds. If the declarers have more, both sides score what they have made towards game. If not, they are lurched and score nothing, and the winners score 162 plus the value of all melds made by both sides. Taking all 162 points in tricks earns a bonus of 100. Game is 1,500 up.

Originally, melds were scored from hand as well as 'on the table'. Dutch players have rejected this feature, unlike their Swiss counterparts, who always meld from the hand but rarely do so on the table. Few tricks at Klaverjas therefore contain melds, and anything higher than a marriage or three-card sequence isn't often seen. It is because the quartet is so rare that it counts in any rank, whereas the Swiss restrict it to Jacks and over.

Swiss equivalents of Klaverjas include Kreuzjass, in which a turned card determines trumps; Schieber, in which the eldest hand either declares trumps or bridges the choice to his partner; Sidi-Barrani, a recent development involving a highly sophisticated system of competitive bidding, and its more advanced variety, Bolshevik, played with a doubled pack. Swiss games recognize more melds than the Dutch, since they may be scored from the hand, and a hand may contain up to twelve cards. The widest range occurs in Zuger-Jass, with sequences of five to nine cards worth from 100 to 300 in increments of 50; a quartet of Jacks for 200, Nines 150, and Sixes 300; and a marriage worth 40 in trumps, 20 in plain suits.

The inventive Swiss also count amongst their innumerable varieties of the game such distinctive forms as Handjass, which may be described as equivalent to Solo Whist; Schmaus, to Bezique; Hindersi-Jass, to Hearts; and Bettel, to Nap. Pandur, borrowed from the Dutch Pandoeren, is a four-hand Solo game with an extensive and intriguing range of bids comparable to those of Boston de Fontainebleau. Novel ideas are explored in four-player Molotov and its three-hand equivalent Mittlere, where one's aim is to take either most card-points or fewest, but not to be in the middle. Both exhibit the unusual feature that play proceeds at no trump until a player is unable to follow suit, whereupon the suit of his discard becomes trump for the rest of the deal. Since about the 1940s, two varieties of no-trump bid have been introduced into certain Jass games. In the bid of *Obenabe* ('from the top down') all Jacks count 2 and all Nines zero, but all Eights count 8 each to restore the pack total of 162. In its complementary bid of *Undenuffe* ('from the bottom up') they rank and count, from high to low: Six 11, Seven-Eight-Nine 0 each, Ten 10, Jack 2, Queen 3, King 4, Ace 0.

Klaberjass, Belote

The Swiss game of Cinq-Cents (not to be confused with one-pack Bezique) is the local version of an international classic two-hander better known as Klaberjass, in a variety of forms and spellings. The name means 'Jack of clubs' ('clover' Jack) and may reflect a form of the game according preference to clubs as trumps.[20]

Klaberjass (international, current). Two players; 32 cards, ranking and counting Ace 11, Ten 10, King 4, Queen 3, Jack 2, 9-8-7 zero. In trumps, the highest is the Jack, worth 20, followed by the Nine or *Menel*, worth 14. Deal six each in threes; turn the next for trumps and place it under the stock.

Players bid to become the maker, thereby undertaking to score more for melds and tricks in return for choosing trumps. Non-dealer starts. If he says 'Take it', the turned suit is accepted as trump and play begins. He may accept it conditionally by saying 'schmeiss': if so, dealer may either accept the schmeiss, in which case the turned suit applies and non-dealer must play, or refuse it, in which case the hands are thrown in and the deal annulled. Or non-dealer may simply 'Pass', in which case dealer has the same three options.

If both pass, there is a second round of bidding. Non-dealer may offer another suit as trumps, in which case play begins, or offer it conditionally by saying 'Schmeiss' as before, or pass. If he passes, dealer may himself offer another suit or pass. He may not schmeiss, and if he also passes the deal is scrapped.

Given the maker and a trump suit, play proceeds by the deal of three more cards each, one at a time. If trumps are the turned suit, either player holding the trump Seven may exchange it for the turn-up.

Before tricks, players vie to see who has the best sequence of three or more cards in suit, for which purpose all cards rank A-K-Q-J-T-9–8-7. A three-card sequence counts 20, four or more 50. A higher sequence beats a lower one of equal length; a longer beats a shorter; if still equal, a trump sequence beats a plain one; if still equal, no one scores.

Non-dealer starts by announcing 'None', '20', or '50' for his best sequence, adding further information as to height, length, and suit so long as dealer continues to claim equality (as at Piquet). Whoever claims the best sequence shows and scores for it, plus any others he may hold, upon playing to the first trick.

Non-dealer leads to the first trick and the winner of each leads to the next. Follow suit if possible, otherwise trump if possible. If trumps are led, the follower must trump higher if possible. A player holding both King and Queen of trumps may announce and score 20 for *bella* upon playing the second of them to a trick.

At end of play each reckons his scores for (a) sequences and *bella*, (b) counters taken in tricks, and (c) 10 for winning the last trick. If the maker has more, both score what they make. If equal or less, he scores zero, and if less, non-maker scores the total made by both. Game is 500 up.

There is a version of Klaberjass played at trick-and-draw, like Bezique, and known as Törteln or Tertelé. Passing reference should also be made to Ely Culbertson's brave attempt to turn Klaberjass into an equivalent of Bridge for two players. 'Jo-Jotte', named after his wife Josephine, includes such features as above and below-line scoring, doubles, and slams.

The spread of Klaberjass is undoubtedly related to its enthusiastic adoption by the Jewish community. ('Smoojas', a nineteenth-century Flemish variety, is from the dialectal *Smoos* for 'Jew'.)[21] The late Robin Goodfellow, a card-game researcher with whom I corresponded for many years, wrote:

Klaberjass . . . is current in almost every capital where European cards are used. Its spread is undoubtedly due to the emigration of Jewish people into the cities of the western world. Every properly brought-up Jewish boy of at least the last generation would know something about *Klobiosh*, even if he did not actively indulge in it. It is also widely played by East Londoners of gentile origin. It has a distinct air of Mitteleuropa about it, and I am inclined to believe, with Ely Culbertson, that its birthplace was probably Budapest.[22]

Substantially similar is a two-hander that entered France around the time of the First World War and has subsequently become France's national card game in a variety of different formats. Belote (formerly 'Belotte', a diminutive of the first element of *belle-bruid*) is virtually Klaberjass but without the *schmeiss* bid and with extra scores for quartets. Later variations include alternative no-trump bids of *sans atout*, in which all Jacks and Nines are low, reducing the pack total to 130, and *tout atout*, in which they are all high and bear their trump values, thus increasing the pack total to 258. Three and four-player versions have also developed, the most advanced being Belote Coinchée, a partnership game with bidding.[23]

Alsós, Felsős

The Budapest connection brings us to Hungary, where a version of Klaberjass known as Alsós, 'the Jack game', occupied the post of national card game until its recent eclipse by Ulti. (The last variation on Alsós was Felsős, 'the Queen game', in which the post of top trump was filled by the Queen instead, making the total playing-points 161 and so preventing ties.)[24]

Alsós is remarkable for incorporating a number of bidding elements borrowed directly from Tarock. From a 32-card pack two players receive eight each or three players six. The next is turned for trump, which may be accepted by one player or passed by all. Two then receive four more, or three three more. If the first trump was passed, there follows a round of bidding in which the lowest suit is leaves (spades), followed upwards by hearts, bells (diamonds), acorns (clubs), and no trump. Cards bear their normal Jass rank and values, except at no trump, where all Jacks and Nines count low. The bidder's object is to win a majority of playing-points for cards captured in tricks, plus 10 for last and melds in hand, these being *béla kassza* (trump K–Q) for 10, *terc* (3-card trump sequence) for 20, *kvart* (4-card trump sequence) for 50, similarly *kvint* or longer sequence for 100, and *vannak* (quartet) for 100, all scorable only if not beaten by a better meld of the same type in an opponent's hand.

The bidder's game score may be increased by a number of factors for fulfilling certain additional feats declared in advance. They include:

tulétroá ('Tous les trois'): to capture trumps J-9–7	2 factors
család ('family'): to capture trumps A-K-Q	2 —
abszolút: to take at least 82 card-points, or 66 at NT	3 —
negyvennégyes ('forty-four'): to win all 4 Aces	4 —
százas ('100'): to take 100+ card points, or 80+ at NT	4 —
kétszázas ('200'): to take 200+, or 180+ at NT	4 —
ultimó: to take last trick with trump-7	5 —
összes adu ('all trumps'): to win all 6 trump counters	6 —
volát: to win every trick	10 —
betli: to lose every trick	10 —

22

Lonely hearts

Reversis: A kind of Trumpe played backward.

> Cotgrave, *Dictionary of the French and English Tongues* (1611)

In these times of jollity . . . the ladies of the French court invented, or rather adopted the game of *Reversis*, so called because its order and construction was entirely the reverse of those already in use . . .

> Taylor, *The History of Playing Cards* (1865)

Le Reversis convertit la tristesse en esbat, & divertit l'esprit de l'homme en s'exerçant avec les belles Dames.

> *Le plaisant jeu du reversy des dames* . . . (1634)

A negative or reverse game is one in which the winner loses or the loser wins. More precisely, the definitions of winning and losing are reversed, and players aim for the exact opposite of what they are normally trying to do. Not all games lend themselves to such treatment. The idea of negative Rummy, Cribbage, or Poker is as mind-boggling as that of negative Snooker; and Lowball is not the 'negative Poker' it is sometimes misdescribed as, but only ordinary Poker played with its whole range of hands reversed in relative value—a purely cosmetic variation that makes no difference to the strategy of play.

Trick-taking games, however, work rather well 'played backward'. In fact, they are better described as 'trick-avoidance' games, to emphasize the fact that they invite a positive approach to strategic play. The object here is to win the fewest tricks or the smallest number of penalty cards contained within them. In either case, the best result is to avoid winning any tricks at all. This is a clear-cut objective and calls for a different approach from games in which the object is to win them. Unfortunately, the degree of skill required (as opposed to the type) is relatively limited. In positive trick-taking games, part of the reward for winning a trick is the immediate right of leading to the next and so exercising some control over the direction of play. But in Hearts and other negative games, the successful avoidance of a trick confers no corresponding advantage. The skill of trick-avoidance is therefore largely defensive and sometimes mechanical: it is rather like always batting and never bowling, which can get boring after a while. Negative games also tend to dispense with the exciting feature of trumps—inevitably so, since trumps, by definition, were designed for winning tricks and capturing the lead.

This may explain why great negative trick games are few and far between. The only one of international repute is Hearts, but, as its myriad haphazard variants testify, it is largely perceived as a light-hearted family or pub game and not taken very seriously. Reversis, the probable progenitor of this somewhat miscellaneous family, was a great game in its day, but, being complicated rather than strategic, and playable only for hard-score (cash or counters), it is unlikely to appeal to modern tastes.

Although the negative principle does not stand up to extensive play on its own account—or perhaps for that very reason—it has come to enjoy considerable success by leading the parasitic life of an optional bid in auction games like Solo Whist and Skat. Misère, a bid to lose every trick played, first appears in a mid-eighteenth-century version of Hombre, where it is played with a trump suit.[1] This intriguing novelty soon migrated into Quadrille, Tarot, and Boston. Boston-players found it more sensible to play the bid at no trump, an option not open to Tarot-players, as tarots are trumps by definition. We may therefore assume that non-tarot games where misères are still played with trumps, such as Dutch Pandoer (Swiss Pandur) derive from the older Hombre/Tarot tradition, while those without trumps stem from its more streamlined Boston branch.

Boston further extended the negative principle in a variety of experimental directions. Besides *misère*, a bid to lose all thirteen tricks, it introduced *petite misère* (lose all twelve after making one discard), *piccolissimo* (win exactly one trick), *piccolo* (win exactly two), as well as the refinement of *misère ouverte*, or 'spread misère', with the player's hand of cards exposed on the table for an additional reward. Misères and spreads remain optional bids under such names as *null* in Skat, *Bettel* in German Solo, *pobre* in Spanish Solo. Bids to take exactly one, two, or three tricks survive mainly in Tarot games, as, for example, *pikkolo*, *zwikkolo*, *tricolo* in Königsrufen, though *uno* and *duo* were once to be encountered in the more alcoholic varieties of nineteenth-century Skat.[2]

Another negative idea is that of *nullos*, a bid of *n* nullos being an offer to lose at least the stated number of tricks. Unsuccessful attempts were once made to introduce this into Auction Bridge, and it may still be encountered in games dating from the first decade or so of the twentieth century. That it may be of Scandinavian origin is suggested by the trumpless game of Norwegian Whist, in which the only bids are Grand and Nullo, and by the persistence in Norway of an elsewhere unorthodox null bid in modern Bridge. A perhaps more skill-demanding type of misère is that in which the aim is to avoid winning the last trick, as in the optional 'misery' variation of English Solo.

In point-trick games, the obvious negative aim is to take as few card-points as possible (see Bassadewitz, below), though as a special bid or optional extra in positive games it usually appears in 'scapegoat' form—i.e., it is merely to avoid taking the most, as in the *Trischaken* bid of Königsrufen and the *Ramsch* of Skat. As an ingenious variation, it may be to take either most or fewest card-points, but not some middling number. Of this type are the Jass game of Mittlere and the unorthodox *Mittelramsch* of Skat.[3]

The distinction between plain-trick and point-trick games is rather blurred when they are played negatively. If the object is to avoid capturing penalty cards, as in Hearts, then the game is a point-trick one by definition, though it feels in practice like a plain-trick game. And a negligibly fine line is to be drawn between the null bid of Skat, where the aim is to take no trick at all, and that of German Tarock, where it suffices to take no trick of any point-value.

Reversis

Early trick-avoidance games are not clearly identifiable. A reference to 'Perde o Vinci' in the Steele document of 1450–80 recalls modern Italian Perdivinci, a negative variety of Tressette; but its literal meaning 'win-or-lose' could denote a betting game as elementary as heads and tails. The nearest Cardano gets to a negative game is a Lowball version of Primiera. More promising is an entry in Rabelais's list of Gargantuan games for 'Coquimbert, qui gaigne perd'—'the winner loses'—a telling title undoubtedly counterparted by the Spanish Gana Pierde often recorded in the sixteenth and seventeenth centuries. (At least one modern French book of children's card games[4] includes Qui perd gagne as a trick-avoidance game without frills or complications.) An English contemporary and probable equivalent of Coquimbert is the Lodam, or Losing Lodam, mentioned in (for instance) *Taylor's Motto* of 1621. Its affiliations are apparent both from Cotgrave's French–English dictionary of 1611, where Coquimbert is identified as a card game called 'loosing-lodam', and from Urquhart's translation of Rabelais, where it is rendered 'at losing, load him'. The latter may suggest the practice of throwing unwanted cards on a trick won by somebody else. (So, indeed, might the name of the unidentified Italian game of Scartino mentioned around the turn of the sixteenth century, in view of the fact that 'scartine' denotes worthless discards thrown to tricks in Briscola.)[5]

The oldest negative game to achieve international repute and subsequent status as a classic is Reversis, first recorded in France in 1601 as 'Reversin'.[6] It soon became sufficiently popular to form the subject of one of the earliest books devoted to an individual card game, *Le Plaisant Jeu du Reversy des Dames* (1634). It appears throughout the *Académie des jeux* series from 1659 onwards, and is not dropped from the gamebooks until well into the nineteenth century. Curiously, although Reversis spread widely throughout Europe, it made no headway in England. Negative games are remarkable for their absence in Cotton, Seymour, and Hoyle, and although Reversis pops up in Jones's Hoyle of 1800, it pops out again from that of Pardon in 1862. As Cavendish observes in his *Card Essays* (1879), 'Modern Hoyles contain Reversis, but no-one ever seems to play it.'

Although it would be misleading to portray Reversis as the direct ancestor of Hearts, itself not so much a game as a conceptual basis on which many different games are built, it nevertheless exhibits many distinctive features that have subsequently found their way into negative games in general. In its oldest form, Reversis was played by four with a 52-card pack. Only forty-eight were dealt, and players each made one discard before playing to eleven tricks at no trump, the only obligation being to follow suit. Cards taken in tricks counted Ace 4, King 3, Queen 2, Jack 1 each. The aim was to take as few card-points as possible, the winner being paid by each of the others according to how many they took themselves. By 1634 various other features had been introduced. The winner of a trick containing an Ace of a different suit from that led paid an immediate penalty on the side, as did the player taking the heart Jack ('Quinola') in a trick—compare the role of the spade Queen as 'Black Maria', or heart King as 'le Barbu'. There was a reward for winning every trick, a feat known as the 'reversis' and surviving in Hearts games under such titles as 'hitting the moon'. Before play, the holder of an Ace could give it to someone else in exchange for a card unwanted by the latter—a practice that brings to mind the general exchange of cards preceding modern games of the Hearts family. By the early eighteenth century the game had developed further complications and optional extras, and was now played with a 48-card pack permanently lacking Tens. The bid of *espagnolette*—to take no tricks at all—appeared in 1828 to testify to the game's continued vitality.[7] In 1876 the *Académie des jeux* includes Reversis under 'current' as opposed to 'historic' card games, but says it is only played in the provinces, i.e. with one foot in the grave.

From the absence of Tens, the play from left to right, and such terms as Quinola and *espagnolette*, Reversis has generally been ascribed to Spain, where it was played under the name Revesino. Thierry Depaulis, however, pointing to the absence of positive evidence for its existence in sixteenth-century Spain, now argues for an Italian origin. He notes that Cotgrave's 1611 French–English Dictionary describes Reversis as having been introduced into France by the Duke of Savoy some ten years previously (which happens to accord well with the 1601 French reference to 'Reversin'), and relates its name to 'Rovescino', which is known from the early seventeenth century and is still used for a negative form of Tressette.[8] Reversis became hispanicized in the mid-seventeenth century, Depaulis believes, when it adopted the heart Jack as a penalty card under the name 'Quinola'. Quinola is certainly a Spanish term, having been applied by the Spanish to various card combinations such as the prime (four cards, one of each suit). Given the Spanish flavour and the subsequent stripping of Tens from the pack, the French may naturally have assumed a Spanish origin for the game and then reinforced it by inventing such terms as *espagnolette*.

Polignac, Slobberhannes, Bassadewitz, etc.

Other negative games of historical interest are worth a mention. In Polignac, best played by four with a 32-card pack, each Jack taken in a trick counts 1 penalty, except for the spade Jack or 'Polignac', which counts two. A player who announces 'capot' before the first card is led may cancel five penalties for subsequently winning every trick, but loses five for failing. Polignac may be regarded as a reverse game based on Ecarté, being originally played with King high and Ace ranking between Jack and Ten. It would be helpful to know which of the family it commemorates: probably not Cardinal de Polignac (1661–1742); possibly Madame de Polignac, who at the court of Louis XIV played cards until she ruined herself;[9] perhaps most probably Prince Paul de Polignac, the last Prime Minister (1830) of the last of the Bourbon kings.

Reminiscent of Polignac is the German game of Slobberhannes, or 'Slippery Jack' (Hannes = Johann = John). In this 32-card game, also best for four, penalties accrue for winning the first trick, the last trick, the trick containing ♣Q, and—if they befall the same player—for incurring all three penalties in the same deal, making four in all. The first to reach 10 is the loser.

Either of these evidently related games may underlie '(The Four) Knaves', first recorded by B. C. Westall in the 1930s.[10] No source is given, but the suit hierarchy is that of Bridge-Whist, suggesting a pre-1912 point of origin. In this 52-card game the Jacks of spades, clubs, diamonds, and hearts respectively penalize their takers by 1, 2, 3, and 4 points, which are subtracted from a plus score of 1 per trick.

Bassadewitz or Bassarovitz, still perpetuated in European Hoyles, is another 32-card game best played by four, the object being to capture fewest card-points in tricks at the rate of each Ace 11, King 4, Queen 3, Jack 2, and Ten 10. (Some accounts[11] value Ace at 5 rather than 11, probably representing an older version of the game.) Bassadewitz is played for a pool of 12 chips put up by the dealer, of which five are won for taking fewest points, four for second fewest, and three for third. The pool remains intact and the same dealer deals again if one player (*a*) wins every trick, in which case he receives four chips from each opponent, or (*b*) takes 100 or more card-points but fails to win every trick, in which case he pays four to each opponent.

Hearts, Black Maria, Le Barbu

Hearts, unadorned, is a simple game in which each heart contained in a trick counts 1 point against its owner and the winner is the player with fewest points when the game reaches a previously agreed ending. Being hardly ever played without adornment, it also serves, like 'Rummy' and 'Poker', as a generic title for a vast family of informal games. Typical is:

Black Maria (*Anglo-American, twentieth century*). Three or more players, four best. From a 52-card pack strip as many Twos and Threes (not of hearts) as necessary to ensure that everyone gets the same number of cards, then deal them around one at a time.

Each player first passes three cards face down to the right, then takes the three passed on from the left. (If more than four play, only two are passed.) Tricks are played as at Whist, but without trumps.

The aim is to avoid taking in tricks any hearts, each counting 1 point against, or 'Black Maria', the spade Queen, which counts 13 against. A player winning every trick, however, scores 26 plus-points, or wins the pool, for 'hitting the moon'.

The winner is the player with fewest penalties at end of play (e.g. when someone reaches 100). If played for hard-score, each pays into a pool one chip per penalty point taken, and the pool is won or shared by the player(s) taking fewest penalties. Alternatively, it can only be won by taking no tricks at all, or by hitting the moon, and is carried forwards until either happens.

(Some schools, in any game of the Hearts family, place restrictions on leading hearts to some or all tricks. This strikes me as unnecessary.)

Variations have been devised to compensate for the fact that Black Maria counts as much alone as all the hearts combined. In one version, the Queen's penalty is reduced to 5; in another, penalties also attach to the spade Ace (7) and King (10); in Spot Hearts, the penalty value of each heart is equivalent to its face value. Other varieties include the dealing of a dead hand of four or so cards, which go to the winner of the last trick, together with any penalties they may contain. This strategic improvement—equivalent to a penalty for taking the last trick—also neatly obviates the need to strip out low cards when other than four are playing.

Hearts first appears in English-language Hoyles in the 1880s.[12] In 1895 the author of *Foster on Hearts* remarks on its increasing popularity and solicits authoritative information as to its origin—apparently in vain, as he adds nothing to our knowledge in his later books. Depaulis suspects an origin in the Benelux countries in view of the long-standing popularity there of such games as Le Jeu du Roi (Koningsspel),SansCœur(GeenHarten),andChasse-Cœur(Hartenjagen).

If Chasse-Cœur is but a lightly adorned version of basic Hearts, the other two are far more interesting. Both are compound games, consisting of a number of deals with different penalty cards, and hence strategic objectives, in each. Le Jeu du Roi is said (by Gerver) to derive from an English game called 'King', though no such creature inhabits any English-language Hoyle that I have ever come across. Elements of both have come together in a series of very similar but non-standardized games entitled Le Barbu ('The Bearded Man') or, as a jocular derivative, Le Bambu, for which a vogue began in France during the 1960s, especially amongst Bridge-players. As the half-dozen or so accounts of the game known to me are all different, I will describe a simplified version of the one that strikes me as most typical.[13]

Le Barbu (*French, current*). Four players, 52 cards. Arrange a scoresheet in four columns, one per player, and twenty-eight rows, one for each deal. The deal passes regularly to the left so that each player deals seven times in all. Deal thirteen each in ones.

The player at dealer's left is automatically the Declarer. Having examined his cards, he declares one of seven possible contracts which he has not chosen before. Of these contracts (listed below) all except Domino are trick-taking games, and all except Domino and Trump score negatively. Trick-games are played to normal Whist rules, but at no trump, except in the game called Trump. Declarer always has the opening lead.

1. No tricks. Each trick taken scores -2 points.
2. No hearts. Each heart taken scores -2, the Ace of hearts -6.
3. No Queens. Each Queen taken scores -6.
4. No King. Taking ♥K (*le Barbu*) scores -20.
5. No last. Taking the last trick scores -20, the penultimate trick -10.
6. Trump. Each trick won scores $+5$ points. (Declarer chooses trumps.)
7. Domino. Declarer lays any card face up on the table. Each in turn must then, if possible, play a card so that it abuts at least one card already in position and contributes to the eventual construction of a layout consisting of four 13-card suit sequences (Ace high, Two low), with one row per suit and one column per rank. First out of cards scores $+40$, second $+20$, third $+5$.

Note that the positive scores eventually cancel out the negatives, producing a zero-sum result. Earlier examples were hard-score games played in two phases, each consisting of the same number and type of deals played in a fixed order. In the first phase all scores were negative and resulted in a number of chips being paid into a pool. In the second all were positive, resulting in the same number of chips being taken back out of it. What has turned a simple 'compendium' game into a compound game of strategy is the 'Yacht' (dice-game) device of running through a set of varying contracts in a selected rather than a predetermined order.

23

Flights of fancy

> So it is more suitable for the thinking person to play at cards . . .
> than at other games.
>
> Cardano, *The Book on Games of Chance* (1564)

I hope to have shown, in the foregoing pages, that cards are not just used for 'idle games of chance'[1] but offer an unparalleled variety of opportunities for the exercise of imagination and creative strategy. To what extent that offer is taken up depends entirely upon the player, for there are at least as many different card games as people to play them, and their appeal is not restricted to a particular type of personality. I also hope to have demonstrated that card games are not one-off patented inventions but have evolved as if of their own accord by the modification and recombination of traditional gaming elements: that they are, in other words, the anonymous products of communal invention or 'folk art'. As such, they are most widely and enjoyably played as players choose to play them, and not as dictated by official rules revealed through the prophet Hoyle.

At risk of sounding pretentious, I believe cards will continue to thrive because they relate so closely to the human condition. For all their variety, they embody a unique and unrivalled gaming idea: that of things mysterious on one side and obvious on the other, whose exercise involves unravelling the mystery from glimpses of the obvious in time to put that understanding to good use. There will always be those who decline the invitation, preferring to surrender themselves passively to the dictates of chance—just as there are those who prefer to mark the backs or slyly peek at the fronts, even when not playing games. But so long as anyone is left to wield a card there will always be intelligent games reflecting the basis set-up of life, which starts us all off from unplanned and unequal opening positions, and itself is nothing if not the ultimate game of 'imperfect information'.

This is not to say that card games are immune from the challenges of the times. One of the most insidious threats of our time is the creeping death of international standardization, with its numbing prospect of total cultural entropy. People no longer acquire their gaming habits at their mothers' knee, the family fireside, and the local hostelry: they pick their tastes up from global media and get the details from standard textbooks, whether directly or by hearsay. Textbook games therefore wield the advantage of social prominence, of fashionable desirability, over traditional games of local or limited extent. The particular threat is obvious. 'Contract Bridge', as Dummett says, 'is undoubtedly a very great game. But if one values card games as manifestations of local cultures, Bridge is a menace: it drives out other games as the grey squirrel drove out the red squirrel;[2] it deals the death-blow to games that have survived for centuries.' There is also the related threat of commercial hijacking, whereby a business interest steals a traditional game, redesigns it beyond recognition, launches it with the complicity of media hype, and so replaces a natural and freely available original with an artificial but profit-making substitute. To this end, rich pickings are to be had from the realm of card games.

Fortunately, I have sufficient confidence in the natural goodness of card games not to be greatly perturbed by either of these threats. The second, though apparently more drastic, is unlikely to make any significant inroads into the production of traditional cards or the pursuit of traditional games. Commercialized card games are nothing new: they flourished in Victorian times with in-house productions of Snap, Happy Families, and Spade the Gardener, and were themselves preceded by a long tradition of non-standard packs perversely redesigned for educational and moralizing purposes. Such perversions may take temporary hold, but do not last. Games players are not always aware of being duped when they buy the product, but if it fails to offer any significantly different gaming experience once the surface novelty has worn off they tend to revert to the original on which it is based. Traditional playing-cards may look old-fashioned, but in fact they are timeless, and therefore—unlike their commercial counterparts—never date.

As to the 'grey squirrel' threat, the status of Contract Bridge is by no means unique or without precedent. Its devotees may well believe it to represent an evolutionary pinnacle above which it is impossible to rise. But so, years before, did those of Whist ('The king of card games, and destined, for many a long year, to retain that distinction', as Cavendish wrote[3] shortly before its demise) and before that of Quadrille, of Ombre, of Piquet, and so on, no doubt right back to the fifteenth-century inventors of Tarot. Timewise, upstart Bridge has some catching up to do before it begins to rival the 150-year reign of Whist, let alone the 550-year longevity of Tarot. All, in their various days, may have ousted a few other flourishing games as the grey squirrel ousted the red, but those they ousted were usually not folk games (which merely went underground, as Anglo-Saxon did under the pressure of Norman French) but their own predecessors in the ousting business. None of them ever succeeded in ousting all its potential rivals, and history shows that, once a fad game has slithered into the comfortable status of 'establishment', many of the old ones return to the same ecological niche, even if lightly disguised with elements borrowed from the new.

This consoling thought may yet be put in doubt by the 'global village' effect of modern communications, which naturally tend to favour the promotion of international and fad games at the expense of local and traditional ones. Software re-creations of traditional games, for instance, are notably restricted to those of greatest international repute, like Bridge, Chess, Backgammon, and Go. But this is only at time of writing. Probably, publishers will increasingly find themselves delving into the repertoire of minor, local, or positively obscure games in order to meet a growing demand for novelty, variety, and the satisfaction of minority tastes. We have already witnessed a parallel in the twentieth-century development of the gramophone, the LP, the audio tape, and the CD. If output in these media initially confined itself to the Bachs and Beethovens of the musical world, it has inevitably expanded to embrace the Bantocks and Butterworths too.

Games to come

Looking forward, then, to the continued evolution of traditional cards and games, we may enquire in what direction such evolution may lead. As the question can hardly be answered without first inventing the games we are enquiring into, which is rather a tall order, it may help to look back at the way card games have developed in the twentieth century.

The phenomenal rise and variegation of Rummy games shows what scope may still remain for the exploitation of simple ideas which perhaps have yet to be tapped. It is amazing what riches were squeezed, in a few decades, out of the elementary principle of drawing and discarding to a stockpile with a view to forming combinations in the hand. Just as no one in 1900 could have foreseen the butterfly of Canasta arising forty years later from the caterpillar of Conquian, so we may be led to wonder which caterpillar games of the present day might not be ready to take flight by the mid-twenty-first century.

Less prominently, some revival of fortune has been enjoyed since 1950 by games of the Eights family such as Mau-Mau. Although this has led to the remarkable commercial success of a proprietary adaptation under the name Uno, it is hard to see a game of universally acknowledged excellence arising from so unpromising a caterpillar, unless it borrows further from something like the Russian Durak, or unless one counts under this heading Bob Abbott's 'Eleusis'.

Tarot games continue to flourish in countries enjoying that tradition, and recent claims of increasing popularity in France are supported there by increasing sales of Tarot playing-cards (as opposed to fortune-telling Tarots). Anglo-Americans interested in extending their card-playing repertoire could hardly do better than explore this exciting field.

From Contract Bridge itself, which needs no bush, we may detect a trend in modern games towards increasing the amount of information available at start of play, and perhaps be tempted to see a future for games entirely based on 'perfect information'. In Chapter 2, however, we noted that card games seem to impose a natural limit on the degree of information which it is proper to impart. For this reason, although such games have been invented, and might be thought to accord with the spirit of the times, none has so far made any lasting conquest.[4] I maintain that this is because such perfection makes no use of the deliberate blankness of the backs of cards, thereby contradicting the fundamental nature of the gaming material.

Two innovations are worth mentioning in this connection. One is a pack of cards designed by Alex Randolph and published in 1987 by Messrs Piatnik, the Viennese card-makers, under the rather meaningless title Indiscretion. In this, the back of each card is distinctively coloured to show what suit is on the face, but not which rank. Several good games have been designed to exploit the corresponding increase of information, and it will be interesting to see how well the concept fares. The other is Abbott's 'Eleusis', which first appeared in 1959.[5] Eleusis uses ordinary cards for a matching game with a difference. The object is to be the first to play out all one's cards to a matching sequence gradually built up on the table, as in Eights or Newmarket. No one, however, knows what the rule of matching is, apart from a non-participating player, the Umpire, who invents the rule to be followed at start of play and secretly writes it down for future reference. Players therefore have to work the rule out for themselves by attempting to add cards to the sequence and noting whether the Umpire accepts or rejects them as according with his secret rule. While not a game of perfect information, Eleusis is the most perfect game of imperfect information imaginable, since the whole point of play is to discover information by the formulation and testing of hypotheses. Because this replicates the manner of scientific enquiry rather well, it has attracted a considerable amount of philosophical attention tending to support our earlier point about card games being intrinsically relevant to the practice of everyday life.

Continuing our enquiry, we may next consider notable games or ideas which, despite promising material, have not so far enjoyed the success or expansion of Bridge and Rummy. Fishing games in particular, such as Scopa and Cassino, are remarkable for their failure to attract a widespread following, and the brilliance of Italy's national game of Scopone remains to be discovered. As this family of games is popular in China, it may yet benefit from expanding east–west relations. Also of the stuff of greatness is the Chinese game of Zheng Shàng Yóu, or its French equivalent Trouduc, as described in Chapter 10.

In the field of tricks, it seems surprising that the evolutionary advances of Bridge have exerted so little influence on reverse games such as Hearts and alliance games such as Solo. In the first case one would expect there to be scope for a game of depth and skill in which players bid for the privilege of nominating the penalty suit and can earn credit for the winning of tricks which contain no penalties. Such games have certainly been devised, but none has yet managed to enter the everyday repertoire of Hoyles. Another approach, represented by the French game le Barbu, has also yet to attract the wider attention it deserves. As to the alliance principle, as opposed to fixed partnerships, it still thrives in such continental point-trick games as Doppelkopf and 'Rufer' varieties of Tarock, but in Anglo-American plain-trick tradition is only vestigially represented by the Prop-and-Cop bid of Solo. The failure of Foster's 'Pirate' to replace Auction as the standard form of Bridge may be regretted by those who find themselves by temperament averse to permanent partnerships, as may the failure of Solo Whist to grow out of gambling garb and allow itself to be taken seriously.

Oh Hell!—Ninety-Nine

A more promising idea is one which only in the twentieth century has developed to within sight of maturity. This is what might be called the 'precision' principle, whereby the object is to capture, not a maximum or minimum of tricks or card-points, but a precise and predetermined number of them. Such a game is simultaneously both positive and negative, since a bid to win (say) exactly seven tricks out of thirteen is obviously the flip-side of a bid to lose exactly six. Successful play therefore calls for a high degree of precision, provided that the mechanics of play offer the players sufficient strategic manœuvrability to deploy it to the full.

The precision principle was foreshadowed in eighteenth-century Boston by such bids as *piccolo*, an undertaking to win exactly one trick, and in Tarock by the self-explanatory *uno*, *duo*, and *tricolo*. The earliest example of a structured game entirely based on this principle is that best known as Oh Hell!, presumably from a technical term often overheard in course of play. (Bowdlerized titles include Oh Well!, Blackout, and Jungle Bridge.) Of unknown origin, it was first described by B. C. Westall in the 1930s. According to Mott-Smith, 'It began to be played in New York Clubs in 1931, and was said to have been introduced from England.'[6]

Oh Hell! is for an indefinite number of players. At each deal a card is turned for trumps, and each player, after examining his hand, declares how many tricks he proposes to win. There is a rule forbidding the last player to declare from announcing a number which would equate the total number of tricks bid with the total to be played, in order to ensure that at least one player will come adrift. Play proceeds as at Whist, and each scores 1 point per trick actually won, plus 10 for succeeding in his bid. For added interest there is a structural resemblance to Knockout Whist, in that the number of cards dealt on the first round is as many as can be evenly divided amongst the players, and each succeeding deal is reduced by one card, so that the final deal is of a single card and only one trick is played. This is all very jolly, but hardly conducive to brilliant play after the first couple of deals. It feels, in fact, distinctly like a drinking game.

The point-trick equivalent would be one in which each player declares in advance how many card-points he aims to win in tricks. Such is encountered in Differenzler, a Swiss variety of Jass. Bids to take specific numbers of card-points are announced before play, and each player subsequently receives a negative score equivalent to the difference between the numbers bid and actually taken. A precise correspondence is rewarded with 10 plus-points.[7]

A more advanced embodiment of this idea is my own game Ninety-Nine, invented in 1968 and first published in 1974.[8] As it has since been republished in various languages from Spanish to

Japanese, thereby attracting something of a following, it may perhaps be acceptably described here as our major illustration of the precision principle.

Ninety-Nine (*Parlett, 1968, revised 1980*). Three players; 36-card pack ranking A-K-Q-J-10-9-8-7-6. Deal twelve cards each. The first round is played at no trump.

Each player discards three cards face down and plays the other nine to tricks. The object of play is to take exactly the number of tricks indicated in code by the three discards. For this purpose,

> each discarded ♣ represents 3 tricks bid;
> each discarded ♥ represents 2 tricks bid;
> each discarded ♠ represents 1 trick bid;
> each discarded ♦ represents 0 trick bid.

(Example: A bid of three tricks may be made by discarding any heart, spade, and diamond, or a club and two diamonds, or any three spades. A bid of nought can be made only by discarding three diamonds, of nine only by discarding three clubs.)

There follows a round of premium bidding to see if anyone will play 'declared', i.e. with bid-cards turned up so that everyone knows how many are wanted, or 'revealed'—the same, except that the bidder also spreads his hand of cards face up on the table before the opening lead is made. Only one player may make a premium bid. If two wish to do so, the elder hand has priority, but a revelation outbids a simple declaration.

Eldest leads, and tricks are played as at Whist—*f,tr.*

Whoever takes exactly the number bid must turn his bid-cards up to prove it; otherwise, they are left face down. Each player scores 1 point per trick actually taken, whether bid or not. Succeeding in a bid earns a basic bonus of 10, plus 10 more in respect of each player who failed. A declared game carries an additional bonus of 30, a revealed one of 60. This goes to the bidder if successful, otherwise to each opponent, whether they succeed or not. Thus the highest possible score on a single deal is 99 points: 9 for tricks taken, plus 30 for being the only player to succeed, plus 60 if the game was revealed.

The trump suit in each subsequent deal depends on the number of players who succeeded in the previous one: if no one succeeded, diamonds; if one did, spades; if two, hearts; if three, clubs.

Game is 100 points. If tied, play another deal. There are various ways of structuring a whole game—e.g., play a fixed number of games, or continue until one player has won a previously agreed number of games.

Variations: Four may play with a full pack, dealing thirteen each and playing ten to tricks. A bid of three diamonds represents either no tricks or all ten, there being no need to specify which. If all succeed, the next deal is played at no trump.

Two may play with a 24-card pack (Nine low), dealing twelve each. Non-dealer may choose trumps or pass this privilege to dealer, who may not refuse it. Only the player who does not choose trumps may declare. Neither may 'reveal', as this would add nothing to the information already available.

Sphinx is a version for three or four more experienced players. The deal is followed by a round of bidding to see if anyone will 'declare' or 'reveal' in return for the privilege of choosing trumps. If so, the declarer announces trumps and everyone then lays out their bid-cards. If not, the trump suit is determined in the usual way. The game is played up to 200.

Ninety-Nine has several points of unusual strategic interest. Whereas most bidding games see a single contract established by one player or side, which the others merely try to defeat, Ninety-Nine enables every player to establish and fulfil a contract at every deal. It also contains an 'alliance' element, in that, whenever a player declares or reveals, the others will find it more profitable to collaborate towards defeating the contract than to concentrate primarily on fulfilling their own. Often, of course, they can do both.

Its best feature lies in the consequences of the precision bidding involved. Since a bid to win (say) three tricks is simultaneously a bid to lose six, each player must start with a clear idea of the destination of almost every card in the hand. One may be needed for winning a trick, and one earmarked for getting off lead when the requisite number has been won; another must be discarded early for fear of taking an unwanted trick later, and yet another held in reserve in case the expected trick-winner fails; and so on. The bidding method introduces a further element of skill, in that the selection of bid-cards alters the shape of the hand, for which purpose players often find themselves confronted with several options. Since the same hand is often biddable in several different ways, the object is not so much to think of a suitable number of tricks and then bid it, as to bid a suitable number of tricks and then make it.

*   *   *

I look forward to seeing whether Ninety-Nine has anything of a future, and whether the precision principle in general will spread into other tricksters as a logical extension of the contract idea. I'm sorry I shan't be here in a hundred years' time to see whether tricks and trumps and bids remain the stuff and matter of the world's great card games. That cards themselves will still be played in thousands of ways that are 'everywhere different, yet everywhere the same' I have no doubt—nor that all will still be traceable, in one form or another, to the unknown inventors of Karnöffel, Tarot, Piquet, and the like.

APPENDIX I

General rules of play

Rules were made
to be displayed
on notice-board
and there
    i
     g
      n
       o
        r
         e
          d

Certain rules are not specific to particular games but serve as a general code of good practice over the card-table. Their purpose is to keep things running smoothly and fairly and to obviate disputes, so that no one's enjoyment of the game is marred by embarrassment, ill behaviour, or time-wasting. The following points are worth taking into account.

Cards

Regular card-players eschew novelty packs, especially those with non-standard faces or gimmicky back designs; they prefer the proper cards for the game, and always have a fresh pack handy for replacement. A sloppy old pack encourages sloppy old habits, and cards should be abandoned when they get sticky or when any of them are so worn with use as to be identifiable from the back by a stain, fold, or tear. It is good practice to alternate two packs of similar back design but contrasting colour, one of them being thoroughly shuffled for the next deal while the other is being dealt out for this. That cards sometimes run unfavourably to a particular player for a long time is not a superstition but an observable fact. By tradition, anyone may call for new cards at any time in the session. (But—also by tradition—at their own expense.)

Cutting

Cards are cut to decide things like choice of seats, partners, and first deal, to which end they normally rank in their 'natural' order from Ace low to King high. If two or more cut equal ranks, they cut again, but only to break the tie between themselves. Instead of cutting, players may draw a card at random from the whole pack shuffled and spread face down on the table.

Partners

In a fixed-partnership game, players may wish to select partners at random. This may be determined by cutting or drawing, the two highest ranks playing the two lowest, and having first choice of seats.

Seating

The order of seating around the table may be randomized by cutting, with highest cut conferring first choice of seat, and so on. Although this practice is rooted in superstition (the aim being to prevent players from fighting over 'lucky' seats or positions), there is also a practical reason for it. Since experienced players who know the company well can adjust their play according to who is sitting on either side of them, it is obviously fair to randomize their relative positions.

Rotation

It is immaterial whether the turn to play passes from right to left around the table (clockwise, seen from above) or from left to right (counter-clockwise), and different games have different traditions. Roughly speaking, counter-clockwise is associated with ancient games and southern European practice, clockwise with northern and relatively modern games.

Scoring

The scoring of a soft-score game (pencil and paper) should be entrusted to the player most reliable as to neatness, numeracy, and objectivity—but keep an eye on it all the same, as no one is infallible. In a two-sided game, it is helpful to follow Contract Bridge practice whereby each side keeps a scoresheet recording both sides' current scores. If playing *for* money, ensure that everyone agrees the final basis of settlement in advance and that it is not increased in mid-play. If playing *with* money or its equivalent (e.g. Poker chips), make provision for players to retire when they are broke. It is silly to allow anyone to leave a game either owing money or feeling that they have lost more than they can afford.

Dealer

Unless tradition or book-rules decree otherwise for a particular game, and for a sensible reason, the turn to deal passes from person to person in the same order as the turn to play. The first dealer may be selected by cutting or drawing the lowest (or highest) card. Normally, though not invariably, it is for the player next in rotation from the dealer—'eldest hand'—to play, bid, or bet first.

Shuffle and cut

The pack should always be shuffled before being dealt. (Some schools restrict shuffling to certain deals, thereby deliberately 'stacking the pack' to produce more startling and dramatic hands. This greatly appeals to children and gamblers, but those who do not follow the practice are advised to steer clear of those who do.) Any player who wishes to may shuffle, but dealer has the right to shuffle last. If you can't shuffle well, practise; and if this doesn't help, get someone else to do it. The important thing is the randomization, not the performance. The shuffle should be followed by a cut.

Dealing

Unless otherwise agreed or specified, cards are dealt face down in rotation around the table, one at a time, starting with eldest and finishing with the dealer. In some games it is customary to deal not singly but in batches of three or four cards at a time. This is not designed to produce 'more interesting hands' so much as to save time and effort. Custom should always be followed in this matter, as the dealer who fails to do so may be suspected of nefarious motives, not to mention bad manners.

Play

It is bad manners to pick your cards up before the deal is complete. (It may put the dealer off his stroke, or cause a card to be faced, which is a waste of time and effort.) In play, restrict conversation to that necessary to the game—gossip can be left to between deals. Make bids clearly and audibly. Play cards smoothly rather than histrionically, decisively rather than hesitantly. If you have to stop and think, do so before touching a card in your hand, as the act of touching first one and then another may be construed as illegal signalling to a partner. (This tends to be accounted dastardly, especially in a non-partnership game.) Don't criticize a partner for their play, or brag about or justify your own. If the rules of the game do not demand that players show the cards they have won, played, or discarded, don't insist on seeing them. (These procedures are open to relaxation in informal play, for example among close friends who are not playing seriously for money and know one another well enough to follow an intuitive code of behaviour. But it is as well to know and follow them, especially when a newcomer joins the group.)

Irregularities

An irregularity of play may be dealt with either by exacting a penalty, in chips or score-points as the case may be, or by attempting to eliminate any unfair advantage it may have occasioned. The second course is better than the first. (Though I have read somewhere that the British tend to prefer penalty exaction while other nations favour positional restoration.) Typical corrections include the following, and should only be relaxed by unanimous agreement.

If the wrong person deals, let it stand. Only annul the deal if anyone *who has not yet looked at their cards* insists on a redeal by the right dealer. (It is obviously unfair to wait until you have seen your cards before having an attack of the superstitions.)

If a card is exposed in the deal, bury it in the pack and continue if everyone agrees; but redeal if anyone insists on it.

If anyone is found to have the wrong number of cards before play begins (this includes any relevant announcement, bid, or bet), gather them in and redeal by the same dealer. Otherwise, players are individually responsible for ensuring that they have the right number of cards, and anyone later found to be in error must be deemed to have lost, unless a replay is agreed by all.

If a card is led or played out of turn, leave it face up on the table and play it at the first legal opportunity to do so.

A card once played may not (except by universal agreement) be taken back, unless (*a*) its play was illegal, and (*b*) the next in turn to play has not yet done so. The misplayed card must then be left face up and played as soon as legally possible.

In case of discrepancy between a card actually played and what its player declares it to be (e.g. the bidder, in a game where trumps must be led, declares spades trump but actually pitches a heart), the card speaks for itself.

A player or side which is found to have revoked is deemed to have lost.

An irregularity counts as condoned, and therefore no longer rectifiable, once the score or settlement for that deal has been made.

Avoiding disputes

Authority is best vested in agreement. It is helpful for a constant group of players to commit to writing, for future reference, agreements made as to how the game is played, what practices are and are not valid, and such 'cases and decisions' as may have occurred and been agreed on. Additionally or alternatively, players may agree to accept as binding the rules quoted in a given book, for which purpose the best book is the nearest one to hand.

It may be possible, and always is desirable, to appeal to an experienced player who is not taking part in the current game.

Game ending

Unless the game is one of the few equipped by definition with a prescribed structure (e.g. a 'partie' at Piquet or a 'rubber' at Whist), it is desirable to decide in advance when to stop, or how to agree on stopping. The simplest is to fix a time limit and, when it expires, to stop as soon as everyone has made the same number of deals.

National suit systems

French-suited cards

English	spades	clubs	hearts	diamonds	
French	*pique*	*trèfle*	*cœur*	*carreau*	(= pikes, clover, hearts, tiles)
German	*Pik*	*Kreuz*	*Herz*	*Karo*	(same, but Kreuz = 'crosses')

English (52)		A	K	Q	J	10	9	8	7	6	5	4	3	2
French (52, 32)		A	R	D	V	10	9	8	7	(6	5	4	3	2)
German (32)		A	K	D	B	10	9	8	7					

English	Ace	King	Queen	Jack (Knave)
French	*As*	*Roi*	*Dame*	*Valet*
German	*As*	*König*	*Dame*	*Bube*

German and Swiss-suited cards

German	*Laub*	*Eichel*	*Herz*	*Schellen*	(= leaves, acorns, hearts, bells)
or	*Grün*	*Eichel*	*Rot*	*Schellen*	(= green, acorns, red, bells)
Swiss	*Wappen*	*Eichel*	*Rosen*	*Schellen*	(= shields, acorns, roses, bells)

German (36, 32)	D	K	O	U	10	9	8	7	(6)
Swiss (36)	D	K	O	U	%	9	8	7	6

German	*Daus*	*König*	*Ober*	*Unter*	
Swiss	*Daus*	*König*	*Over*	*Under*,	% = *Banner* (equivalent to Ten)

Latin-suited cards

Italian	*bastoni*	*spade*	*coppe*	*denari*	(= batons, swords, cups, coins)
Spanish	*bastos*	*espadas*	*copas*	*oros*	(= clubs, swords, cups, coins)

Italian (40)	R	C	F			7	6	5	4	3	2	1
Spanish (48, 40)	R	C	S	(9	8)	7	6	5	4	3	2	1

Italian	*Re*	*Cavallo*	*Fante*	(= King, Cavalier, Footsoldier)
Spanish	*Rey*	*Caballo*	*Sota*	(= King, Cavalier, Servant)

Glossary

Pray, Mr Dousterswivel, . . . will you have the goodness to supply us with a few thumping blustering terms of art?

Walter Scott, *The Antiquary*

age Order of priority in making the first lead, bid, or bet, as reckoned around the table starting from player immediately next to the dealer, who is known as eldest and enjoys greatest priority. Also edge; and see also youngest.

alliance A temporary partnership, lasting only for the current deal (as in 'prop and cop' at Solo Whist).

ante In gambling games, an obligatory stake made before play begins—usually by every player, sometimes only by the dealer.

auction A period of bidding to establish the conditions of the game, e.g. who is undertaking to win, how many tricks constitute a win, which suit is trump, etc.

bettel Same as misère.

bid An offer to achieve a stated objective (e.g. a given number of tricks) in exchange for choosing the conditions of play (e.g. a trump suit). If the offer is not overcalled by a higher bid, it becomes a contract.

blank (1) In card-point games, a card worth nothing. (2) A hand without courts, consisting only of numerals.

blaze A non-standard Poker hand, consisting solely of court cards.

card points The point values of cards in point-trick games (as opposed to nominal face values).

carte blanche Same as blank (2).

carte rouge A hand in which every card counts towards a scoring combination (Piquet).

chicane A hand which, as dealt, contains no trumps.

chip A gaming counter, especially in Poker.

combination A set of cards matching one another by rank or suit and recognized by the rules of the game as a scoring feature.

complex See card-point games.

contract See bid.

counter (1) An object representing a score or partially won game. (2) A card with a point-value, in point-trick games such as Skat and Pinochle.

court (cards) King, Queen, Jack, etc., as opposed to numeral or pip cards. Also called face-cards, and originally coats.

cut To lift off the top portion of the pack and either (1) reveal its bottom card, so as to make a random decision such as who deals first; or (2) to replace it beneath the lower half, so as to ensure that no one knows what the bottom card is.

cut-throat All against all; without partnerships.

dead hand See widow.

deadwood Penalty cards remaining in opponent's hands when one player has gone out (chiefly in Rummy).

deal (1) To distribute cards to the players at start of play. (2) The play ensuing between one deal and the next.

declare (1) To announce the contract or conditions of play (number of tricks intended, trump suit, etc.). (2) To show and score for a valid combination of cards in hand.

declarer The highest bidder, who declares and then seeks to make good the stated contract.

deuce The Two of any given suit.

discard (1) To lay aside an unwanted card or cards from hand. (2) To throw a worthless or unwanted card to a trick.

doubleton Two cards of the same suit in the same hand, no others of that suit being held.

draw To take, or be dealt, one or more cards from a stock or waste-pile.

drinking game Typically, one that results in a loser rather than a winner, in order to decide who pays for the next round.

dummy A full hand of cards dealt face up to the table (or, in Bridge, dealt to one of the players, who eventually spreads them face up on the table) from which the declarer plays as well as from his or her own hand.

elder, -est (See age.) The player obliged or privileged to make the opening bet, bid, or lead. Also called age, forehand, pone, etc.

exchange (1) To discard one or more cards from hand and then draw or receive the same number from stock. (2) To add a specified number of cards to hand and then discard a like number. (3) To exchange one or more cards with a neighbour, sight unseen.

finesse To play, when holding both, a possible winning card instead of a certain winning card, in the hope of making an extra trick.

fish (1) In 'Fishing' games, to capture a card or cards by matching their face value(s) (Chapter 11). (2) A gaming-counter, originally fish-shaped.

flush A hand of cards all of the same suit.

follow (1) To play second, third, etc. to a trick. (2) Follow suit: to play a card of the same suit as that led.

forehand Same as eldest (German *Vorhand*).

frog The lowest bid in certain American games of German origin; from German *Frage*, 'request'.

f,t,r Shorthand used in this book (see Chapter 6) for rules of following to a trick.

gambling game Technically, one in which cards are not played but merely bet on.

game (1) A series of deals or session of play. (2) The contract, or conditions of the game; e.g. 'Solo in hearts'. (3) The target score; e.g. 'Game is 100 points.'

go out To play the last card from one's hand.

grand A bid equivalent to no trump in some games, a slam in others.

hand (1) The cards dealt to an individual player, which he either plays from or bets on, depending on the type of game. (2) Same as deal (2).

hard score Scoring done with coins, chips, or counters, as opposed to a written or 'soft' score.

head To play a higher card than any so far played to the trick, especially in games such as Ecarté where it is obligatory to do so if possible.

honours Cards attracting bonus-scores or side-payments, usually to whoever holds and declares them, occasionally to whoever captures them in play.

kitty The pool or pot.

lead To play the first card; or, the first card played.

line, above/below (Bridge) Scores made for tricks contracted and won are recorded below a line drawn half-way down the sheet, and count towards winning the game; overtricks, honours, and other premiums are scored above it and mainly determine the size of the win.

marriage (1) King and Queen of the same suit. (2) In Patience, any two cards in suit and sequence.

matadors Top trumps, sometimes with special privileges (especially in Hombre).

meld (1) A combination of matching cards attracting scores or privileges, or winning the game. (2) To declare such a combination.

middlehand In three-hand games, the player of intermediate priority. (German *Mittelhand*. See also age and forehand.)

misère A contract or undertaking to lose every trick.

miss A dead hand, especially in Loo; see widow.

negative game One in which the object is (1) to avoid taking tricks or penalty cards, or (2) to avoid being the loser, there being no outright winner.

null (1) In point-trick games, a card carrying no point-value; also blank. (2) Same as misère (German).

numerals Number cards, as opposed to courts. Also called pip cards, spot cards, spotters, etc.

ouvert(e) A contract played with declarer's cards spread face up on the table for all to see.

overcall To bid higher than the previous bidder. (Suit overcall = bid to entrump a higher-ranking suit; majority overcall = to take a higher number of tricks; value overcall = to play a game of higher value or to capture a greater total of card-points.)

overtrick A trick taken in excess of the number required to win.

pair Two cards of the same rank.

partie A whole game, as opposed to a single deal, especially at Piquet.

partnership Two or more players whose interests are bound together as a team and who therefore play co-operatively rather than individually. A partnership may be either fixed in advance and last for the whole session, as at Whist and Bridge, or vary from deal to deal, as at Quadrille or Solo, in which case it is better referred to as an 'alliance'.

pass In trick-games, to make no further bid; in vying games, to pass the privilege of betting first but without dropping out of play.

pip A suitmark printed on a card, or the number represented—e.g. the Deuce shows two pips. (Originally 'peep'. In manufacture, numeral cards were 'peeps' and court cards 'têtes'.)

plain suit A suit other than trumps.

plain-trick games Also called 'simple' trick-taking games: those in which importance attaches only to the number of tricks taken, regardless of the cards comprising them, as opposed to point-trick games.

point (1) The smallest unit of value, score or reckoning. In various games distinctions may be drawn between card-points, which are notional values attached to certain cards, the object being to capture a minimum number of them; score-points, which are points credited to a player's account; and game points, which might loosely be described as 'bundles' of score-points and may be affected by other bonuses. (2) The total face value of all cards held of any one suit (Piquet).

point-trick games Also called 'complex' trick-taking games: those in which win or loss is determined not by the number of tricks taken but by the total value of counters contained in them, as opposed to plain-trick games.

pool Same as pot.

pot A sum of money or equivalent, to which everyone contributes initially or throughout play, and which is eventually awarded (in whole or part) to the winner.

prial ('Pair-royal'): a triplet; three cards of the same rank (Brag, Cribbage).

rank (1) The denomination of a card (e.g. Ace, Two, King, etc.), as opposed to its suit. (2) The relative trick-taking power of a card (e.g. 'Ace ranks above King').

rearhand The player with least priority, or youngest, usually in three-hand games (German *Hinterhand*).

renege To fail to follow suit to the card led, but legally so, by exercise of a privilege granted by the rules of the game, as in Spoil Five.

renounce Strictly, to play a card of any different suit from that led—the same as 'renege', if done legally, or 'revoke', if not. Loosely, to do so only from a non-trump suit, thereby renouncing all hope of winning the trick.

revoke To fail to follow suit to the card led, though able and required to do so, thereby incurring a penalty.

riffle A method of shuffling. The pack is divided into two halves which are placed corner to corner, lifted, and allowed to fall rapidly together so that they interleave.

round (1) A period or phase of play in which all have had the same number of opportunities to deal, or bid, play to a trick, etc. (2) Round game: one playable by an indefinite number of players, typically three to seven.

rubber A contest won by the first side to win two games; i.e. best of three.

ruff To play a trump to a plain-suit lead.

run Same as sequence (Brag, Cribbage).

sans prendre A bid to play with the hand as dealt, without benefit of exchanging, thereby increasing the difficulty and hence scoring value of the game.

sequence A scoring combination consisting of three or more cards in numerical sequence or ranking order.

shuffle To randomize the order of cards in the pack. See also riffle.

simple See plain-trick games.

singleton A card which is the only one of its suit in a given hand.

skat (or scat; German, from Italian *scarto*, 'discard'). In effect, the same as widow.

slam (or grand slam) The winning of every trick, or a bid to do so.

small slam As above, but every trick bar one.

soft score Score kept in writing or on a scoring device, as opposed to cash or counters (hard score).

solo (1) Originally, the same as sans prendre. (2) A bid to achieve a given objective playing alone against the combined efforts of the other players.

soloist One who plays a solo.

spread Same as ouvert.

squeeze In trick-taking games, a situation in which a player is forced to weaken himself in either of two suits but has no way of deciding which to play from.

stock Cards which are not dealt initially but may be drawn from or dealt out later in the play.

stops Cards which terminate a sequence, in games of the Stops family (Newmarket, Pope Joan, etc.); or those which are not dealt initially and whose absence from play prevents the completion of sequences.

straddle An obligatory stake made, before any cards are dealt, by the second player around, the first having put up an ante.

straight In Poker, a five-card sequence.

suit A series of cards distinguished by the presence of a common graphic symbol throughout; or, the symbol (suitmark) itself.

talon The undealt portion of the pack; same as stock. (French, from its use to denote the remainder of a loaf when one or more slices have been cut from it.)

tourné(e) A bid to turn the top card of the stock and accept whatever suit it shows as trump.

trey The Three of any suit.

trick A set of cards equal to the number of players, each having contributed one in succession.

trump (From triumph): (1) A superior suit, any card of which will beat that of any other suit played to the trick. (2) To play such a card, or ruff.

turn-up A card turned up at start of play to determine the trump suit.

undertrick A trick less than the number required to win the deal.

upcard A card lying face up on the table, or the faced top card of the waste-pile at Rummy, Patience, etc.

void Having no card of a given suit.

vole The winning of every trick; same as slam. (French, from Spanish *bola*.)

vulnerable (Bridge) Describes a side which, having won one game towards the rubber, is subject to increased scores or penalties.

waste-pile A pile of discards, usually face up, as at Rummy, Patience, etc.

widow A hand of cards dealt face down to the table at start of play and not belonging to any particular player. One or more players may subsequently exchange one or more cards with it. See also miss and skat.

wild card One that may be used to represent any other card, with or without stated restrictions. Typically the Joker in Rummy games, Deuces in Poker.

younger, -est The player last in turn to bid or play at the start of a game (usually, in practice, the dealer). See age.

Notes

Chapter 1

1. *National Playing Card Survey*, Waddingtons Playing Card Co. (now part of Waddingtons Games Ltd.), Leeds, Apr. 1981. Over 2,000 adult interviewees in over 145 locations in Great Britain were asked 'Which of these card games have you played in the last twelve months?—Rummy, Whist, Bridge, Canasta, Solo, Poker, Pontoon, Brag, Newmarket, Cribbage, Other, Not Played [47%], Don't know [4.5%]' Responses as to frequency of play were: Never, 40%; less than twice a year, 7%; less than four times a year, 7%; less than once a month, 7%; less than weekly, 2%; at least once a week, 13%; only at Christmas, 5%; only on holiday, 3%; only when visiting friends who play, 2%.
2. Ostrow, A., *The Complete Card-Player* (New York, 1946), pp. 10–12.
3. Crawford, J., *How to be a Consistent Winner in the Most Popular Card Games* (New York, 1953).
4. Parlett, D., *Poker and Brag* (Sevenoaks, 1980).
5. Italian card games are regularly surveyed by Giampaolo Dossena, in *La Repubblica* (Rome) and formerly *La Stampa* (Turin). See also Depaulis, Dummett, Grupp, McLeod, von Leyden, and others in the *Journal of the International Playing-Card Society*, (*passim*).
6. See the Gaming Act (1968) and some interpretations in *Lotteries and Gaming* (National Council of Social Service, 1972).
7. Sketchily but invaluably surveyed by Arthur Taylor in *Pub Games* (St Albans, 1976), pp. 56–75.
8. Ostrow, appendix to 2nd edn. (1949) of *The Complete Card Player*.
9. Burke, P., *Popular Culture in Early Modern Europe* (London, 1978), pp. 124–5, noting especially 'Motifs may be said to "wander" or "float" from one [folk] tune to another.'
10. A useful gaming concept introduced by Abbott, R., in 'Under the Strategy Tree', *Games & Puzzles*, No. 36 (London, May 1975), pp. 4–5.
11. In the words of the Religious Society of Friends (Quakers), to which I belong: 'Gambling by risking money haphazardly disregards our belief that possessions are a trust . . .' (*Christian Faith and Practice*, London Yearly Meeting, 1960, para. 567).
12. See Halliday, J., and Fuller, P. (eds.), *The Psychology of Gambling* (London, 1974).
13. I am indebted to John McLeod for helpful additions to the train of thought at this point.

14. Adapted by substituting 'pack of cards' for 'chessboard' in Abrahams, Gerald, *The Chess Mind* (London, 1951), p. 34.
15. Scarne, J., *Scarne on Cards* (London, 1974), p. 4.
16. For an exploration of game as ritual, see Huizinga, J., *Homo Ludens* (Switzerland, 1944; Eng. trans. London, 1949), pp. 10–18.
17. Game theory compounds this confusion by referring to the outcome as the 'pay-off'.

Chapter 2

1. Cardano, Girolamo, *Liber de Ludo Aleae* (1564); also Gould, Sydney (trans.), *The Book on Games of Chance* (Princeton University, 1953).
2. Curiously, most board games exhibit a common element of inequality in that possession of the opening move is a distinct advantage, whereas in many card games the lead may be an advantage or disadvantage depending on the situation.
3. See Abrahams, G., *The Chess Mind* (London, 1951) and *Brains in Bridge* (London, 1962). Also relevant is the article on strategic clarity by Robert Abbott entitled 'Under the Strategy Tree', in *Games & Puzzles*, No. 36 (May 1975).
4. Quoted in Avedon, E., and Sutton-Smith, B., *The Study of Games* (New York, 1971).
5. Most are for two players. See Parlett, D., *Card Games for Two* (Sevenoaks, 1978, 1983).
6. McLeod, John, 'Ulti', in *JIPCS* (May 1976), p. 15. McLeod tells me that many such methods of ending games are to be found throughout what was once the Austro-Hungarian empire.
7. See Schreiber, W., *Die ältesten Spielkarten* (Strasburg, 1937), p. 7.

Chapter 3

1. Despite legends to the contrary, *naipe* does not derive from Flemish *knaep*, 'paper', nor does it perpetuate the initials of one Nicolas Pépin, nor is 'Jackanapes' from 'Jack' plus Spanish *naipes*.
2. Denning, T., *Spanish Playing-Cards* (The International Playing-Card Society, 1980).
3. For detailed information on cards as cards, see Hoffmann, Detlef, *The Playing Card—an Illustrated History* (Leipzig, 1973); Beal, George, *Playing-Cards and their Story* (London, 1975); Mann, Sylvia, *Collecting Playing Cards* (2nd edn., London, 1973); Janssen, Han, *De Geschiedenis van de Speelkaart* (The Hague, 1985); and relevant sections of Dummett, Michael, *The Game of Tarot* (London, 1980).
4. Burke, Peter, *Popular Culture in Early Modern Europe* (London, 1978), p. 94.

Chapter 4

1. For a well-known (and expanding) list of early dates, with commentary, see Dummett, pp. 10–11.

2. Monreal, Luis, 'Iconographía de la Baraja Española', *JIPCS* xvii (Feb. 1989), p. 92.
3. Schreiber, W. L., *Die ältesten Spielkarten* (Strasburg, 1937), p. 48.
4. For further comments on *naibbe* see Dummett, p. 43, and Pratesi, Franco, 'Italian Cards—New Discoveries', *JIPCS* xvii (Feb. 1989), pp. 107–12.
5. The best-known copy of John's lost text is in the British Museum and dates from the 1470s. It is one of several roughly contemporaneous copies which may have been made from the earliest surviving copy (1429).
6. This reference first appears in Père Menestrier, *Bibliothèque instructive et curieuse* (Trevoux, 1704).
7. Schreiber, p. 8.
8. Chatto, *Facts and Speculations on the Origin and History of Playing Cards* (London, 1848), pp. 90–1.
9. Dummett, p. 34.
10. Dummett, p. 37.
11. References listed in von Leyden, R., *Ganjifa: the Playing Cards of India* (London, 1982), pp. 41–2.
12. Rosenfeld, Hellmut, 'On the Morphogenesis of Games . . .', *JIPCS* ix (1981), pp. 69–82.
13. Mayer, L. A. (Ettinghausen and Kurz, eds.), *Mamluk Playing Cards* (Leiden, 1971).
14. See Dummett, M., and Abu-Deeb, K., in their review (*JIPCS* iii (Feb. 1975), pp. 43 ff.) of Ettinghausen, Richard, 'Further Comments on Mamluk Playing Cards', in *Gatherings in Honour of Dorothy E. Milner* (Baltimore, 1974).
15. Wintle, S., 'A Moorish Sheet of Playing-Cards', *JIPCS* xv (May 1987), pp. 112–22.
16. Dummett, pp. 63–4.
17. See Ch. 6, under 'Trick-taking games'.
18. For another interpretation, including verbal as well as visual relationships, see Rumpf, Marianne, 'Zur Entwicklung der Spielkartenfarben in der Schweiz, in Deutschland und in Frankreich', in *Schweizerisches Archiv für Volkskund*, xvii: 1–2 (Basel, 1976), pp. 1–32.
19. Dummett, pp. 21–2, and 'The Portuguese Suit-System in the Central Mediterranean', in *JIPCS* xvii (May 1989), pp. 113–24.
20. Dummett, 'The Game of Ganjifa', in von Leyden, n. 11 above, p. 53 and notes on pp. 58–9.
21. For an Oedipal interpretation of which, see Olmsted, Charlotte, *Heads I Win—Tails You Lose* (New York, 1962).
22. See Field, Albert, in Correspondence on 'De Poli Unmasked', *JIPCS* xiii (May 1985), pp. 114–17, as corrected in xiv (Nov. 1985), p. 46; also Decker, Ron, 'Who's Who in Court Cards', in *JIPCS* xvi (Feb. 1988), pp. 90–6.
23. See Turner, K., 'The Paston Letters reference', in *JIPCS* xiii (May 1985), pp. 117–18, and, on the 1461 reference, Turner's earlier communication, in vii (May 1979), p. 97.
24. Taylor, E. S., *The History of Playing Cards* (London, 1865), p. 103.

Chapter 5

1. Huizinga, J., *Homo Ludens*, p. 11.
2. Schröder (ed.), *Das Goldene Spiel von Meister Ingold*, in *Elsässische Litteraturdenkenmaler aus dem XIV–XVII Jahrhundert*, iii (Strasburg, 1882).

3. Steele, Robert, 'A Notice of the Ludus Triumphorum . . .', a paper read to the Society of Antiquarians on 31 May 1900, *Archaeologia*, lvii (1900), pp. 189–200. See also Decker, Ron, 'The Steele Manuscript', in *JIPCS* xvii (Feb. 1989), pp. 73–7.
4. Cohen, J. (trans.), *The Histories of Gargantua and Pantagruel* (London, 1955).
5. Fischart, *Affentheurliche Naupengeheurliche Geschichtklitterung von Thaten und Rahten der . . . Herrn Grandgolchier Gorgellantua* (1617); also Rausch, Heinrich, *Das Spielverzeichnis im 25 Kapitel von Fischarts 'Geschichtklitterung'* (Strasburg, 1908).
6. Cardano, *Liber de ludo aleae* (see Ch. 2 n. 1); see also Dummett, esp. pp. 356 and 366–70.
7. Chatto, *Facts and Speculations on the Origin and History of Playing Cards* (London, 1848), p. 120.
8. Chatto, p. 126.

Chapter 6

1. As reported by Borvo, Alain, in *L'Aluette—anatomie d'un jeu de cartes* (Nantes, 1977), p. 18.
2. The word *knob* is related to *knubble*, which may be a cognate of *Karnöffel*. See wordlist in von Leyden, *Karnöffel: das Kartenspiel der Landsknechte* (Vienna, 1978), pp. 32–3, and cf. slang meaning of knob with literal meaning of Karnöffel ('hernia').
3. At Loo, the opening lead must be one's highest trump. The required lead of a trump at games like Pitch and Nap is not a genuine exception, since the leader is free to choose any suit as trump.
4. A rare exception is the Danish game of Brus (Ch. 14).
5. The most accessible modern account of Ganjifa, by Michael Dummett, is in von Leyden, *Ganjifa: the Playing Cards of India* (London, 1982).

Chapter 7

1. Depaulis, Thierry, 'Un document important pour l'histoire des toutes premières cartes en France', *JIPCS* x (May 1982), pp. 118–20.
2. Depaulis, private communication.
3. Cavendish, *Card Essays* (London, 1879), pp. 63–4.
4. Depaulis, private communication.
5. Hughes, Barrie, *The Educated Gambler* (London, 1976), p. 93.
6. For an international survey of casino Blackjack, see Hughes, above, pp. 108–20. Card-casing is expounded at length in Edward O. Thorp's *Beat the Dealer* (New York, 1966).
7. Taylor (from d'Ambly), *The History of Playing Cards*, pp. 358, 370, 373.
8. Taylor (or d'Ambly), making the same reference (p. 295), renders the quotation 'jugando a la veyntiuna', i.e. Twenty-One, not Thirty-One. Unless this is a slip of the pen or an error of transmission, the whole history of Pontoon will have to be rewritten. Fortunately, it has yet to be written.

9. Chatto, 'Facts and Speculations on the Origin and History of Playing Cards' (London, 1848), pp. 114–15.

10. See Welcome, John, *Cheating at Cards* (London, 1963), pp. 60–160.

11. Depaulis, private communication.

12. From the *Jüdisches Lexikon* (Berlin, 1930). See Rudolf von Leyden, 'Kvitlakh: a Jewish Card Game', in *JIPCS* xi (May 1983), pp. 103–6; also Kissel, Robert S., 'Kwitlech: the "Kosher" Cards of Glician Jews', in *JIPCS* xviii (Feb. 1990), pp. 86–100, continued in issues of May, August 1990.

13. See Gupta, Kashaul, 'Gambling Game of Naqsh and Ganjifa Cards', in *JIPCS* viii (Nov. 1979), pp. 29–39.

14. See Mann, Sylvia, *The Dragon Cards of Portugal* (Published by Sandford for the International Playing-Card Society, 1973), pp. 60–5.

15. Laycock, D., 'Three Native Card Games of New Guinea and their European Ancestors', *Oceania*, xxxvii (Sept. 1966); also 'Three more New Guinea Card Games, and a Note on "Lucky"', xxxviii (Sept. 1967).

Chapter 8

1. The word 'vie' is discussed in this context by 'Cavendish', in *Card Essays* (London, 1879), p. 60.

2. See Schreiber, *Die ältesten Spielkarten* (Strasburg, 1937), p. 160.

3. First described in the *Académie universelle des jeux* of 1718. Depaulis tells me that the earliest French references date from 1610 and 1640.

4. Schreiber, p. 153.

5. Discussed by Depaulis in an article on 'Le Flux', in *Le Vieux Papier* (Paris, Apr. 1982).

6. See Kopp, Peter, 'Die drei ältesten Innerschweizer Kartenspiele und ihre Regeln', in *Der Geschichtsfreund*, 139 (1986), pp. 23–36.

7. Taylor, *The History of Playing Cards* (London, 1865).

8. Chatto, *Facts and Speculations . . .*, p. 120.

9. I paraphrase Gould's translation of Cardano in *The Book on Games of Chance* (New York, 1953), pp. 22–6.

10. Depaulis, 'Une boîte à jeux du musée de Cluny', in *La Revue du Louvre* (Paris, Feb. 1987), No. 1.

11. Warton, *History of English Poetry*, vol. iii, p. 311, cited by Taylor, *The History of Playing Cards*.

12. I quote verbatim, but do not see how Cotgrave arrives at his figures.

13. Depaulis, 'Brelan, Brelan, Brelan', in *Bulletin de la Société Archéologique, Historique et Artistique*, 286 (Paris, Oct. 1982), pp. 389–96.

14. Barnes, *Juegos de Naipes Españoles* (Vitoria, 2nd edn., 1984).

15. Taylor, Arthur, *Pub Games* (St Albans, 1976), p. 64.

16. Taylor, above, pp. 66–7.

17. 'In carde playinge he is a goode greke | And can skyll of post and glyeke' (Roy, *Rede Me*). Depaulis, again, is to be thanked for this reference.

18. Bowle, the Rev, 'Observations on Card-playing', in *Archaeologia*, viii (1786).

19. I have not examined Hoyle's Treatise on Brag, but the commentary on it in Dowling, Allen, *The Great American Pastime* (New York/London, 1970),

pp. 23–40, raises some problems. In particular, it is questionable whether the second stake (vying) involves a draw, as Dowling or Hoyle implies, as all other contemporary descriptions relate the draw solely to the third stake (thirty-one). And the third bragger, which Hoyle does not and Dowling cannot identify, is surely the Ace of diamonds in its capacity as an outright winner in the first stake. Perhaps Hoyle's reticence about promoting this treatise (Dowling, p. 25) was due to misgivings as to its accuracy.

Chapter 9

1. Yardley, Herbert, *The Education of a Poker Player* (US, 1957; London, 1959).
2. Berne, Eric, *Games People Play: The Psychology of Human Relationships* (1964; Harmondsworth, 1967).
3. Spanier, David, *Total Poker* (New York, 1977).
4. Films, with writer and director: *The Cincinnati Kid* (Lardner/Jewison, MGM, 1965); *Big Deal at Dodge City* (US title *A Big Hand for the Little Lady*) (Carroll/Cook, WB, 1966); *The Hustler* (Carroll/Rossen, TCF, 1961); *The Driver* (Hill/Hill, TCF, 1978).
5. I owe this reference to Prof. Evert Sprinchorn of Vassar College, New York.
6. Whether or not it appeared in the 1845 edition of Anners, which I have not seen, is subject to conflicting reports.
7. Also by 'Aquarius', in *Italian Games at Cards and Oriental Games* (London, 1890).
8. Dummett, pp. 45–51.
9. Cited in Coffin, George, *The Poker Game Complete* (London, 1950), from researches conducted by Louis Coffin, former Treasurer of the US Playing Card Co.
10. Actually A-K-Q-9-8; see 'Quinola', *Nouvelle académie des jeux* (Paris, 1876), p. 360.
11. I regret that I have lost this reference, which I found by chance in a late 19th-cent. American travel book. Something similar is reported in Coffin, n. 9 above, p. 15.
12. See the Introduction, by Poker historian Oliver P. Carriere, to Dowling, Allen, *The great American Pastime* (New York/London, 1970), pp. 9–17.
13. 'Trumps', *The American Hoyle* (New York, 1880).
14. Quoted in Blackridge, J., *The Complete Poker Player* (New York, 1880).
15. Keller, J., *The Game of Poker* (New York, 1892).
16. Foster, R. F., *Practical Poker* (London, 1904).
17. Foster, R. F., *Foster's Complete Hoyle* (London, 1897), p. 175.

Chapter 10

1. Daniel Daynes (and Thierry Depaulis), 'Jeux d'élimination', in *Sud-Ouest Dimanche* (Bordeaux), No. 2022, 5 June 1988.
2. Quoted by 'Cavendish' in *Card Essays* from a letter reported in Polwhele's *Reminiscences*, 1773.
3. *Cecilia, or memoirs of an heiress*, ix, iii (*OED*, s.v. 'snap').

4. Pennycook, Andrew, *The Book of Card Games* (St. Albans, 1982).

5. Philips, Hubert, *The Pan Book of Card Games* (London, 1960), p. 223.

6. McLeod, John, 'Modern Chinese Card Games', *JIPCS* viii (Feb. 1980), pp. 74–7.

7. Literally, 'arse-hole'. The game is also reported under the name Petit Cul, which hardly changes matters, and, more mysteriously, as Association 1901, commemorating the date of the French law governing associations. Daniel Daynes, 'Le Trouduc', in *Sud-Ouest Dimanche*, 27 Dec. 1987. I thank Thierry Depaulis for this enlightenment.

8. This and other adders are described in Pennycook, n. 4 above.

9. Quoted by Hartmann in his introduction to *Games and Gamesters of the Restoration* (London, 1930), from the Clarendon State Papers, vol. iii, 1656.

10. Goldsmith, *The Good-natured Man.*

11. Robert Reid, of the Queen's University, Belfast.

12. From Berloquin, P., *Cent Jeux de Cartes Classiques* (Paris, 1975).

Chapter 11

1. A quotation reported by, if not invented by, Pardon in *The Card Player* (London, 1862).

2. Dummett, pp. 62 and 177.

3. For this, Depaulis refers us to Dangeau's *Journal* of 1684 and the *Inventaires du mobilier de la Couronne*, 1687.

4. 'E un guioco per uomini, uomini veri, non per fannulloni o frivole donne o gente che con le carte vuole arricchire o pagare il pedaggio per esse ammessi nella buona società . . .'

5. See Parlett, *The Penguin Book of Card Games* (London, 1979), pp. 361–3.

6. Described in Dummett, p. 332.

Chapter 12

1. 'Coon Can' in *The Standard Hoyle* (New York, 1887), pp. 480–1; 'Conquian' in *Foster's Complete Hoyle* (New York and London, 1897).

2. Culin, Stewart, *Chess and Playing Cards* (Smithsonian Institute, 1896).

3. Pennycook, *The Book of Card Games* (St. Albans, 1982), p. 457.

4. Dummett, pp. 181 ff.

5. Taylor, E. S., from d'Ambly, from Bullet, *Recherches historiques* (Lyons, 1757).

6. For Spanish and Italian games see, respectively, *Juegos de Naipes Españoles* (Vitoria, 1975) and Dossena, Giampaolo, *Giochi di Carte Italiani* (Milan, 1984).

Chapter 13

1. For Cribbage and Pontoon Patiences, see Parlett, *Teach Yourself Card Games for One* (Sevenoaks, 1986).

2. 'Cavendish', *Patience* (London, 1890).

3. See Ross, A. S. C., and Healey, F. G., 'Patience Napoléon', in *Proceedings of the Leeds Philosophical and Literary Society*, vol. X, pp. 137–90. A summary

entitled 'The Origins of Patience' appeared in *Games & Puzzles*, No. 40 (Sept. 1975), pp. 10–13.

4. Whitmore-Jones, M., *Games of Patience*, Ser. II (London, undated, *c*.1890–1900), p. 12.

5. Referred to and dated in Casanova's *Histoire de ma vie*. Dummett, p. 106, from Hoffmann, D., and Kroppenstedt, E., *Wahrsagekarten* (Bielefeld, 1972).

6. See n. 3.

7. 'J-R-W', *Besique* (London, 1863).

8. Rabouge in Anton, F., *Encyclopädie der Spiele* (Leipzig, 1889); Crapette or Cripette, in Mary Whitmore-Jones (between 1890 and 1910). As 'Robuse', it forms a topic in *The Master Book of Mathematical Recreations* (New York, 1968), from a 1943 Dutch original by F. Schuh. Schuh draws a careful distinction between 'puzzles' and 'problems', but then, curiously, treats 'games' and 'puzzles' as interchangeable.

Chapter 14

1. Triomphe in 1480 (Depaulis, private communication), Trump in 1522, Spanish Triunfo in Vives, 1539 (Dummett, pp. 178–9).

2. This is based on Dummett's study, pp. 164–91, but Dummett carefully refrains from suggesting such a clear-cut line of development.

3. The aristocratic Italian inventors of Tarot need not have been unacquainted with Karnöffel because it was German: the question, as Dummett observes (p. 191), is whether they would have encountered a game played by the lower orders.

4. For Ganjifa, see Ch. 6 n. 5.

5. Von Leyden, *Karnöffel: das Kartenspiel der Landsknechte* (Vienna, 1978).

6. Schreiber, W., *Die ältesten Spielkarten* (Strasburg, 1937), pp. 93–4.

7. Dummett, p. 189.

8. Dummett, pp. 184–91.

9. Grupp, C., *Kartenspiele* (Wiesbaden, 1975).

10. Game description from *Spillefuglen* (Copenhagen, 1952), pp. 121–3.

11. Line from an old play, according to 'Captain Crawley' (G. F. Pardon) (*The Card Player's Manual*, London, 1876)—who, however, had a habit of inventing quotations.

12. Le Truc was sketchily described in Lanes, E., *Manuel des jeux* (Paris, 1912), and a reconstruction of it was published by Sid Sackson in *A Gamut of Games* (London, 1969). See also Dummett, 'Bluff, Counter-Bluff', in *Games & Puzzles*, No. 5 (Sept. 1972), pp. 16–17. Depaulis tells me that Lanes's reference to the Midi as its area of play has been too broadly misinterpreted, and that it is restricted to the particular regions cited. (Roussillon, capital Perpignan, is the French rump of pre-1659 Catalonia.)

13. Details of Truco from Juan Capagorry, *El Juego es Cosa Seria* (Uruguay, 1978); Rodolfo, I. Henry, *Truco: Reglamentación y Técnica* (Buenos Aires, undated, *c*.1976); Mario Tobelem, 'Los Trucos del Truco', in *La Revista del Snark* (Buenos Aires, July 1976).

14. Borvo, Alain, *L'Aluette: anatomie d'un jeu de cartes* (Nantes, 1977), p. 24.

15. Depaulis, private communication.
16. *Cavendish on Piquet* (9th edn., London, 1896).
17. Depaulis, private communication.
18. Rausch, H., *Das Spielverzeichnis im 25 Kapitel von Fischarts 'Geschichtklitterung'* (Strasburg, 1908).

Chapter 15

1. 'Assez connu et pratiqué dans presque toutes les compagnies, sans qu'il ne fût besoin de le mettre dans ce livre.' In Daniel Martin's French/German reader *Le Parlement Nouveau* (Strasburg, 1637), Triomphe is associated with the Alsatian Trümpfspiel, which bears remarkable points of similarity although it is a point-trick rather than a plain-trick game.
2. For dates and discussion of Homme/Bête, see Depaulis, Thierry, 'Un peu de lumière sur l'Hombre (Part III)', in *JIPCS* xvi (Nov. 1987), pp. 46–8.
3. *Das neue königliche L'Hombre* (Hamburg, 1908); *Nieuwe Beschrijving der meest gebruikelijke Kaartspelen* (Amsterdam, 1828). I thank Thierry Depaulis for these references.
4. *Juegos de Naipes Españoles* (Vitoria, 1984), p. 31.
5. Grupp, C., *Kartenspiele* (Wiesbaden, 1975).
6. Crowne, *Sir Courtly Nice*, iii, 22.
7. From *ramasser*, 'to pick up'. Described in Parlett, *The Penguin Book of Card Games* (London, 1979).
8. Werner, E., and Sandgren, T., *Kortoxen* (Helsingborg, 1975).
9. Mauscheln in Grupp, C., *Kartenspiele* (Wiesbaden, 1975); Mousel in *Spillefuglen* (Copenhagen, 1952).
10. From 'An Old Man's Chatter' (West Donegal dialect), undated (but 1905–19), in *Dermot O'Byrne: Poems by Arnold Bax*, ed. Lewis Foreman (London, 1979), p. 31.
11. The holder of a matador is normally not obliged to play it, even if a trump is called for when he holds no other trump. Nor does the lead of a low matador force the play of a higher one; but the lead of a higher one does force the play of a lower one if no other trump is held. The Five-finger is thus a very powerful card, being entirely unforceable itself, but uniquely able to force the other two.
12. Arthur Hall, *Account of a Quarrell* (1576).
13. In *Ancient Ballads and Broadsides published in England in the sixteenth century . . . as preserved in the library of Henry Huth* (London, 1867).
14. Rich, *Greene's newes from heaven and hell.* I am indebted (again) to Thierry Depaulis for many of the references in this section.
15. Chatto, *Facts and Speculations . . .* (London, 1848), p. 126.
16. The British Museum holds a version of this engraving and text dating from 1609 (*The Revells of Christendome*), with Henry IV of France playing against a monk.
17. Carleton, *Fardorougha*, xvi (*OED*).
18. *Foster on Five Hundred* (London, 1909), p. 21.
19. Cowell, *Thirty Years Passed Among the Players in England and America . . .*

(New York, 1844), cited in Coffin, George, *The Poker Game Complete* (London, 1950), p. 15.

20. Asserted by Rausch, H., in *Das Spielverzeichnis im 25 Kapitel von Fischarts 'Geschichtklitterung'* (Strasburg, 1908), under 'Marsch'; supported by Bernhard, K., *Strossburjer Wibble* (Strasburg, 1856).

21. *Nieuwe Beschrijving der meest gebruikelijke Kaartspelen* (Amsterdam, 1828), see also n. 3 above.

22. Catherine Perry Hargrave, *A History of Playing Cards* . . . (New York/London, 1966, text 1930), p. 348.

23. Janssen, Han, *De geschiedenis van de speelkaart* (Rijswijk, 1985), p. 283.

24. In Pole's *Handbook of Games* (London, 1890).

25. In *Cassell's Book of Indoor Amusements* . . . (London, 1881), p. 122.

26. By Edmond Taylor, in *The Fossil Monarchies* (London, 1963).

Chapter 16

1. Depaulis, Thierry, 'Un peu de lumière sur l'Hombre', in *JIPCS* xv. 4 and xvi. 1 and 2 (May, Aug., Nov. 1987).

2. No longer extant, but mentioned by Chatto (*Facts and Speculations* . . ., 1848, p. 145) and others. See Depaulis, above.

3. Taylor (from Boiteau d'Ambly) *The History of Playing Cards*, p. 394.

4. Both by Cardinal De Luca, the first in his encyclopaedia *Theatrum veritatis et justitiae*. See Depaulis, n. 1 above.

5. Depaulis, n. 1.

6. Dummett, p. 174.

7. Dummett, p. 490.

8. Dummett, p. 498.

9. Depaulis, n. 1.

10. This account, from Anton's *Encyclopädie der Spiele*, seems more logical than Hoffmann's in *Der Meister in allen Kartenspielen*.

11. *Foster's Complete Hoyle* (London, 1897), p. 2.

12. Rumpf, Marianne, 'Zur Entwicklung der Spielkartenfarben', in *Schweizerisches Archiv für Volkskunde*, xvii. 1–2 (Basel, 1976), p. 4.

13. Depaulis, n. 1.

14. Depaulis, n. 1.

15. Werner, E., and Sandgren, T., *Kortoxen* (Helsingborg, 1980).

16. 3–5 players, 36 cards in *Spillefuglen* (Copenhagen, 1952); 4 players, 40 cards plus two Jokers in Pedersen, S., *Spillebog for Hus, Hjem og Kro* (Copenhagen, 1983).

17. Wilks, Abraham, *The Handbook of Solo Whist* (London, 1898; a revision of Wilks, A., and Pardon, C., *How to Play Solo Whist* (London, 1888).

18. In his contribution on Solo to *The Whist Table* (London), an undated but probably pre-1896 'Treasury of Notes on the Royal Game'.

Chapter 17

1. Quotations from *The Oxford English Dictionary*.

2. See Dummett, pp. 178–9.

3. The elderly Daines Barrington calls it Whisk as late as 1787, in his 'Dissertation on the History of Playing Cards' (*Archaeologia*, viii).
4. 'E.B.', in *A New Dictionary of the Terms Ancient and Modern of the Canting Crew* (1700), omits the Ace of trumps, probably by oversight; all four appear in Grose, *A Dictionary of Buckish Slang* . . . (1811, republished as *A Dictionary of the Vulgar Tongue* London, 1981).
5. William Pole, *The Evolution of Whist* (London, 1895).
6. Chatto, *Facts and Speculations* . . . (London, 1848).
7. Barrington, n. 3 above.
8. *Admiral's Widow—Life and Letters of the Hon. Mrs Edward Boscowan from 1761 to 1805* (London, 1942), pp. 38, 172.
9. By Mr Hoare, of Bath, one of the party, according to Chatto.
10. By Andrew Pennycook, in conversation.
11. Dalton, William, *Saturday Bridge* (London, 1907).
12. In a letter to the *Bridge Magazine*, May 1932, quoted by Mackey, n. 14 below.
13. One surviving copy is held by the Bodleian Library, but a facsimile edition was published by Bibliagora (Richmond-upon-Thames) in 1986.
14. Mackey, Rex, *The Walk of the Oysters* (London, 1964).
15. See Preobrazhensky's Russian Etymological Dictionary (1910).
16. Foster, R. F., *Foster's Bridge* (London, 1901).
17. *Saturday Bridge*, p. 26; source unstated, but probably German or French, as it is transliterated as 'ieralasch' and 'ieralache'.
18. According to the Russian authors of *The Laws of Vint* (London, 1900).
19. From *Spillefuglen* (Copenhagen, 1952).
20. Dalton, n. 11 above.
21. Buller, *Contract Bridge and its Development from Auction* (London, 1929).
22. Manning Foster, *Bridge-Plafond* (London, 1933).
23. Mackey, n. 14 above.
24. In his Introduction to Manning Foster, n. 22 above.

Chapter 18

1. The history of Tarot cartomancy and occultism is traced in Dummett, *The Game of Tarot* (London, 1980), pp. 93–163.
2. 'King, Queen, Knight, Jack' sounds better, but 'Cavalier' is preferred for its distinctive initial. In some traditions the Jack or Valet is a 'Maid'.
3. The Joker derives from a Jack (see Ch. 15, under 'Euchre'), and bears no relation to the Fool in Tarot.
4. The identities and order of the Tarot trumps remain an endless topic of research and discussion, most of which may be followed in the pages of the *Journal of the International Playing-Card Society*.
5. The word 'tarocco' was a mystery even to 16th-cent. Italians. See Dummett, p. 178.
6. Dummett, p. 201.
7. For the origins of Tarot, see Dummett, pp. 65–92.
8. Dummett discovered the Mineo game after publication of *The Game of Tarot*. He is convinced that there are no others (private communication).

9. For a practical English-language guide, see Dummett, *Twelve Tarot Games* (London, 1980).

Chapter 19

1. Dummett, p. 367.
2. See Dummett, pp. 355–70, and Kissel, R., 'Bohemian Bulka—the Missing Link in the History of Trappola', *JIPCS* xvii (Aug. 1988), pp. 9–19.
3. Honl, Ivan, *Z Minulosti Karetní Hry v Čechách* (Prague, 1947), pp. 57–63. On p. 69 is reproduced the title-page of *Šest a dwadcet*, or *Trapulky do bulky* (Krakow, 1822), where it is described as 'hry mrawopočestné'— 'a decent game', if I interpret aright.
4. Anton, F., *Encyclopädie der Spiele* (Leipzig, 1889).
5. Omasta, V., and Ravik, S., *Hráči Karty, Karetní Hry* (Prague, 1969), p. 92.
6. Dummett, p. 365.
7. Dossena, *Giochi di Carte Italiani* (Milan, 1984), p. 169.
8. Thierry Depaulis, private communication.
9. See entries 137 and 131 in Lensi, *Bibliografia Italiana di Giuochi di Carte* (Florence, 1892; ed. Dossena, Ravenna, 1985).
10. Depaulis, private communication. Detailed description of main game and variants based on Renaudet, B., and Ehrhart, P., *La Manille et la Manille Contrée* (Paris, 1972).
11. Depaulis (ibid.) traces this error to 'Gégé', *Historique et règle du jeu de la Manille* (1883), and points out that only the non-talking form (later called Manille muette) is described in 1776 and at Bordeaux in 1845.
12. *Foster's Complete Hoyle* (London, 1897).
13. Mott-Smith, *Culbertson's Card Games Complete* (New York, 1952).
14. Taylor, A., *Pub Games* (St Albans, 1976).
15. See van Groningen, S., *Het Kaartspel* (Blaricum; undated, post-1935), pp. 134–6, and English account in Parlett, D., *Card Games for Three* (Sevenoaks, 1978), pp. 230–5.

Chapter 20

1. Dummett, pp. 561–2.
2. Hoffmann, *Der Meister in allen Kartspielen* (Hamburg, 1873).
3. A. van Baerland, *Dialogi XLII . . .*, including a *Dialogus unus de ludo chartarum* by Augustinus Reymarius. (I am indebted to Thierry Depaulis for this reference.)
4. *Dizionario Etimologico della Lingua Italiana* (Florence, 1950–7).
5. Daniel Martin, *Le Parlement Nouveau* (Strasburg, 1637).
6. Hoffmann, n. 2 above, pp. 150–2. This game also features a rule similar to that of Ganjifa, whereby players on lead are obliged to play out their unbeatable cards (see also Dummett, p. 54n.).
7. Hoffmann, n. 2 above.
8. da Costa, Mário Pinheiro, *Sueca: Tratado do Jogo de Cartas* (Oporto; undated, post-1978).

9. Foster, *The Official Rules of Card Games* (Cincinnati, 1926), p. 211.
10. Original game in Hoffmann, n. 2 above; variations in Pennycook, *The Book of Card Games* (St Albans, 1982).
11. Pennycook, above, p. 623.
12. This streamlining of the Ace-11, Ten-10 system is often encountered in European games and applies to some versions of American Pinochle.
13. Private communication.
14. Anton, *Encyclopädie der Spiele* (Leipzig, 1889).
15. Hagen, P., ed., *Spillefuglen—I* (Oslo, 1970), p. 53.
16. Hammer, Paul, *Die deutschen Kartenspiele* (Leipzig, 1811), is a patriotic collection of German folk games at cards and includes many others not previously recorded. (Cited by Hoffmann, see n. 20 below.)
17. A practical survey of the family is provided by McLeod, J., in 'Rules of Games: Schafkopf', *JIPCS* vii (Nov. 1978), pp. 38–47.
18. *Das Frauenzimmer Lexicon* (Leipzig, 1715). Depaulis (private communication) cites recent etymologies deriving *Scharwenzel* from Czech *červenec*, 'red Unter/Jack', in reference to their noteworthy role. Wolfgang Suma, in *Grand mit Vieren!* (Berlin, 1982, p. 28), favours a derivation from *wenden*, 'to turn, move about' and its intensive form *wendsen*.
19. Pedersen, *Spillebog for Hus, Hjem og Kro* (Copenhagen, 1983), p. 144.
20. See extensive bibliography in Hoffmann, Detlef, and Dietrich, Margot, *Das Skatspiel: Geschichte—Bilder—Regeln* (Munich, 1982). Of particular importance is Stein, Oskar, *Geschichte des Skatspiels* (Berlin, 1887).
21. Hertefeld, A., *Illustrirtes Skat-Buch* (Breslau, 1884). Translated by 'Professor Hoffmann' (Angelo Lewis) as *The Game of Skat* (London, 1893).
22. Lemmer, Ernst, *Skat Taktik* (Leinfelden, 1969), p. 28.
23. See Wergin, Joseph Petrus, *Wergin on Skat and Sheepshead* (McFarland, Wis., 1975); also Eichhorn, J. Charles, *American Skat* (Chicago, 1898); Foster, R. F., *Foster's Skat Manual* (New York, 1906).
24. Wergin, above, p. 299; also Kempson, Morehead, and Mott-Smith, *Hoyle Up-to-Date* (London, 1952), p. 144.

Chapter 21

1. It can easily be derived from the card-exchange procedure of, say, Ecarté/Triomphe. A search through *The Game of Tarot* reveals no Tarot example earlier than the 18th cent. Dummett (p. 318n.) does quote the Italian Speroni (1500–88) as noting 'In some games you draw new cards as play proceeds . . .'; but this need not imply trick-and-draw. It fits Piquet, for instance.
2. Gerver, Frans, *Le Guide Marabout de tous les jeux de cartes* (Verviers, 1966).
3. See Pratesi, Franco, 'Italian Cards: New Discoveries—4. Tarot in Piedmont in the XVIth Century', in *JIPCS* xvi. 1 (Aug. 1987), pp. 31–2, and Dummett's supplementary comments in xvi. 2, p. 66.
4. *Das Frauenzimmer Lexicon* (Leipzig, 1715).
5. The Sixty-Six Research Circle referred to by Claus Grupp in *Schafkopf, Doppelkopf* (Leinfelden, 1976) is no longer contactable.

6. Grupp (above).
7. McLeod, John 'Ulti', in *JIPCS* iv (May 1977).
8. Capagorry, Juan, *El Jeugo es Cosa Seria* (Uruguay, 1978).
9. Dossena, Giampaolo, articles in *La Stampa* (Milan), 2 and 23 Feb. 1985.
10. Dossena, in *Giochi di Carte Italiani* (Milan, 1984), quotes the *Dizionario della Lingua Italiana* as ascribing a Bàzzica reference to 1562, and derives many 17th–18th-cent. references from Lensi's Bibliography of 1892. Depaulis tells me that Bàzzica, as described in *Il giuoco pratico* from 1753, was a cross between Brelan and Thirty-One.
11. Bijou Books, F. Warne, London.
12. 'Berkeley', *Bezique* (1901).
13. Described in Parlett, *The Penguin Book of Card Games* (London, 1979).
14. Grupp, n. 5 above.
15. In *Culbertson's Card Games Complete* (New York, 1952) Morehead and Mott-Smith remark, 'In the writings of Damon Runyon and others, the game is frequently mentioned, as Klob, Klab, Kalaber, and, often, Kalabriàs.' Having re-read Runyon as a piece of extra-curricular research, I find that he always calls it 'Klob', except in *The Lacework Kid*, where 'Klabriasch' is said to be played in Germany.
16. Lehner, K., and Wyss, S., 'Zur Geschichte der Spielkarten im Raume Schaffhausen', in *Zeitschrift für Schweizerische Archäologie*, 30 (1973), pp. 185–204. (Cited by Dummett and McLeod in an article on Jass in *JIPCS* iii (Feb. 1975).)
17. Here and elsewhere in this chapter I am again indebted to Thierry Depaulis and his seemingly inexhaustible fund of first references.
18. Cf. Truc, in which, for much the same reason, the Eight is referred to as the Six.
19. Description and comments from Haes, J., *Klaverjassen*, in series Ken uw Sport (Amsterdam; undated, probably 1970s).
20. Kenneth Konstam, in the original version of *Teach Yourself Card Games for Two* (London, 1954), in fact quotes a form with clubs preferred. 'Clover Jack' also appears as *Kleverbub and Kleenbub* in Daniel Martin's French–German reader, *Le Parlement Nouveau*, of 1637. See also Rumpf, Marianne, 'Zur Entwicklung der Spielkartenfarben in der Schweiz...', in *Schweizerisches Archiv für Volkskunde* xvii. 1–2 (Basel, 1976), p. 10.
21. Gerver, n. 2 above.
22. For Culbertson, read Geoffrey Mott-Smith, the real brain behind *Culbertson's Card Games Complete*.
23. A bid may be doubled, or *contrée*, or (dialectally) *coinchée*.
24. Details of Alsós and Felsős are from chapters by Kovács, E., in Gedeon, D., Villányi, A. (eds.), *Kártyások Koönyve* (Budapest, 1986), pp. 82–96.

Chapter 22

1. Dummett, p. 498, traces it to the 1757 edition of *Das Neue Königliche Ombre*, where it is called *devole*. Lord Aldenham, in *The Game of Ombre* (London, 1902), p. 51, defines *devole* as an unintentional failure to win a single trick, and identifies the deliberate negative bid as *contrabola*, or 'countervole'.

2. 'Professor Hoffmann' (Angelo Lewis), *The Game of Skat* (London, 1893; a translation of Hertefeld's *Illustrirtes Skat-Buch*).

3. For *Mittelramsch*, see Hoffmann (above).

4. Boulanger, J., *Jeux de cartes* (Paris, 1978), p. 58.

5. Dossena, *Giochi di Carte Italiani* (Milan, 1984), p. 40. Dummett, however (pp. 426–7n.), suggests that Scartino implies a game in which excess cards are thrown out before play begins, as in skat.

6. In a letter of Henry IV, 13 Nov. 1601. This and most of the following historical notes on Reversis derive from unpublished material kindly imparted by Thierry Depaulis.

7. In Lebrun, M., *Manuel des jeux de calcul et de hasard . . .* (Paris, 1828). For a detailed description of full-blown Reversis, see McLeod, John, 'Rules of Games No. 5: Reversis', in *JIPCS* v (May 1977), pp. 23–30.

8. See Dossena, Giampaolo, *Giochi di Carte Italiani* (Milan, 1984), and *Giochi dai Molti Nomi* (Reggio Emilia; undated, perhaps 1985).

9. Taylor, E., *The History of Playing Cards* (1865), p. 345.

10. Westall, B. C., *Games* (Associated Newspapers Ltd.; undated, 1930s).

11. Including *Hráči Karty, Karetní Hry* (Prague, 1969).

12. The earliest I know is in *Trumps' New Card Games* (New York, 1886); but Hargrave, C., in *A History of Playing Cards* (1930; repr. New York, 1966), p. 189, mentions a pack designed for the game 'Heartsette', published in Britain in 1883.

13. This version is a cross between that in Chicandard (and others), *Jeux d'intérieur* (Paris, 1965), pp. 31–2, and one described to me by John McLeod. A very neat 32-card version appears in Berloquin, P., *Cent jeux de cartes classiques* (Paris, 1975), pp. 128–30, together with a reference to Roger Gouze's novel *La Partie de Bambu* (Julliard), which includes rules and strategies, and credits this version to Robert Mitterrand.

Chapter 23

1. An occultist appraisal emanating from Alice Hutton, *The Cards Can't Lie* (London, 1979), p. 21.

2. Dummett, p. xxvi. I recollect using the same image in 'On the Cards', *Games & Puzzles*, No. 38 (May 1975), p. 41.

3. 'Cavendish', *Card Essays* (London, 1879).

4. Several such games are described in Parlett, *Teach Yourself Card Games for Two* (Sevenoaks, 1978).

5. The original version of Eleusis is best described in Abbott, R., *Abbott's New Card Games* (New York/London, 1963). A more elaborate version was published in 1977. Eleusis has since found its way into other gamebooks, often without acknowledgement—as in Pierre Berloquin's *Cent jeux de cartes classiques* (Paris, 1975), where it is renamed Delphi. See also Romeburg, H. Charles, 'Simulating Scientific Enquiry with the Card Game Eleusis', in *Science Education*, 63. 5 (1979), 599–608.

6. See Westall, *Card Games* (Associated Press; undated, 1930s), and Morehead and Mott-Smith (eds.), *Culbertson's Card Games Complete* (New York, 1952).

7. See Egg, G., *Puur, Näll, As* (Zurich, undated, post-1970).
8. *Games & Puzzles*, No. 22 (Feb. 1974). Fullest account in Parlett, D., *Original Card Games* (London, 1977). The version described here is a revision of 1989.

General Index

Index of Card Games

Page numbers in **bold type** are main entries.